The Early Image of
Black Baseball

The Early Image of Black Baseball

*Race and Representation
in the Popular Press,
1871–1890*

James E. Brunson III

McFarland & Company, Inc., Publishers
Jefferson, North Carolina, and London

LIBRARY OF CONGRESS CATALOGUING-IN-PUBLICATION DATA

Brunson, James Edward, 1954–
The early image of black baseball : race and representation in
the popular press, 1871–1890 / James Edward Brunson III.
p.   cm.
Includes bibliographical references and index.

ISBN 978-0-7864-4206-5
softcover : 50# alkaline paper ∞

1. Baseball — United States — History — 19th century.
2. Negro leagues — History — 19th century.
3. African American baseball players — Public opinion.
4. African Americans in mass media — History — 19th century.
5. Athletes in mass media.   6. Public opinion — United States.
7. United States — Race relations.   I. Title.
GV863.A1B785 2009   796.3570973'09034 — dc22   2009019060

British Library cataloguing data are available

On the cover: *Colored Sporting Fraternity*,
James Brunson, watercolor, 15" × 12½", 2008

Manufactured in the United States of America

McFarland & Company, Inc., Publishers
Box 611, Jefferson, North Carolina 28640
www.mcfarlandpub.com

To my wife, Kathleen,
and my daughters,
Takkara Keosha and Tamerit Kaisha

Acknowledgments

Many people and institutions helped in the making of this work. Close friends like Willard Draper urged me to write a history of colored baseball. Further encouragement came from university colleagues Laverne Gyant, Admasu Zike, Don Bramlett, Walt Owens, and my wife, Kathleen.

My work has been particularly nurtured by the NINE Conference and its welcoming members. I am thankful to John Thorn, Larry Gerlach, Trey and Geri Strecker who have supported my efforts. Special thanks to the late (and great) Bill Kirwin who invited me to present my first paper in 2006.

A few individuals who played baseball together in the 1950s and early 1960s have inspired the writing of this manuscript. These were my father, the late James Brunson, and my uncles Jo Nathan Sanders and Solomon Johnson. They played semiprofessional baseball for the Pirates, an all-black independent club of Chicago that crossed bats with white and black teams throughout the Midwest (Illinois, Indiana, Iowa, and Wisconsin).

Research for the book took me to destinations throughout the country. I want to thank the following institutions: Northern Illinois University, University of Texas–Austin, University of Chicago, University of Illinois at Champaign-Urbana, University of Illinois–Springfield, University of Memphis, Chicago History Museum (formerly the Chicago Historical Society), University of Maryland at College Park, University of California–Berkeley, Emory University, DuSable Museum (Chicago), Newark Public Library, Tulane University, Library of Congress, and especially the St. Louis Public Library.

Table of Contents

Preface

The stereotype, then, as the primary point of subjectification in colonial discourse, for both colonizer and colonized, is the scene of a similar fantasy and defense — the desire for an originality which is again threatened by the differences of race, colour and culture.

— Homi K. Bhabha, *The Location of Culture* (1994)

There is no romance free of what Herman Melville called "the power of blackness," especially not in a country in which there was a resident population, already black, upon which the imagination could play; through which historical, moral, metaphysical, and social fears, problems and dichotomies could be articulated.

— Toni Morrison, *Playing in the Dark* (1992)

This book explores an era that preceded the Negro Leagues: the Colored Leagues. It considers three issues: black images, representations, and the colored sporting fraternity. By "black" image, I mean any likeness, figure, motif, or form that appears in or could be associated with the sports medium. By "representations," I mean visual and verbal images that fashioned the colored baseballist in the postbellum Gilded Age. This work also attempts to frame a black community that fascinated literary and graphic artists. The "colored sporting fraternity" included men and women whose cultural history — both the familiar and unfamiliar — has been partially portrayed, but little examined. This book, as a whole, examines how visual and verbal images sought to mediate, contain, and unleash the figure of blackness, both on and off the green diamond. Black images of the sporting fraternity in general, and the baseballist in particular, proliferated in the years immediately following the Civil War. They flourished in mass-produced and mass-circulated media — in monthly magazines that reflected the fears and desires of the genteel leisure–class; in weekly and daily newspapers that dispatched "newsy stories" throughout the country; in weekly sporting and theatrical journals that catered to a presumably rougher crowd; and in photographs that sought to counter negative racial/ethnic stereotyping through the agency of black authorship.

What makes this book unique is that, simply put, no comparable work exists. It explores the late 19th century colored sporting world through images of adoration and abomination during a turbulent period in North American history. Of course, well-received histories of colored baseball in the postbellum period have gained some traction over the past few years. But this is not a comprehensive look at colored baseball; it is a limited historical and cultural sampling. The history of the black baseball image, from its invention in the late 1860s to its emergence as a media phenomenon in the early 1880s, must be framed within a bare-bones outline of the story of the modern sporting world from the beginning of the Reconstruction Period through the end of the postbellum Gilded Age. While this study includes an analysis of representations of the Cuban Giants (East Coast) and the New Orleans Pinch-backs (South), my primary cultural work privileges the Midwest. Why? For starters, I am a Midwesterner (a long-time fan of the Chicago White Sox). And, in general, the Midwest has been overlooked in discussions of colored baseball. Although most readings have privileged the Cuban Giants as the first black professional baseball team, this work refutes the common wisdom of that notion. It also questions the common wisdom that privileges them with the invention of that dubious practice, "negro" comedy.

This book argues that the cultural phenomenon which clearly finds parallels with blackface minstrelsy, at least in the eyes of scholars who have attempted to address the topic, is far more complicated. This book zeroes in on the Black Stockings of St. Louis, and if anyone merits consideration for introducing "negro" comedy, it is Henry Bridgewater's colored aggregation. The other colored clubs examined in this work are the Cleveland Blue Stockings, the Uniques and the Blue Stockings of Chicago, and, of course, the Blue Stockings of St. Louis. This book represents these colored aggregations as part of a larger social network that unified the colored sporting world, bringing together seemingly disparate black images that have yet to be fully explored, examined, or appreciated. It peers into the hidden lives of colored baseballists, sporting men and women, whose black images have been pored over with the eye of an art historian and cultural critic.

But this book does something else. It begins by acknowledging that the dearth of visual images and the surplus of verbal images seemingly put this cultural history at a disadvantage. It recognizes that the very idea of visual culture depends upon our ability to conceive its relation to art history and aesthetics, the phenomenon of writing, and to speech and the study of language, literature, and philosophical discourse. Writing stands at the nexus of language and vision, epitomized in the figure of the rebus or hieroglyph, the "painted word" or the visible language of gesture-speech that precedes vocal expression. The relation of the colored sporting fraternity to the postbellum Gilded Age baseball world comes into view through reflection on differences between art and non-art, visual and verbal signs, and ratios between different sensory and semiotic modes. It exposes how the colored sporting fraternity challenged those in power by constructing a "hidden transcript," a dissident political culture manifested in representations of sartorial expression, aesthetic style, and other cultural practices.[1]

The argument of this book is that black images, both visual and verbal, can be used to reconstruct the integral relation of representation to perceptions of the colored sporting fraternity. Baseball representations are significant to this discussion because they became an integral part of the professional entertainment industry, within which mass-media, mass-production, and mass-circulation provided environments where the black image might be easily reproduced. Our first national theater — blackface minstrelsy — played a crucial role in the formation of the professional entertainment industry. And the mask of blackness as a commodity penetrated marketing practices throughout the business world (commercial advertising being exemplary); but minstrelsy's entrepreneurial links to the commodification of baseball have been largely overlooked. Blackface minstrelsy dovetailed neatly with baseball, and the medium transformed the black image of the colored baseballist into an ambivalent figure: ballplayers became men of mark and marked men, both celebrated and overlooked. The validity or vulnerability of certain assumptions conventionally accepted among baseball historians and critics and circulated as "knowledge" is central to any understanding of our national pastime. To understand blackface minstrelsy or give it meaning is to speculate about how journalists, especially sportswriters, transformed aspects of their social grounding into aspects of language, and the ways they told sports stories, fought political wars, and represented civic debates in their texts. Blackness is a "playground for the imagination."[2]

The black image of the colored baseballist in particular and the colored sporting fraternity in general bore the burden of what Walter Benjamin called the mark and the absolute mark. The latter is naturally imprinted; the former, by contrast, emerges. But the opposition between mark and absolute mark does not exist, for the mark — in this instance, skin color — is always absolute and in its appearing is similar to nothing else. Turning up as it does on the living, the mark of skin color in the baseball sporting world retained linkages to guilt and innocence. Skin color, especially the construction of blackness, enriched the country's creative possibilities. While marking or supplying physically significant characteristics with internal value equivalents, sharpening, by visual antithesis, their conceptual unity, the work of the postbellum Gilded Age artists shows its "flaws best in written form." Benjamin associates painting with the mark as a visual form that appears on the human body and can acquire etiological, genealogical, moral, affective, and theological meanings. He insists on the decisive role of language in relation to painting.[3]

The exclusion of the colored baseballist from the spaces of visual culture — from periodicals, tobacco trading cards, studios and galleries, and fine arts museums — exemplifies a central principle of high modernism. It illustrates perfectly the difference between modernity (of which the baseballist was a conspicuous symbol of national pride) and modernism (an aesthetic of purity that rigorously guarded against representations of the black invasion of leisure class life) in the 1870s and 1880s. Both painting and sculpture commemorated white, not colored, baseballists. And the high arts were not alone in this exclusion. But my project, to quote Toni Morrison, "rises from delight, not disappointment" from what I know about the black image, the colored sporting fraternity, and representation. As an art historian and a newcomer to the writing of baseball history, the author's viewpoint will be rather like a sociologist examining social artifacts (census reports, employment records, and city directories), a cultural historian combing baseball and other sporting archives, an art critic analyzing an array of black images. This book is an exploration of a lost world, a baseball landscape that has been mapped but rarely traveled.

Introduction

In 1878 *Harper's Weekly* published Solomon Eytinge Jr.'s *Base Ball at Blackville—"The White Stockings" against the "Black Legs"—First Blood for the "Black Legs,"* a woodcut illustration comically depicting a segregated sporting event where two colored clubs cross bats. The baseball grounds resemble a wide-open wilderness. No enclosed grandstand restrains the crowd. Fashionably attired men, women, and children congregate on a grassy hill, adding to the scene's circus-like atmosphere. Three figures—two seated players and one standing bleacher fan—form the picture's triangular composition. Other players lolling about and transfixed by the scene frame the foreground. The Black Legs' pitcher braces for what will not happen: the batter making contact with the ball. Instead, the White Stockings' slugger takes a pitch to the face.

Base Ball at Blackville is an offensive black image which—along with other black images from Eytinge's notorious series—appeared at a crucial time in North American history. The subject matter of *Base Ball at Blackville* belonged to an era of violence, disenfranchisement, and accommodation that shaped the social contours of Reconstruction and the post–Reconstruction era. Significantly, *Blackville* imagined a culturally segregated black leisure class, the newly emancipated who lived along the nation's social margins. By lampooning a fictitious clan called the "Blackville" family, the woodcut did more than deride black leisure class life: it mocked the "colored" sporting fraternity. *Base Ball at Blackville*, then, did not simply provide opportunities for genteel middle-class readers to indulge in untroubled contemplation or ribald humor. Rather, Eytinge's work is the locus of historical, political, and social practices that found symbolic expression in visual and verbal representations.

In the 1870s and 1880s, black images of the colored sporting fraternity—baseball barons, ballplayers, umpires, fans, prizefighters, musicians, tonsorialists, gamblers, and other underworld types—proliferated and circulated widely throughout the country. Among the more dubious legacies of postbellum Gilded Age culture, the period of economic ascendency in the United States following the Civil War, is that artists and writers had distanced themselves from the social system that had grown up around them. Historian Neil Harris explains: "Satire, caricature, and irony evolved into familiar weapons. Increasingly, artists and writers did not fasten upon specific political targets but upon the spirit of the age.... The picture presented was not a pretty one, and the intellectual at war with his world gave later commentators plenty of ammunition." Harris points out that newspapers, magazines, and above all, photography, expose the period as the most vividly portrayed era that had ever existed: "our sustained photography memory of American history begins in the 1860s and 1870s." And "chroniclers who provided influential accounts of the period" contributed to the hostility towards the colored sporting fraternity. Those visual and literary artists whose black images represented the colored sporting fraternity succeeded in shaping some mainstream perceptions and attitudes towards black Americans. Many remain unknown, "hidden frequently from the sight of their contemporaries or subsequent chroniclers because their accomplishments were not recognized by the official guardians of culture."[1]

The Early Image of Black Baseball: Race and Representation in the Popular Press, 1871–1890 offers another foundational story in the history of baseball. The remarkable thing about this story is not so much its retrieval from the cultural margins of North American history as its buried treasure: titillating sports fragments that need to be unearthed and reexamined. Its baseball forms provide a parallel vision of the larger forces of modernization and urbanization reshaping black American life, and reveal how visual and literary artists alternately resisted and adapted negative stereotypical black images to these forces. As this story makes clear, the black image in baseball forms rarely presents a single story, or a single meaning. Thus, the cultural meaning of baseball representations remains to be fully explored by art and cultural historians.

What, then, are baseball forms? And more precisely, how are we to understand black images in baseball forms? Eytinge's *Base Ball at Blackville* exemplifies a little understood phenomenon in art historian Henri Focillon's "life of forms," the moment when an image undergoes a decisive evolutionary transformation. For Focillon, the progenitor of an image is another image, and the principle of life that links them is form. But as the iconologist W.J.T. Mitchell reminds us, Focillon's theory did something more radical than simply model the evolution of artistic forms on the development of biological organisms; it turned the analogy around and modeled biology on the evolution of images.[2]

This study asks how black images are produced, where they come from, and how they evolve. But, as an art historian, I also query: what is a medium? What is the text's intent/function? Who is the artist/author? Classification by artist/author offers a reliable taxonomy, an art historical equivalent to the "species" in natural history. A species is the basic classificatory unit or "taxon" for biological organisms. All members of a species (human beings, for instance) share a "family resemblance: at two levels, one visible and the other invisible: they "look similar," and they maintain this similarity "through successive generations."[3]

Eytinge's mastery of the black image and technique of woodcut illustration found perfect theme not only in baseball forms, but also in his other representations of the colored sporting fraternity. His black and white illustrations are, at times, tonally shaded to create spatial depth and racial identification. Contrasting Eytinge's black images with Thomas Worth's black images illustrates the life of baseball forms. Based on Eytinge's original conception of the colored sporting fraternity, Worth's *Darktown Comics* is a crude melding of human and animal forms. Worth's lithographs made the transition from hand-coloring to chromolithographs, where bright colors glazed the surfaces of black and white prints. Worth's *Darktown Comics*, in reality, belong among other black images produced by visual artists for the lithographic firm of Currier and Ives, portrays the evolution of the black image in baseball forms from the Reconstruction and post–Reconstruction era. This example perhaps offers a confirmation of Focillon's theory of the "life of forms in art": a synthesis of vision and technique, subject matter and style that "is immersed in the whirlpool of time" and yet "belongs to eternity."[4]

Examining selected black images that emerged in the postbellum Gilded Age, this present work addresses the life of the black image as it is portrayed in print and visual culture within the framework of the sports medium. This larger framework of racial and ethnic stereotyping includes the colored sporting fraternity and allows a more nuanced and differentiated account of the "black image." Far from a simple or singular image, blackness in 19th-century baseball representations is internally divided by strains of literary narrative and visual-verbal iconography drawn from numerous sports sources. More than simply tracking the colored sporting fraternity in baseball representations, I suggest how visual/literary artists and their contemporaries used these works to reconfigure the black image for new cultural circumstances and changing political projects. Given the colored sporting fraternity's seemingly inconspicuous role in the late 19th century, I postulate that this image-repertoire was embraced for its symbolic potential to contain, to mediate, or to address an emergent aesthetic sensibility that transcended, critiqued, and supplemented spaces and places traversed by the black body. In other words, the sports medium shows how colored sports refracted the black gaze within its own social frame of reference. From Solomon Eytinge's *Blackville* series (1874–1885) to Moses Lenore Tucker's cartoons (1890–1891), the black image of the colored sporting fraternity invoked black leisure class life. This study shows how the colored sporting fraternity became established as an American cultural icon, and the effect it had on social perceptions, racial attitudes, and national policy.

Photographic portraits and photographically derived representations also circulated in the sporting world. Photographic portraiture is unique among baseball representations because these images always make reference to an existing element of reality — that is, to a real person. Art historian Richard Brilliant writes: "To real persons we tend to give names, and to portraits we also try to give names. A real, named person seems to exist somewhere within or behind the portrait."[5] For the colored sporting crowd, the photograph mattered. W.J.T. Mitchell elaborates: "The connotations of photography — its technical, scientific, progressive modernity, its cheapness and democratic availability, its middle-brow, petit-bourgeois social position, its mythic status as a natural and universal language — all commend themselves to American national ideology."[6] Photographic representations of the colored sporting fraternity are relics of the past, traces of what have happened. They imply a set of prior questions about the relationships between nations and media. A modern nation is not a natural fact: its origin, history, and destiny are the stuff of myth, made and not given. Several black baseball books heavy on photography — most recently, in the works of David Craft, Bruce Chadwick, Phil Dixon and Patrick J. Hannigan, Larry Lester and Sammy Miller and Dick Clark, Mark Rucker and Peter C. Bjarkman, Jerry Malloy, and Mark Chiarello and Jack Morelli — seemingly aestheticize and idealize by rendering things pictorial.

During the late 19th century, photographers, engravers, and lithographers immersed themselves in the sporting life, advertising their services and wares to the baseball fraternity. Between 1881 and 1888, portraits of ballplayers, teams, owners, and sporting men became a lucrative niche market, perhaps partly motivated by the commercial success of illustrated periodicals like *Frank Leslie's Weekly*, *Sporting Life*, *The New York Clipper*, *The National Police Gazette*, *Harper's Illustrated Weekly*, and *Harper's New Monthly Magazine*. Such media are not just materials, but material practices that involve technologies, skills, traditions, and habits. These practices made it possible for images of the colored sporting fraternity to be embodied as word pictures — not just products of newsprint and ink, but of printing presses and printing rooms, telegraph offices and dispatches, telephones and telephone switchboards, newspaper distribution centers and social outlets (hotels, restaurants, grocery stores, tonsorial parlors, train station depots, newspaper exchanges, betting parlors, gambling dens, billiard halls, saloons, club houses, race tracks, and, of course, the baseball grounds). This cultural web included a whole set of material practices that brought the black image together with an object to produce word pictures.

Sol White's *History of Colored Baseball* first brought the Cuban Giants back to life in 1903. Then in the 1990s, the history of this black image in baseball experienced its second resurrection when sports enthusiasts and authors interested in the Negro Leagues coupled with Ken Burns's magisterial *Baseball*, which mobilized the new technology of digital video to create a new animation of the dead, resurrecting late 19th-century colored ball. But as baseball historian Bruce Chadwick notes, "[T]he most difficult challenge of all is the journey into uncharted areas, one with few maps, paths or landmarks for guidance."[7]

Perhaps the dearth of good visual (and marketable) material on black baseball explains why Chadwick's publishers enlisted artist Mark Chiarello, whose baseball paintings are instantly recognizable, as if sports fans had already seen them, as if they had always existed, like the widely circulated early 20th-century Major League Baseball cards. But this resurrection the black image was restricted neither to print nor digitized forms. Chiarello had resurrected the heroes of the Negro Leagues as baseball cards (ironically, something they never enjoyed in their lifetimes). The subject matter for his vibrant watercolors derives from baseball's photographic archive. In 2007, Chiarello's mastery of baseball realism and painterly style found its perfect habitat in the digitalization of Robert Peterson's classic work, *Only The Ball Was White*.

Baseball art history books are few, and scholarly works that examine the visual culture of postbellum Gilded Age colored baseball are even scarcer. While a few books contain photographs and other cultural artifacts, typically, images supplement text, and visual analysis is beyond the authors' scope. Paintings, drawings, ceramics, sculpture, and other high art baseball forms are practically non-existent and few cultural and art historians have analyzed the available visual material. An exception is baseball historian David Zang, who analyzed photographs that depicted Moses Fleetwood Walker. For postbellum Gilded Age baseball, no specialty books, digital videos, or trading cards exist either. But the crucial point is not that late 19th-century colored baseball history needs 21st-century surrogates to resurrect it, but that its native habitats — primarily mass-produced objects — have yet to be fully explored. I present this study, then, as an analysis of the colored sporting fraternity from the postbellum Gilded Age. Art and cultural historians may give priority to other black images if the subject was to enter their accounts. For present purposes, I think it makes sense to concentrate on this buried treasure and leave other black images to be exhumed later.

This book explores a complex social institution that contained not only newspapers, sporting and theatrical journals, advertisements, cartoons and illustrations, and lithographs, but also individuals, with a history of practices, rituals, habits, skills, techniques, and a set of material objects and spaces. Black images engaged in a dialogue with baseball images, revealed through multiple traces of old baseball forms (sculpture, painting, and ceramics) and the "habitats" (including, photographs, lithographs, and cartoons) where black images took form and thrived. There is something appealing, even redeeming, about the concept of the sports medium functioning as a place or space that addresses the black image in its native habitats. As artistic productions, these baseball landscapes should be studied and enjoyed to appreciate iconic black images previously relegated to visual culture's lost world.

The print media enlarge our understanding of the colored sporting fraternity in general and baseball representations in particular. This work considers several periodicals. *The Sporting News*, a St. Louis publication established in 1886, covered dog-fighting, prize-fighting, pedestrian-walking, horse-racing, billiards, college football, theater, and baseball. It soon became the dominant American publication covering baseball and even acquired the nickname "The Bible of Baseball." Established in 1845, *The National Police Gazette* was a sensational tabloid, with lurid coverage of murders, prostitution, Wild West outlaws, theater, and boxing. Known primarily for its voyeuristic engravings of scantily clad strippers, burlesque dancers, and prostitutes, *The Gazette* expanded its format to include sports and began reporting on "The National Game" in the early 1880s. *The New York Clipper*, a weekly journal published from 1853 to 1924, covered circuses, dance, music, the outdoors, sports, and theater. Philadelphia's *Sporting Life* devoted coverage to all sports but became the mouthpiece of the national game. Eye-catching column headers veiled the topics covered: "Aquatic" (Boating and Regattas), "Piscatorial" (Fishing), "The Trigger" (glass ball and clay pigeon shooting), "The Wheel" (Bicycle Racing), "The Ring" (Boxing), and "Baseball."

These periodicals and others create challenges for studying baseball representations in mass-culture and high art objects. The latter provide a habitat for formal studies of white ballplayers filled with grace, dignity, and presence — Thomas Eakins's *Base Ball Players Practicing* (1875), Isaac Broome's *Base-Ball Vase* (1876), and Douglas Tilden's *Our National Pastime* (1888-89) immediately come to mind. These works catch players in moments of abstraction, perhaps deep thought or reverie — unaware of being seen. But these works also show that baseball images were not confined to mass-produced objects: they also found visual expression in the work of painters and sculptors. The "habitats" or "landscapes" of white baseball images were many, and their mobility permitted them to migrate back and forth between high art and mass-culture. However, they not only point to the significance of high art as a sports medium, but to the limitations imposed on the black baseball image.

Baseball historian Steven Riess describes the sporting fraternity as an informal brotherhood of pleasure-seekers who backed, participated in, and attended various sporting contests. Sporting men measured manliness by skill at chasing women, drinking, gambling, fighting in taverns, and the frequenting of fashionable sporting houses. How can the term sporting be so iconic as to invoke many forms, each embedded within a larger social framework? Its ambiguity refers at once to pleasure seekers, the acts themselves, and the social spaces to which it belonged. What W.J.T. Mitchell calls the dialectics of species and specimen, stereotype and individual, class and member, the sporting fraternity cuts across all these levels of attention.[8]

The Early Image of Black Baseball uses this taxonomy not to simplify or systematize the discussion, but to complicate the question by expanding its possibilities. Could women be pleasure seekers? Could colored women be sports? What about Chinese immigrants? To these questions, I respond yes. The print media show that colored women and Chinese immigrants participated in the National Pastime, both as spectators and participants. Sporting culture permitted colored women a measure of autonomy; they shunned acquiescence in the face of mistreatment and injustice, and exercised some control over their lives. Blues women, for instance, engaged in sporting life and challenged middle-class notions of womanhood. Middle-class black women were not the only black women who engaged in community-building. For black men and women, the baseball grounds constituted social spaces or places of leisure-class life free of working-class culture. Imagining themselves in baseball uniforms was enormously important in terms of constructing social identities based on something other than wage labor, presenting a public challenge to negative racial stereotypical images, and reinforcing a sense of dignity that was perpetually being assaulted.

Chapter One looks at the Blue Stockings and the Uniques of Chicago in the early 1870s. In a transition space between professional and amateur baseball nines, this black image raises the specter of the black leisure class, racist fears of civil rights, and the modern anxiety that the newly emancipated masses might claim a place in the professional game. The discussion situates these anxieties in the language and imagery used to assert the racial politics of leisure, and depicts the "Blues'" inability to contend with the Uniques in the struggle for the Colored Championship of the United States.

Chapter Two explores riverboat culture, the golden era of the steamboat on the Mississippi that reached its peak between 1870 and 1890. The term "boom" found expression in riverboat vernacular, and sportswriters applied the metaphor to local baseball. Between 1875 and 1877, segregated colored nines boomed in St. Louis and, like other phases of the economy, they witnessed national game trends toward large-scale enterprises, eliminating and absorbing small companies. These years, which also overlapped the Reconstruction era (1863–1877), exposed the "boom" in the struggle for black civil rights.

Chapter Three examines visual and verbal representations of the black sporting crowd. These images suggest that sporting men and women — athletes, musicians, dudes, waiters, tonsorialists, and underworld others — fashioned and were fashioned by black community institutions, wage labor, and white-dominated public spaces. These black images depict a sporting world where race, class, gender, sexuality, and violence coalesced. While discussing the life of the colored sporting fraternity in general, this chapter gives particular attention to the Midwest, especially St. Louis.

Chapter Four provides an art historical context or case study for the baseball photograph. The photograph of the Cuban Giants as Colored Champions of 1887-1888 says something about the limited opportunities for representations of professional black clubs. This portrait of the Cuban Giants, what I call "men of mark and marked men," is an aesthetic object which distills the relation of the New Negro to the National Pastime's economic development, labor unrest, and racial segregation. It captures perfectly the new self-stylized black male and the cult of celebrity.

Chapter Five shows how blackface minstrelsy penetrated the sporting world on many levels — burnt corkers played ball, journalists narrated colored games as blackface farce, and colored nines engaged in "negro" comedy. While most historians credit the Cuban Giants for this innovation, this historical analysis presents other possibilities. It begins with baseball minstrelsy's prehistory, before the Cuban Giants. "Comical coaching," for instance, appeared much earlier; and if any club deserves credit, it is the St. Louis Black Stockings. This story offers St. Louis as a unique case study of the relationship between blackface minstrelsy and baseball.

Chapter Six explores representations of the sporting life of the Callender Minstrels and Henry Bridgewater's Black Stockings B.B.C., which thrived in several habitats and helped fashion the new self-styled black male as public spectacle. This story queries whether blackness was a metaphor for the social excesses of the postbellum Gilded Age — or for the cultural expressivity of the aesthetic movement (1877–1887). That mass-produced objects formed the native habitats of these genuine colored artists reveals much about the process by which blackness is pictured.

The conclusion assesses baseball images as the principal currency of media. Baseball images, not language, are the main currency of bulletin-boards, telegraphic dispatches, sports pages, commercial advertisements, and black bodies. Midwifed by these technologies, Henry Bridgewater's Black Stockings entered the daily lives of the sporting fraternity. Despite the available evidence revealing the centrality of Bridgewater's efforts to modernist thinking and critical involvement in baseball and civil rights, this is the first study to explore how this "man of mark" helped fashion the cult of black baseball celebrity.

CHAPTER ONE

Dust from Many Diamonds:
Trauma, Memory, and the
Colored Championship

A National Transformation shaped by the compelling forces of Reconstruction and accompanied locally by an epochal disaster, Chicago's Great Fire of 1871, profoundly influenced the transition of African Americans into a new way of life in triumphant, postwar Chicago ... for the first time, the character of societal transformation accorded African Americans unfettered expressions of agency, choice, accountability and respect.

How could one discover the strategies by which dominant power groups in the United States developed mechanisms to engineer a "forgetting" of traumas that they originally inflicted on victims (such as slavery or the decimation of Native Americans)?

The Uniques, a colored club, of this city, claim that they are champions, and desire to play the Franklins. The Franklins refuse to play the 'niggers,' as they call them, except for $250 a side, and have deposited $100 with Tom Foley, and if the Uniques desire to play them, they can deposit another $100 alongside of the Franklins,' and the game will be played at anytime they wish.[1]

In 1865, *Harper's Illustrated Weekly* allegorized the National Pastime as an act of civil rights legislation (**fig. 1**, page 15). *The Great National Game* depicts a black male figure that embodies the United States. Patriotically dressed in a striped shirt and cap, a colored ball-player prepares to whack a star-covered sphere. The enlarged baseball is suspended just below members of Congress who watch the game. Now a citizen, the player clutches a bat inscribed with the word "15th Amendment." Holding up his pantaloons and supporting civil rights legislation is a belt inscribed "41st Congress." Poised to take a whack at citizenship, a white woman (holding a bat inscribed "16th Amendment"), an Inuit (the Alaska Purchase or "Seward's Folly"), and Chinese immigrants (Naturalization Act of 1870). But "Our Colored Brother" wards them off: "Hi Yah! Stan' back Dar: It's Dis Chile's Innin's Now."

The Great National Game transforms the embedded difference of civil rights legislation into a national sport. The batting "team" shares an exotic strangeness; sartorial display enhances race and gender difference. The Eskimo's costume appears ill-suited for the game; the Asian of Chinese descent sports his native dress; and the costume of the white female cradling the bat, like Daniel Boone holding a musket, is too revealing. Marginalizing this grouping along the composition's edge, the colored batter's powerful form dwarfs their smaller bodies. The batter's elbow forces the hooded figure to raise his right hand and lean away in defense, fearing he might be swatted. Not unlike the colored batter's massive, sculpted physique, the 15th amendment and baseball are young, new and, in this instance, strong.

The pastoral landscape is hardly idyllic. For some, undoubtedly, it portrays a world turned up-side down. In the background, white spectators witness the black figure's potential skills and witness the event's spectacle. On the most basic level, the black image conjures the potential threat of a new social order: a huge black man ascends the post–Civil War center stage. His body, resting on the weight of his bent right leg, leans toward the smaller figures. And viewers wonder whether the batter will make contact with the ball. *The Great National Game* offers the first visual glimpse of the "fifteenth amendment club slingers."

The Great National Game offers an allegorical representation of the colored baseballist, a black image that depicts the figure preparing to take a whack at citizenship during Reconstruction (1863–1877). The illustration mediates post–Civil War trauma; that is, emancipation and civil rights expose how the black image of the colored baseballist remapped the black body for changing political projects and cultural circumstances. The image invites us to question how the allegorical figure reinforces certain cultural and political perceptions, and whether the image engages viewers in a "mental sketching" of dread, fascination, or fantasy. The reciprocal relation between *The Great National Game* and the viewer fosters the mental sketching of the action and the action's mental sketching of the viewer. The action is the fantasy scene of the figure stepping up to the plate; the fascination is that the batter does not gaze at a regulation-size ball, and the unseen twirler (the federal government) lobs a big fat one. The dread of not being able to capitalize on "fat ones" like civil rights amendments reveals that success was not guaranteed. Surely spectators — primarily white male citizens — had something to say about it. Social opportunities for blacks, both on and off the green diamond, remained extremely limited.

The Great National Game is also allegorical because it characterizes the baseball landscape. By baseball landscape, I mean a sports medium, the actual or lived spaces of the colored sporting fraternity, journalists, photographers, painters, and illustrators. As the hallowed site of the first organized competition in 1846, the Elysian Fields, of Hoboken, New Jersey invoked the baseball landscape as contested ground, mediating the idyllic mythos of baseball: pastoral vs. urban origins, leisure vs. labor, gentlemanly wagering vs. blacklegs gambling, or inclusion vs. exclusion. While Congress was passing the 14th amendment guaranteeing equal protection under the law, the National Association of Amateur Base Ball Players was drawing baseball's first color line by denying membership to the Pythians, an all-colored team from Philadelphia. Following the formation of the National Association of Professional Ball Players in 1871, coupled with the exclusion of colored baseballists, literary and visual artists mediated a bewildering array of secondary images in the baseball landscape, black images of the colored baseballist cast in the role of the serpent in the idyllic baseball garden. The iconic emblems of the baseball landscape — ball, bat, uniforms, spectators, players, and wide-open field — expose a host of crucial ambiguities. They refer at once to the black body in the illustration, the illustration itself, and the genre (political cartoon or baseball illustration) to which it belongs.[2]

THE GREAT NATIONAL GAME.

Our Colored Brother. "HI YAH! STAN' BACK DAR: IT'S DIS CHILE'S INNIN'S NOW."

Figure 1. The Great National Game, *Punchinello*, 1870

The Great National Game symbolizes post–Civil War trauma because it invokes the black body as an "object of both love and hate, affection and fear, forms of overestimation such as worship, adoration, and veneration, and of devaluation or underestimation — horror, disgust, and abomination." The best evidence for traumatic black images is the passion with which the literary and visual artists sought to destroy or kill them. The value or life of black baseball images becomes most interesting when they appear at the center of the socio-political crisis framed by Reconstruction. The colored baseballist represents not only the surplus value of black images generated by the politics of exploitation, misery, and inequality, but also the surplus value that transforms both visual and verbal forms into "bearers of ideological fantasy."[3]

In the colored sporting world, where positive black images published for public consumption were relatively rare, *The Great National Game* proved an ambivalent image that wandered the cultural wilderness of the sports medium in search of baseball habitats. Baseball photography, more specifically, photographs of colored baseballists, like this illustration, thrived as another habitat. Sadly, I have yet to find individual or team photographs from the 1870s. Of course, this doesn't mean that photographic images don't exist. Nor does the lack of evidence mean that colored baseballists did not sit for photographs. And it would also be wrong to link this absence to economics or cultural sophistication. Despite limited artifacts from the 1870s, it would seem odd if colored clubs had not posed for studio portraits — young colored men caught up in baseball mania, immortalized themselves in baseball portraiture as well. Nonetheless, surviving black baseball images demonstrate the migration of the colored baseballist from the habitat of baseball photography to the habitat of illustrated engravings. When illustrated magazines and journals reproduced baseball portraits — often woodcut engravings derived from photographs — colored baseballists were noticeably absent. For the white sporting fraternity, this absence or oversight probably mattered very little; the relation of baseball celebrity to fifteenth amendment club slingers seemed incompatible. Even when sportswriters deemed the exploits of colored baseballists exemplary, visual images failed to make the cut. And for colored newspapers, the surplus value of black images remained dubious, a "minor skirmish" in the larger theater of social conflict that focused on "real values" such as food, shelter, and employment.[4]

By 1868, the colored sporting fraternity and baseball representations had emerged in Chicago. And in the years roughly corresponding to the Reconstruction Period (1868–1878), print media reported the exploits of colored aggregations. This spread baseball fever. In 1875, *The Times*, a Chicago newspaper, reported: "There is war in Africa. Yesterday, the colored Blue Stockings of St. Louis, played the colored Uniques, of Chicago, a match game of baseball on the grounds of the White Stockings, and walloped them to the tune of 12 to 8." This hyperbole use of the war metaphor had as much to do with baseball vernacular as with negative racial stereotypes. Beginning with the Civil War, if not earlier, newspapers across the country played a crucial role in stigmatizing segregated black communities, labeling them with epithets like "Africa" and portraying their inhabitants as criminals. This ambivalence fashioned colored baseballists as objects of adoration and abomination.[5]

In 1870, the number of city baseball teams increased exponentially at all levels of the sport. "Daily newspapers regularly reported the results," notes historian Ray Schmidt, who has demonstrated that Chicago has long been regarded as one of the capitals of baseball, dating back to the earliest days of the sport's professional era in the 1870s. After the Civil War, veterans returned to civilian life and organized contests among amateur teams, intercollegiate teams, company teams, and boys' teams. One of the first all-colored nines was the Blue Stockings: "This outstanding ballclub claimed the state's 'colored championship' after winning a late season series from the Rockfords, another all-black team." Broadening Schmidt's historical summary, Leslie A. Heaphy identifies one sporting account that claimed the Blue Stockings had been around for many years by 1870. She also shares team rosters for the 1870-71 baseball seasons.[6]

Of course Heaphy and Schmidt know that their black baseball narratives are only metapictures, constructed out of scattered fragments, buried treasures sketched out in relation to personal concepts. Like periods of history, baseball stories achieve reputations. But almost every ball club, even the most overlooked colored nine, "will eventually find a champion to discover unnoticed virtues or unknown difficulties mastered." Historian Neil Harris reminds us: "Successive generations of biographers present dramatically different views of their subjects." The Blue Stockings' social drama is not simply a popularization of historical understanding, nor a mere vehicle for reporting and representing historical knowledge. Baseball narrative is a key element in the process of historical thinking and discovery, not just a descriptive afterthought or afterimage, but a constitutive element, a speculative, theoretical construction. Perhaps more than any baseball history, 19th-century colored baseball requires the aid of art and cultural historians to reconstruct black images embedded in words and pictures.[7]

This narrative resurrects images of Chicago's postbellum colored sporting fraternity. Specifically, it identifies an image-repertoire that circulated across print media engaged in racial and ethnic stereotyping. The combination of baseball and civil rights, critics complained, had transformed American citizens of African descent into creatures of legislative enactment. Sports journalists dubbed them "amendments," political appendages of the National Pastime. However, the means of representation links black images of the colored sporting fraternity. Yet the representation of black baseball images is a symptom of their indispensable role to sporting life. Sportswriter Louis Meacham observed: "Chicago has enjoyed a wide range of experience in base ball, having witnessed its representation in nearly every possible shape, but not until yesterday had an opportunity been afforded for seeing how the American citizen of African descent does it."[8]

These black images raised the specter of the leisure class, racist fears of civil rights, and the modern anxiety that the newly emancipated masses might claim a place in the professional game. Yet these social attitudes would evolve during the 1870s, along with black images the sporting world used to fashion a presumably all-white professional league. Prior to the establishment of the National Association of Professional Base Ball Players (NAPBBP), powerhouses like the Forest Cities of Rockford, Illinois, and the Chicago White Stockings expressed ambivalence toward the fifteenth amendment club slingers. The print media situated this ambivalence in the language and imagery that asserted a racial politics of baseball and the challenges facing the colored sporting fraternity.[9]

The Colored Sporting Fraternity of Chicago

On Sunday afternoon, 11 July 1858, the Chicago Police raided a "negro gambling den" on Harrison Street, just east of Wells Street. They arrested keeper Anthony Merrick, Thomas Viven, Harry Johnson, George Robinson, Thomas Scott, Silas Johnson, Mark Lee, William Moore, Joseph Hansen, Wesley Hall, George Clay, Robert Goodloe, Charles Bailey, Thomas Wilson, and Roe Fisher, alias Maggie Morse. Merrick's gambling house was formerly kept by two colored women known as Big Liz and Indian Sal. That same weekend, on the same

THE SPREES OF A SPORT.

"notorious" corner, police descended upon a black-and-tan dance saloon and arrested whites and blacks on charges of disorderly conduct for nightly drunken revels. Among the citizens of color swept up were C. Peterson, Elijah Parker and Marshal Rogers.[10]

Contrary to the optimism embodied in the "fat one" lobbed toward the batter in the *Great National Game*, the grim reality of the 15th amendment, five years later, found members of the Blue Stockings Base Ball Club living in an established vice district "swarming with harlots, footpads, pimps, and pickpockets and crowded with brothels, saloons, and dives of every description." George Brown and William Johnson, for instance, lived in "Shinbone Alley," next door to the powerful colored gambler Stephen Stamps. According to police accounts, Stamps ran a "coon" gambling den and saloon in an old frame building on Monroe street east of Wells. During a raid of his resort, one officer, watching the activities from the building's roof, in the comedic fashion of the Keystone Cops, fell through the glass transom or skylight. The derisive term "coon dive," writes historian Cynthia Marie Blair, represented a means of classifying resorts of sexual leisure considered doubly uninviting to traveling white businessmen or an affluent local sporting fraternity. But there was always a bordello, billiard hall, saloon, or dance hall located in the colored part of the city, which formed the social headquarters of gamblers, well-dressed thieves, and confidence men.[11]

Knowing what happens in these cultural spaces permits us to understand the social formation of the colored sporting fraternity, identify unfamiliar black images from its postbellum image-repertoire, and unveil black images that invoke and constrain the colored baseballist. Despite the racial ambivalence, not all members of the colored sporting fraternity (dudes, dandies, aesthetes, etc.) have been examined; nor has the figure been painted, drawn, or sculpted in the fashion of high art. Black images of the colored sporting life thrive in the print media, and the birth of black images and their evolving baseball landscape reveals how places of leisure were also places of work for some segments of the black working class, particularly women who had few opportunities outside of domestic service.[12]

Historian Steven Reiss describes the sporting fraternity as an informal brotherhood of pleasure-seekers who sponsored, participated in, and attended various sporting contests: "All part of the male bachelor subculture these sportsmen measured manliness by skill at chasing women, drinking, gambling, and fighting" in the faceless taverns, gambling halls, and fashionable sporting houses (**fig. 2**). The iconic term sporting invokes many forms, each embedded within a larger social framework. Its ambiguity refers at once to pleasure-seekers, the acts themselves, and the social spaces to which sporting belonged. What iconologist W.J.T. Mitchell calls the dialectics of species and specimen, stereotype and individual, class and member — the colored sport cuts across all these levels of attention. For the colored sporting fraternity, baseball helped increase race pride, provided its members a sense of self-worth by vicarious identification with athletic heroes, and gained the black community local, regional, and national attention. Baseball, argues Reiss, was the most important 19th-century sport of the black community. Thus, newspapers accounts devoting significant attention to the colored sporting fraternity deserve serious consideration.[13]

I invoke the term sporting fraternity not to simplify or systematize its usage but to complicate the question by expanding its possibilities. Could women be pleasure seekers?

Opposite: **Figure 2. The Sprees of a Sport,** *National Police Gazette,* **1882**

A FATAL FLIRTATION.

Figure 3. A Fatal Flirtation, *National Police Gazette*, 1884

Could colored women be sports? To answer both questions: yes. The *Gazette* divulges how sporting culture permitted colored women a measure of autonomy; in the face of mistreatment and injustice, they shunned acquiescence and exercised some control over their lives. Historian Robin Kelley has identified places of leisure as places of work for some segments of the black working class. Sporting culture gave colored women access to the expanding and diversified urban economy: access to money, and opportunity to establish a degree of self-sufficiency in a labor market offering extremely low wages and few alternatives. Angela Davis shows how the black blues women of the 20th century challenged middle-class notions of womanhood, and engaged in community-building. Colored sporting women were, as historian Cynthia Marie Blair relates, much more than symbols of the fragile boundaries separating zones of morality and immorality. Sumptuary display and conspicuous consumption suggest that linkages of material culture to the sporting fraternity impacted the search for additional sources of income (**fig. 3**).[14]

The female baseballist (or 16th amendment club slinger) depicted in the *Great National Game*, particularly her hour-glass form and shapely legs, operates within the baseball landscape. Sporting representations of female baseballists ranged from burlesque to soft pornography to prostitution. The sartorial display of their legs and stockings intersected the world of theater, prostitution, and by 1869 — baseball. The Cincinnati Red Stockings fashioned an aesthetic style that other professional ball clubs would emulate, exposing shapely legs in a sensuous spectrum of colored hosiery. But *Sporting Life* condemned the female baseballist: "The Cincinnati Club managers should be ashamed of renting its ground for a purpose of degrading the national game.... The female baseballists meet with condemnation whenever they appear." The *New York Times* declared them "more circus than is popularly supposed." While many critics found such linkages between women and the sporting fraternity problematic, entrepreneurs sought to capitalize on them and their lucrative possibilities.[15]

The female figure of the theatrical stage depicted in the pages of *The Police Gazette* helped to define the sporting crowd (**figs. 4, 5**). One main feature of the journal was the depiction of female performers. These photoengraved portraits of voluptuous bodies depict white women in costumes and poses. Just as the *Police Gazette* published and sold photographs of female entertainers — for the delectation of the national sporting fraternity — the theater and sports journal often reinforced links between leisure and sexual pleasure in urban cities like St. Louis. Sporting resorts like Deagle's Theater, Looney's Varieties, and Esher's Varieties — at times, dubbed "houses of ill-repute" — showcased female "cocktail" singers and dancers, offering artistic freedom to perform bawdy songs and dances. In 1873, the aspiring actress Stella Dickson, alias Moore, came to St. Louis from Olney, Illinois. Described as a "beautiful actress of sweet sixteen," Dickson obtained an engagement at one of the variety shows. One newspaper reported that she also performed as a sex worker. Angered by the report, the actress instituted a $20,000 libel suit against the newspaper. Following its own investigation, another local paper declared Dickson's case "rather thin."[16]

Actresses, songstresses, dancers, and strippers shared social spaces often reserved for sex workers (male and female). The exposure of real and imagined flesh framed them as objects of sexual pleasure. Certain representations of legs covered in white tights and exposed white arms give the visual impression of partially nude figures (**fig. 6**). Voluptuous in form, they recall the full-figured women depicted by the Flemish artist Peter Paul Rubens

LILLIE GRUBB,

ONE OF THE FAIREST FLOWERS OF THE ADONIS GARLAND OF PRETTY YOUNG WOMEN.

[Photo by Falk.]

Figure 4. Lillie Grubb, *National Police Gazette*, 1885

(1577–1640). Theatrical costumes mapped the contours of the female form and exposed body parts that would normally be concealed. In saloons, concert halls, and other sporting resorts of Chicago, police accounts identified gaudy women of all ethnic groups who wore bodices cut so low that they didn't amount to much more than a belt, scarlet dresses that never came below their knees, and multi-colored stockings and fancy shoes. The role of stockings as an aesthetic form of sartorial display will be explored in Chapter Six.[17]

In the 1870s, Vina Fields ran a large pleasure palace at 138–140 Custom House Place in Chicago. Although Fields and all of her girls or "boarders" were mulattos, it was not a "coon dive": colored men were not allowed. During the Chicago Columbian Exposition of

Figure 5. M'lle Dalizel, *National Police Gazette*, 1881

1893, Fields boasted more than 60 women. Fields appears to have left her Custom House Place address between 1904 and 1907. In 1905, she resided at 1834 South Dearborn, remaining there until 1910. Her well-furnished establishment harbored the handsomest women and charged the highest prices, and the white male customers were comparatively safe from robbery. Fields deliberately fashioned resorts in accordance with Victorian ideals of leisure; in a rare interview, she suggested links between the idea of home and the inner workings of high-status bordellos. The police never raided Field's establishments. She rigidly enforced her own rules and regulations and never had to call the police for assistance. Fields used her wealth to finance her daughter's expensive education.[18]

Like others who sought to liberate themselves from the social and moral constraints of period, female baseballists were chided as little more than prostitutes. When baseball promoter Henry H. Freedman brought his show to New Orleans, for instance, the *American Nashville* noted their exotic jersey shirts,

ANNIE HART.

ONE OF THE SHAPELIEST AND MOST STATUESQUE OF THE DIVINITIES OF THE VARIETY STAGE.

Figure 6. Annie Hart, *National Police Gazette*, 1885

knee breeches, colored stockings, and red caps. Critics called their revealing attire indecent and threatening (**fig. 7**). But one startled male spectator invaded the field and seized a player by the neck. It was his sister. After his arrest, Freedman was run out of town by angry citizens who believed he was soliciting young girls for prostitution.[19]

The rage for using female baseballists to advertise cigarettes was started by Cuban tobacco manufacturers. By the 1880s, the cigarette manufacturer Lewis Ginter had produced over eighty sets of cigarette cards, including a set of women baseball players. Goodwin & Company, maker of Old Judge and Gypsy Queen Cigarette brands, is believed to be the first business to create baseball cards and other sports cards. The first cards were small, 1½ inches by 2½ inches, and printed on thick cardboard. Old Judge issued more than 2,000 different baseball cards, plus cards for other sports and non-sports. While nudity and truly risqué advertisements were seldom used to sell the early cigarette brands, titillating portraits of female baseballists capitalized on theatrical photographs of actresses and dancers.[20]

In New York and Atlanta, tobacco dealers encouraged sporting establishments to display photographs of models dressed as female baseballists. *The Constitution* reported that "a cigarette picture sensation is agitating certain good people in Atlanta." The pictures displayed in a window at the Kimball House depicted "nine handsome female baseball players in attitudes common in that popular game." Crowds gathered daily to view "the graceful forms" of the female baseballists. A prominent lawyer attempted to buy a set of the pictures but was informed that only tobacco dealers could purchase them, and then only as advertisements, so the attorney claimed to be a dealer and purchased 5,000 cigarettes to secure six sets of photographs. Critics declared the images indecent and immoral, and newspapers joined the crusade against the photographic display of "the luscious baseball nine."[21]

Anthony Comstock, agent for the New York Society for the Suppression of Vice, joined the crusade, seized the "pretty pictures" wherever found, and issued a stringent order to dealers to suppress similar cigarette advertisements. Dealers argued that they were no more immoral than the portraits of actresses exhibited in the barrooms of leading hotels and photographic establishments (**fig. 8**). Dealers assured fashionable sports that the cigarette photographs had been all taken in New York, and that young women had been especially employed to sit for them. Some of the more defiant dealers announced their intention to legally contest Comstock's right to seize their property. The combined efforts of the Atlanta and New York dealers failed.[22]

The baseball landscape contains architectural objects, buildings that not only say something about the sporting fraternity but broader American society as well. These buildings' capacity to influence social and intellectual life established their role as status signifiers in the history of the world's religious and political institutions. Their changing revelations affected domesticity, urbanity, and civic awareness. "Buildings, in the form of records," writes historian Neil Harris, "belong to different creatures: the architects, the developers, the owners, the tenants, the municipality, and in some cases, even the visitors." While Harris does not discuss how aged structures, demographic shifts, municipal catastrophes (fires in Chicago's case), and urban renovation help define the composition of ethnic/racial populations, the sports medium offers insights into how older buildings in predominantly black communities came to be labeled as barbarous legacies of a repudiated past.[23]

My earliest memories of movie palaces in downtown Chicago suggest how buildings "became vulnerable to victimization as symbols of systems being repudiated." In the 1960s,

THE DAISIES OF THE DIAMOND FIELD.

HOW THE GIRLS SHAKE THEIR PETTICOATS AND GO IN FOR VIGOROUS AND ATHLETIC EXERCISES WHICH DEVELOP THE MUSCLE, EXPAND THE CHEST, AND KEEP THE BLOOD FROM STAGNATING.

THE GENIUS OF ADVERTISING COULD NO FURTHER GO—AN ENTERPRISING PROPRIETRESS OF A BAGNIO PLACES A PHOTO-LITHOGRAPH IN HER WINDOW SETTING FORTH THE CHARMS OF THE INMATES; NEW YORK CITY.—See Page 3.

Figure 8. An Enterprising Proprietress of a Bagnio, *National Police Gazette*, 1880

theater owners collaborated with the public schools to promote movie-going as an educational and cultural experience (White schools had been engaged in this practice since the 1950s). On such occasions, my teachers required the finest dress code and the best behavior; before and after the film, we dined at a downtown restaurant. When my all-black sixth grade class attended *The Sound of Music* (Loop Theater) and *Russian Adventure* (McVickers Theatre) in 1966, I remember that while white schools were seated on the main floor, the white male ushers escorted the black schools to the balcony. Despite these peculiarities, the opulent and majestic movie palace became an object of adoration.

These experiences suggest how movie houses represented symbols of social segregation in the mid–1960s, transforming pleasure spaces into sources of shame. On Chicago's Southside, I spent my youth at neighborhood theaters (the Regal and the Metropolitan or "Met"). Getting to the "show" early usually guaranteed choice seats (balcony or main floor). At downtown theaters, I could not claim any seat in the house until white audiences abandoned the theaters (probably between 1967 and 1969). In 1967, my friends and I enjoyed *The Dirty Dozen*, starring Jim Brown, at the State-Lake Theater. As white audiences fled

***Opposite:* Figure 7. The Daisies of the Diamond Field, *National Police Gazette*, 1882**

what musician George Clinton would later call "Chocolate City" for the "vanilla suburbs," downtown movie houses suffered from lowered expectations. Traditionally, they dealt with heavy traffic patterns and required aggressive, routinized systems of maintenance. The theater had to be cleaned every night. Ushers, who had previously helped to keep order and collected excessive trash between viewings, gradually disappeared. With the demand for midnight showings, the movie houses were poorly cleaned, and rodent infestation followed. It was not unusual to hear audiences scream or see them scamper as rats scurried across their feet. Street gangs also infiltrated the theater, and patrons could be robbed. Theater owners no longer seemed concerned with bad publicity. Anger and anxiety accompanied this transformation — the disappearance, disfigurement or remodeling of the social landscape exposed the inevitable pains of aging. Movies palaces became symbols of fear and dread. Old Comiskey Park was also contested terrain. Irish toughs robbed unsuspecting black boys, and we knew to never leave the park through the gates facing the Bridgeport neighborhood! As a medium, then, buildings are messengers.[24]

Between 1860 and 1870, Chicago's black population rose from 1,000 to 3,691, representing an increase of 286 percent. According to historian Christopher Reed, this demographic phenomenon resulted from the wartime flight of hundreds of former slaves, plus Civil War veterans who participated in community building by constructing an "imagined" community of those who shared the vicissitudes of life on the battlefield. Almost two-thirds of the native born blacks came from the South, and of these, almost a third were from Kentucky, and the next largest number from Virginia. "Being virtually invisible," Reed adds, "Chicago offered African Americans neither the overt hostility that led to violence and riots elsewhere in the North nor the malignant neglect commonly associated with proscription in the workplace, schools, and church." Nearly 80 percent of the black population lived in the area bordered by Sixteenth Street to the south, Lake Michigan to the east, and the Main and South branches of the Chicago River to the north and west; at the time, this area comprised the First, Second, and Third wards. A close look at the 1870 Federal Census Report for the Third Ward suggests that occupations for blacks, while varied, were primarily nonskilled.[25]

The Reconstruction amendments enacted between 1865 and 1870, and other pieces of congressional legislation dramatically influenced life in Chicago. During a meeting of the city's colored electors, held at Mt. Olivet Baptist Church in 1870, the following proclamation was read: "Whereas, We, the colored citizens of Chicago, recognizing with pride the great boon bestowed upon us through the earnest exertions of the great Republican party of the United states, to-wit, the right of enfranchisement, we therefore pledge ourselves, each and every one, to support and maintain the principles of said party." Among these colored electors were William C. Phillips and C. B. White, members of Mt. Olivet. The church had been a source of black leadership since 1850. It had opened its brand new building in 1868, under the leadership of the Reverend Richard DeBaptiste, a nationally known minister and civil rights leader. In 1869, DeBaptiste organized Illinois' first Colored Convention to fight for black civil rights. After its destruction in the Chicago Fire, the congregation rebuilt the church on the same site in 1877.[26]

While the black community suffered from the Chicago Fire, Reed argues the trauma of this "fiery holocaust" offered no new challenge to the collective black psyche: "Compared to the traumas of bondage, liberation, combat, and postwar civilian adjustment, it took on the aura of being just another in a series of life's major tragedies and disappointments." But following the fire's aftermath, the bulk of the city's gamblers and prostitutes infiltrated the black community—stretching the demimonde to an area three blocks long and fifteen blocks wide. It transformed the "Black Hole" into a collection of saloons, gambling joints, and bawdy houses at Washington and Halsted Streets, a vice area bounded by Sangamon, Halsted, Lake, and Monroe Streets. "No part of Chicago was rebuilt more quickly than the saloons, brothels, gambling houses, and other resorts and habitations of the underworld. What was later called the "Levee District" infringed upon black residential areas and threatened black middle-class families that lived there.[27]

Historian Thekla Joiner shows how the combination of demographic factors and racial conflict exacerbated the potential for violence within the sporting fraternity of Chicago. Joiner makes two crucial points. First, the modest size of the colored population made the everyday encounters of working-class life especially unstable and bloody. Second, colored men, also by virtue of their small numbers, found themselves without a network or group of loyal friends and were vulnerable to physical assaults. Local bordellos and gambling dens employed colored men as porters, waiters, and janitors, and colored women as maids and prostitutes. Colored laborers routinely encountered drunken, boisterous young men eager to demonstrate their manliness. Attempting to control wild white bachelors at their wildest, colored men became convenient targets for local toughs who failed at faro and lost at lust.[28]

While Joiner states that it was not unusual for groups of whites, frequently Irish toughs, to bulldoze colored citizens by crowding them off the sidewalks and into alleys or streets, members of the sporting fraternity could perpetuate violence. Following the Excelsiors vs. Forest Citys contest in 1868, for instance, both Chicago and Rockford fans and players rushed to the commuter trains. Crowding themselves into one of the cars, Forest City players confronted a colored fan. A "prominent member of the Forest City Club" pushed the man's hat over his eyes, and put his hands over his mouth. Laughter and cries of "put the darkey off" followed. The man agreed to depart the train if his company was objectionable. But as a paying customer, he stressed his right to ride the train. Cries of "put him off" were renewed. The conductor ordered him off, shoved back the crowd to make room, and gave him a push. A "prominent" but unnamed ballplayer kicked him, and the "poor fellow" landed on the street. Amid laughter and jeers, the car proceeded on its way. The abused man walked home. Among the team's prominent players: Albert Goodwill Spalding and Roscoe Barnes. Members of the sporting crowd would continue to view blacks as minstrel figures and went about business as usual, disregarding Reconstruction amendments and civil rights legislation.[29]

How the journalist comically restages the violent scene reveals much about racial attitudes. What would this scene mean to baseball fans? To engage minstrelizing black images as an "amusement" at fairs or summer resorts was fairly prominent. Participants had opportunities to throw baseballs at "wooden darkeys" or "a live Ethiopian" target. These cultural practices dovetail neatly with other situations where literal or symbolic violence against blacks proved acceptable. While newspapers remapped the baseball landscape, their stories were anything but transparent, self-evident, or unmediated entities. And such narratives should remind us that the sports medium simulated older narrative forms: advertisements, police and court records, gossip and city life columns, and business reports that represented the colored sporting fraternity in recognizable, if not ambivalent black imagery, the comedic antics of minstrelsy and the transgression behavior of crime. The sports medium, then, did not remap the habitat of the black image for the baseball landscape so much as it was already mapped by the nature of sensational newspaper accounts that made the black baseball representations look like those earlier stereotypical figures.[30]

By the 1860s, hotel employment afforded young colored men opportunities beyond unskilled labor. Hotels organized colored ball clubs, hosting contests to entertain guests. In the baseball world, the gentlemanly deportment of the hotel waiter and the manly prowess of the baseballist constituted signifiers of identity and social status. And through skilled performances on the green diamond, colored hotel waiters could imagine shedding degradation and collapsing class distinctions between themselves and wealthy whites. Working at Chicago's Old Sherman House and Wright's Opera House Restaurant, for instance, some young colored men figured among the city's finest baseballists. The *Tribune* reports: "A match game of baseball will be played on Monday at Excelsior Grounds, between the colored waiters of Wright's Opera House restaurant and the waiters of the Sherman House. A large attendance is expected." This elite white spectatorship included the Sherman House's traders and financiers, and the Crosby Opera House's crowd of singing and dramatic stars.[31]

The relation of sports institutions to the emergence of the colored sporting fraternity of Chicago shows why the lives of black images are so complex. It expands our understanding of the postbellum dialectics of power and desire within baseball representations. When the police blotter narrates the social drama of the "Black Hole," black images are thriving: "Joseph Lewis and Allen Gunnale (colored)" were taken into custody for making a race course of Clark Street. But the construction of the racial and racist stereotype is not a simple exercise of the black image as a technique of domination. It is what Mitchell calls "the knotting of a double bind that afflicts both the subject and the object of racism in a complex of desire and hatred." The ocular violence of racism splits the object of representation in two, rending and rendering it simultaneously hypervisible and invisible, an object of abomination and adoration.[32]

The Blue Stockings: Prized Objects and Offensive Images

In *The Great National Game*, the baseball holds a central axis in the composition. Suspended in space, between twirler and batter, the star-covered sphere mediates the action. The action, one might argue, centers on the ball. As the batter, on-deck batters, and spectators hold it under their watchful gaze, they seem spellbound. It is a prized object. What should be obvious is that the represented object is not a baseball at all. Its unusual size has something to do with the object's detailing. Five-pointed white stars cover its dark surface. Had the artist depicted the ball in naturalistic proportions, the stars would have been difficult to see. On the surface, the constitutive elements of the flag (stars and stripes signifying the original thirteen colonies and the union of the states) help refashion the colored baseballist as a U.S. citizen. The baseball is, then, a kind of trophy. Sometimes it is quite explicit, as when the Blue Stockings appeal for recognition in a local amateur baseball tournament; or when the touring Chicago Uniques defeat the Philadelphia Pythians on the latter's home turf, and declare themselves Colored Champions of the United States.

The connection between social status and citizenship in a post–Civil War society is central to *The Great National Game*—but what is it doing in baseball? Let me cite one interesting example, Isaac Broome's *Base-Ball Vase* (**fig. 9**). When the Otto and Brewer Pottery Company (Trenton, New Jersey) employed Broome in 1873, he was engaged by John Hart Brewer to create special sculptural designs for the Philadelphia Centennial Exhibition (1876). A portrait painter, sculptor, and fresco artist, Broome produced a series of works in Parian ware, sculptural imitations of marble, both in surface and tint. Among Broome's works were two covered vases that flanked Otto and Brewer's display in the ceramics area of the Manufacturer's Building. The nationalistic spirit of these vases, inspired by the formation of the National Base Ball League, attracted so much attention that one vase was moved to the Art Gallery of Memorial Hall a month after the fair opened. In 1887, Brewer gave one of the vases to the National League of Professional Baseball Players to serve as a pennant trophy. *Baseball Vase* became the first American work of ceramics to be officially classified as art.[33]

Base Ball Vase not only commemorates the national spirit but elevates the national sport to high art. From its pedestal rises a gradually tapering vase, suggestive of a baseball bat. The lower portion consists of a series of bats banded together by a strap. It depicts three figures sculpted in-the-round: the batter, the catcher, and the pitcher. In raised relief, along the vase's middle band, are smaller, running figures. Self-absorbed, the ballplayers display manly vigor as they contest one another, and their gestures

Figure 9. Base Ball Vase, Isaac Broome (Detroit), 1876

PRESENTATION OF A CHAMPION BAT TO THE "RED STOCKING" BASE-BALL CLUB, CINCINNATI, OHIO, ON ITS RETURN HOME.—[SKETCHED BY J. A. GERVIS.]

Figure 10. Presentation of a Champion Bat to the Red Stocking Base-Ball Club, J.A. Gervis, *Harper's Weekly*, **1869**

move in narrative fashion, at least in the mind's eye, around the vase. Along the middle register, a player reaches out to catch a ball. These figures also display a gritty naturalism — wrinkled long-sleeve shirts, rolled up past the elbow, reveal bulging biceps; there is stitching on the shoes. On the uppermost register, a laurel wreath circles the smoothly rendered spherical cap which mimics a leather-covered baseball, complete with stitching. It idealizes the celebrity status of a champion.

The *Baseball Vase* also commemorates the nation's centennial anniversary. The cream-colored trophy, comprised of several registers, fashions a primordial habitat for both our National Game and our national symbol, the American Bald Eagle. The bottom register's leather-bound rack mimics bound reeds. At the base, encased baseballs surround a fluted stem. The eagle displays massive thighs and razor-sharp talons; the ball players' sinewy lower bodies mimic these physical characteristics. Perched upon the summit of the vase cover, an eagle watches vigilantly over the ballplayers. Both the ballplayers and the bird invoke the nation's virility and self-adoration.[34]

Baseball trophies are objects of "conspicuous consumption" and "sumptuary display" (**fig. 10**). The 19th-century theorist Thorstein Veblen coined these terms to define a new leisure class that had emerged in the postbellum Gilded Age. But in material terms, baseball awards took multiple forms in the 1870s. When they took on the image of a baseball, trophys made direct associations to the other objects in baseball landscape. On the other hand, baseball tournaments offered other forms of desire that transformed sumptuary display into a thing; championship objects acquired more than one name, more than one identity. In 1867, the baseball tournament of Detroit honored players not only with gold and silver objects but with greenbacks, blue and red silk field flags, and wine sets. Of course, this practice was hardly uncommon. But the emerging reverence for gold and the persistent decline in the prestige and, ultimately, the acceptance of silver bears contemplation: silver ice pitchers, silver mounted balls, silver-mounted opera glasses, silver tea sets, silver tobacco boxes, silver stars (badge), gold-mounted rosewood bats, regulation-size gold balls, gold badges of baseball design, and gold-mounted opera glasses competed as objects of conspicuous consumption.[35]

The problem with scrutinizing these prestigious symbols is that they have too many meanings, and too many of them are contradictory. Baseball narratives set the silver ball in motion as an object of adoration. In 1870 Conger and Webb, a Chicago jewelry business, agreed to design, craft, and present a silver ball to the champions of the local amateur tournament. Amateurs sought to mobilize around the silver ball, an ideal representation of gentlemanly deportment, manly prowess, and athletic skill. As an object of dread, the silver ball witnessed the decline of the amateurs and the rise of professionals. For the amateur clubs, the professional baseballist would become the new gold standard. Examining meanings in the baseball landscape and reasons for its aesthetic appeal reveals racial formations at the intersection of social status and national citizenship.[36]

The Blue Stockings Base Ball Club consisted of ambitious and aspiring young colored men, including some post–Civil War migrants to Chicago who caught the baseball fever. Hoping to take advantage of cultural opportunities created by the birth of the National Association, black players voiced dissatisfaction because they were not permitted share in the "energetic and free-wheeling spirit" that pervaded the amateur tournament. The national and local press published the colored nine's eloquent grievances. On the baseball grounds, in saloons, betting parlors, newspaper offices, and in the city's segregated communities, the sports became a medium to argue for and against civil rights. While Republican and Democrat newspapers took sides, sometimes quietly, some accounts exposed the plight of the colored baseballist and revealed how the sporting press sometimes collaborated against them behind the scenes.

Chicago papers reported some Blue Stockings games. In fairness, there could be many reasons for omissions. If teams with less social standing wanted column space, newspaper sports editors required them to submit game results, and perhaps the Blue Stockings' team secretary failed to submit results. When we think of the Blue Stockings' exploits, we should not focus on any single figure, but rather the confrontation of two images — the silver ball and the colored baseballist — and the struggle for baseball representation in Chicago.

Many Blue Stockings players were Kentuckians by birth and migrated north following the Civil War. Ironically, Kentucky agreed to join the Union only after President Lincoln exempted the state from emancipation, so during the Civil War, black enslavement continued. Hence, the Blue Stockings shared this kinship with Abraham Lincoln, who was also born in the "Bluegrass State" and made Illinois his home. It is also illuminating that many of these Kentuckians embodied baseball representations of the mulatto — black images that some whites thought aesthetically pleasing — and preferred its dark tint over the darker image. Historian Michael Lomax imagines the mulatto ballplayer as a prestigious symbol because lighter skin complexions made them better situated to organize ball clubs. Mulattos controlled wealth vastly disproportionate to other members of the colored community. Lomax cites the Philadelphia Pythians, members of the city's mulatto elite. His analysis is edifying: "For the mulatto elite, baseball served as a means to elevate the race from its political, economic and social plight." But the Pythians were not the only black image of the mulatto ballplayer. Moreover, the social drama of the colored sporting crowd allows us to track both the evolution of the black image and this prestige symbol as an object of desire.[37]

While reviving an era is rather complex, the baseball landscape cannot be understood without contemplating the mulatto and its potential impact on the dominant white population. Fragments from newspapers, city directories, and census reports offer the subject as part of the larger baseball narrative. The 1870 Federal Census Report of Chicago is instructive. Race/gender demographics of the first, second, and third wards (where most blacks lived) include the social classification of the term mulatto. The Third Ward, for instance, lists 1095 blacks and 261 mulattos. But the demographic patterns are illuminating: white men married to black/mulatto women, with mulatto children; black men married to white/mulatto women, with mulatto children; mulatto men married to white women, with mulatto children; single/divorced white/black/mulatto women with mulatto children; black families with mulatto children; black and white families with white/black/mulatto servants (one black railroad engineer had a domestic servant from Bohemia); and, interestingly, white children with black/mulatto families.

The dominant white sporting fraternity believed that the primacy or attainability of whiteness differentiates representations of the tragic from the comic, or leisure from servility, or colored from white society, but all these utopian aspirations begin to look splintered, complicated, and illusive. Bridget T. Heneghan explains: "The challenge of locating the exact position where white might become black — the question that concerned upwardly or downwardly mobile whites — settled finally upon, and within the body of the mixed race slave." Heneghan's study of the antebellum period points out that blackface minstrelsy and "tragic mulatto" stories differentiated the tragic from the comic. Literary and visual artists would use minstrelsy — much like blackface performers — to deride colored baseballists. Minstrelsy, as I explore later, says something about the black baseball image; however, in the Chicago sporting world and in print culture the protocols of blackface minstrelsy (the performance of "negro dialect" vernacular and the masking of Negroid facial features) had yet to penetrate baseball representations.[38]

While journalists identified mulattos in crime stories and tragic events, they rarely identified mulatto ballplayers in the 1870s. But in the 1880s, journalists (and perhaps readers) began to obsess over euphemistic descriptions like "light saddle-colored," "bright colored," "yellow," "saffron," "mustard," "lemon," "dusky," and "molasses-colored." By 1883, this fascination would include baseballists. One sportswriter, for example, called the Black Stockings "dusky blondes." Other journalists called players William Davis and Isaac Carter, both of the Black Stockings, mulattoes. When the local print media did promote the spectacle of the mulatto ballplayer on the green diamond, they targeted the black image as a viable commodity or product.[39]

Between 1871 and 1878, the Blue Stockings team rosters included Robert Johnson, 2b; Zacharias Daniels, ss; George Brown (or Browne), c; Durias H. Hampton, lf ; Charles Wing, p; Henry Smith, cf; Charles Adams, rf; Flint B. Carter, 1b; Thomas Brown, 3b; Thomas Hamilton, 3b; and William P. Johnson, p. *The Lakeside Directory of Chicago* and census reports breathe life back into these men. Born in Tennessee, 21-year-old Thomas Hamilton was a coachman. Missouri-born waiter Robert Johnson resided at 88 Harrison. Another waiter, Zacharias Daniels, lived at 318 Clark and had migrated from Alabama in 1866. At least three players were from Kentucky: 16-year-old barber Henry Smith, 19-year-old waiter Thomas Brown (a mulatto), and 25-year-old waiter Charles Adams.[40]

George Browne and William P. Johnson are interesting because their occupations invoke "symbols of repudiation." With Missourian George Brooks, Kentuckian Johnson co-owned a saloon at 480 State Street. Both saloonkeepers were 25 years old. The 31-year-old Browne, an Ohioan, worked as their bartender. All three men were mulattoes and lived at 77 S. Halsted. Sporting establishments often had barkeepers, streetwise figures who exemplified modern urban life. "The bartender," the *Tribune* observes, "is a gentlemanly person, and has the happy facility of blending these various elements into harmony, just as he mixes gin and sugar." While saloons sought to maintain a tone of respectability, barkeepers developed ties to gamblers, pimps, and athletes. Overtime, saloons degenerated into all-night houses and fell under the control of hack men. For mid–19th-century purveyors of "high culture," baseball, variety shows, saloons, dancing halls were hardly more reputable than brothels or "sporting houses."[41]

Indeed, colored institutions like "negro saloons" prompted entrepreneurs to contemplate the formation of a professional colored baseball league. Given the city's search for professional talent, sportswriters who had witnessed Browne perform as catcher claimed him an object of civic pride. As captain of the Blue Stockings, Browne "displayed an energy and judgment, and enforced a discipline, of which a certain high-priced team we know of stands sadly in need." Writers gushed at his athleticism, his ability to hold "foul tips," snag "flys" and "bound" from the catcher's crouched position. Browne's skill behind the plate would have "excited the envy of [Bill] Craver" of the White Stockings. His "throwing to second base was such that the plan of stealing from first was altogether abandoned" by other teams. For sportswriter Louis Meacham, Browne had no superior and few equals — white or colored. In fact, Meacham compared him to the best professional catchers in the country — unsurpassed by Tom "Reddy" Miller of the St. Louis Brown Stockings, John Clapp of the Philadelphia Athletics, or James Laurie "Deacon" White of the Boston Red Stockings. Browne's discipline, personality, and manly form projected his rise to baseball celebrity as an ambivalent black baseball image.[42]

Colored nines exploited the press to insure that their accomplishments remained in circulation. The literary evolution of the black baseball image in Chicago did not begin with detailed sports accounts, but with sketches or "notes," "announcements" or "results" from local games. Newspapers had few resources, but more importantly, little interest in covering every game played across the city, so journalists merely edited and published games results submitted to newspapers. The Rapids, Hunters, Mohawks and Red Stockings regularly submitted their reports.

Newspapers and sports journals have always played a role in communicating baseball happenings. The formulaic nature of baseball, won and lost results, have the desired effect of interweaving baseball sketches into a larger narrative: On 2 July, the Rapids beat the Star Juniors 9 to 0, in seven innings. On 8 July, the Rapids beat the Mohawks by the score of 21 to 13. On 9 July, the Rapids clubbed the Star Juniors by the score of 37 to 24. On 4 August, the Pioneers crushed the Rapids by the score of 72 to 36. On 6 September, the

Fourth Avenues crushed the Rapids, 48 to 14. On 23 October, the Rapids beat the Alpines 14 to 6, in six innings. On 29 October, the Rapids beat the Alpines, in a return game, 48 to 36. On 22 June, the Rapids beat the Griswold Scrubs 34 to 7 in seven innings. On 1 October, the Hunters defeated the Monitors by the score of 35 to 20. On 9 October, the Hunters defeated the Union Turners by the score of 29 to 0. On 16 October, the Protections defeated the Hunters by a score of 8 to 2. On 12 June, the Red Stockings captured the Red Hands, by 23 to 14. On 24 June, the Gray Stockings beat the Red Stockings 19 to 2.[43]

Black images reside within newspapers the way organisms reside in a habitat. Like organisms, they move under the weight of the sportswriter's pen from one habitat (baseball grounds) to another (sports columns), so that the visual image on the green diamond can be reborn in the verbal image of the print medium. It is why Mitchell's notion of a "life of images" is so inevitable. Black images need places to live, and that is what a sports medium — newspapers, uniforms, baseball grounds, tournaments, or trophies — provide as objects of representation. Addressing the whole issue of economics and exchange, they link the exploits of colored clubs to narrations of counting, recounting, giving of accounts, telling, tallying, and totaling. In short, relations between stories and storage became part of our cultural memory.[44]

The Blue Stockings reinvigorated the sporting scene, expanding the city's public amusements and changing the baseball landscape. Chicago had strong amateur organizations, but in 1870 the city also had a professional team, the White Stockings. Tom Foley, manager of the White Stockings (and former player of the Excelsiors), also owned a billiards establishment, covered bets, and brokered sporting events. Chicago also had horse-racing at Dexter Park, whose infield contained a baseball diamond where the White Stockings played their home games.[45]

Civic leaders financed the Chicago White Stockings, and the club attained a notorious national reputation. In its efforts to recruit a professional nine, the organization, backed by "a genuinely impressive group of leading citizens," doled out cash advances of up to $500 to convince top players to move to Chicago. The team offered players $1200 per year, $200 more than Cincinnati salaries. Among the White Stockings' supporters were billiard magnate Tom Foley, *Tribune* publisher Joseph Medill, and Palmer House Hotel proprietor Potter Palmer, also well-known in theater, billiards and horse-racing circles. Club president, City Treasurer David A. Gage, had at his disposal $100,000 to $300,000, personally embezzled from his office. He was indicted in 1873.[46]

The White Stockings were one of the first professional teams to organize a stock company, but due to the novelty of the idea, they could not obtain legal incorporation until 1871. Illinois law did not acknowledge such a thing as a baseball corporation. To get around this legality, the club finally used a statute allowing the incorporation of benevolent, religious, educational, literary, musical, and missionary societies. Critics wondered if the corporation would only benefit gamblers. They viewed the plan as putting the team on a thorough gambling basis, to be used like a race horse or bull terrier in the experienced hands of the sporting fraternity, essentially for the purpose of generating economic capital. Some newspapers agreed. *The Republican* snarled: "If the notorious gamblers and players will confab on the field, and then if players give away runs by three at a time, is it any wonder people talk?"[47]

While it seems clear that gamblers, civic leaders, and wealthy members of the sporting fraternity had plenty of amusements to distract them, they expressed fascination with the Blue Stockings vs. Pink Stockings contest. Of course, they could view the game as an extension of the long-established rivalry with the city of Rockford.

> The Chicago Tribune of Wednesday contained a lengthy account of the game at Ogden Park last Tuesday by the "Rockfords" of this city and the "Blue Stockings" of Chicago (both composed of colored base ballists) in which the Tribune says the Rockfords are the protégés of the Forest City Club; that the latter had taken pains to educate the colored club, and promised them $100 if they beat the Blue Stockings in Chicago. Both assertions are false. The Forest City Club knew nothing of the existence of the "Rockfords" until they played the "Blue Stockings" here a short time since. The "Rockfords" paddle their own canoe, and stand on their own bottom.

There was little altruistic in all of this. Money, business, and civic pride mattered. The manager of the White Stockings, Tom Foley, probably helped broker the colored contest.[48]

Of course, this black image possessed a "kind of vital, living character that makes it capable of feeling what is done to it." It is, as Mitchell maintains, an animated living thing, an object with feelings, intentions, desires, and agency. But racial attitudes transformed proficiency into an offending image. Offensive images take up residence on the frontlines of social and political conflicts. Part of the black baseball image's offensiveness had to do with the menial labor positions held by colored baseballists. Playing as hotel nines, colored waiters proved a perfect postbellum foil for graphic artists, who often ridiculed their menial position. For instance, Moses L. Tucker's *Charge for Paper* shows how colored waiters mediated between corporate greed and irate consumers (fig. 11).

Charge for Paper.

Drummer (indignant at being charged with writing paper at a Texas hotel): How did I come to be charged with writing paper? I never had any.

Waiter (desiring to mollify him): May be not, sar. Hit's de paper de bill was made out on.—[Texas Siftings.

Figure 11. Charge for Paper, Moses L. Tucker, *The Republic* (St. Louis), 1888

While his simian-like facial features and handwringing gesture invoke the expression "mon-key-see-monkey do," the waiter as the proprietor's surrogate withstands the white patron's indignation. But colored baseballists who toiled as waiters, porters, doorkeepers, servants, kiln-workers, roustabouts, hostlers, and carriage drivers proved to be more than menial laborers.

Nothing prepared Chicago for the Blue Stockings vs. Pink Stockings contest: "The colored troops will perpetuate a game this afternoon at Ogden Park. The dark side of the Forest Citys and the emblems of bad luck of the Chicagos will with ball and bat assault each other no white washing will be allowed, as the boys are going out for a day of pleas-ure and don't propose to work. Game will be called at 3 p.m. It is reported Senator [Hiram] Revels will act as umpire and Fred Douglass will score." If Douglass attended the event — he enjoyed the national pastime — newspapers don't mention him; R.C. Rickhoff, of the Potter Palmer Base Ball Club, umpired the contest. Nearly a thousand spectators, of all shades of complexion, witnessed the battle between colored clubs. Sportswriter Louis Meacham expressed astonishment at their excellent play. The Blue Stockings, "composed of hotel and restaurant boys, smart, keen and active, good batters, fine fielders and the best base run-ners that we know of among amateur clubs," had an easy walk-away with the Rockfords. Completely "out-fielding their opponents and batting in a style that would do the White Stockings proud," the Blue Stockings won by a score of 48 to 11.[49]

Viewed as a form of surrogacy, a stand-in for the professional rivalry, these amateur contest spectacles intuited the fascination, dread, and fantasy associated with the fifteenth amendment club slinger: the vacillation between ineptitude and proficiency. Prior to the event, the colored nine did not receive detailed coverage, but after their second game against the "Pinks," the "Blues" went from relative unknowns to media darlings. Follow-ing an unanticipated spectacle of "excellent play," four newspapers published detailed accounts.[50]

The Blue Stockings were certainly a good team, but local media sketches fail to tell the club's entire story. When the press introduced the regional rivalry between the Blue Stockings and Pink Stockings, the three-game series had already begun. According to the *Register*, they had met earlier on the Rockford Fairgrounds: the Pink Stockings beat the Blue Stockings, 27 to 17. But media accounts suggest the rivalry began in late-August. Why does this oversight matter? Newspapers found it expedient to cover the best white amateur clubs, yet given Meacham's crucial observations, we find it difficult to believe that the Blue Stock-ings simply came from nowhere. Colored baseballists, it seems, worked for the Palmer House Hotel; this might explain why R.C. Rickhoff umpired. Of course, Meacham understood how colored baseballists threatened the status quo, particularly catcher Browne's high-cal-iber skill. Simply calling the Blue Stockings political appendages fails to account for their remarkable power to project offensive images. Mitchell writes: "The psychological forces that lead people to be offended by an image are invisible and unpredictable. But when peo-ple set out to offend an image, to censure, denounce, or punish it, their behavior is out in the open where we can look at it." The image evoked by the Blue Stockings battery of Browne and Johnson was that the colored nine probably played better than the best white amateur clubs.[51]

Conspicuous Consumption: Trophies, Tournaments, and the National Pastime

When the Amateur Organization of Chicago announced the Tournament Championship in late August 1870, the Blue Stockings submitted an application for participation. Approving their decision to challenge the white aggregations for the silver trophy and other prizes, the *Tribune* retorted "Why Not?" The Blue Stockings boasted the skills to hold their own against any local club, except the professional White Stockings, whom they considered formidable. Yet this declaration seems odd, considering that the White Stockings played the prominent white amateurs and beat them all in convincing fashion. They thrashed the Athletics, Amateurs, Actives, and Aetnas by the crushing scores of 75–12, 48–2, 41–1, and 36–8. They also pummeled the Memphis Bluff Citys, amateur state champions of Tennessee, by the score of 157 to 1.[52]

When the Amateur Association denied the Blue Stockings' application to the tournament, the offending black image of the fifteenth amendment club slinger took on a life of its own, mediated between white and colored baseballists and subject to virulently prejudicial distortions. And this slippery nature triggered the actions of William P. Johnson and George Browne. On 10 September, the editor of *The Clipper*, Frank Queen, published Johnson's appeal to the Garden City's sense of fair play. As club secretary, he wrote: "We, the Blue Stockings (colored), of Chicago, made an application to play in the amateur tournament now in progress in this city, at Ogden park, but were not admitted, for what reason I cannot tell, unless it is because they are afraid of us beating them." On 20 September, *The Times* reported that Browne, captain of the Blue Stockings, had not submitted a formal application; *The Post* repeated the falsehood. Browne shot back: "*The Post* knows nothing of the facts when it says he did not do so." He was correct: tournament organizers had declined their petition. This distortion should be read as a literary construction, a cliché that obscures more than it reveals: the fifteenth amendment club slinger had penetrated the idyllic baseball landscape.[53]

The *Evening Journal* brought to life the black image that illuminated the Blue Stockings: "There is a base-ball club in this city composed entirely of colored young men, employed as waiters at hotels. They are gentlemanly in appearance and deportment — *and can play ball.*" Newspapers sketched black images of the Blue Stockings that fulfilled the social fantasies of the white amateur clubs who considered colored baseballists below their social status: "No one who is at all acquainted with the material of most of the amateur clubs of Chicago will believe that the colored boys were ruled out because of any apprehension that the respectability or social position of the white chaps would suffer from being brought in contact with them."[54]

This time the *Tribune*, often sympathetic to the Blue Stockings, sided with the Amateur Baseball Association. The paper's editorial board supposed that the five amateur clubs viewed the Blue Stockings of insufficient strength to be entitled to consideration. However, their social standing also had something to do with the matter: "Very naturally it would, as young men belonging to our leading amateur clubs are all respectable and of good standing, some of them being connected with the best families of Chicago." Joseph Medill's bias perhaps reflects his political biases. The newspaper's publisher became mayor in 1871.[55]

The facts proved antagonistic to this theory. The racial fear that young colored men would sweep the amateur tournament championship influenced white aggregations to rule out the Blue Stockings. More importantly, despite the poorly organized tournament and intermittent rain showers, the black image of the Blue Stockings conjured financial success. If the Blue Stockings had been admitted, "the novelty of the thing allied to the extreme probability that the colored boys would successfully defeat the white clubs, would have attracted thousands of spectators." Without them, not more than a score of spectators attended any one game, and the tournament treasury, dependent on gate receipts, was "as empty as space." *The Evening Journal* declared the tournament a "regular failure — a perfect fizzle" because the organizers denied the Blue Stockings. The editor concluded that Conger and Webb rescind their offer "until the tournament of all the amateur clubs shall have decided which is the 'champion club.'"[56]

Rival newspapers were relentless in their attacks against the *Tribune*. *The Evening Journal* added: "The assumption that the colored club of Chicago is not strong enough 'to be entitled to consideration' shows that the *Tribune* is on the wrong scent." It reminded the *Tribune* that, a few weeks earlier, sportswriter Louis Meacham had declared the Blue Stockings would test the mettle of any amateur club in the city. Quoting to *The Times*, *The Evening Journal* quipped:

> Let them have the silver ball, and let the rest of the prizes go to blazes, with the exception of the one offered to the most popular base-ball reporter, which should be promptly given to the person who is willing to stoop to win the favor of the senseless managers of the played-out amateur tournament.

The Evening Journal's editors suggested complicity, declaring that the baseball reporter's tournament prize had been unquestionably won by the *Tribune's* Louis Meacham.[57]

The sporting fraternity, civic leaders, and newspapers pressured white amateurs and, after private negotiations, the association reached an agreement to play a series of games against the Blue Stockings. Four points are significant. First, the tournament winner (Aetnas) refused to play the Blue Stockings. Second, the association selected a picked nine from the city's five crack clubs. Third, the association would play under an anonymous moniker: the Independents. And finally, baseball coverage was disappointing. Louis Meacham, celebrated for introducing the box score and providing running reports of important ball games, reduced this historical event to brief notes with no box scores.[58]

According to historian Leslie Heaphy, the Blue Stockings and Independents played five games: 21, 23, 25, and 28 September 1870. Using *The Times* as a major source, Heaphy notes the Blues won once 17 to 9, but the Independents beat the "stalwart youths of the blue hose and dusky faces" by scores of 24 to 8, 17 to 15, and 25 to 24. While Heaphy's evidence is instructive, no single major newspaper carries all the game results. Plus, another game was played on 6 October 1870. Regardless, the reportage of other major newspapers (or lack thereof) is illuminating and raises revealing questions: Why are these accounts important? How might full accounts impact their social status? Why might the Independents as losers be an equally offensive image? What, then, are the implications of all this for the black image of the colored baseballist?

The trauma of social inequality reified the black image of the colored baseballist as incompatible with the prized object of the silver ball. And newspapers sought to protect the social status of the Amateur Baseball Association. The *Tribune* reported only two of the contests, and Meacham's reportage shrewdly rotated the terms "picked nine" and Independents. *The Republican* mentioned just one contest. *The Times* provided the most consistent coverage, but no paper carried batting line-ups, detailed accounts, or even attendance figures. Only *The Times* carried a box score, which the Blue Stockings submitted to prove their victory. Perhaps the mere report — the image of defeated amateurs — was enough to indict the image as being offensive: "The 'Blue Stockings' (colored), and the Independents (white), or rather a nine selected from all the crack amateur nine of this city, contested a game yesterday afternoon at Ogden Park." In October, the *Tribune* felt obligated to address an inquiry related to a club that felt slighted by the tournament: "Can the amateur clubs of Chicago challenge and play the Aetnas for the championship this year?" Meacham responded to this inquiry, presumably submitted by supporters of the Blue Stockings. After stating that the amateur clubs were not compelled to play "every inferior club," the question could be tested by issuing a challenge and, further, the matter could be deferred to the Judiciary Committee, whose decision would be final.[59]

One final example illustrates how good the Blue Stockings were. On 6 October 1870, the colored nine crossed bats with the Independents. *The Times* announced: "The Blue Stockings, colored, and the Independents play their return game at Ogden Park this afternoon, a prize of $100 has been raised for the winners, and a lively game is anticipated." Apparently the first four contests had not settled the question. The match was hotly contested, and accounts differed as to who won. *The Times* reported that the Independents defeated the Blue Stockings, by a score of 25 to 24. But the *Tribune* disagreed: "Darkness necessitated the calling of the game at the close of the eighth inning, when the score stood 23 to 22 in favor of the Blue Stockings. The burden of proof rested with the Blue Stockings who claimed the $100 purse, and forwarded the score result by innings." *The Times* offered no retraction, but the Blue Stockings submitted evidence, and the sports editor published a follow-up article: "The Blue Stockings claim that in their late game with the Independents, the game was called at the end of the eighth inning, and in proof of their claim they state that they have been given the $100 purse, and they also forward the following score of the game by innings." Neither the Independents nor the purse holder (probably Tom Foley) challenged the black team's claim.[60]

"Colored Champions of America": The Chicago Uniques

For the sporting fraternity of Chicago, and for baseball critics, the Uniques transformed the colored baseballist into a gold standard. Between 1870 and 1871 the Blue Stockings battery of William P. Johnson and George Browne jumped to the Uniques, another colored nine. On 30 May 1871, the Blue Stockings faced the Uniques for the colored championship. It was a rout: Uniques 39, Blue Stockings 5. While the print media represented the primary habitat for this "unique" black image, it had national circulation. The Uniques are significant for at least two reasons. First, they continued the struggle begun by the Blue Stockings for social inclusion in the segregated sporting world. Second, the Uniques established themselves regionally and nationally, something no colored nine had accomplished, prior to that time. Thus, the Uniques continue a whole sequence of evolving black images from the Chicago Blue Stockings to the St. Louis Black Stockings to the Cuban Giants.[61]

A closer examination of who organized the Uniques informs a discussion of what this team did for baseball in Chicago and colored baseball in the United States. George Browne and William P. Johnson were keys to its organization. As the nucleus of the Blue Stockings, Browne and Johnson were not the only baseballists to jump clubs; Thomas Henry Hampton, Zachary Daniels, and William D. Berry also left the Blue Stockings. In 1871, the management of the Uniques consisted of George G. Mead, vice president; William D. Berry, corresponding secretary; and Harry P. Hall, manager. Mead, a 38 year-old mulatto, was a store porter; 29-year-old Berry was a brick mason; Hall, a gambler, also worked as a barber. In 1874, Hall became team president; Berry, team manager; and H. Beauford, vice president.[62]

The Uniques 1871–78 team rosters included the following players: Zacharias Daniels, ss (1871–74); J. Tyler, c (1871, 1876); George Browne, c (1871–76); Durias H. Hampton, lf (1874–75); Robert Johnson, 3b (1871–76); John Shaw, 1b (1871–76); Benjamin Dyson, 3b (1876); C. Deveney, rf (1874–76); George Overland, rf (1875–76); Jim Simms, rf (1871); Simon Johnson, 2b (1875–76); James Lewis, (1878); James Houck, 3b (1878); John Chrisop (1878); Frank Spears, ss (1878); Thomas Watkins, 1b (1874); William Powell, ss (1874–76); R. Reynolds, cf (1878); W.C. Sutcliffe, p (1878); T. Hambleton, ss (1871); William P. Johnson, p (1871–74); and William D. Berry, 2b/secretary (1871–1876).

The black image of the colored baseballist is not simply a racialization of the baseball landscape, a mere vehicle for representing social knowledge. The baseball landscape is also a key element in the process of image-making and racial formation as such, not just a sports medium or messenger, but as a constitutive element, a post-emancipation construction. The socio-cultural formation of the black image of the fifteenth amendment club slinger explores the very nature of the shock or trauma that images can produce, and tries to identify ways a black image passes from civil rights legislation to prestigious symbol or minstrelsy. This is especially true of cultural historians, who weave baseball images into complex narratives, representations of the struggle for dignity and autonomy. Perhaps more than traditional historical narratives, cultural histories require the aid of visual and literary artists who might project a voice into black images, or construct iconic symbols that say something about colored sports.

The black image of the colored baseballist, as represented by the Uniques of Chicago, embodies the fantasy of being colored champions of the United States. It appears in ongoing competitive local rivalries with white amateur nines, the Alerts and Garnets. It finds expression in the amateur state tournament championship. It defines the highly competitive regional rivalry with the colored aggregations of St. Louis, especially the Blue Stockings. It also attains baseball celebrity when it builds an archive of black baseball imagery highlighted by an east coast road tour and a victory over the famed Philadelphia Pythians.

While the print media often transformed the colored baseballist into an offensive image, sports accounts could also be a nurturing habitat for them to thrive and flourish. Baseball coverage of the Uniques is scanty between 1871 and 1877, but does offer a few batting line-ups, box scores, and, sometimes, sports narratives. In their inaugural contest against the Alerts at White Stockings Park in 1871, the Uniques won by a score of 17 to 16. Other than contests with the St. Louis Blue Stockings, no games against colored nines appear. However, newspapers do offer some scores against white nines: the Uniques beat the Alerts, 33 to 4; the Uniques beat the White Stockings Juniors, 9 to 7; they defeated the Garnets, 18 to 9 and 17 to 16, and lost, 12 to 10. Nevertheless, Chicago sports accounts are disappointing, and much of the club's coverage comes from another baseball town: St. Louis.[63]

The significance of the so-called mythic title as a dignified emblem of socio-cultural dissent cannot be overemphasized within the cultural context of claims to the Colored Championship of the United States and the social context of skin color making claims on professional and amateur clubs. The Uniques initiated a historic event. Prior to the aggregation's east coast tour, no colored club had scheduled long-distance travel. This was no small feat. As Michael Lomax explains, the home team's inability to guarantee the visitor's travel expenses or to share huge gate receipts (or betting pools) imposed limitations. National tours required both economic (money) and labor capital (leisure time). So if the Uniques failed to accomplish anything else, this entrepreneurial effort embodied freedom and self-determination.

In 1871, the Uniques organized a two-week tour of Washington, D.C., Baltimore, MD, Philadelphia and Pittsburgh, PA, and Troy, NY. They scheduled colored contests with the Mutuals of Baltimore, Alerts of Washington, D.C., Oclias of Troy, Pittsburgh's, and Pythians of Philadelphia. They played at high-profile and enclosed facilities, including the professional grounds of the Washington Nationals and the Philadelphia Athletics. They split a series with the Alerts, losing 30 to 19, and winning 24 to 18. They defeated the Mutuals and the Pittsburgh's, but I have not authenticated results against the Troy and Pittsburgh clubs. The celebrated games against the Pythians are noteworthy: the Uniques won the first game of the series by the score of 19 to 7, and the Pythians returned the favor by winning the second contest, 22 to 16. The Uniques returned home three weeks prior to the Great Chicago Fire, which began on 8 October 1871.[64]

While local newspaper accounts reported the scores of these games, the secretary of the Uniques also dispatched telegraphic accounts to Chicago newspapers. When the Pythians and Uniques met at Philadelphia before a large crowd, the Chicago aggregation routed their celebrated rivals: according to the box score that appeared in the *Philadelphia Inquirer*, they scored 3 runs in the 1st inning, 3 in the 3rd, 3 in the 5th, 4 in the 6th, 2 in the 8th, and 4 in the last inning. Following the noteworthy victory, a jubilant club secretary dispatched the following proclamation: "This club, composed of young men of African descent, having inflicted the first defeat of their experience upon the Pythians, of Philadelphia, the colored champions of the east, now lay claim to the title of colored champions of America."[65]

In 1874, the Uniques tested the local and state amateurs at the Peoria Tournament. First prize was $200 cash and gold medal; and, second prize was $75 cash. Of the local clubs, the Uniques proclaimed themselves champions of Chicago. The Franklins thought differently. When the Uniques challenged them, they "refused to play the 'niggers,' as they call them, except for $250 a side." Later, they upped the ante to the astonishing sum of $300. But black images functioned within a polarized logic of this sort. On the one hand, this diminution of the colored aggregation to an epithet had political linkages: *The Times* sports account, rather more like an editorial, chastised the Uniques: "If the colored boys are wise they will do nothing of the kind; not that there is danger of their losing, but for the reason that if they are not worth playing with for sports, then they are not worth playing with at all." Members of the Franklins worked for *The Times*, and their jobs allegedly prevented them from participating in the tournament. On the other hand, the press celebrated the Uniques, who played in the title game for the first place money and state championship. The *Times* reported: "The tournament opened this morning with a match between the Uniques of Chicago and the Nationals of Peoria in which the former walked away with their opponents by a score of 33 to 1." The Uniques also defeated the White Stockings of Monmouth, by a score of 39 to 36. But in the championship, the Socials of Chicago defeated the Uniques by a score of 30 to 16. The Uniques went on to defeat the Nameless Club, by a score of 27 to 18, taking second place in the tournament.[66]

Between 1874 and 1878, the Uniques engaged in a battle for baseball supremacy at the regional level against the perennial colored powerhouses of St. Louis, Missouri. According to sports accounts, St. Louis nourished a thriving baseball culture and, by 1875, the "Mound City" boasted 15 colored clubs. The earliest evidence for contact between the aggregations of St. Louis and Chicago occurred in the fall of 1874, when the Napoleons and Uniques played a two-game series in Chicago. *The Times* announced: "The Uniques, of Chicago, and the Napoleons, of St. Louis, two colored base-ball clubs, will play a match game this afternoon on the Twenty-third street grounds for the championship of the Northwest. An admission fee of 25 cents will be charged." While both Chicago and St. Louis newspapers reported the upcoming "championship of the Northwest," the results of the contests never appeared in print.[67]

In 1875, the nucleus of the Napoleons reorganized as the Blue Stockings. While the Uniques might have boasted the better club, the exploits of the Blue Stockings, who split 10 games with their Chicago rivals, dominated media accounts until the rise of Henry Bridgewater's Black Stockings (see next chapter). However, a powerful strain in St. Louis sports narratives treats the Uniques as baseball celebrities, as a celebrated black image of the colored baseballist. *The Times* reported: "Blue Stockings of St. Louis vs. Uniques of Chicago. The colored organizations play to-day for the 'Championship of the West.' The rivalry runs high and we have no doubt that the sons and daughters of Ham will turn out in form at the Grand Avenue Park, where the game takes place." Even though the print media framed postbellum narratives of the black image of the colored baseballist as the fifteenth amendment club slinger, the most interesting sports accounts of the Uniques elude the simple classifications, presenting a complex sporting world complete with politics, history, culture, and economics.[68]

And this is the beginning of the story. "Dust from Many Diamonds" shows that the colored baseballists of Chicago used literacy — writing — to help to control their image. The Blue Stockings used the national media to voice their complaints of social exclusion, perhaps believing they would find support within the broader sporting fraternity. Two relatively unknown figures emerged in 1870, William P. Johnson and George Browne. Prior to Bridgewater's famed Black Stockings, these players arguably formed the nucleus of perhaps the greatest colored baseball run in the Northwest. Browne's celebrity status achieved regional, if not national attention. Someday, Cartes de'visite (small albumen prints mounted on cards 2½ by 4 inches) or baseball photos of the Browne and Johnson will be discovered at some garage sale or antique fair. They competed in the Peoria Tournament, made an east coast tour, and established an ongoing regional rivalry. Just as the colored sporting fraternity sought to displace the black image of the colored baseballist with that of colored champion, the print media slowly melded the black image to narratives of blackface baseball minstrelsy.

"During the last three decades of the 19th century, the period known as the Gilded

Age," writes art historian Joshua Brown, "one of the most popular ways to decorate the home was by purchasing lithographic prints." Some prints exploited the nostalgia of white customers for an imagined simpler time, before the trauma of the Civil War and the unrest of the Reconstruction era. Baseball lithographs and engravings show black figures cavorting in bucolic surroundings, scenes that mocked not only civil rights legislation but social freedom as well, but few black Americans were customers for these lithographic offerings. Although the colored baseballist would become an object of minstrelsy mania in post–Civil War America, how the sports medium represented the colored sporting fraternity throughout the country also intuited a sense of solidarity against collective oppression and community-building. The black image of the colored baseballist thrived in print culture, and it nurtured both the Blue Stockings and the Uniques of Chicago. But the black image of the colored baseballist and the colored sporting fraternity thrived in New York, Cleveland, St. Louis, New Orleans, Indianapolis, and other baseball cities. The chapters that follow explore a synthesis or deeper truth of what the colored baseballist might say about the black image of the other and a mirror of the self.[69]

CHAPTER TWO

"Fifteenth-Amendment Club-Slingers": Colored Base Ball and the St. Louis Sporting Fraternity, 1875–1877

Henry Jackson Lewis's *The National Game* depicts, on first glance, a baseball contest between white and colored clubs (**fig. 12**). The event takes place in an enclosed ballpark, and Lewis tilted the ground plane to provide an aerial view. Despite the excitement on the

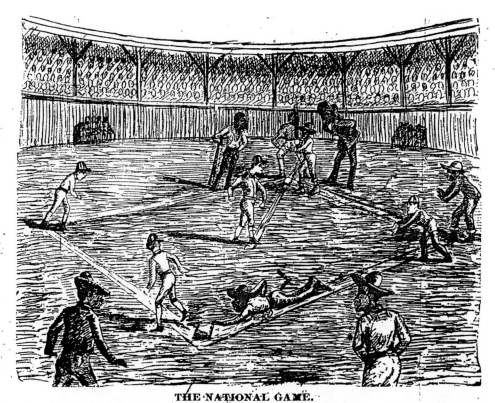

THE NATIONAL GAME.

A pen picture of a game between the "Neversweat" and Neverwash" clubs of this city. (For particulars you must witness the game.

Figure 12. The National Game, Henry Jackson Lewis, *The Freeman* (Indianapolis), 1890

46

green diamond, seemingly sedate spectators cram the wooden grandstands, but only as floating heads, with no flailing arms or waving hats or handkerchiefs. White players occupy the defensive positions; the white uniforms, consisting of long-sleeved shirts, knickers, stockings, and baseball shoes, cover the battery, first, second, and third base. The colored club occupies the offensive position, or so it seems; most of them — excluding the on-deck batter to the right-side of the foul line (or is it the umpire?) — sport wide-brim, high-crown hats, short jackets or long-sleeve shirts, and cuffed pants. The remaining players rest on benches along the grandstand walls.

Anticipating that the base runner will attempt to steal third, the pitcher throws to the third baseman. The third base coach leans slightly forward, extending both arms outward and hands upward, signaling the runner to remain at second. The base runner dives back into second base. An exceptional figure in a dark suit and wide-brimmed hat bends over slightly behind the batter. Compared to other figures around home plate, his proportions are gigantic. Is this towering figure a coach, manager, or umpire? (Lewis often inserted into his cartoons allegorical journeys through giant and miniature worlds.) Finally, two foreground figures further complicate this scene. Are they colored spectators or outfielders? If they are outfielders, why are they on defense? Their uniforms and dark complexions suggest that they belong to the colored nine.

Despite the roughly hewn figures (other works reveal Lewis to be a superb draughtsman), his woodcut engraving demonstrates that the black baseball image (albeit in a caricatured form) had penetrated colored newspapers in the late 19th century. This panoramic view also says something else: despite baseball segregation, the notion of colored and white clubs remained crucial to the baseball landscape. It suggests something about the national pastime's pastoral mythology: the colored aggregation looks like a bunch of "rubes," countrified ballplayers caught up in the urbanization of professional leisure class entertainment. Having extra capital to waste on baseball uniforms reveals something about wealth and "conspicuous consumption." And the image says something about making do: uniforms do not necessarily make the man or woman.[1]

This chapter explores representations of the colored sporting fraternity in the postbellum Gilded Age, the period of economic ascendency in the United States following the Civil War. Between 1875 and 1877, the print media show that segregated nines flourished in St. Louis and, like other phases of the U.S. economy, the colored sporting fraternity witnessed the National League trend toward large-scale enterprise and the elimination and absorption of smaller companies. Politically, these years overlap the Reconstruction Period (1863–1877), and they expose how the colored sporting fraternity, struggles for civil rights. Some sportswriters called black players fifteenth amendment club slingers.[2]

Fifteenth-amendment critics complained that the combination of sports and civil rights had transformed the American citizen of African descent into a creature of legislative enactment. For a number of reasons, sportswriters often represented the colored baseballist with contempt. On pseudo-scientific anatomical grounds, their bodies could not withstand the physical play: tender shins and red hot grounders proved incompatible to the national game. Furthermore, the baseball grounds belonged to the domain of white men. By playing on the green diamond, colored baseballists stepped outside their class position to indulge in leisure activities reserved for the white sporting fraternity. And some critics dubbed colored baseball a mirthful spectacle. Of course, these fallacies did not hold water. Yet sports journalists called colored baseballists "amendments," political appendages of the National Pastime.[3]

If some sports journalists represented colored baseballists as political appendages of the National Pastime, some graphic artists delineated the humorous side of that character, deriding black bodies through racial caricature and unjustifiable exaggeration. While many publishing houses and illustrator-cartoonists come to mind, Harper and Brother's *Blackville Comics*, Currier and Ives' *Darktown Comics*, and Thomas Worth's prodigious artistic output capture perfectly the postbellum black image-repertoire of baseball that circulated across media, especially blackface, the "cooning" of the colored baseballist. Worth became one of the best-known artists for the New York lithography firm of Currier and Ives, beginning that association in 1855. In the 1870s Worth contributed to *Harper's Weekly* (a book and magazine publishing house), and produced genre scenes of horse racing and the urban bustle of middle-class life. Worth's *Darktown Comics* was inspired by the work of another *Harper's* graphic artist, Solomon Eytinge, Jr., who in 1874 introduced the notorious *Blackville Comics*. Both Eytinge and Worth offer case studies for exploring the colored baseballist in a racialized context.

Worth's *The Champions of the Ball Racket: At the close of the Season* (1885) (**fig. 13**) parodies a baseball team photograph by arranging the poorly uniformed figures and props in an immediately recognizable scene: standing and sitting rows of colored baseballists pose

THE CHAMPIONS OF THE BALL RACKET.
At the close of the Season.

Figure 13. The Champions of the Ball Racket: At the Close of the Season, Thomas Worth, *Currier and Ives*, 1885

for the photographer. In the immediate foreground, two crossed bats and three balls are artistically arranged and displayed before the ball club. Here the similarities to a team photograph end. This is no distinguished photographic portrait of colored baseballists (*Cuban Giants, Colored Champions*, discussed in Chapter Four, comes to mind). The candid "photograph" does not depict what art historian Alan Trachtenberg terms "illustrious Americans," nor does it represent what William J. Simmons called "men of mark." Instead, these figures suggest "marked men," conspicuous symbols of "blackface-on-black violence."[4]

It is easy enough to see how the symbolic violence of the image satisfies the requirements of racial caricature and blackface. Colored baseballists seem barely human, re-imagined as absurd physical distortions with bulging eyes, large rubbery lips, and elongated swollen limbs (hands, arms, legs, and feet). These distortions invoke the phenomenon of "multistability," the coexistence of contrary or simply different readings in a single image. The central-seated figure, a portion of its covered face wrapped in a kerchief, conjures a moke (broken down horse) or jackass: pointing skywards, the kerchief's knotted ends mimic elongated ears. The bandaged, standing figure to the seated figure's left invokes similar racial epithets.[5]

Crude racial jokes emerge: there are other "appendages." The sitting figures suggest vulgarity, replete with sexual overtones. Four players, their legs gapped wide-open, insist that viewers inspect them for proof of manhood. A fifth figure, to the far right, lying in repose, offers a peak at his rounded buttocks; as if to accentuate its contour, a large patch covers the seat of his pants, which seem more like long underwear. The seated man to the far left conjures a phallic emblem: long arms and hands cradle his head, and the light, vertical space between the darkened arm and the oval formation of the lips suggest "black male sexual demeanor." Thus, oral or genital amusements, as Eric Lott defines them, become a spectacle of vulgarity.[6]

Champions of the Ball Racket vividly illustrates how the blackface mask offered a way to play with white collective fears of the colored baseballist while at the same time maintaining some symbolic control over them. What is the meaning of bruised and banged-up champions? Why depict colored champions with arm in sling, bandaged and swollen feet, swollen faces wrapped in kerchiefs, or held upright by crutches? While baseball's pseudo-scientific notion of "fifteenth amendment club slingers" suggests a straightforward collaboration with *Champions of the Ball Racket*, the comedic portrayal of the racially and anatomically unfit forces a lack of masculine vitality back on to the battered ball club. Worth exemplifies for Eytinge the symbolic violence of their work and the possibility of the "seeming counterfeit" mask engaging in racial pleasure.

While my study doesn't begin with baseball's segregated origins in 1867, it does present an interesting starting point. Postbellum Gilded Age colored baseball has been the subject of a growing body of scholarship — most recently important works by David Zang, Mark Ribowsky, Michael E. Lomax, and Lawrence D. Hogan — and becomes an object of great consequence in the social history of the National Pastime. Baseball's pursuit of "willow wielding and leather hunting" held the black community in its grip. For colored clubs, participation in the national game, an essentially segregated fair, promoted both economic empowerment and social uplift. Segregated nines reveal the struggle to form lasting institutions in their own image.[7]

There is something paradoxical in saying this, insofar as colored baseball has often been viewed as a novelty, full of comedic antics that invoked the specter of blackface minstrelsy. Eric Lott defines blackface minstrelsy as "an established nineteenth-century theatrical practice, principally of the urban North, in which white men caricatured blacks for sport and profit." Blackface minstrelsy penetrated baseball forms on many levels — burnt corkers, sportswriters and, as contended, colored nines. Historian David Roediger notes that the aftermath of the Civil War brought an outpouring of minstrelsy, most of whose political content attacked emancipation, black civil rights, and an alleged favoritism toward the "nigger." As early as 1875, the "burnt cork" profession of white performers appeared on the green diamond. These Ethiopian Sketches of American Life penetrated baseball's circus-like atmosphere — parades, bands, and crowds — capitalizing on the game's entertainment possibilities. Burnt cork artists shared the print media's ambivalence toward the fifteenth amendment club slingers. Newspapers further blurred the boundary between genuine colored baseballists and their burnt cork counterfeits. While the relation of blackface farce to baseball is beyond the scope of this book, its origins are intriguing.[8]

Representations of the colored sporting fraternity in general and colored baseball in particular should be incorporated into the baseball master narrative. Between 1875 and 1877, baseball accounts show that the colored sporting fraternity of St. Louis built a remarkable institution. They tell a story that has been framed by actual historical incidents of people, places, and rituals, and by written narratives of journalists recounting events related to the colored sporting fraternity.

This social drama shares many historical and narrative elements that literary critic Cecil Brown associates with the folkloric narrative of Stagolee. According to Brown's classic work, Stagolee belongs to the St. Louis sporting world of bordellos and prostitution that linked sex and class to criminality. "Many scholars do not want to know who the real Stagolee was," writes Brown, "because he was not a hero." This antihero's world was far more complicated. The "Stagolee paradigm" inverts certain events and permits the assignment of values and meaning — a process that transforms actual historical incidents (narrative events) into oral literature (narrated events) by recounting them from the viewpoint of the desires of people hearing the story.[9]

Social drama informs our understanding of colored (and colorful) nines, heroic figures, and sporting traditions. First, social dramas identify members of the colored sporting fraternity as real people, places, and rituals. Second, social dramas reveal how journalists narrated certain events but not others. While journalists represent the colored sporting fraternity in actual historical incidents, these titillating fragments also offer traces or signs of black urban life. Collectively, they dramatize the actions of the participants — a "black ethos" — or the performers' character for survival. For purposes of this study, these representations are viewed through the political lens of black citizens' eroding civil rights.[10]

Social dramas invoke the pursuit of leisure and pleasure. Of course, literary and visual artists mediated black images. But if the sports medium includes and constitutes not only creators and the social spaces of the baseball landscape hypothetically reserved for them, then we should consider the subjects of the social drama as well. Penetrating the historical accounts of this richly-textured archive illuminates the impact of these representations on baseball's master narrative.[11]

Sports Medium: "Treating Buildings as Events"

Social spaces are constituent components of the sports medium. The 19th-century sports medium suggests how the black community worshipped at the altar of baseball and participated in the cult of the sporting fraternity. With the growth of political and social organizations, disposable income, and leisure time, the black community secured architectural spaces that could address political and social needs. One such building was the St. Louis Union, located at 1015 Christy Avenue. Renamed for the St. Louis Union Society, the facility housed a colored benevolent association headed by the black political leader, Charles H. Tandy. Other accounts called the building Union Hall, Little Rock Hall, Little Rock Church, and Rock Church. The St. Louis Union served both sacred and secular functions. Its exterior and interior spaces mediated between public displays (marches, parades, and speeches), private gatherings (political meetings and dances), and colored institutions (the Attuck Blues/Attuck Guards, the Eighth Ward Republican Club, the Young Men's Central Registration Club, the Hayes and Wheeler Club, and others claimed Union Hall as their own). Colored Republicans cherished the structure as Rock Church, an oasis for empowering the politically disenfranchised. The colored sporting crowd called the building Little Rock Church. If journalists marked Union Hall as the liminal space between work and play, between adoration and abomination, colored institutions constructed an architectural space (along with other social spaces) that transmitted both sacred and profane messages.[12]

Union Hall transmitted racial and gendered images. When a reporter covered an event commemorating the anniversary of emancipation in St. Domingo, he noted the presence of thousands of colored people. Marveling at how they marched around Union Hall to the band's lively musical strains in military style, his visual account shifted. He wrote: "[S]cores of dusky beauties gathered in the galleries and on the platform" to hear the remarks of Charles H. Tandy. Ornamenting the architectural surroundings, his nameless society belles functioned as commodities, objects subject to the sporting pleasure of the male (but also female) gaze. The well-worn phrase "dusky beauties" frequently appeared in late19th-century baseball narratives of colored games; it demonstrated an underlying current of sporting-male ideas and activities that glorified urban heterosexual male freedom and bachelorhood.[13]

Newspaper accounts transformed Union Hall performances of the raucous, strange, and modern into an ethnographic tableau of the colored sporting fraternity. When police officers and reporters descended on the famous Christy Avenue dance house, well known as "Little Rock Church," they captured and conveyed "thirty colored amazons" to the Third District Station. Why the story remained silent as to reason for the police raid is not as important as what brought them. In the 1870s, colored women performed in sporting resorts, and concert and dance halls. In a similar raid at Henry Bridgewater's Saloon (later associated with the Black Stockings, 1882–1890), a large number of mulatto women were arrested for performing the Can-Can and bawdy songs full of double entendres. The Can-Can, a sexually-explicit dance performed in Parisian theaters and cabaret halls, derived from North Africa.[14]

While journalists attempted to frame buildings as part of what they saw and what they heard, they recognized in these social spaces an inimitable lifestyle and ethos that prevented the colored sporting fraternity from being imprisoned altogether by definitions which the larger society tried to impose. They understood that St. Louis epitomized riverboat culture, the golden era of the steamboat on the Mississippi that reached its peak between 1870 and 1890. The term "boom" is instructive. Historians credit the newspaper publisher Joseph B. McCullough with the word's origin. While the epithet found expression in riverboat vernacular, local sportswriters applied it to baseball. St. Louis was a sporting town, and Cecil Brown argues that colored roustabouts and Octoroon ladies embodied the era. Colored politicians, saloonkeepers, gamblers, tonsorialists, waiters, porters, swells, pimps, prostitutes, and ballplayers also belonged to the period. My subject dovetails neatly with Brown's thesis because it maps similar cultural markers that express the social drama of living.[15]

Some critics might dismiss this approach to understanding the colored sporting fraternity, saying that it conforms to vulgar perceptions of black culture. Historian Wilson Jeremiah Moses asserts, "Most scholars who concern themselves with nineteenth-century black culture are attracted by its rich and colorful folklore, its exuberant religiosity, and its earthy peasant traditions." It is true that the black community of postbellum St. Louis, like any other black community, had its itinerant elements and underworld characters. But there was another side to the colored sporting fraternity; it contained musicians, aspiring thespians, writers, thinkers, and political powerbrokers who were, in Moses's words, "racially responsible, and worthy of respect." In the 1870s, black intellectuals penetrated civil rights activism and literate culture in St. Louis. These men and women "who had come of age before or during the Civil War" believed in racial advancement, literary activity, political activism, education (not just the industrial arts) and voiced their aspirations through colored societies and clubs. They sponsored the Catholic Benevolent Society, United Brethren, Crummel Club, Ira Aldrich Literary and Dramatic Club, Attucks Guard Militia (originally the Blue Attucks Guard), Colored Waiters and Coachmen's Society, and, of course, numerous baseball clubs.[16]

The struggle for civil rights helps to frame members of the colored sporting fraternity, and it illuminates Charlton H. Tandy, James W. Wilson, Henry Bridgewater, William P. Dye, Charles Starke, Reuben Armstrong, William Roberson, James A. Johnson, and William H. Berzey — all mulattos — in socio-political terms. Many of these men briefly labored as river men; there were riverboat women as well. Cecil Brown explains: "After emancipation, the operation of a riverboat without a crew of black freight hands, called roustabouts or rousters, was inconceivable." The figure of the roustabout was connected with the vice district through prostitution and gambling. Some critics called "rousters" a foul-mouthed, violent crowd; others dubbed roustabouts "macks," "swells," or ladies' men. And the impact of the river man's presence on the colored sporting fraternity was significant. Politicians transformed river men into a powerful voting bloc for the Republican Party. Charlton H. Tandy began his political career as a river man, and he built his political clout with roustabouts. Linkages between the Republican Party, mulattos, and the colored sporting fraternity provide insight into the fifteenth amendment club slingers.[17]

An Urban Slumming Spectacle: Pursuing Gilded Age Leisure and Pleasure

Just a few months after they received their freedom, on January 11, 1865, St. Louis blacks founded a black organization fight for voting rights. On March 30, 1870, when the Fifteenth

Amendment went into effect, they got that right. When St. Louis blacks went to the polls for the first time in the fall of 1870, the Republican Party had already "won their allegiance as the party of Lincoln, emancipation, and black rights." Although they were only 6 percent of the population, blacks made their presence felt, because, according to the Democratic St. Louis republic, they "had the balance of political power in the city." Because Republicans had passed national legislation and three amendments that helped secure black citizenship rights, black St. Louisans were loyal to the party of Lincoln.

On 1 April 1875, the colored citizens of St. Louis paused to celebrate the passage of the 15th amendment to the constitution. One principal feature of the celebration was a public parade. The Attucks Guard, a colored militia, headed by J. Postlewaite's Western Reed Band and officered by Captain William H. Berzey, proceeded to Union Park, where the Grand Marshall reviewed the procession. In the evening, the Ladies' Mutual Aid Society, an organization composed wholly of teenagers, joined them. Ladies and gentlemen from other colored societies, attired in full dress and regalia, commenced a number of beautiful evolutions and drill exercises, keeping step to the music. Charlton H. Tandy delivered the commemorative oration.[18]

Enterprising young boys prepared for another gala: the opening of the baseball season. Colored boys between 15 and 17 years old had established ball clubs, including the Franklin Juniors, Brown Stockings Juniors, and the Colored High School nine. The Colored High School nine defeated the older Brown Stockings in a hotly contested game, in which few errors were made. Young colored sports also hustled the streets. One gang hanging around Grand Avenue Park established a concession, charging white patrons one dollar for carriage room on the grounds. One writer warned: "As Mr. Solari purchased the addition to the park expressly to accommodate Brown Stocking patrons, he deserves, and no doubt will get, their custom." The boys also gambled. And for the purposes of waging bets, newsboys and bootblacks patronized Tom Kelly's Saloon. In another example, police arrested the youngish James Gay for selling the *Sporting Gazette*, which critics called "a filthy sporting sheet ... devoted exclusively to detailing the doings of houses of infamy in St. Louis and Chicago." After Judge Cullen perused the paper, he placidly declared nothing indecent about it, and dismissed the case. Later, the "Terrible Judge" fined another colored youth, Charles Mouthey, $5 for tossing a baseball on Sunday. The social drama of modern urban life makes visible the grittiness of the "sporting spirit" that permeated the black community.[19]

A Tour of St. Louis; or, The Inside Life of a Great City (1878) offers the social drama of tenement people as part of an ethnographic tour, an urban slumming spectacle for genteel readers safely ensconced within their Victorian homes. Among other tourist sites, the narrative introduces the Third District and condemns its inhabitants for their urban squalor, immorality, corruption, and popular misery. A sizable colored population ekes out its existence in the midst of poverty, and it shares in all forms of vice. Promiscuity ethnically mixes roustabouts, vagrants, children, and women. They live in neighborhoods with picturesque names: "Vinegar Hill," "Castle Thunder," "Clabber Alley," and "Wild Cat Chute." Yet no mention is made of the political hostility towards civil rights. Thus, *A Tour of St. Louis* represents modern life's "actuality in its mundane ugliness."[20]

A Tour of St. Louis indicts not only the tenement people but also the Gilded Age, exposing urban squalor, immorality, failed social reforms, and popular misery. Authors

James A. Dacus and William Buel offered no redeeming features. Nor do they refer to base-ball or how the game brought diverse communities together. Other publications did address this issue. *The Republican*, for instance, reported a contest between white and colored nines: Kerry Patch 24 vs. Clabber Alley 16.[21]

A Tour of St. Louis finds itself in the fundamental grip of popular notions about the impotence of the masses. Its representations of tenement life are highly racialized and gen-dered constructions. No mention is made of white political hostility towards civil rights. Its failure is neither surprising nor difficult to read. As Neil Harris relates, it is easy to get the Gilded Age wrong because getting it right requires much research and consideration. Thus, my strategy uses leisure culture as an instrument, not merely to recover baseball, but through it to recover insight into the pursuit of pleasure via the sports medium.[22]

St. Louis had a ward system of government based on the population's ethnic compo-sition. A majority of the colored population lived in the Third District's Eighth Ward, which was divided into a fiefdom of saloons, each one sponsoring political meetings, gam-bling, and prostitution. Like other wards, the eighth had an unofficial mayor or political boss, and in the "Bloody Third," colored sports served this role. Social clubs engaged in political organizing as well, but were only unofficially connected to the Republican and Democratic parties. They had a liminal function, providing sites where colored and white could meet on an equal basis. Whites attended musical shows, dances, and benefits, and made political speeches. From the outside, these socio-political spaces proved frightening because they represented a world in which mainstream rules and conventions were literally inverted: black man on top.[23]

Members of the white sporting fraternity engaged in the ethnographic spectacle of urban slumming often found more than they bargained for — sometimes, it was black women on top. Saloonkeeper Thomas Kelly was well known to colored sports. The former pugilist promoted prizefights, financed gamblers, and sponsored social benefits. Kelly gambled on prizefights, horse races, dog fights, and baseball. He patronized "notorious negro dens" and bawdy houses. One such excursion led to physical confrontation. Upon entering a sport-ing house — its name suppressed by the media — Kelly got into an altercation with Estella Clark. Enraged by Kelley's advances, Clark drew a knife and cut him across the forehead and hand. Kelly promptly filed a complaint. During the court case, Clark smiled and lis-tened with evident satisfaction to his story. She was no stranger to the police blotter, and the story described her as "one of the worse specimens of the commonest kind of negro wenches."[24]

This scenario shows that neither racial segregation nor the threat of violence hampered the pursuit of leisure and pleasure. Angela Davis's study unveils how blues songs performed by black women expressed male violence against them. It informs my critique of the post-bellum period because it helps to complicate themes of resistance and acquiescence in the 1870s. As Brown argues, the blues ethos developed as a form of resistance to prevailing con-ditions in the Third Ward. It combined realism and poetic imagination. Brown points to the stylish figure of Mama Lou, the first to sing blues commercially. She performed at Sarah "Babe" Conners's White Castle, a sporting resort reserved for wealthy white men. Mama Lou verbally abused customers and performed bawdy songs. Her dark skin contrasted sharply with Babe Conners's yellowish complexion and, of course, her mulatto "inmates" who had been imported from New Orleans for her guests' entertainment.[25]

The White Castle belonged among the few illicit black enterprises that enjoyed police protection. But Conners was not hidden. Strikingly tall, she was hard to miss. In the 1870s, one police blotter provided the earliest image of her in action. In a sensational story involving two Cyprians riding in a hack screaming, shouting, and acting in a disorderly manner, the journalist recounted what caught his attention. He found the woman exceptionally tall (nearly "seven feet"), muscular, and fashionably dressed in a green silk gown and matching shoes. Henry Bridgewater and Sarah Conners were friends, and prominent members of the western sporting fraternity. When police raided Bridgewater's fancy ball, they arrested nine women who may have been Conners's "Cyprians." Behind bars, the "young, bright, fashionably-dressed mulattoes" stripped every vestige of clothing, performing the Can-Can and bawdy songs full of double entendres. Interestingly, the reporter recognized them, identifying the women as "some of the elite of the Senegambians."[26]

Adoration and Abomination: The Mulatto and the Colored Sporting Fraternity

The black image of the mulatto is an oral narrative that is based in both social events and oral literature. Journalists relied heavily on police reports, and the interviews of witnesses. It is a figure that acquired expansive importance, especially when newspapers prominently identified the mulatto with the illicit and immoral behavior of the colored sporting fraternity (**fig. 14**). The mulatto possessed a looming black presence in St. Louis, a mythological object of adoration and abomination in the sense that W.J.T. Mitchell meant when he wrote: "The idol, like the black man, is despised and worshipped, reviled for being a nonentity, a slave, and feared as an alien and supernatural power." This leads us to a conception of an oral literature in which the mulatto is an archetypical figure.[27]

As a form of oral literature, the mulatto of the sporting fraternity is based on facts. But like much of oral literature, as Cecil Brown explains, it is a combination of facts and fictions. As oral literature, it is a verbal performance — a mode of verbal communication. Throughout the 1870s, journalists identified the black image of the mulatto in crime and sex stories through titilating epithets — "light saddle-colored," "bright colored," "yellow," "saffron," "mustard," "lemon," "dusky," and "molasses-colored" figured prominently. Yet adjectival descriptions of colored baseballists other than "colored" or "negro" or "darkey" rarely surface in St. Louis newspaper sports accounts until the 1880s. The "eyewitness accounts" are the narrative events. They show that elements of crime and sex stories are derived from the figure of mulatto as protagonist/antagonist: the emphasis on the black-white parentage that differentiates the tragic from the comic, or leisure from servility, or colored from white society. Mitchell explains it this way: "The stereotype is an especially important case of the living image because it occupies precisely this middle ground between fantasy and technical reality, a more complexly intimate zone in which the image is, as it were, painted or laminated directly onto the body of a living being, and inscribed into the perceptual apparatus of the beholder."[28]

Much of what may seem obscene in saloons, gambling dens, dance houses, bordellos and ballparks may not be when experienced in the context of social drama. Promoters strongly encouraged ladies' attendance at ball games, but women understood the social risk

ICHARD K. FOX. }   tor and Proprietor. }   NEW YORK, SATURDAY, NOVEMBER 4, 1882.   [VOLUME XLI.—No. 267.   Price Ten Cents.

LIVE COON SANDWICH.

THE PICTURESQUE RESULTS OF MISCEGENATION AS ILLUSTRATED DAILY IN THE PERSON OF AN ETHIOPIAN SWELL AND HIS CAUCASIAN FAMILY IN THE STREETS OF NEW YORK CITY.

Figure 14. Live Coon Sandwich, *National Police Gazette*, 1882

that the national game invited a reputation for low-class and unladylike behavior. For instance, prostitutes and their pimps attended ball games. The rise of the black pimp, Brown shows, reflected the burgeoning concept of sportsmen. Of course, not every female spectator was a sex worker (nor every sport a pimp). Yet colored women faced challenges in the pursuit of social freedom and economic opportunities, and found their desire the subject of public scrutiny. One example (from Atlanta, Georgia) details the embarrassment of two

Gonsalvo —"And you say that dress is composed entirely of ribbons?"
Helen—"Well I guess they used a little thread in putting it together"

Figure 15. Untitled, Moses L. Tucker, *The Freeman* (Indianapolis), 1891

fashionable ladies in a phaeton who were unjustly removed from the baseball grounds. Colored women struggled to find social spaces where they could ease their worries about middle-class notions of womanhood — submissiveness, gentleness, purity, modesty, and piety (fig. 15).[29]

Gus Solari's provision to accommodate ladies at Grant Avenue Park is illuminating. Solari's grand pavilion may have excluded certain members of the female species for whom it had been hypothetically constructed: women of color. And it seems highly unlikely that white and colored ladies would have shared pavilion seating. Despite the passage of civil rights legislation, many public spaces remained highly segregated. Businesses ignored the law and refused to seat or serve colored citizens. In 1875, a confectionary store refused to seat Miss Susan Gibson and Miss Julia Colman. When the young girls refused to leave, a dispute ensued. They were arrested and charged with vandalism; Charlton H. Tandy bailed them out.[30]

While these narrated events reinforced stereotypical associations between violence and colored women, similar literary expressions penetrated the sportswriters' baseball narratives. When journalists reinforced certain views of the colored sporting fraternity, they meant both men and women. This is most vividly illustrated by the dissonance between one sports-writer's comedic sketch of the colored sporting fraternity at the ballpark and the sobering reality of the talented colored performers. When the journalist caricatured the spectators as a blackface mob, his fascination lingered on the therapeutic effects of baseball: "Quite a large delegation of the colored sporting fraternity threw down their razors, shears and wait-ers and went out to see the game." But his view might equally have been: "The enthusi-asm of the colored spectators proved quite the spectacle. And because there are fifteen colored clubs in the city, they may freely choose to attend one of their many weekly con-tests."[31]

Documenting the number of colored clubs in St. Louis has entailed a close examina-tion of city newspapers and regional papers. The number of organized, segregated colored nines is impressive, including the Black Stockings, Blue Stockings, Brown Stockings, White Stockings, Green Stockings, Sunsets, Franklins, Olives, Lindells, Atlantics, Napoleons, Moonlights, Hartfords, Kirkwood Wheelers, and Webster Blue Stockings. But the Blue Stockings were the perennial powerhouse and had few serious competitors in the 1870s.[32]

To play on the city's professional grounds, colored clubs had to generate revenue or possess money to lease them. Proprietors Gus Solari and the McNeary brothers controlled the professional ballparks. Solari expanded Grand Avenue Park, erecting a grand pavilion, with special viewing for ladies. The McNeary brothers increased seating capacity as well, adding covered stands for ladies, and making them suitable for paid admission. The Stocks baseball organization built a new ballpark for its professional nine. Teams could schedule, then, at Red Stockings Park (Compton Avenue Park), Grand Avenue Park (Empire Base Ball Park or Brown Stockings Park), or Stocks Park. When these grounds were unavailable, colored aggregations crossed bats at the Fairgrounds, Lafayette Park, Concordia Park, and Union Park.[33]

Park owners hired white baseballists to officiate colored games. The Brown Stockings' Ned Cuthbert, George Bradley, and Denny Mack officiated; and the Red Stockings' L.C. Waite also umpired colored games. One colored umpire appears in print: James Pollack umpired the Green Stockings (colored) vs. Lyons Clubs (white) contest, and his officiating gave general satisfaction.[34]

One colored baseballist, Albert Pierce, offers a case study of the sporting fraternity and race relations between 1875 and 1877. Pierce exemplified the baseball image of the mulatto as an ambivalent figure. Playing catcher and shortstop for the Sunsets and the Black Stockings, he displayed athletic ability and charisma, and the local press enshrined his hero-ics in print. Serving as mascot for the Brown Stockings, Pierce attained a reputation for gambling on the superiority of the team pitchers. The *Globe-Democrat* reported: "[Pierce] won $200 on a ten-to-nothing game, and "probably doubled it yesterday." The "Browns" adorned Pierce in blue regimentals and, for good luck, took him around with them: "He 'toted' the bats onto the grounds ... beautifully, and undoubtedly his presence helped to win the game." But Pierce was also ridiculed in the press. When the Browns played the Mutuals, rain stopped the contest with the latter winning. Pierce's absence elicited specta-tor antagonism: "Where was that lucky nigger?" He would later attain national recognition as cyclist, pedestrian, and jockey, with exploits personifying the fears and desires of the col-ored sporting fraternity.[35]

Diamond Dust: Al Pierce and the Cult of Baseball Celebrity

On Sunday afternoon, September 13, 1875, the Blue Stockings and the Sunsets crossed bats at Red Stockings Park. The game began as a lopsided affair, the Blues leading through five innings by a score of 8 to 2. But the Sunsets rallied to beat their rivals by a score of 18 to 13. Albert Pierce caught for the Sunsets and played well. *The Times* thought his performance worth mentioning. The account credits a heroic effort and notes his pluck and energy, following a first inning incident in which one nail split from his finger. Pierce kept his place, put out twelve men, assisted five times, and supplied one offensive run.[36]

By the 1870s, the figure of the mulatto embodied the national celebrity of Al Pierce. The print media portrayed Pierce, the black image of the mulatto, as an all-around athlete. In 1882 *The Clipper* noted his accomplishments as cyclist, pedestrian, and jockey. Two years prior, the prestigious theatrical and sports journal had informed its readership of Pierce's participation in bicycle races at Brooklyn, New York, and England. Working for the Brown Stockings, Pierce attained his gambling reputation on the superiority of the team's pitchers. He displayed baseball talent on the green diamond, and the local press enshrined his heroics in print. Pierce personified the colored sporting fraternity.[37]

In the 1870s, prominent colored clubs marked Pierce as a good ballplayer. He covered shortstop for the Sunsets when they opened the championship season against the Chicago Uniques and the Blue Stockings in 1876. The Blues defeated the Sunsets by scores of 24 to 18 and 22 to 11. Against the Uniques, the Sunsets fared no better, losing 13 to 9. One writer expressed fascination with the players' skin color. Colored clubs, quipped *The Times*, "involuntarily adopted [Al Goodwill] Spalding's 'different color' business, ranging in line, from the rich coffee color to the undiluted ebony."[38]

In July 1876, Pierce joined the Black Stockings. On Sunday, 28 July, the colored nine defeated the Independents, a colored club from Topeka, Kansas, by a score of 18 to 14. Pierce's shortstop debut proved disappointing. One journalist noted, "Al Pierce did not strive with the brilliancy of a Wright at short." Pierce jumped to an Illinois club, the Aurora Senegambians, who recruited him to play against the Elgin Adelaides, another colored club. The Senegambians lost by a score of 45 to 44. Jumping from club to club was not a new practice, and for big-money contests, baseball nines routinely raided each other's teams. The Sunsets, for instance, secured the services of Frank Spears, the colored catcher of Chicago, to play against the Uniques.[39]

Pierce played regularly with neither the Sunsets nor the Black Stockings, and his name is absent from two noteworthy game reports, where Hershfield worked behind the batter. It is impossible to ascertain how many games Pierce played, but he seems to have always followed the money trail and lucrative sporting opportunities.[40]

Professional baseball offers insight into the rise and growth of the entertainment industry. In 1874, the Browns' organization secured the services of east coast players and a team manager. Team salaries totaled $15,000. When a writer asked why he joined the Browns, Jack Chapman replied: "Very rich and nice people form the company. Its officers are mostly millionaires, who desire their city ably represented in baseball. The people 'turn out' there in the thousands, and all are agog with the baseball excitement. Five thousand people witnessed our practice." Wealthy baseball towns and famed players brought to life sporting images that invoked financial reward and celebrity status.[41]

In 1875, Pierce joined the Browns organization and served as water boy, bat carrier, and mascot. The sobriquet "mascot" derives from the Provencal word "masco" meaning "little magician." According to Larry G. Bowman, mascots fended off the "hoodoo' (bad luck) placed upon their teams by opposing mascots or fans. The mascot was prominently displayed during parades to the opposing club's ballpark. On the grounds, the mascot glared at the opposing team and mascot, extended his arms, and shook his fingers and hands at them. The mascot chattered to men on the field and entertained fans by dancing, singing, and prowling about the bench area.[42]

Bowman's assessment might apply to Pierce's role with the Browns, and his gambling success marked him as a talismanic figure. The *Globe-Democrat* noted that that he "won $200 on a ten-to-nothing game," and "probably doubled it yesterday." Pierce became legendary and returned to the Browns the next season. They adorned Pierce in blue regimentals and, for good fortune, took him around with them: "He 'toted' the bats onto the grounds ... beautifully, and undoubtedly his presence helped to win the game." In one game, Pierce was absent, and rain stopped the Mutuals' thrashing of the Browns. Spectators jibed: "Where was that lucky nigger?"[43]

Pierce exploited the post–Civil War physical culture movement, which found linkages to the birth of modern athletics in Europe, especially England. He placed second in the all–England professional one-mile race at the Molineaux grounds. Walking, running, and cycling tournaments lured him with prizes, travel, and celebrity status. Frank Hart and Isaac Murphy, both colored contemporaries, probably inspired him. Hart was a famed pedestrian, winning gate-money and championship belts. The jockey Murphy became the highest paid athlete in the United States. Pierce's own exploits intensified his prestige as sporting man.[44]

Tonsorial Artistry: Sporting Places and James A. Johnson's Blue Stockings

Baseball became big business. In 1875, the *Globe-Democrat* identified four classes of ball players: legitimate amateurs who received no remuneration of any sort and always paid for their own traveling expenses; regular stock company professionals who played for an annual salary; cooperative professionals who shared the profits of their enterprises; and semiprofessionals, or gate-money amateurs, who did not like being called professionals but wished to imitate that class in the matter of making money out of the game. Colored teams like the Blue Stockings, Sunsets, and White Stockings fit among the latter categories and engaged in similar business practices. Park owners shared gate receipts (normally forty percent) or paid a "heavy guarantee" (a fixed amount of $250) to visiting teams. Such arrangements attracted regional play, like the Chicago Uniques to St. Louis or the Blue Stockings to Chicago.[45]

James A. Johnson managed the Blue Stockings, a perennial powerhouse of the 1870s. *Gould's Directory for St. Louis*, 1872 lists him as a colored barber residing at 806 N. Main. Between 1875 and 1876, *Gould's* lists his business at 517 Chestnut. In 1877 the directory locates him at Morgan, corner of 6th Avenue. One account described him as "a bright mulatto, a fellow of considerable snap, and somewhat stylish in appearance." Johnson talked fluently and had "more than average intelligence for a colored man." By 1879, the tonsorial artist had two chairs in his shop and employed two other barbers. He also had a chair on a riverboat steamer packet.[46]

Entrepreneurs like James A. Johnson operated the Blue Stockings within the social fabric of the national economy (professional white baseball). William Smith, Robert J. Wilkinson, Joseph H. Mahoney, and William Roberson — successful tonsorial artists — backed Johnson's Blue Stockings. These sporting men were race-conscious, civic-minded, and political. Roberson and Wilkerson were aristocrats of color. They pushed industrial education for colored youth. Johnson operated by *any means necessary*: while he displayed a willingness to operate within the framework of a biracial institutional structure, emphasizing self-reliance and racial cooperation, Johnson did not suffer social indignity lightly. For instance, he retained Lt. Governor Charles P. Johnson and Joseph Colcord as legal counsel and commenced a suit for $10,000 against Louis Eber, an established restaurateur who refused to serve him.[47]

Johnson secured leasing agreements with park owners and scheduled games, but his Blue Stockings could not have been successful without exploiting the club's most valuable assets, the players. Here, I find Michael Lomax's thesis instructive:

> Afro-American baseball entrepreneurs had to locate black players and develop their skills to a level that would match, and at times surpass white players in the major and minor, semi-professional, and college ranks. Moreover, they also had to keep their player rosters intact, as a means of operating over a period of time.

Team rosters included: Phil Smith, c; William Richardson, 3b; George Taylor, 2b; Henry Day, ss; (?) John W. Collins, p; William Pitts, rf; (?) Sharp, 1b; James Grant, cf; (?) Casey, lf; Joseph Bailey, 1b; Andrew Goodall, 2b; (?) Green, rf; (?) Hays, 1b; (?) Jones, rf; W. Brown, 2b; (?) Lillie, 1b; (?) Harris, rf; Aaron Filley, 1b. Taylor, Richardson, Goodall, Grant, Day, and Pitts were mulattos.[48]

However, prior to Johnson's aggregation, there was the Napoleon Base Ball Club. When print media covered the Napoleons in 1874, the team had scheduled a professional road tour. The roster of the Napoleons included Bill Richardson, pitcher; Phil Smith, catcher; J. Joiner, 1b; George Taylor, 2b; Joseph Bailey, 3b; Henry Day, ss; William A. Pitts, lf; James Grant, p; William Webb, cf; and G. Turner, rf. Taylor, Day, Pitts, and Webb were mulattos. While no scores appear in the print media, demonstrative proof of the team's image of formidability emerged in another context. When Johnson organized the Blue Stockings in 1875, Smith, Richardson, Day, Pitts, Grant, Taylor, and Bailey jumped to the new Club.[49]

Preserved fragments of Joseph Bailey's life deserve special attention. *Gould's St. Louis Directory*, 1870-71, lists Bailey as a colored laborer living at 703 N. Main. Bailey and James A. Johnson lived in the same neighborhood, and they undoubtedly knew each other. Between 1872 and 1876, directories also classified Bailey as a laborer; however, he moved to 1715 N. Main, and by 1891, he had moved to 3917 Florissant Avenue.[50] Bailey played for the Blues (mid–1870s), the Eclipse (1883–1886), and the Euchres (1886). In 1881 he testified in court regarding the bulldozing of colored men at the polls: "Went to precinct 39 to vote but they wouldn't let me vote. I was a Union man and had a union ticket; yes, had a Republican ticket; have been a Republican three or four years, ever since I was a free man; they wouldn't let me vote."[51] In 1882 police officers arrested him for gambling at Dolan's Saloon, an establishment patronized by colored sports. They also arrested Ed Davis, a Black Stockings' player of 1883.[52] While Bailey never played for the Black Stockings, he always played against them. Bailey played several positions, and time didn't lessen his skills. In 1884 a reporter called him "the longest thrower of any colored player in the state."[53]

In 1875, the *Globe-Democrat* reported: "The Blue Stocking Club, a colored organization, is desirous of being challenged, and a note dropped to James A. Johnson, 615 Washington Avenue, will receive prompt attention." This was the address of William Roberson's Shaving and Bathing Saloon, a fashionable and elegant establishment with tonsorial and Turkish Bath Departments (**fig. 16**). His operation, previously located at 410 Market Street, had comparatively small beginnings, but expanded; Roberson added many departments, securing finer and finer tonsorial artists, until it ranked second to none in the city. With stylishly carpeted floors, painted and frescoed walls, costly mirrors, and marble bathing tubs, it was aptly called the "Marble Palace." A grand opening marked the tenth anniversary, inviting all its white patrons to the celebration. Joseph William Postlewaite, a colored bandleader, played inspiring music.[54]

Music was an important aspect of black modern life, and the musical talents of the colored sporting fraternity intersected with the baseball entertainment industry. Many members of the colored sporting fraternity were gifted musicians. William Pitts was a talented vocalist, and Andrew Goodall performed serenades and campaign songs—both men played for the Blue Stockings. But

Figure 16. Shaving and Bathing, *The St. Louis Times*, 1874

Postlewaite, by all accounts, dominated the musical scene. When journalists recounted hops sponsored by baseball organizations, they noted the presence of Postlewaite's Quadrille Band. When the Empire Base Ball Club hosted their annual ball in 1876, they hired the famed colored composer and bandleader. Fashionable white clubs danced to Postlewaite's orchestra, and they performed annually: "The music was furnished by Postlewaite's Quadrille Band, and it was all that could be desired."[55]

In the baseball sporting world, the colored aggregation's moniker was fairly common. Of course, there were the Blue Stockings of Chicago (colored) and the Blue Stockings of St. Louis (white), both amateur nines. The Blue Stockings of St. Louis (colored) left no written account of the team name. Lawrence D. Hogan views nicknames from the early period of baseball history as quaint and traces them to local sources. Some names were chosen for their braggadocio quotient. Hogan considers the Philadelphia Pythians' nickname original because it did not derive from some white club. "Pythian" comes from the ancient Greek athletic and musical competitions held in honor of Apollo, chiefly those at Delphi. Versed in ancient history, many colored intellectuals linked ancient Greek civilization and its athletic events to ancient Egypt, an imagined ancestral homeland. Therefore, it would not be surprising if founders of the Pythian organization, among them Octavius Catto, selected the name for its African associations.[56]

The intellectual climate of St. Louis probably influenced the selection of the colored nine's moniker. There is reason to believe, for instance, that black literary culture was aware of the historical symbolism of blue stockings. In 1875, the Reverend John C. Learned addressed a small audience at LaSalle Hall, on the "Blue Stockings of the Eighteenth century." Learned asserted: "In the eighteenth century women did not have the right of suffrage or want to vote, but sometimes went to saloons and drinking houses to vote generally for husbands when candidates for office; but not withstanding this they expressed no desire to cast a ballot. A woman one hundred years ago was laughed at if found with a book in her hand, or found writing or doing anything to cultivate their minds. If found doing this, they were dubbed 'Blue Stocking.'" The Enlightenment touches displayed Learned's romantic tastes, of course, but they were also well suited to the era of the fifteenth amendment club slingers. Some colored baseballists probably looked back upon the past, noting the amazing transformations that had taken place within a space of a century in the social conditions of their colored brethren.[57]

Baseballists immersed themselves in militias, politics, and civil rights. Like baseball, precision drilling complemented these young colored men's youthful enthusiasm, both politically and socially. Colorful uniforms held symbolic meaning, functioning as a metonymy of black male virility. Turning out in full force, they presented a fine appearance, with their colorful costumes and military bearing. Among the baseballists who served in the Attucks Guard were William A. Pitts (Blue Stockings), George D. Thompson (Aetnas), and Andrew Goodall (Blue Stockings). Pitts also served as captain of the Eighth Ward Hayes and Wheeler Club, and Goodall belonged to the Eighth Ward Republican Club. Thompson, another mulatto, fought with colored roustabout Henry Sheridan and shot him in the leg after receiving several knife wounds. On the green diamond, members of the colored sporting fraternity were fierce rivals; off the green diamond, they maintained uneasy political and social alliances.[58]

Residential segregation made it possible for the colored sporting fraternity to establish a vibrant social network and provided opportunities for cultural expressivity. Ballplayers from the Blue Stockings and other colored clubs also served in local militias. As early as 1873, the colored baseballist had developed cultural ties to the Attucks Blues, a colored militia of St. Louis. Membership in the Attucks Blues, like other militia groups, was expensive in time and money. The men were required to buy their own uniforms, maintain their state-issued equipment and arms, and purchase their own camp and garrison equipment, tents, practice ammunition, flags, instruction books. Financing their own armories, they drilled as often as three nights each week, with no pay.[59]

Local white militias had an ambivalent relationship with the Attuck Blues and banned them from participating in drill competitions. The Attucks Blues challenged the best white companies in St. Louis, but both militias refused to meet them. The colored militia was also involved in controversy. In July 1877, local militias were called out to quell a national railroad strike that had spread to St. Louis. Only two units reported: The Simpson Battery (white) and the Attucks Guard (colored). According to John Viessman, the Attuck guards, numbering 40 to 60 men, were held at the armory and not deployed. Although no complaint was made against them, the riots associated with the 1877 Railroad Strike signaled the end of the Missouri's colored militia units.[60]

There Is War in Africa: Gamblers, Ballplayers, and Hatchet Men

Cracking open the door of the gambling establishment wide enough to see two white men, a black man entertains their questions (**fig. 17**). A figure with his back to the viewer wears a top hat and sack suit. The profiled figure to the right sports an evening or full dress suit—a "swallow tail" coat, high collar shirt, cravat, and bowler hat. Holding the handle of his walking stick close to the lips, the absorbed sporting man listens with anticipation. Holding the door with his left hand, this "sable cerebus" guards the hellish gates of the sporting underworld.

A Colored Cerberus depicts a prominent role played by black men in the underworld gambling culture. In the 1870s, gambling was never conducted with open doors, and most establishments shunned publicity because it

A Colored Cerberus.

Figure 17. A Colored Cerberus, *The Republican* (St. Louis), **1888**

was dangerous. Colored doorkeepers (sometimes wearing aprons, as in the illustration) stood guard at doors and knew every policeman in town, but rarely barred unsuspicious-looking strangers. Once past this "sable cerberus," men climbed numerous flights of stairs, threading their way through devious passages with doors at annoying intervals, to reach a vista of anterooms, with generous luncheons heaped on tables, and more rooms beyond. *A Colored Cerberus* aptly portrays the surreptitious journey down the River Styx under the sentinel's watchful gaze.[61]

The black image of the mulatto penetrated underworld gambling culture. Doorkeepers, number callers, runners, and assistants worked in well-heeled white gambling establishments run by Pete Manning, Robert C. Pate, and Pete Pearl. At Number 11 South Fifth Street, Peter Manning employed Peter Ross as the doorkeeper. The colored doorkeeper had a symbolic presence with an American Orientalist appeal, imagined as Moorish guards. One account described Ross as a "heavy-set, light-colored negro" with "English mutton-chop whiskers and heavy mustache, and quite a fine-looking man." At 114½ North Sixth Street, "two light colored mulattoes" assisted white dealers; their main work appears to have been furnishing the gamblers wine and other refreshments. At North Fourth Street, proprietor Robert C. Pate employed "a tall, firmly built mulatto with a smooth face" who turned the box [in keno] and loudly called out the numbers on the ivory balls. This "negro was assisted by a dapper-looking young negro with side whiskers, who seemed the most comfortable man in the establishment." Yet this curiously exotic figuration of the black dandy through the sports medium, a formal recognition that it demands to be feared and admired, leads straight to the colored sporting fraternity (**fig. 18**).[62]

Figure 18. Untitled, Moses L. Tucker, *The Freeman* (Indianapolis), 1890

Other than Henry Bridgewater, of the famed Black Stockings, no colored gambler created more press than Charles Starke (although, there were more notorious figures). Described as "a bright-looking Quadroon," Starke owned a gambling saloon as early as 1870. *Gould's Directory* lists his establishment at 405 South 4th Avenue. And like the raids conducted against other gambling houses in 1873, police arrested Charles Starke, and Judge Cullen fined him for maintaining a nuisance. When the school board removed his children from an all-white school in 1873, he began his civil rights work. As part of the Colored Republican Club, he was active in the national election of 1876. By 1878, *Gould's* listed his saloon at 811 Christy Avenue; for the next twenty years, it would remain at this location, directly across from Bridgewater's Saloon at 814 Christy Avenue (**fig. 19**).[63]

The linkages among saloonkeepers, gamblers, bordello madams, and baseballists were part of a larger colored sporting community of the Northwest, especially Chicago and St. Louis in the 1870s and 1880s. John "Mushmouth" Johnson came to Chicago from St. Louis in 1875, and established his career as the gambling lord of the Southside. Madam Vina Fields came to Chicago from St. Louis in the 1870s, and operated a bordello for white men; Fields and her girls were mulattos. When the Sunset Colored Club of St. Louis needed a defensive player to compete against the Uniques, they secured Chicago catcher Frank Spears. George Browne and William P. Johnson, the star battery of the Uniques, also had links to

Figure 19. Wanted Equality, *The Freeman* (Indianapolis), 1891

Chicago saloonkeepers. Johnson co-owned a business with George Brooks, who was born in St. Louis, but came to Chicago after the Civil War. They were all mulattoes.[64]

In the mid–1870s, the sporting fraternity witnessed the Chicago-St. Louis rivalry for the Colored Championship. Ballparks intensified performances on and off the green diamond. Chicago's White Stocking Park mediated between the gambling crowd and baseballists: it was a space where messages and representations of hippodroming thrived and circulated. When the Blue Stockings and Uniques crossed bats on the baseball grounds of the White Stockings in 1875, the Blues beat the latter 12 to 8. The defeated Uniques invaded local newsrooms and balked that their manager, Harry P. Hall, had offered their pitcher $10 to "throw" the game. Being a "little hatchet man, [Hall] had owned up and said he refused the proffered bribe, but that Dyson, the catcher had yielded to the charms of $25 and sold them out. They discovered the treachery at the end of the seventh inning, and changed catchers, but too late to win the game." *The Chicago* Times averred: "There is war in Africa."[65]

Regional newspapers celebrated the exploits of the Blue Stockings. In 1876 the colored aggregation toured the West, playing the Brown Stockings of Kansas City; the Independence Club of Topeka, and the Eagles of Lawrence, all colored nines of Kansas. The Blue Stockings walloped the Browns 30 to 2 and defeated the Eagles 13 to 11. The team secretary dispatched results to the *Globe-Democrat.* The Black Stockings vs. Blue Stockings rivalry is instructive. Playing a two-game series, the Blues walloped the Blacks 30 to 19, but the Blacks returned the favor, defeating the Blues 15 to 9. This rivalry culminated in the early 1880s. In 1877, the Blues and Hartfords contested for the colored championship. While no results have been found, it appears that the Blues lost because weeks later, the Black Stockings played the "colored champion" Hartfords.[66]

Following this brief history of the colored sporting fraternity of St. Louis, I offer some summary thoughts about the sports medium. In the late 1870s, white press coverage of colored baseball practically dried up. This disparity coincided with the national elections of 1876, and the end of Reconstruction. After reporting thirty colored games in 1876, the city's many newspapers printed only three contests in 1877. In 1878, the *Globe-Democrat* stated that the newspaper would only publish game results that the editor deemed "sufficiently interesting." White baseball barons and journalists colluded to eliminate the competition, and colored clubs became the first casualties: the Blue Stockings, Sunsets, and White Stockings seemingly vanished. While certain white clubs continued to receive some coverage, it varied in direct relation to political and civic clout. But this exclusion represented only part of the strategic plan to restrict labor, squeeze out undesirable teams, and consolidate the market.[67]

CHAPTER THREE

Dudes, Macks, Land Ladies, Waiters, Tonsorialists, and Aesthetes: The Colored Sporting Fraternity

The sporting crowd's colored "dude" may be brought into focus with Henry Jackson Lewis's 1890 cartoon (**fig. 20**). The beholder witnesses an encounter between two men. Breaking his stride long enough to display an impressive walking stick, the immaculately dressed Chicago Dude gazes contemptuously at the hometown Indianapolis Dude. The for-

'hicago Dude:—"Say, Cully, are there any dudes in this town?"
ndianapolis Dude:—No sir, but there are lots of wood-bees.

Figure 20. Untitled, Henry Jackson Lewis, *The Freeman* (Indianapolis), 1890

mer is taller: a stranger in town, haughty in his statuesque pose. They exchange words. "Say, Cully, are there any dudes in this town?" says the Chicago Dude figure on the left. The smaller and wimpish Indianapolis Dude replies: "No sir, but there are lots of wood-bees." While asserting that only "wood bees" (would-be dudes) live in Indianapolis, his presence evokes a poor imitation.[1]

But what exactly is funny about this scene? Is it just colored dudes? Would it be funny if both figures appeared in rumpled clothing? Or is there something more, something in the content of what they are saying, something which takes the question seriously? Why is it funny, that is, odd, strange that the Indianapolis Dude puts down his hometown? What makes this remark truly odd is that, as any "wood bees" would tell you, sartorial dandyism is a symbol of power and status in the colored male sporting fraternity. Contrasting with the smooth-shaven and seemingly youthful face, the Indianapolis Dude's hunched and disheveled form, wrapped in a frumpy suit, resembles a plodding figure. The beholder, slightly elevated above him, looks down upon him as well. He cowers. Elegantly attired and sophisticated, the Chicago Dude is startling. Given his piercing gaze, accentuated by the furrowed brow, the Chicago Dude denies his counterpart's claim to dudedom. His erect form, the right hand poised atop the walking stick, and the right leg positioned in front of the left, stereotypes the flashy colored figure. The Van Dyke beard and moustache, the diamond-studded high collar, cuffs, and pinky ring, along with the double-breasted high waist coat transform black leisure class life and the male sporting world into visual-verbal performance.

This cartoon not only says something about the Lewis artist, but also about Edward E. Cooper, the publisher of *The Freeman*. Cooper's perceptions informed Lewis's subject matter. In the late 1880s, his socio-cultural sensibilities mapped Cooper's editorial and journalistic practices. Cooper had the artist project him as an urban sophisticate who enjoyed modernity's fascination with beautiful things, theatricality, and self-absorption. Henry Jackson Lewis and Moses L. Tucker, cartoonists of the colored weekly, depicted Cooper as artisan-craftsman (**fig. 21**). But the image of Cooper the aesthete competed with the image of Cooper the sporting man. Cooper imagined himself as a baseball magnate, but his involvement in the organization of the Indianapolis Black Stockings projected dudish behavior — attitudes he vigorously condemned.

For Lewis, the colored dude was another matter. Clearly, the location for the scene is neither Indianapolis nor Chicago. Projected against a white background, the figures could be anywhere; or, nowhere in particular. What, then, do they signify? Perhaps desire. They invoke the fraternal brotherhood of dudedom. Lewis's strutting peacock says something about gender in a world of the colored sporting crowd. The Chicago Dude displays his body as an objet d'art. Leaning back ever-so-slightly, he provides an almost full frontal exhibition of his body. Upon closer inspection, the left leg extends before the right leg rather awkwardly, bracing the body delicately against the walking stick. The left hand rests against his left side, with the arm locked at the elbow. A diamond jeweled brooch radiates intensely, casting an illuminating aura. Yet there is something devilish about his angular facial features (v-shaped mouth and flared nostrils) and facial hair. His wolfish grin, quite frankly, conjures an image of urban danger.

Of course, Lewis did not invent the dude. Since the 1870s, representations of swaggering colored men in the new male sporting culture had been appearing in the sports

Figure 21. Race Gleanings, Moses L. Tucker, *The Freeman* (Indianapolis), 1890

ENVY.

medium. By law or custom, resorts, baseball grounds, theaters, saloons, billiard halls, brothels, and gambling dens functioned as messengers that helped fashion the colored sporting fraternity. Its subjects not only consisted of artists, writers, athletes, musicians, saloon owners, waiters, and tonsorialists, but also dudes, dandies, macks and flaneurs, activists, tonsorialists, lawyers, waiters, gamblers, athletes, hustlers, thugs, and roustabouts. Lewis's cartoon is important, then, because it projects desire and suggests that desire can be found anywhere. And that desire suggests the colored sporting fraternity sought to establish an identity composed of images that radiated new forms of value in the collective, political unconscious of their beholders (fig. 22).[2]

Figure 22. Envy, Henry Jackson Lewis, *The Freeman* (Indianapolis), 1889

Historian Wilson Jeremiah Moses might classify these images as symbols of the New Negro, postbellum representations of black Americans following emancipation. While Moses's work focuses on the New Negro of the lost world of black literary societies, this chapter explores another sort of black cultural production: the hidden history of the colored sporting crowd. Some members participated as gamblers; others as journalists, players, managers, and owners. While some shifted between these roles, others developed complex social identities. Whether enjoying life inside or outside this charmed fraternal circle, colored men worshipped at the altar of baseball and participated in the cult of sporting fraternity.[3]

The colored sporting fraternity struggled to monitor the porous boundary between dandies and dudes, pretty players and pretty uniforms, and manliness and effeminacy. Baseball in general also expressed this ambivalence. Following a St. Louis Browns vs. Chicago White Stockings contest in 1881, for instance, *The Republican* sought to distinguish between displays of sartorial expression and technical proficiency: "The team from Chicago are prettily uniformed and play a pretty game. But then it takes hard, as well as pretty work, to win a game from the Browns." One might argue that the sports journalist implicated the "Chicagoes" in dudish behavior — the substituting of sumptuary display for athletic proficiency. Dudes could not play ball. Another account explained, "Somebody has dubbed the local club the 'dude team.' It is a misnomer. There are no dudes on it. The men were signed as ball players and will prove such. They are dandies, but not dudes." The dude conjured a marked man.[4]

Understanding the dude requires unpacking the meaning and value of black images that complicate our understanding of the colored sporting fraternity. The question of black images and value cannot be settled by arriving at a set of values and then, as Mitchell shows, proceeding to their evaluation. As active players in the sporting world of establishing and changing values, black images are capable of introducing new values into the sporting world and thus threaten old ones. When one thinks of the dude, dandy, aesthete, or flaneur, for instance, a black image does not traditionally come to mind. They are typically imagined as white figurations of modernity. However, as black figurations of the postbellum period, they belong to what W.E.B. Du Bois described as the "peculiar sensation" of "double-consciousness, this sense of always looking at oneself through the eyes of others." But as cultural critics like Barbara L. Webb point out, such representations relate to the broader concept of self-making, which becomes especially relevant in terms of black postbellum identity.[5]

The peculiarity of capitalist commodity production is its all-engulfing nature. None can escape, and the colored sporting fraternity succumbs to the clutches of that which initially fascinates them but from which they retain a certain distance. Citing Walter Benjamin's critique of the flaneur, Esther Leslie explains how surrender under protest transforms the poet, the dandy, the gambler, the rag-picker, and the prostitute into modern heroes. The modern hero is tragic, writes Leslie, "skewered on the contradictions of capitalist modernity. However, he is not nostalgic or sentimental about the past, rather he is engaged in finding strategies to survive the present.... His protest was to use idleness as a rebuke to a burgeoning economy of commodity manufacture and increased productivity."[6]

Benjamin's definition of modernism also appeals to the understanding of black images in the politics of self-making. Benjamin's "rag-picker" aptly characterizes how modernism not only picks up the usable, but also turns the old and discards into something new: "Walter Benjamin is right: the destructive character leads to liberation." Such representations construct the "hidden transcript," a dissident socio-political culture that manifests itself in the performances of the colored sporting fraternity, and is expressed through an "infrapolitics" of resistance and survival. Robin Kelly explains: "Politics is not separate from lived experience or the imaginary world of what is possible; to the contrary, politics is about these things. Politics comprises the many battles to roll back constraints and exercise some power over, or create some space within, the institutions and social relationships that dominate our lives."[7]

"Dudish Behavior": Our Man About Town

In 1885, the *Cleveland Gazette*, a colored weekly newspaper published by Henry C. Smith, introduced a new sporting column: *Our Man About Town*. Its iconic figure portrays the "dude" as a discerning observer of black modern life, a flaneur (**fig. 23**). Wedged between society columns and advertisements, this visual/verbal image represents the relation of American modernity to the colored sporting fraternity. The profiled body is a caricature for sure — dwarfing the puny body, the massive head has an uncanny ability to hold it aloft. A plug gives form to the massive cranium. In an effort to survey the world, it seems to lurch forward. Its hair and brushy mustache are immaculately groomed. A monocle rests against a large, bony nose; a squinting eye holds it in place. Thin lips purse a black cigarette billowing smoke.

OUR MAN ABOUT TOWN.

Figure 23. Our Man About Town, *The Cleveland Gazette*, 1885

Our Man About Town strides from right to left across an amorphous background, its shadowy body marked upon the surface of the white paper. Its wispy, if not fragile, form borders on the effeminate. Tight-fitting clothes mock its contours. Impeccable dress frames its aloofness. A handkerchief is neatly tucked in the coat's breast pocket. Terminating at the knees, the coat fits tightly about the upper torso; the tugging lapel, just above closed hands, suggests a snug fit across the chest, where an unseen button and a buttonhole meet. Arms are pressed tightly against the body, forming a right angle. Firmly clasped hands, fingers interlocking tightly between one another, extend slightly away from the body; and yet, guardedly protecting the body's social space against any undesired encounter. A black walking stick provides additional protection — pressed against his right side, it counters the arm's positioning with a sharp diagonal that mimics the extended right leg. The tight-fitting pantaloons reveal little, if any, muscle tone; the cuffs drag along an imagined ground plane, again suggested by the squiggly black shadow.

Our Man About Town is an allegorical figure, a postbellum critic of the colored sporting world. On the one hand, *Our Man About Town* represents some gritty realities of black modern life. Its presence penetrates cultural spaces and social institutions: saloons, gambling dens, baseball parks, theaters, resorts, and the church. Even before the column's debut in 1885, its verbal representation had carefully tracked the colored (and colorful) cast of sporting characters since 1883. Smith knew something about the sporting fraternity. An extremely gifted man, Smith was a newspaper baron, musician, politician, and baseballist. He twirled for the Blue Stockings of Cleveland, Ohio, and played competitively throughout the 1880s.

On the other hand, *Our Man About Town* narrates the aspirations of the colored sporting fraternity. Colored baseball in Ohio attained national prominence — and not just for Moses Fleetwood Walker's tenure as catcher for the Toledo Blue Stockings in 1883. That same year, the Blue Stockings challenged the Black Stockings for the colored championship of the United States. But Smith also raised crucial issues about his teammates, public issues that situated him precariously between sporting life and the demimonde. And their urban corruption and moral decay furnished sensationalized stories that permitted the *Gazette* to compete with white dailies. *Our Man About Town* transformed James A. Smith into Henry C. Smith's surrogate figure, a critic who covered aspects of the colored sporting fraternity.

Our Man About Town specifically relates the colored sporting fraternity to the "lost world of the New Negro," an apt phrase derived from the work of historian Wilson Jeremiah Moses. For Moses, the legitimate roots of black cultural production were not confined to plantation folklore, the blues style, and proletarian iconoclasm. Black language and literature was fashioned not only by plantation laborers and the urban poor but by the more literate classes. He observed: "We shall never really appreciate the nature of black American language and literature until we have reconstructed the cultural and intellectual life of literate, urban nineteenth-century black America." This study zeroes in on the literary image of colored sporting culture: the lost world of businessmen, journalists, gamblers, billiardists, baseballists, and managers — black images that built upon the apocalyptic and moral struggles of the Civil War. But these black images of the colored sporting fraternity expose complex social identities: aesthetes, dudes, and skilled and unskilled working-class laborers. The figure of James A. Smith was exemplary. Whether enjoying life inside or outside of this charmed circle, Smith — *Our Man About Town* — worshipped both at the altar of baseball and participated in the cult of the sporting fraternity.[8]

Smith's highly complex black image suggests that colored sporting men achieved social status and engaged in a form of leisure class life rarely enjoyed by most blacks in the postbellum period. It exposes a world where gentility, refinement, manliness, toughness, and violence coalesced. It shows that this lost world intersected with the leisure class world of summer resorts, where womanizing, alcohol, baseball, gambling, and other dubious activities claimed center stage. It reveals the complex relations between the colored sporting fraternity, baseball, and the print media. Print culture plays a crucial role. Members of the colored sporting fraternity were, in one sense, "race rebels," young black men who engaged in subtle and not-so-subtle but conscious acts of rebellion and resistance during the period when social segregation and Jim Crow politics tightened its grip on black modern life.[9]

Our Man About Town does not exhaust its role as an agent of surveillance society, nor as a sign of the society of spectacle. There remains the question of what constitutes this image. Its monstrous head seemingly absorbs information, sometimes signified by the lengthy verbal texts accompanying the human figure. While his monocle invokes high-toned aloofness, it is symbolic: a highly specialized lens, an aperture upon the black world. The strategically placed solid black marks — shoes, shadow, walking stick and cigarette — serve not only as dudish props, but also signifiers of the modern black urban landscape. One suspects that, given his pleasure-seeking, *Our Man About Town* maintains an aura of invincibility — immaculately attired as he leisurely strolls, this colored dude is equally dangerous both with pen and walking stick. Its stories depict the figure as engaged and detached from dangerous situations. Its criticism, it seems, often falls on deaf ears, as evident in the law's unwillingness to close down disreputable places.

In 1883 the vogue word "dude" and the image it embodied proliferated in the print media. While the term had referred to the devotees of the aesthetic movement, the national press encountered the dude everywhere. It embodied a "fastidious man." Its female forms "*dudine*" and "dudettes" appeared in 1883 and 1885 respectively. "A number of this ancient order," wrote *The Times*, "may be observed at the Casino, on the Polo Grounds, on Ocean Avenue, or in certain Marine Villas." The *Post-Dispatch* wrote, "[T]he dude is the acme of propriety and good taste. He wears no jewelry other than a ring, and invariably dresses in dark and quiet colors." The dude understands that, "clothes make the man," insisted the *DuQuoin Tribune*. High-toned barbershops are objects of aesthetic delight. The dude has an effeminate spot for palatial establishments with tall French-plate glass mirrors, luxuriant chairs, costly cosmetics, and other niceties. He shaves, pomades, bandolines, crimpes, bangs, and atomizes with perfume. Women manicure his fingers. He is indolent. He shows no "inclination to be of any use in the world.... The true dude dies, but never works."[10]

There was no consensus as to what constituted the dude aesthetic. The sporting fraternity appropriated the dude vernacular and aesthetic. On and off the field, baseballists fashioned the contours of the male sporting fraternity. Teams, for instance, embraced the term: "Dude" base ball clubs sprang up around the country. And there were colored and white dudes. Newspaper publisher Eric Elder Cooper identified the dude of the colored sporting crowd: "There are too many lazy, good-for-nothing colored loafers in the city, who infest the saloons, the ball park and other places. They ought to be made to go to work or leave town. They are nuisances." Cooper added: "No class of men know the Negro as so well as the editor.... Who knows the vain woman, the dude, the barber or the crooked preacher so well? He knows them all for he has dealings with them, and you never know a person until you have dealt with them." A discerning observer of black modern life, Cooper (a flaneur himself) railed against its seedier elements. Eyeing dudes with suspicion, the editor viewed them as predators. Cooper derided their attire, patent-leather shoes, garish jewelry, and Old Judge cigarettes — popular with the sporting crowd because they included base ball cards — clenched between pearly teeth. While dudes ranged between 20 and 60 years old, some were older. The dude aesthetic constituted a scale of sliding signifiers, ranging between effeminacy and manliness.[11]

The *Gazette* has demonstrated that the dude was hardly an innocuous figure, but as newspapers circulated visual/verbal images of dudedom, the dude aesthetic intersected with ideals about manhood, manly labor, and its products. If *Our Man About Town* says anything about black manliness, it is this: looks can be deceiving. Perhaps, *Our Man About Town* conjured how the racial camouflage of the sporting world (light complexion and bony high-bridge nose) served as a form of intimidation, creating anxiety with the broader sporting fraternity. One can only imagine what it meant "to pass for white" in the white world and live in the black world, as many colored sports did. James A. Smith, alias *Our Man About Town*, moved uncontested throughout the colored sporting world; he embodied an ambivalent figure of adoration and abomination, reporting not only on baseball but on immorality and corruption. Yet *Our Man About Town* succumbed to one of the sporting fraternity's most important unwritten rules: honor among thieves.[12]

"Better with His Brush Than on a Crap Table"

In the 1880s, young colored laborers were greatly hindered by many white employers' indifference and hostility to their career aspirations. In 1885, it struck another personal cord with Henry C. Smith after James H. Morris and Powhattan Henderson lost their very public positions. Henderson had worked in the Customs House, and Morris, the only colored street car conductor in the city, allegedly lost his position for taking off a day to attend a private picnic — "so the report says." His light mulatto complexion had probably secured the initial appointment. Morris had been Smith's former teammate on the Blue Stockings. No reason had been given for Henderson's termination, but the darker-complexioned man had aligned with Cleveland's aristocrats of color. The "Blue veins" (as Smith derided them) pushed Henderson for a clerkship in the Supreme Court of the United States. For Smith, Henderson had never identified with the mass of colored people in the city. There were, in his opinion, more worthy candidates.[13]

"No field of employment," writes historian David A. Gerber, "was as much associated with blacks as domestic and personals service." Blacks were not only highly visible in such occupations; they were particularly over-represented in Ohio's service work force. Working as a chef, steward, or waiter in private clubs or luxurious dining rooms, aboard passenger boats or railroad dining cars, fine restaurants or hotels — though servile and tedious — lent some prestige to the work. James A. Smith's employment opportunities are illuminating. In 1880, he toiled as a waiter at the Stewart Club House, in 1883, he worked as a city whitewasher, and by 1884, he had returned to the hotel service industry, working as a pastry chef for the Forest City House. The 26-year-old married man and expectant father needed steady employment. Smith and his 22-year-old wife, Josie, both mulattos, maintained a close relationship with Smith's family. The *Gazette* reports: "Mrs. James Smith, of High Street, left the past week to visit relations in Wrightsville, PA., and Baltimore, MD. Mr. Smith leaves Sunday." When the expectant mother traveled between Maryland and Ohio, her mother-in-law, Mrs. W. H. Smith, accompanied Josie. *The Gazette* celebrated the birth of their child in 1884.[14]

Smith came to Henry C. Smith's attention, perhaps through the musical world, a cultural space shared by both men. Smith augmented his family income as a basso vocalist, violinist, and trombonist. They also would have been acquainted with each other through the Blue Stockings ball club. Immersed in the activities of the colored sporting world, Smith belonged to the Owl Club. He spent leisure time (and money) on pool, billiards, baseball, and gambling. He was not good at the latter, and the *Gazette* jibed: "[Smith] will do better with his brush than on a crap [*sic*] table." But the editor viewed him as an ally, a political protégé, but also as a family man on the road to potential ruin. Here was a young man, an individual who needed direction. Why not offer flaneurie? Smith knew the colored sporting world underbelly. His personal views — though filtered through Smith's political lens — could offer critical perspectives, "newsy" (if not gossipy) items that outsiders like Harry C. Smith could not. Distancing himself from the illicit behavior — even as he endorsed the colored baseballist — Smith's newspaper often criticized their socio-political antics. *Our Man About Town* confronted excessiveness in all its forms: drinking, fighting, gambling, racketeering, wasteful spending, blue veinism, infidelity, race-mixing, and traveling.[15]

While men and women found opportunities for the pursuit of pleasure in black and tan saloons, the baseball grounds exploited not only the colored woman's involvement in the pleasure industry but intensified the ballpark as a site of illicit social behavior that had, at least for Smith's newspaper, a social dimension. For colored women who spent their time at ballparks, saloons, gambling houses, dance halls, and brothels, the press typically exploited their physical presence as the site of male pleasure, particularly for the delectation of readers titillated by the penetration of sexual seduction into other forms of urban leisure. For instance, when the Blue Stockings and Black Stockings played, *The Leader* reported the presence of colored ladies: "There were handsome black eyes watching the home team from the grandstand, and it is quite probable that our boys wanted to appear so fine before their fair admirers that in trying to outdo themselves they made some very grave errors, so the girls should let the boys down as lightly as possible in getting defeated, for they were in a certain measure slightly responsible for it."[16]

Throughout the mid–1870s and early 1880s, sportswriters transformed spectacles of colored ladies into scenes of sporting pleasure. Ballparks paralleled other social spaces where fashion, language, behavior, and skin color received intense scrutiny. When Bridgewater's Black Stockings debuted at Red Stocking Park, the press described the diversity of spectators as condiments: "pepper, salt and mustard as to complexion." He stressed the presence of "several dusky beauties" that didn't stay long because "the men were too busy betting on runs and innings to play them much attention." The diverse crowds that attended Cleveland's sporting events reminded spectators of the permeable boundary between sexual desire and the ballpark. Thus, baseball accounts should not only be read alongside sporting narratives, but alongside social narratives linking the black community to modern leisure-class life.[17]

Our Man About Town covered all aspects of colored sporting culture, challenging the "manner in which several married women with hard working and respectable husbands are carrying on." A dozen could be named without taking "our pencil from this paper," colored women who rendezvous at Euclid Street, Bank Street, and the corner of Wood and St. Clair Street. *Our Man About Town* asserted, "they are foolish enough to think that they are never seen by respectable colored men." The trade a few women carried on to obtain the means for fine dresses disgraced colored society. When the ballplayer Moses Fleetwood Walker opened his saloon on High and Sheriff Streets in 1885, the popular drinking hole became another social space for immoral behavior and violent confrontation. *Our Man*

About Town queried: "Who are the three women, wives of respectable colored men, who were seen in a private room over Walker's Saloon ... one of them was in bed with a white man and all of them half nude? The Man About Town will give their names next week." While relaxing at Fleetwood Walker's Saloon, John Glover and Gus Barber, of the Owl Club, got into a physical confrontation. Glover disparaged Barber's wife by circulating an allegation, and Barber rapped him in the mouth.[18]

Our Man About Town also incriminated married men. Not content with slipping up to the Owl Club and playing "rounce" (roulette) and "shooting craps," James Smith wrote, these "Gay Lotharios" frequented a pleasure house on Cross Street. Some of the stories had political subtexts. While attending the opera, for instance, *Our Man About Town* observed colored sport and provocateur Powhattan Henderson and a lady "who, if colored, resembled a white lady so much we came to the conclusion she was white." Amusingly, the story required an apology: "Mr. Powhattan Henderson attended the opera Sunday evening, May 3rd, with a colored young lady." For the colored sporting fraternity, interracial dating was hardly uncommon. *Our Man About Town* witnessed: "Two festive owlets met their (white) lady lovers on St. Clair Street and adjourned to Hatch and Thompsons for refreshments in broad day time last Thursday afternoon, and of course the Man About Town had to go in also. In our next issue, we shall make some startling disclosures, and Oh! The fun."[19]

In 1885, Smith's newspaper reported on the upcoming baseball season. While the brief notice celebrated the return of Henry Bridgewater's famed aggregation, the narrative casted a disparaging eye at the ongoing antics of the local ballplayers: "The Black Socks, of St. Louis, carries fifteen men this year—three batteries and an extra man.... Will somebody send the police up in the Owl Club (Saloon) and Black's Gambling Room long enough to root out some of Cleveland's base-ballists of color who months ago showed efficiency in that direction on the League Park?" The Owl Club and Charles Black & Company's establishment had become so notorious in 1885 that *The Leader* dubbed them "the ante-chambers of hell." They hosted several quite prominent and respected colored men, including one or two church members, some of whom, after playing cards till midnight, were compelled to depend upon the dealer's generosity for car fare to get home. Gambling raids were frequent, and in such incidents, James A. Smith, alias *Our Man About Town*, found himself arrested with other members of the colored sporting fraternity.[20]

Our Man About Town first surfaced in the *New York Globe*, a colored weekly published by T. Thomas Fortune. Fortune's own column took into account the journalist's role to the black masses. An inspired Henry C. Smith understood Fortune's empathy for the complex lives of the black urban community. In 1883, when *Our Man About Town* first strolled through Cleveland's streets, the dude was simultaneously drawn toward the sporting fraternity and the black middle-class. Smith took hold of the "givens of the experience and then tossed them, as it were, into the crucible of dreams." What Walter Benjamin adduces as "the intoxication of empathy" felt by the flaneurie—the melding of all knowledge of the customs of another age and our rights and obligations as citizens—Smith understood as the race's unique origins in non–Western culture and its unique history in the New World. Convinced that the flaneur was the virtuoso of this empathy, Smith's protégé readily accepted the new sporting role.[21]

Smith's newspaper wrote, "As expected, the general inquiry the past week has been who is the Gazette's Man About Town?" Few people knew his identity. His writings drew criticism, derision, condemnation, and threats of violence: "Pot Henderson, we understand, told local reporter [Ernest] Orsburn, 'we would get our cranium "creased" first thing we knew.'" *Our Man About Town* overheard two Owlets criticizing the column's contents and roundly cursing and questioning its opinions. One man asserted, "[O]ur damn head ought to be broken." In 1885, James Smith appears to have been exposed, yet he seemed unfazed by threats from his fellow Owl Club members: "The rumor that Jim Smith is the *Man About Town* is correct. Now what are you going to do about it?"[22]

The Blue Stockings and Cleveland Baseball

The Blue Stockings shed additional light on the Owl Club Saloon. On April 9, 1883, *The Leader* observed: "Should the St. Louis Colored Base Ball Club visit Cleveland while on their Eastern tour, an opportunity will be given them to decide whether they are champions or not, as they claim." In 1882, the national media celebrated the Black Stockings of St. Louis as colored champions. Following the end of Reconstruction, their exploits helped spark renewed interest in the colored sporting fraternity and colored baseball. Several of Cleveland's prominent colored baseballists participated in this renewal, and H.W. Wilson, Edward Wilson, James Morris, Charles Stanley and Edward W. Doctor scheduled a meeting to consider the challenge received from the Black Stockings. At the meeting, they founded the Colored Base Ball Club and elected the following officers: president, George Myers; secretary, William Sabb; and, treasurer and manager, H.W. Wilson. They agreed to play the Black Stockings.[23]

Here, George Myers and Henry C. Smith merit special consideration. In 1879, Myers came from Baltimore with knowledge of the barber's trade and soon obtained a position as foreman of the black-owned barbershop at Cleveland's Weddell House. Myers was an entrepreneur, avid book collector, and sporting figure. In the 1880s, Myers collaborated with white businessman Liberty Holden, editor of the *Plain Dealer*. When Holden opened the Hollenden Hotel (which refused black people service), he engaged Myer to establish what became "the best barbershop in America." Myers maintained a large library and reading room in his home which he made accessible to friends. His interaction with the colored sporting fraternity began at the Weddell House, which sponsored a colored ball club. What linked Smith and Myers was not only entrepreneurialship and civic enterprise, but also the sporting fraternity and baseball. Smith's newspaper served as an important source of black enlightenment. Smith was a race man, and his newspaper emphasized the study of racial history, finding a source of pride and inspiration in the race's past. The *Gazette* refused to shrink from association with Africa and often reported on African political affairs. Devoted to his music, Smith arranged and performed personal compositions. He was critical of colored musicians who refused to compose or perform dance music. And Smith loved baseball. Between his political and business trips, he found time to play on the green diamond, including with the Blue Stockings.[24]

Newspaper sports columns published the Blue Stockings team roster: H.W. Wilson, ss and team captain; Henry C. Smith, p; W. Milligan, lf; Charles Stanley, c; Edward Doctor, 1b; Powhattan Henderson, rf; James H. Morris, cf; William Sabb, 2b; Edward Wilson, 3b; William B. Morris, substitute; and George A. Myers, manager. *The Leader* hyped the event: "The colored base ballists, as will be seen by the list published above, have organized a good, strong team, and from what is known of their practices so far, they will make it exceedingly lively for any of the colored teams in the country who wish to cross bats with them. They will lead the St. Louis Black Stockings a merry race." The press acknowledged that the Black Stockings contained the pick of the best colored baseballists in the country, and attracted attention from the sporting classes throughout the city. But the Blue Stockings contained the best colored baseballists of Cleveland: "[A]lthough recently organized, [the Blue Stockings] has put in two weeks' hard practice, and will, no doubt, make a creditable showing by playing a strong game."[25]

Following a professional tour that included games against the Saginaws, the Findlays, and the Daytons — professional and semiprofessional white organizations — the Black Stockings arrived in Cleveland with a road record of 3–3. On Wednesday, May 9, the colored clubs crossed bats at Kennard Street Park or "League Park," home of the National League Blues (1879–1884). Before a crowd of 500 spectators, the Black Stockings defeated the Blue Stockings 11 to 5. The batting of the "Blacks" was good, and the team scored runs in practically every inning, taking and keeping the lead from start to finish. Both the local press and Blue Stocking organization petitioned Bridgewater's club for another game, but it never materialized.[26]

During the Black Stockings visit, the Owl Club, owned by Charles G. Starkey (or Starky), generously received them. The 29-year-old Starkey began his career as a carpenter, but by 1883, his establishment offered billiards, choice liquor, wines, and cigars. It also contained a tonsorial department and reading parlor and catered dinners and sponsored raffles. The Blue Stocking ballplayers, billiardists, gamblers, and other sporting men who fraternized at the Owl Club Saloon were called "Owlets." For young men not associated with the colored elite or blue-vein society, Starkey's resort became a crucial social outlet. However, the Owl Club also became affiliated with illicit activities, which the *Gazette* viewed with suspicion. Yet Starkey's resorts prospered because of his political links and the relative apathy of the police department.[27]

When Henry Bridgewater visited the Owl Club, his sporting aura illuminated the billiard hall. A noted "exponent of the western sporting fraternity and expert billiardist," Bridgewater crossed cues with Andrew Williams, of Columbus, Ohio, playing three-ball carom for $100 per game. Williams won the match. Still awestruck by Bridgewater's sporting aura and fueled by his exotic stories of the "Mound City," George W. Doctor and other Cleveland "boys" traveled to St. Louis, but their brief visit was disastrous because the town was a muddy mess, and Doctor complained that Bridgewater failed to reciprocate their hospitality. Doctor stated that Bridgewater, the "famed billiardist," whom Williams conquered so nobly, "showed up" pretty poorly. Bridgewater was "willing to play again for a cool hundred, but is not terribly enthusiastic over his 'seemingness.'" Unmoved by his disinterest, the Owl Club's "dice sharks and system players" persisted. H. W. Wilson agreed to back Williams, 500 points up, straight rail billiards, for $100 and the colored championship of the Northwest, to be played in Cleveland —"Stakes and Man can be found at the Owl Club."[28]

Our Man About Town immortalized Henry Bridgewater as "the famous billiard player." Honorific epithets and titles also elevated his Black Stockings to the black baseball pantheon, transforming them into cultural icons. Of course, the Cleveland "boys" understood

Figure 24. They Conspire Against Country, Henry Jackson Lewis, *The Freeman* (Indianapolis), 1890

the relation of manly prowess to celebrity status because they worshipped Bridgewater's sporting aura. However, gaining the colored sporting fraternity's devotion required not only the aura of celebrity status, but prima facie evidence of successful aggression. Such was the pantheon of the sporting fraternity in general, and the colored sporting crowd in particular, which Bridgewater embodied as an object of manliness, technical proficiency, and sartorial dandyism. The Cleveland boys, then, engaged in a shrewd mimicry and a systematic display of the self-as-spectacle — often with a very happy effect.[29]

   To contemplate defeating him on the baseball diamond or on the billiard table — in essence, to assume the honorific title "colored champion" — prefigured what Thorstein Veblen

Figure 25. "Country's" Skill Wins, Henry Jackson Lewis, *The Freeman* (Indianapolis), 1890

called prima facie evidence of successful aggression. Henry Jackson Lewis's *They Conspire Against Country* is exemplary (**figs. 24, 25**). The cartoon portrays three colored men at a billiard table: two urban con men and a rustic newcomer to the city. The billiard table separates them. The center figure whispers to his partner. "Country" leans across the billiard table, overhears their vile scheme, and beats his opponent. Taking pleasure in the easy pickings, the so-called rube mounts his bony horse and skedaddles with two fists full of cash. The dudes are wiser; "Country is richer."[30]

Within the social space worshipped by the colored sporting fraternity — the billiard den — pool sticks function as phallic symbols of masculinity. Urban headgear signifies dudishness, and *They Conspire Against Country* shows sporting gents perfectly at ease wearing them. Headgear provides an allegory of the social boundary between rural and urban life; in short, contested ground. The wide-brimmed pillbox scarcely distinguishes the dudish hustler from his countrified kin because Country's hat appears brand-spanking new. Yet its picturesque quality recalls an antiquated antebellum style, buttressed by the figure's relative isolation in the composition. By contrast, the dude's upturned brim is weather-beaten and tattered. These qualities symbolize urban corruption. Over time, the urban scene has transformed one southerner into an incompetent hustler. While the upturned brim, battered and torn, betrays his rustic origins, the "would-bee" hustler brazenly sells out his country-kin. Country's dandified opponent sports a bowler or derby, arguably the most sophisticated headgear. If wide-brimmed pillow box hats conjure style, the plug invokes dudish ineptness.

Other clothing also reveals meaning in these images. The dudish manipulator sports a high-collared shirt, cravat, vest, plaid pants, and the knee-length Prince Albert frock coat. The frock was especially popular with professional men. Country's competitor also dresses well, wearing a full-cut suit, high-collar shirt, four-in-hand tie, and plug. Although we can trace the aesthetic contours of the black dude's sartorial vestments in *They Conspire Against Country*, they seem overstated, as if Lewis melded figure and interior space into one aesthetic object. Seemingly crammed into a corner of the room, the billiard table, racked balls, and pool sticks dominate the compositional arrangement. The zooming perspective of the sharply tilted ground plane, floor boards, and billiard table recall Vincent Van Gogh's *Night Café* (1888). The table structures not only the scene's action but spatially distances predator from prey by driving a wedge between them. Note how the "wood-bee" leans against the table. The ornamental quality of his plaid pantaloons competes for attention with the highly wrought table leg. Pool sticks intersect and, seemingly, puncture his emasculated body. However, their zigzag patterning and phallic potency direct the viewer's attention to Country and not to his opponent. If fashionability marked high status for the colored sporting crowd and expertise at billiards marked manly prowess in a leisure-class world, impotency marked the appalling horror of everything linked to and dreaded by dudedom.

Whether *They Conspire Against Country* best characterizes the Owl Saloon Club is a moot point. The baseball landscape stages an allegorical battle: in the Owl Club Saloon, the heraldic device of the bird of prey conjured the subjectivity of animal imagery — the idyllic emblem of the owl invoking the apt phrase, "sporting man." The centrality of animals is deeply linked with baseball motives of domination. As Mitchell argues, animals stand for all forms of social otherness: race, class, and gender are frequently figured in images of subhuman brutishness, bestial appetite, and mechanical servility. Baseball deployed animal metaphors as team monikers and emblems of male virility. Animal and human figures converged on the baseball landscape, a sports medium where the dialectics of stereotype and individual found metaphoric expression. But how did the owl metaphor function? At a minimum, the owl represented the dominion of humanity over nature; at a maximum, the owl embodied the dominion of one colored sporting man over another, expressed by the figure "man-as-animal."[31]

By challenging Bridgewater's image, the Cleveland boys hoped to acquire via transmission the honorific title of sporting man. The baseball landscape differentiated player from non-player, dandy from dude, predator from prey, and men of mark from marked men. The Owl Club Saloon restaged this struggle: a sports medium that mapped the symbolic geography of martial triumph, rendered magically efficacious by the imagery itself, by ritual use of the object, or by both together. In short, the Cleveland boys and Bridgewater alternated between maker and beholder, simply interchangeable positions within the restaged scene.[32]

Opportunities to transform ones' self into an object of aesthetic display were not limited to the Blue Stockings. In August 1883, the *Gazette* reported that the Cincinnati Brown Stockings, Louisville Mutuals, and Geneva Clippers — all colored nines — were anxious to play the Cleveland team. The Blue Stockings also sought games against the colored nines of Detroit and Columbus. However, the Clippers aggressively pursued the Blue Stockings, and Geneva captain O. D. Carman challenged them to a game in his city on October 11. When Myers failed to respond, Carman sent another correspondence, boasting that the Clippers could beat or scare any colored club in Northern Ohio. The Blue Stockings would gladly meet the challenge, but they had one major problem: composed of waiters and barbers, the team's job responsibilities restricted their road tours, so they failed to meet several challenges and scheduled few road games. Editor Smith publicly chastised 25-year-old George Myers for his organizational skills:

> The base ball club of this city certainly cannot amount to a great deal, or else it would not allow a little town like Geneva to raise a base ball club of which it (our club) is afraid. They have challenged the club of this city three or four time and say it is impossible for them to see or hear from Manager Myers, of our club. Does he go in his hole and drag it in after him?

Failing to hold their contested terrain against the Black Stockings, Carman and the Clippers mocked the manliness of the Blue Stockings. In the sporting metaphor of fishing, the Clippers repeatedly challenged the Blue Stockings but could not get a "bite."[33]

In April 1884, the Owl Club's prominent members reorganized their baseball team. To raise funds, they formed the Base Ball Stock Company and agreed to host a promenade concert featuring Professor Byron C. Freeman's orchestra. Ladies and gentlemen volunteered their services: Alice Doctor, of the well-known Doctor family was one of colored society's best soprano vocalists; Henry C. Smith, of *The Gazette*, was an accomplished cornetist; Edward Stewart was tuba performer; George Moody was an accomplished pantomime; Alonso Cunningham served as costumed Drum Major; Albert Roberts and Walter Revels were popular song and dance specialists; and the billiardist Andrew Williams was an accomplished vocalist. J.A.D. Mitchell, A.H. Bowman, Daniel Fairfax, Henry Davis, and Henry C. Smith handled ticket sales through *The Gazette*. The Base Ball Association's entertainment at Halcyon Hall was well attended and proved financially successful. Following the gala, Smith agreed to solicit contests for the city's premiere colored aggregation and sent public announcements to other colored nines interested in securing dates and terms, specifically to the Springfields and the Chicago Gordon Base Ball Club. However, when the association showed little interest in "coming to the front," Smith suspected mismanagement and raised questions. *The Gazette* quipped: "Who has it and how much money was made at The Base Ball Association concert? Come, answer — the patrons want to know." The association's baseball club apparently never materialized.[34]

Perhaps frustrated by his former teammates, Smith organized the Excelsior Base Ball Club (a moniker obviously inspired by the Excelsior Band). Envisioning a competitive colored nine, Smith scheduled games against the Keystone Colored Base Ball Club of Pittsburgh, strong hotel clubs, and independents. Because of his many concerts across the city, Smith's colored aggregation enjoyed the benefit of a supportive fan base. Of course, Smith's newspaper marketed his beloved Excelsiors and carefully inserted "plugs" throughout his City Department column: "Take the Cedar Avenue through cars to the Base Ball Park.... Don't fail to see the colored base-ball club play on Tuesday, the 24th inst.... The Excelsior Base-Ball Club, colored, will play at the Gentleman's Driving Park.... The (colored) ball club of this city will give a grand promenade concert Thursday, June 9th, at Hallnorth's." Smith also played third base on the Cleveland Newspaper Ball Club against the Detroit Newspaper Ball Club.[35]

Other former Blue Stockings player, H.W. Wilson pursued sports as a path to economic opportunity. Wilson combined baseball and gambling into an economic base beyond the constraints of servile employment. In 1884, the Wilson brothers (H.W. and Edward) worked at the Lake Minnetonka summer resorts — a financially rewarding venture that attracted young colored waiters. But the resort's attraction was not limited to servility; it offered the colored sporting fraternity opportunities to join baseball clubs, gamble, drink, and pursue women. In 1885, the Wilsons worked for Cleveland's Lake View House and played for their colored nine. The Lake View "boys" consisted of H.W. Wilson, p; D. Clifford, c; Edward Wilson, 1b; George Snowden, 2b; George Moody, 3b; R. Williams, ss; John Brock, cf; Charles A. Lett, rf; and John McKee, lf. In 1885, the Lake View boys traveled to New York, where they defeated the "Kent House Boys" 7 to 5. In the second game of the series, the Lake View boys defeated their rivals again, 17 to 6. Wilson made a "lovely catch," and George Moody made a "beautiful stop and throw." In April 1886, Wilson organized an independent ball club, which would contest colored nines in Ohio and the newly organized Southern Colored Base Ball League. In 1887, Wilson joined the Keystone B.B.C. of Pittsburgh, Pennsylvania. Later, he managed the Pickwick B. B. C. of New Orleans. Wilson fancied himself a gambler.[36]

Between 1884 and 1887, Charles H. Griffin established a reputation as a competitive baseballist. In 1884, he served as player-manager for the Union Base Ball Club. The Unions played local and regional teams, and challenged any colored club in the State. They also crossed bats with local hotel clubs, including the Weddell House and the Forest City House. The colored aggregation crossed bats with the Pittsburgh Stars, defeating them by a score of 10 to 4. They lost for the first time, 16–8, to a picked nine, consisting of the best players from the Weddell, Forest City, and Kennard House boys. In 1884, Griffin's Unions posted a record of 16–2. In 1885, the colored nine reorganized and, in the first game of the season, again defeated a picked nine from the hotels, 14 to 1. In 1887, the baseballist reorganized his nine simply as the "Griffins" and opened with a 22–21 victory against the "Samuel Moore" club at the "Old Kennard Street Grounds." Charley Griffin's team made regional tours, as well. In 1889, Griffin played for the "Z" Base Ball Club, managed by the gambler Charles Black.[37]

The Colored Sporting Fraternity of Cleveland

Between 1883 and 1885, the *Gazette* politicized the dude aesthetic of the colored sporting fraternity. The gambler Phillip Hurst mapped out the streets heavily trafficked by the young dudes, dubbing the Garden Street trains the "Colorado Branch" and Garden Street Road trains the "African Branch." *Our Man About Town* and *Local Gossip* observed baseballists, gamblers and several other young colored gents "sporting very fine gold watches." Matt Scott and Edward Doctor (both of the Blue Stockings), George W. Doctor, Gus Barber, Byron W. Bucker, Andrew Williams, and Isaac Turner displayed their handsome time pieces. Sartorial display is interesting because of its widespread usage in the postbellum Gilded Age, when pocket watches typically affixed with fobs became required equipment for all railroad workers. Public performance was not limited to sartorial display: Lloyd Johnson, of the Union Base Ball Club, had a "patent on that 'dude walk' of his." In another instance, while attending church, *Our Man About Town* expressed amusement at the spectacle of young colored men sporting "pompadours." One man resembled something trying to fly: "Billy Kersands mouth, in its palmiest days, couldn't equal the average kinky-haired 'pompadour.'"[38]

The purchase of prestigious commodities linked the colored sporting fraternity to what historian Robin Kelly calls "the pursuit of leisure and pleasure." This male-identified culture unified colored baseballists within a "dudish" inner circle. *Our Man About Town* often identified the "coming dude." Edward Doctor and Sam Smith, for instance, formed a partnership called the "dudish manipulators." The *Gazette*, in the sporting vernacular, averred: "Freeze this last word." When ballplayer Charles A. Lett quit working at the railroad, *Local Gossip* doubted his manliness. The columnist sneered that the dude's "light suit" would not permit railroad labor. Lett took a waiter position which allowed more leisure time. In a world where stylish performances carried a great deal of social meaning and were signifiers of power (or the lack thereof), young men often imagined themselves as so-called "shadies" who supplied others with entertainments which society at once desired and abhorred. Matt Scott, for instance, gave a stag party to a few intimate friends over the Thanksgiving holiday but made no effort to conceal his activities. Whether or not "dudish manipulators" acknowledged what Moses calls the apocalyptic and moral struggles of the Civil War and Reconstruction, the life of the black working-class influenced the attitudes, values, and behaviors of the colored sporting fraternity.[39]

Shaped by socio-political concerns of the mid–1880s and told through the cultural prism of racial uplift, the didactic and rhetorical character of *Our Man About Town* obscures the oppositional meanings embedded in negative stereotypical associations. And it would do well to understand the socio-political history and cultural character to which these associations belonged. This requires mapping the colored sporting fraternity of Cleveland and examining its domestic and personal services to whites (a path which required patient saving, hard work, ambition, and little luck) on the one hand, and its relation to the more lucrative enterprise of supplying whites with entertainments (a path that offered "shady" opportunities for making a fast buck while maintaining a respectable image).[40]

While these criticisms alluded to the potential dangers of the sporting world, such as squandering ones' wages on unnecessary material goods, they expressed concern about the looming threat of idleness, corruption, and immorality. Yet the young members of the colored sporting fraternity expressed ambivalence towards conventional respectability. The Owlets, for instance, made it a point to attend festive events sponsored by colored society. When the Eureka Club hosted its annual ball, Matt Scott, Edward and George Doctor, Thomas Spencer, Charles Starkey, and Mr. and Mrs. James A. Smith attended the gala affair. When George Myer and Henry C. Smith of the Young Men's Social Club sponsored its annual "hop" in 1884, "Owlets" Al Roberts and James A. Smith attended. The Young Men's Social Club filled the gap between aristocrats of color and the demimonde of the colored sporting fraternity. In Henry Smith's view, they offered race pride and racial solidarity, sources of racial inspiration and confidence lacking in the Blue vein society.[41]

Music was an important aspect of black modern life, and the musical talents of the colored sporting fraternity intersected with the baseball entertainment industry. Many members of the colored sporting fraternity were gifted musicians. Andrew Williams, the billiardist who defeated Henry Bridgewater, was a talented vocalist who performed at the Base Ball Association Ball. Another "Owlet," Albert Roberts, played guitar, sang, and danced. While serving as a waiter at a summer resort in Minnesota, Roberts performed "character selections" in a musical concert. Charles Starkey's quartette performed several selections at a baseball concert, as well. Musical performances — not unlike the live organ and prerecorded music of ballgames today — made for a festive atmosphere. Henry C. Smith's Excelsior Reed Band performed throughout Ohio and provided entertainment for picnics, festivals, excursions, balls, and sporting events. Smith often collaborated with Professor Bryant C. Freeman, another popular colored musician. Freeman, who performed at the Baseball Association Ball, displayed his proficiency with the violin by performing classical European pieces. The rotund Freeman also played for dances and ballgames. And James A. Smith (*Our Man About Town*) himself was a basso vocalist, violinist, and trombonist.[42]

Our Man About Town charged the Owl Club and Black's Gambling Room with catering to corruption and immorality. The columnist surnamed the gambler Charles G. Starkey "the Prince of Wales." But only one member of Cleveland's colored sporting royalty proved bold enough to claim gambling as an occupation: Phillip Hurst. *Local Gossip* quipped that Hurst had opened a banking house, serving as a money lender and political provocateur. *Our Man About Town* questioned Hurst's loyalty to the Republican Party in 1885. Claiming his Republican birthright, Hurst denied the accusation. He claimed no association with Madison Tilly, or anyone who peddled Democratic tickets. *The Gazette* thought differently. Hurst and Starkey had secured funds from the coal baron and Democratic strategist Thomas Axworthy to publish a colored democratic newspaper. "Spending money freely among the colored boys" or buying colored votes, Axworthy made the proprietor of the Owl Club Saloon, Charles Starkey, and Phillip Hurst, his lieutenants.[43] *Our Man About Town* linked the Owl Club and Black's establishment to the Democratic Party through another source: the "Blue vein" society. John P. Green, for instance, belonged to Cleveland's aristocrats of color. Green, a lawyer, enjoyed a long, cordial friendship with Cleveland's oil baron, John D. Rockefeller. Green's political support included, at least for a time, the "crap shooters and gamblers."[44]

Equally notorious were Charles Black's business enterprise, pleasure resorts, social clubs, and baseball teams. Black began his career in 1878, innocently enough, as a waiter. By 1883, the 30-year-old had established at least two important services: black-owned gambling resorts and money lending. *Our Man About Town* tracked Black's movements throughout the city in the 1880s, especially the constant relocation of his illicit resorts: "Charlie Black has removed his place of business, and cannot be found on St. Clair Street anymore." In 1886, William Clifford and Charles Black financed a pleasure resort with "more commodious and elegantly fitted apartments." The "Z" Club, as it was called, offered the choicest wines and cigars, pool, billiards, lunch, reading rooms, and tonsorial parlors. In 1888, the Z Club added a "ticker" to receive baseball news by the innings. The owners left nothing wanting in the line of service and pleasure.[45]

In 1889, Black served as manager and treasurer of the Z Base Ball Club, whose members comprised former baseballists of the Blue Stockings, Clippers, and Unions. Frank Doctor was team secretary. The team included: W. Nelson, c; James Jackson, p; F. Johnson, 1b; Charles Griffin, 2b; H. W. Wilson, ss; John Jackson, lf; W. Stanard, cf; R. Gross, rf; and O. Hall, substitute. Newspapers reported local games against the Genevas, the Shamrocks (white), and the Woodlands Club (white). The Z Base Ball Club brought out large crowds. In a game against the Woodlands Club, the colored nine drew nearly 2,000 spectators. The Woodlands defeated the Z Club, 22 to 12. The colored aggregation also made road tours. They visited the Brooklyn Alpine Base Ball Club, captained by James H. Porter and managed by Charles A. Johnson.[46]

James A. Smith embodied a new patterning of race relations that favored, to some degree, mulattos. While disagreements raged over what constituted the dude, particularly within the colored sporting fraternity, it seems certain that ambivalence existed towards them. This is not to say that skin color did not matter, but class, gender, and educational training were also important. When a newspaper correspondent asked Blanche Kelso Bruce, the Register of the Treasury, to comment on the present condition of black America in 1883, Reconstruction's first full-term black U.S. Senator from Mississippi (1875–1881) offered a surprising response. Bruce, who figured among the colored social elite, had just walked his young son — a "pretty baby boy with dark, wavy hair and a clear olive complexion, tastefully dressed and carrying in his hand a tiny lunch basket"— to kindergarten. While Bruce emphasized the importance of black educational opportunity, he quipped: "[W]e have the dude, the colored dude, full-fledged and as pronounced as the white race can produce." As he climbed the Treasury Building steps, Bruce laughingly howled: "[W]e have the dude."[47]

Frank Grant Is Quite a Ball Player: The "Colored Dunlap"

A photographically derived portrait of Frederick Ulysses Grant depicts the colored baseballist as a member of the Cuban Giants (**fig. 26**). The chest-length portrait appears to derive from a team portrait that has not been uncovered. First, the figure is in a team uniform. While this may not seem important, individual photographs of the period were often of action poses: holding a bat or glove or sliding. This image imitates tobacco or baseball cards, yet cards were not made for 19th century colored ballplayers. Second, the figure is part of a larger composition. The rounded shoulders have been closely cropped, suggesting that the sitting player had been sandwiched between teammates. Finally, Frank Grant's intense eyes link him not only to unseen players but also to the camera operator who had instructed them to avert their gaze from the camera's eye.

Another aspect of Grant's image is his skin complexion. The engraver, perhaps in an attempt to emphasize noticeably Negroid physical features, accentuated Grant's full lips by tightly compacting and cross-hatching black marks to model not only the bone structure but darken the skin. The photograph probably rendered him much lighter: the *Buffalo Express* described the light-skinned Grant as a "Spaniard." Sports journalists often employed euphemistic terms like Spaniards, Portuguese, or Arabs to describe the black image of the mulatto baseball player. Yet this did not stop sportswriters from engaging in the misrepresentation of his skin complexion by calling him the "ebony second baseman" or being as "black as a raven."

The portrait belonged to a biographical sketch devoted to Frank Grant which first appeared in the Harrisburg *Telegram*. The paper's proprietor and publisher, J. M. Place, supplied the *Gazette* with both sketch and portrait,

Figure 26. Frank Ulysses Grant, *The Cleveland Gazette*, 1890

which may have been further doctored by an artist at the *Gazette* who lettered the moniker "Cuban Giants" across the jersey. Between 1886 and 1890 Cuban Giants uniforms did not have the moniker. It seems odd that the *Telegram* would not have a photographic portrait of Frank Grant in a Harrisburg uniform.

On the green diamond, Frank Grant was a dandy. Having played for several white organizations (Meriden, Connecticut; Buffalo, New York; Ansonia, Connecticut; and Harrisburg, Pennsylvania) and colored aggregations (Cuban Giants) in the postbellum period, Grant established a reputation as an excellent hitter and slick fielder. He played second base so skillfully that he was called "The Black Dunlap," evoking comparison to Fred Dunlap, a white professional player at the same position. While playing for the Buffalo Bisons, Grant did some fine defensive playing against the Pittsburgh Alleghenies. Several of his marvelous stops and catches displayed great showmanship. His arm strength and range were so exceptional that some observers derided his defensive play as a "circus act."[48]

Grant was also a sporting man. Following the loss of a game, for instance, the Buffalo Bisons manager discovered that bad play had been due to drinking, so team directors fined several players, including Frank Grant. As a member of the colored sporting fraternity, he dressed stylishly: "[Grant], the colored second baseman, of the Buffalo's is immense, when he lays aside the team uniform. He electrified Broadway recently by appearing in a blue corduroy coat, black and white striped trousers, yellow gloves, patent leather shoes with light drab gaiters, a slate colored Fedora hat and a gold headed cane." In 2006, Frank Ulysses Grant was elected to the National Baseball Hall of Fame in Cooperstown.[49]

Macks, Pimps, Land Ladies, and the St. Louis Sporting Fraternity

Henry Jackson Lewis's *She Was Practicing* reveals the uniqueness of colored sports' dress and fraternal deco (**fig. 27**). A male suitor appealing to his girl's father wears an exceedingly extravagant outfit that perfectly captures Brown's description of the "mack." The open black box-back coat reveals an equally black cravat and a white shirt with a standing collar that keeps his chin high in the air. Wrapped around his waist is a thick plaid sash. Knuckle-length sleeves almost cover his hands; his left hand clutches a metal-tipped walking cane. His right hand appears to hold a white Stetson. Oversized, black-striped pants hang over the suitor's shoes. *She Was Practicing* makes the suitor's membership in the world of the sporting crowd readily apparent. Recurring motifs such as box coats, white Stetsons, high collars, knuckle-length sleeves, and metal-tipped canes not only represent a testament to aesthetic style, but they also project individuality.

Figure 27. She Was Practicing, Henry Jackson Lewis, *The Freeman* (Indianapolis), 1890

The mack or pimp, an emblematic figure of the period to be sure, was elevated to the status of folk hero. The critical question is why the mack invoked an exalted status in the colored sporting fraternity? Or more broadly, why has sartorial expression represented a subversive refusal to be subservient? And is there a relation between the land lady and the mack?[50]

It is difficult to understand the pimp's image in postbellum period cities like St. Louis, without considering how they embodied the sporting spirit of the Mound City. According to cultural critic Cecil Brown, career politicians hired colored men to help to manipulate political elections and control and police brothels. Colored female sex workers were directly threatened by attacks from white sporting males who unleashed pent-up frustration against visibly independent, autonomous, and sometimes materially successful women. "Brothel bullies," writes Brown, "were middle- and lower-middle class males who were seldom arrested for their crimes." Most women (certainly not all, as demonstrated), were unable to defend themselves against strong men, and the courts refused to view them as legitimate victims. Pimps were their main defense against brothel bullies. "Black men were hired to live in the brothels, providing physical protection and performing services such as buying the groceries, repairing the house, and serving the guests.... The pimp became a negative figure for white men, but for most black people in areas like Deep Morgan and Chestnut Valley a hero."[51]

Brown introduces us to St. Louis, which included a range of social types by the mid–1890s. Among them are pimps or "maquereaux," shortened to "macks," a term used today in black urban society. "The mack of St. Louis," writes Brown, "was a well-dressed sportsman who wore the finest clothes and lived in Chesnutt Valley." The mack qualifies as a marginalized figure because he is the ultimate expression of putting one's body in the marketplace. It combines aspects of the sauntering flaneur and the self-conscious dandy. Brown adds:

> The pimp, like many of the new type of black sportsman who inhabited American cities in the 1890s, was "an incipient version of the bourgeois consumer": he could dress in nice clothes as though he was prosperous, but he might not have had a dime in his pockets. Like the flaneur, the mack didn't generate commodities as middle-class manufacturers did, nor did he consume enough commodities to make a difference.

Sartorial expression is illuminating. The folkloric hero Lee Shelton (also known as "Stagolee") wears tailored shoes known as "St. Louis flats." They practically have no heels, and the long pointed toes extend upward. On top of the shoes are tiny mirrors that capture electric light, refracting it upward as flaming sparks. Dovetail colored spats cover them. Gray-striped pants hang over his spats. The flaps of his black box-back coat fall open to reveal an elaborately patterned red velvet vest and a yellow embroidered shirt, with a celluloid standing collar that keeps his chin high in the air. Knuckle-length sleeves almost cover the gold rings on his manicured fingers; his left hand clutches the gold head of an ebony walking cane. The other hand holds a long cigar. On his head is a high roller, milk-white Stetson. Along the hatband is an embroidered picture of his favorite girl, Lillie Shelton.[52]

Arna Wendell Bontemps confirms the "mack" as a "gaudy breed." His description of them, derived from original sources, occurs in his novel:

> They wore gay embroidered shirts, and on their fingers, below the knuckle length sleeves, flashed diamonds and polished nails. Their finery seemed even to exceed that of the fancy

women who supported them. Gold money made into jewelry was customary, also high-roller hats, with nude women or boxers or racing horses worked in small eyelets in the crown.

Macks also wore fancy waist-coats, peg-topped trousers, gaudy neckties, and other accoutrements of the dandy. The flaneur and the mack did not generate commodities as did middle-class manufacturers, nor did they consume enough commodities to make a difference. Henry Sweeden, the 22-year-old proprietor of a "negro dance hall," is an interesting character in this regard. Formerly employed at a saloon opposite Deagle's Varieties, the slim built, 5'9" mulatto, was known for his gray suit and cape. Macks functioned as facilitators, the in-between, individuals who made their living on the luck of what the city could provide. If organized baseball clubs wore uniforms to avoid the appearance of property through sartorial expression, the mack took over the streets and imbued it with their own kind of competitive display and improvised stylistic freedom.[53]

As Brown makes clear, "land lady" and "boarding house" are code words for "madam" and "bordello." He elaborates: "We can gather [that] the 'boarding house' was a house of prostitution and that the 'land lady' was a madam." Prototypical linkages between the pimp and the land lady find expression with Emma Baptiste and her male "inmates." In 1873, the press identified James Lewis — "a dark complexioned Italian looking man of about thirty"— as "a hanger-on at the negro house of prostitution of Emma Wilson." He was accused of murdering the 26-year-old John Anderson, who, along with a party of fellow workmen, accosted Wilson's frail inmates. Lewis was described as a well-dressed man who looked quite respectable. While papers called Lewis a "white Italian," it seems likely that he was a mulatto because he had a brakeman position, and to identify as colored would have cost him a job. In 1881, bartender J. C. Clark and roustabout patron Henry Wise participated in a fight at Baptiste's house of pleasure. Wise called Clark "a pimp," which enraged him so that he struck the patron with a chair. Wise then pulled a knife and disemboweled the barkeeper. Such social dramas express, according to Brown's thesis, the drama of living. It is also what Mitchell calls an offensive image, an urban performance that insults, degrades, and humiliates female subjects of representation and by extension, all other women as well.[54]

"The Dude of Saratoga": *Baseball/Waiter Subculture*

In 1883, an east coast reporter in search of the dude covered the summer resort circuit at Saratoga Springs. While the reporter regrettably discovered only three dudes, "the greatest of these was a negro." His clownish description bears all the traces of minstrelsy. The colored dude dresses as gaudy as a circus wagon, and he is twice as handsome. His natural skin color resembles a new rubber shoe. His mouth is as handsome as a gash in an over-ripe watermelon. No pains and but little expense is spared in his get up. The neck-tie is the reddest of the red, the gloves are white kids, and the tops of his gaiters are dove-colored. He condescends to act as a waiter at one of the large hotels for a few hours each day. During the large leisure of that class, and while his fellows are playing baseball on South Broadway, or pitching quoits on back streets, the black dude clothes himself in all his wardrobe's glory and promenades Broadway. And during his triumphal march, the carriage drivers cease from troubling and the busmen are at rest; little dogs laugh to see such a sport,

Figure 28. Fred May's Close Call, *National Police Gazette,* **1883**

and the tallyho coach "hath not where to blow his horn." Colored waiters always make a fine appearance while strolling on Broadway.[55]

While meant to poke fun at the colored sport, this stereotypical narrative unleashes the subversive potential of the baseball/waiter subculture. When the reporter cast his optics over the flamboyant figure, he beheld both the theatricality of the black masculine self and conjured a minstrelizing figure of leisure class life. For the reporter, the figure conjures humor and horror: ostentatiousness, combined with a perceived disdain for labor, signifies the effortlessness of the colored dude aesthetic. As the story mocks its subject, the reader is nonetheless drawn to a black performance inextricably linked to the universality of exchange in commodity society: resort hotels, circus wagons, new rubber shoes, watermelons, red neck ties, kid gloves, gaiters, quoits, baseball grounds, and laboring bodies. Colored waiters, like the colored sporting crowd, were subordinated to the market.

While the colored dude was expected to refrain from laborious work, when before the public eye, his laboring body made certain demands upon the aesthetic self to conduct a leisure class life in due form (**fig. 28**). Talented colored laborers of summer resorts — waiters, athletes, musicians, and thespians — were, it seems, better suited than less-talented laborers for obscuring all appearances of effort. The only residue left after deduction of this effective work could be classed as a performance of leisure. Hotels provided one of the few opportunities for colored laborers to exploit their talents — the Base Ball Club of the West End Hotel Long Branch furnished colored guests with musical and literary entertainment. Wilson Corey and J. Willard performed a duet entitled "Jamie, my Jamie"; Corey also sang sacred music at church socials. Joseph Middleton performed solo selections. J. H. Paynter rendered "Rienzi's Address" and "The Gladiator" by J. Wilson of Lincoln University. Stanislaus K. Govern, manager of the Clarendon Base Ball Club, Manhattans, and Cuban Giants, performed with the Ira Aldridge Dramatic Company. Govern also managed a society concert at Putnam's Opera House in Saratoga Springs. Alexander Plummer, of the Gordon Base Ball Club (and officer in the United Headwaiter's Union No. 1, of Chicago), established himself as a cornetist.[56]

Colored waiters also held annual receptions and balls that included music, dancing, and recognition awards. Following cultural tradition, they honored exemplary performance by presenting costly gifts to one other at the close of the resort season. In 1883, the waiters of Ocean Grove awarded Fred Nichols, headwaiter at the Metropolitan Hotel (and ball club's manager), a handsome pitcher, valued at $25. In one Saratoga Springs gala, the headwaiter and his officers presented Robert N. Smith a gold-headed cane. That same year Joseph Marshall, the headwaiter of the Leland Hotel, received an elegant Japanese tea set. In 1884, headwaiter C. H. Lansing received a silver tea set from the waiters of the Grand Union Hotel. In 1886, the waiters of the Clarendon Hotel presented their headwaiter, Charles H. Clifton, a gold watch and chain. That same year, the waiters of the Werden Hotel presented their head waiter, W. A. Wayland, a gold-headed umbrella, as a token of their esteem. Solid gold badges were presented to the most popular third waiter of the large hotels. In 1888 Charles E. Nelson, of the Saratoga, beat out Mr. Nesbitt, of the Congress Hotel. Colored waiters also may have been following a tradition among blackface performers to award colleagues with jewelry (diamonds and gold watches) and other expensive objects, knowing that, under financial duress, they might have to pawn them.[57]

For some colored politicians, the image of college-educated colored men serving as waiters was appalling. When the Colored Press Association held its national conference in 1883, delegates expressed strong views on the topic. In his paper on industrial education, P. H. Murray observed: "The education that our young men receive simply raises their aspirations above rough labor without qualifying them for anything else." Those who could not preach or teach sought refuge in the corridors of hotels and behind barber chairs. Murray lamented: "[M]any of our young educated for teachers spend their vacation, at Long Branch and Saratoga flying about the dining tables in white jackets" (fig. 29). While Murray failed to name these hotels or others in the United States, young colored men could be found working at the Clarendon, the Ocean House, the Mansion House, the United States, the Grand Union, the Cataract, the Congress, the Metropolitan, the West End, the International, the Ocean Grove House, the Ashbury Park, the Broughton House, the Lakeview House, the Kent House, the Peabody House, the Gayoro House, the Leland, the Laclede, and the Lindell. Murray also did not mention that hotels provided opportunities for the sporting crowd to wager on contests where waiters doubled as ball players.[58]

This social camaraderie linked waiters of color to other members of the colored sporting fraternity, including the tonsorial artist. If the colored dude embraced aesthetic style, it was because the tonsorial artist helped fashion him as an objet d'art. For dudedom, tonsorial artists performed head work, painted and powdered them, atomized and primped them, and supplied cuffs and collars. Being natty dressers and well-groomed, tonsorial artists had an artistic cast: "His attire is artistic in color and form and his pose is artistic as he waves the razor, or snaps the shears or plies the shampoo process.... Under his cunning hands the sufferer from dust and heat becomes transformed and returns to the world a thing

Figure 29. Long Branch Dives, *National Police Gazette*, 1887

of beauty." *The Globe* adds: "Mark Hamilton, tonsorial artist of the Broughton House, sustains his wide earned reputation by his steady hand and the first class work it performs." *The Globe* identified the tonsorial "studio" or "shop" of Charles H. White, which enabled its proprietor to prepare all head work in a most artistic manner. Al Jones of the Chicago Gordon Base Ball Club operated tonsorial parlors, and John "Bud" Fowler followed the trade when baseball opportunities were scarce. However, the tonsorial artist could resurrect the image of the laboring black body. When the National Colored League collapsed in 1887, for example, players stranded around the country had to work their way home by doing turns at barber chairs and waiting tables in hotels. Thus, the tonsorial artist was also an emblematic figure of the colored sporting crowd.[59]

Our Famous Tonsorialists

On 5 March 1881, *The Evening Chronicle* ran Koken & Boppert's ad for "Razors, Hones, Strops, Barber's Supplies, And Toilet Articles" (**fig. 30**). The woodcut illustration accompanying the text is crudely rendered. Two black-faced figures stage a comical scene: a chase occurs through an open, grassy field and against either the rising or setting sun. The razor-wielding antagonist awkwardly pursues his foe with an open razor in the right hand; stamped onto the blade is "Koken." The left hand forms a clenched fist. The fleeing figure leaps over

Figure 30. Koken & Boppert, *The Evening Chronicle* (St. Louis), 1881

a small mound with the intention of distancing himself from the razor-wielding antagonist. These figures, one wearing a short jacket and the other wearing a vest, romp towards
the viewer, or at least in the direction that leads past him. Just above the razor, to the right,
is the date "1881"; closer inspection shows that the last numeral "1" has been partially hacked
up to change it from a "0." Note its curvilinear form and how it tapers along the edges.
This image had been used the previous year. While its recirculation saved money, the image's
resurrection buttressed negative stereotypical associations.

The image hints that a wood chopper hewed the figures out with a dull broad ax. The
hastily-carved design was probably intended to represent men, but the execution would
hardly warrant the assumption. Note the sharply angled hairstyles. Their lower torsos, especially the legs, are about as pliable as thin paper match sticks, while their crotches look like
shovel bottoms. Upon their blackened faces are expressions of desperation, with bugged-
out eyes wondering where and when this chase will end.

The artist chose this funny yet thematically violent image to relate to the sporting
crowd. The image is funny because its message had a built-in audience. Postbellum newspapers carried stories of razor-wielding blacks, reinforcing notions that they were violent
and dangerous. Of course, razor-wielding blacks gave meaning and value to "Blackville"
and "Darktown," segregated social spaces full of marginalized figures and urban violence.
But given the many narratives of black crime and black violence, one might argue that St.
Louis practically invented the razor-wielding black horror.[60]

Indispensable to the tonsorial profession, the razor was converted into a weapon of
war. One postbellum critic has argued, the "African Weapon" or, in "negro" dialect vernacular, the "rahzer," belongs to the "kettle-colored race." So general has become the use of
the razor among the descendants of Ham that it is considered the stereotypical weapon of
choice. In the right hand of those tinged with African blood — blacks, mulattos, and
Octoroons — the razor becomes one of the most formidable weapons. The author offered
readers an amazingly descriptive and meticulous illustration:

> [The black] opens and swings the blade of the instrument until its back almost touches the
> back of the handle, clutches the handle near its junction with the blade with his index and
> middle fingers the handle and that part of the steel between the razor rivet and the keen edged
> blade, anchors his grasp with his thumb, and then with a chopping machine assails his enemy.

Of all concealed weapons, none deserved to be more severely tabooed, the author concluded, than the "rahzer."[61]

The deployment of razors among colored baseballists (male and female) and spectators typified the potential threat of violence among colored sports. Real and imagined narratives filled the sporting columns. *The Police Gazette* declares: "There are no less than six
colored clubs who claim the charcoal championship of the country. These clubs are located
respectively, in St. Louis, Cincinnati, Cleveland, Pittsburg [*sic*], Philadelphia and Washington. This is a dispute that hundreds would enjoy seeing settled, even if the contestants are
compelled to fall back on their razors." Describing a game's outcome between the West Ends
(colored) and the Hartfords (white), for instance, *The Courant* offers the following pun:
"The Hartfords Beat the West Ends by a Close Shave." Sports narratives implicate female
baseballists as well. During practice of the Dolly Varden's, a colored female professional
baseball club, Captain Ella Harris pulled a razor from her pink stockings. Finally, *Sporting*

Life detailed a raucous melee between colored nines that resulted in casualties and arrests. *The Police Gazette* describes this event as an "old, original style of ball playing":

> The game was very exciting, a vast amount of interest being taken in it, in fact, the interest was so great that it brought back days of early ball playing, and pistols, razors, knives, bats, & c. were freely used. By the time the two nines and the spectators had done one another up pretty well, the police arrived and escorted them all to jail, where they had an opportunity to reflect upon the advantages attending the more modern style of playing.[62]

But the colored sport hardly monopolized the razor as a weapon. Newspapers accounts show that the razor in the United States had a peculiarly violent social history. A sampling of violent crimes committed by the Germans, Dutch, Irish, Italians, English, and other ethnic groups is staggering. Victims and victimizers cut across race, ethnic, class, gender, and professional lines. The "rahzer" appears to have been, then, a weapon of choice for many Americans, European and Asian immigrants not excluded.[63]

That being said, portraits of colored tonsorialist artists bring together conspicuous consumption and the sporting crowd. They appear among advertisements for an array of products devoted primarily to the male sporting culture. These ad pages, which appear in *The Police Gazette*, represent a billboard of signs, an image-text field in which portraits of sporting men vie with patent medicines and quack remedies (for syphilis, gonorrhea, sexual potency, headache, stomach disorder, and neurasthenia), condoms and sex toys, pornographic photographs, sporting goods, employment, and mind reading. These "proprietary articles" say, among other things, something about the potential dangers of the sporting world. For example, "Tarrants Extract" claims to cure gonorrhea, gleet, and all diseases of the urinary organs; an oval seal accompanies the text. Along its border is the phrase "*ultimum et unicum remedium*," "the last and only remedy" (**fig. 31**). The oval inset depicts a medieval doctor holding a scepter encircled by a serpent. With his left hand extended outward, the bearded old man appeals to the viewer. The Dude Novelty Company sells condoms. For men who indulged too much in masturbation during their youth, "L. S. Franklin, Music Dealer" offers a remedy for lost manhood, emissions in small parts, varicocele (soft tumors in the scrotum), nervous debility, and so on. While portrait sketches may have conferred "colored" tonsorial artists celebrity status, they also projected against this cultural backdrop those urban dangers that made them "marked" men.

Richard Fox's decision to publish portrait sketches was marketing genius. No publication exploited illustrated portraits of sporting men quite like Fox's sporting journal. Around 1882, *The Police Gazette* began publishing illustrated portraits of ballplayers, managers, and owners. They joined the portraits of pedestrians, prizefighters, and baseballists. Around the same period, relatively unknown members of the sporting fraternity across the country demanded recognition and began submitting photographs and short biographies for publication. Lawyers, clerks, firemen, policemen, saloonkeepers, hotel proprietors, gamblers, politicians, and tonsorial artists figured prominently. The evidence for this is a weekly illustrated column that acquainted readers with small community celebrities from around the country. These portraits projected an aura of manliness, leisure class life, and the cult of the sporting fraternity.

Prior to 1890, colored sporting portraits did not appear. Richard Ohmann describes this phenomenon as "charting social space." According to Ohmann, the print media, especially magazines, helped establish and announce the social status of these middle-class homes. They provided a range of information and interests that linked middle-class readers conversationally with others of the same social circle, and culturally linked them with like-minded readers across the nation. "In this they collaborated with the reconfiguration of social space," writes Ohmann, "and with the new styles and meanings of consumption." While Ohmann's sample concludes that blacks had no place on the agenda of the new cultural producers, *The Police Gazette* portrays them as a rebellious social force on the one hand, while on the other hand, they represent some participation in human social relations.

How did the commodities of pleasure fashion the black image of the colored sports? Ohmann offers an answer: the sports medium exploited gaps between race, class, gender, and the commodities of pleasure. It constituted the reader as one who could bridge them. The visual portraits of colored sports offer verbal explanations of the black images, but only two images reference race because the visual markers for stereotypical blackness fail to expose the colored sports. One portrait is described as an excellent portrait"; another is called "an accurate portrait of the gentleman in question." Where race seems ambiguous, the text is quick to mark the figure as colored. The others offer no such bridge; the reader is supposed to make sense out of the arbitrary connection between Negroid features and the colored sporting fraternity. As for images of well-dressed colored men, the class implications could be troublesome. One can only imagine how the white sporting gents of small southern towns (three pictures depict southerners) responded to the portraits of local colored celebrities. Modernity, Ohmann argues, was never just felt as progress. It often reassured its audience that old values and social relations were still somehow present and dependable. One portrait, for instance, drolly marks the tonsorial artist's propensity for violence by describing him as "quick with a razor."[64]

Column headers typically read: "Our Famous Tonsorialists." Others introduce the celebrity by name. Photo-mechanically reproduced as halftone images, these portraits appear in the first column. Derived from photographs, the head-to-shoulder portraits capture perfectly the well-dressed, distinguished colored sitters casting furtive glances at the beholder or looking away from the camera's eye, giving the impression that they are caught up in reverie. The sitters are juxtaposed, like their white brethren, with remedies for exhausted vitality, syphilis, and gonorrhea, and Fox's "spicily illustrated" stories by French authors (Emile Zola, Hector Malot, Jules De Gastyne and Adolphe Belot). The captions designate some material things that cannot be seen in the portraits (bicycles, hotels, barber shops, dances, and friends). The photographic backdrops are stripped away. What remains is the figure of the sitter, allowing the beholder to focus specifically on the famed sporting man.[65]

These portraits project the colored tonsorialist as an objet d'art. The coiffure is exemplary. The pure delight derived from exquisite coiffures and the thought of costly and beautiful pomades, scents, bay rum, and cosmetics was, in some measure, an enjoyment of the tonsorial artist's sense of expensive tastes masked as exquisiteness. In the portraits described, the sitter's coiffure is closely cropped, black, glossy, and delicate. The hair seems more wavy or straight than curly. This may represent natural or artificial effects since fancy headwork

Opposite: **Figure 31. "Have You Seen Him?,"** *National Police Gazette*, **1883**

HAVE YOU SEEN HIM?

A Reward of $1,000 Will be Paid for the Arrest of Sylvester Young, late of Louisville, Ky. ...

A reward of $1,000 will be paid for the apprehension of Sylvester Young, late cashier Newport News and Mississippi Valley Co., who fled from Louisville, Ky., July 31, 1891. Arrest for grand larceny. Description: Age, 41 years; height, 5 feet 3 or 4 inches; weight, about 120 to 125 pounds; eyes brown, medium size, full and bright; eyebrows long, thin and black, and eyelashes of same color; complexion, sallow; mustache, dark brown or black, not heavy; hair, black, streaked with gray, medium length; face, oval in form and countenance serious; chin, not prominent; mouth well formed, but not large; teeth regular and good; nose medium, with slight tendency toward bulbous and end rounding rather than pointed.

The portrait of Young, which appears above, was taken ten years ago, but is an excellent resemblance of him as he appears without a moustache

He is slightly stooped and round-shouldered, and a little bowlegged; his gait is hurried and nervous, walking with head down as if meditating, and his body from waist leans a little forward. His head is high, tapers noticeably from the crown to the base, and is broadest over the ears. He wears a No. 15 collar and a No. 6 shoe, his feet being somewhat slim. His hands are skinny and dark.

All communications should be addressed to Jno. Echols, third vice-president N. N. & M. V. Co., Louisville, Ky., or to Thiel's Detective Agency, 700 Olive street, St. Louis, Mo.

OUR FAMOUS TONSORIALISTS

R. B. Brown, well known Sport and Barber of Knoxville, Tenn.

R. B. Brown is one of our most popular tonsorial artists of Knoxville, Tenn. Mr. Brown, or Prof. Brown as he is generally called, is connected with the well known establishment of Jones, Martin & Co., at No. 427 Gay St. He is a genial and a jolly good fellow. His record for shaving is 3½ minutes, for a haircut 7 minutes. Mr. Brown besides being a first-class tonsorial artist is also a dancing-master, hence he is called Prof. Brown. He takes great interest in all matters pertaining to sport, and is a constant reader of the POLICE GAZETTE, and says "It's the only sporting paper in the world worth reading." He not only reads sport but he wagers money on all important events, and has never been known to show the white feather.

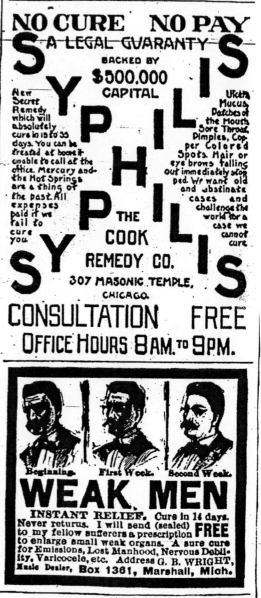
Figure 32. Our Famous Tonsorialists: R. B. Brown, *National Police Gazette*, 1893

included the aesthetic skill for transforming curly or wavy hair to straight. And given ads for hair products that made curly hair straight, its aesthetic appeal in the tonsorial artist "studio" would make common sense. Historian David W. Zang argues that photographic team portraits of the colored baseballist Moses Fleetwood Walker support his view that the player straightened his hair. The sport's coiffure, then, was where the beautiful and the hon-

orific met and blended. The beholder's view of the maker's "fancy"
headwork revealed an appreciation
of its superior honorific character,
melding celebrity status to the cult
of the sporting fraternity.[66]

The sporting fraternity's love of
photographic portraiture perhaps
appropriated from athletic men of
mark provided profusely ornamented images with the insignia of
affluence and authority in *Our
Famous Tonsorialists*. R. B. Brown,
well known sport and barber of
Knoxville, displays facial hair, commonly known as mutton-chops or
chops, and connects his thick side-
burns with his mustache while leav-
ing his chin clean-shaven (**fig. 32**).
Otto H. Riley's biographical sketch
describes the clean-shaven tonsorialist from Conneaut, Ohio, as "a
bright young gentleman well known
to the trade as an artist of merit"
(**fig. 33**). Known as "The Lightning
Razor Manipulator of the Southwest
and Little Wonder of Little Rock,"
John Little serves as tonsorial artist
of the McCarthy Light Guards (**fig.
34**). Little claims the title, "colored
champion fancy hair-dresser of the
Southwest." C. V. McCoy operates
the Ocala House barber shop,
Ocala, Florida (**fig. 35**). After learn-
ing the trade in Chicago, the mus-
tachioed McCoy relocated his
successful business to Florida. His
coiffure resembles a pompadour.

OUR FAMOUS TONSORIALISTS.

Otto H. Riley, a Bright Young Gentle-man Well Known to the Trade as an Artist of Merit.

Otto H. Riley, whose portrait we present above, is a
clever young tonsorialist of Conneaut, O. Mr. Riley
is an admirer of all athletic sports. He is quick with
the razor, and can shave a customer in three minutes.

Figure 33. **Our Famous Tonsorialists: Otto H. Riley,**
National Police Gazette, **1893**

However, not all members of the black sporting fraternity are tonsorial artists. Sidney A.
Clark serves as Tallapoosa Hotel's headwaiter, in Tallapoosa, Georgia. Clark claims to be
one of the leading sports of the South, a champion bicycle rider, a highly respected gentleman, and an ardent admirer of pugilism and all athletic exhibitions (**fig. 36**).[67]

Our Famous Tonsorialists represents what Thorstein Veblen called "an addiction to
sports," not only in direct participation, but also in sentiment and moral support, a char-
acteristic of the leisure class.[68] In these straightforward portraits, however, the colored ton-

14

THE NATIONAL POLICE

JOHN LITTLE,

The Lightning Razor Manipulator of the Southwest and Little Wonder of Little Rock.

Above will be found an excellent portrait of John Little, of Little Rock, Ark., where he is known as the lightning tonsorial artist of the McCarthy Light Guards. Little is also credited with being the colored champion fancy hair-dresser of the Southwest.

DEATH ON THE BOX.

[SUBJECT OF ILLUSTRATION.]

G. B. French, a New York dramatic agent, hired a cabman of a hansom cab to take him up town recently. After proceeding some distance Mr. French noticed that the horse appeared to be without a driver, al-

Figure 34. Our Famous Tonsorialists: John Little, *National Police Gazette*, 1893

|4   THE NATIONAL POLIC:

OUR FAMOUS TONSORIALISTS

:. V. McCoy, the Popular and Handsome Barber of Ocala, Fla.

C. V. McCoy, whose likeness adorns this column, is le proprietor of the Ocala House barber shop, Ocala, la. He is a young and energetic man, and is »ing a prosperous business. He learned his trade in hicago and locate l in Ocala three years ago, where) is now running the leading barber shop of the wn. He is a man of good qualities and has a host of lends.

TOBACCO USERS SMILE SOMETIMES

Figure 35. Our Famous Tonsorialists: C. V. McCoy, *National Police Gazette*, 1893

sorial artist is never depicted with the "rahzer." The material and intellectual life of the "colored" sporting man speaks for him via verbal and visual images. *Our Famous Tonsorialists* charts the social space of the black sporting fraternity not only by merging the colored aesthete within its own peculiar commodity culture but also by rendering leisure class life as the domain where material and physical excesses could lead to potential ruin.

14   THE NATIONAL POI

SIDNEY A. CLARK, SPORT,

Head Waiter, Champion Bicycle Rider and Gentleman, of Tallapoosa, Ga.

Sidney A. Clark is a highly respected colored gentleman of Tallapoosa, Ga. He is the champion colored bicycle rider of that Southern State. Clark is considered to be one of the leading sports of the South, and is an ardent admirer of pugilism and all athletic exhibitions. He is the head waiter of the Tallapoosa Hotel. The above is an accurate portrait of the gentleman in question.

IMPORTANT NOTICE.

Figure 36. Our Famous Tonsorialists: Sidney A. Clark, *National Police Gazette*, 1893

CHAPTER FOUR

Men of Mark and Marked Men:
Black Baseball Representation

The male-dominated photograph depicts twelve baseball players and the manager posed in front of a sparsely crowded grandstand, possibly alongside home plate (**fig. 37**). Six players stand behind six sitting teammates. The smartly dressed figure of the manager

Figure 37. "Cuban Giants. Colored Champions. 1887. And. 1888." Front row: William T. Whyte, Clarence Williams, Abe Harrison, S.K. Govern (manager), Ben Boyd, Jack Frye, Frank Allen. Back row: George Parago, Ben Holmes, Shep Trusty, Arthur Thomas, George Williams, Frank Miller.

sits in the middle, flanked by three players on either side. His dark suit contrasts with the relatively light baseball uniforms. Most of the players sport similar uniforms: light caps; light, short-sleeved collared shirts over dark, long-sleeved jerseys; thickly-knotted dark cravats tucked inside their shirts; thick, dark belts holding up light, heavy-looped knickers; dark stockings; and tight-fitting, ankle-length boots.

All the signs of the postbellum baseball team photograph are here. Conventionally arranged — formally and casually posed — the standing ballplayers place either one or both arms behind their backs or rest them alongside their bodies. Two cradle base balls, extending their arms slightly outward and upward away from their bodies. Perhaps they represent the elite position of the pitcher, also known as a "twirler." The seated players support bats between their legs. To the far right, one has a glove resting on his knee. Six additional bats, a catcher's mask, and glove lay strewn and stacked haphazardly at the players' feet. Of the six standing figures, four look to the right (the viewer's left), one to the left (the viewer's right), and the figure to the far right, not unlike the standing player just behind him, looks directly at the camera. Overall, everyone appears of solemn expression — no one smiles. Names are handwritten across each player's chest; below them, inscribed across the ground plane, is the manager's name. Everyone, except the manager, is relatively dark in complexion. Above the baseball aggregation, emblazoned in three rows, is: "Cuban Giants. Colored Champions. 1887. And 1888."[1]

Cuban Giants, Colored Champions commemorates the black ball club's meteoric rise to national greatness amid a specific cultural context. First, the photograph says something about the limited opportunities for visual representations of professional colored clubs. The artistic evidence for representations of colored baseballists, particularly baseball trading cards and fine art images (painting, sculpture, and drawings), is exceedingly rare. Photographs and photographic engravings, particularly in the 1880s, depict individual and team portraits. Second, the photograph allows us to contemplate baseball both as a national and global metaphor. The democratic medium of photography aptly captures the visual struggle for baseball supremacy: manliness, physical prowess, and the cult of celebrity. The picture depicts "men of mark and marked men" — an aesthetic object that captures the relation of the colored baseballist to the National Pastime's economic development, its labor unrest, and its racial segregation.

Between September and October 1888, the Cuban Giants of Trenton, New Jersey, had a team picture taken, a commemorative photograph that set these baseballists apart from their competitors by acknowledging them as the winners of two straight colored championships. The photographic moment was precipitous — in late August the Cuban Giants donned their new uniforms and went on to win twenty-nine successive games, which included the tournament for "the colored championship of the world." Few colored or white nines could have equaled their record: 129 games played; 105 won; 23 lost; and one tied. Managers John "J. M." Bright and Stanislaus Kostka Govern had every reason to be proud of this team not only because they played peerless ball, but because their deportment defied criticism as well.[2]

During the mid–1880s, it was not unusual for white clubs to challenge one another for the imagined world championship. Colored clubs engaged in similar cultural practices. However, news coverage of colored and white teams contending on the national stage for baseball supremacy was another matter. In September 1887, the world champion St. Louis

Browns agreed to play the champion Cuban Giants at West Farms, New York, with 15,000 spectators expected to attend. It would not be their first meeting. Commenting on the peculiar coaching styles displayed in the first game, *The Sporting News* invoked racial epithets masked as bawdy humor: "On their last eastern trip the Browns went over to Trenton, N.J., and played the 'Cuban Giants,' the crack colored club. With the bases full [Walter Arlington "Arlie"] Latham came to bat and gave them the bunt gag, and every nigger on the nine commenced yelling murder."[3]

According to Michael A. Lomax, the unconventional playing styles and coaching of both clubs would have provided an interesting spectacle. But the contest never occurred. Why? *The Police Gazette* queried, "Was it really pride or was it cowardice that prevented the St. Louis Browns from meeting the Cuban Giants last Sunday at West Farms?" Some critics contended the Browns had drawn the color line, but the article complicated this view for those sporting men who relied on fair play and square dealing:

> The Cuban Giants are an uncommonly strong team, and one that is liable to take a game from any professional team in the country. The real trouble lay right here, St. Louis had several disabled men, and it was faint-heartedness on their part, as they were afraid they would be beaten. Therefore they resorted to this cowardly means of backing out by saying that they would not play with niggers.

Thus, *Cuban Giants, Colored Champions* not only represents "men of mark" but "marked men." The triadic structure of representation (photographer, medium, and beholder) complicates our understanding of the 19th century colored baseballist.[4]

Men of Mark or Marked Men: "An Appealing Visual Product"

Cuban Giants, Colored Champions could have been photographed at Trenton or at Hoboken, New Jersey. The Giants' home grounds, which "the boys claim cannot be beaten for beauty, are at Trenton, N. J., but they play more by request at Hoboken." The answer, however, remains unknown. What is known is that studio portraits hardly compared to those taken by operators at the baseball grounds. Simulating exterior settings inside the studio was a common cultural practice, both with good and bad results. To re-imagine the baseball grounds, studio settings combined painted canvas backdrops with real dirt and turf, real and artificial rocks, and tree stumps to recreate bucolic scenes. Other canvas backdrops relied solely on hand-painted or printed (lithographed) surfaces to create the illusion of the panoramic baseball landscape — faux foliage, stone facades, beaten earth, and grassy patches (shaggy rug fragments) round out a utopian vision of the nation's simpler rural past. Canvas backdrops were also painted with cultural landmarks, beaux-arts architecture reminiscent of baseball park or race track building facades. Even the individual ballplayer functioned as a prop, designed to enhance team photographs (and to add missing or newly acquired players) — one figure was cut from an individual portrait and pasted onto an imagined baseballscape. Photography helped transform the idyllic setting into a theatrical space, making the ball grounds as much of an attraction as the team.[5]

In addition to cultural (verbal and visual) representations, social formations of race, gender, and class also helped shape baseball aggregations, mapping colored nines as objects of mass spectacle. A prime example of this occurred with baseball's first world championship series between the Metropolitans and the Providence Grays in 1884. All three games were played in New York. Known for its diversity, if not complexity, New York City was the nation's premiere metropolis, sheltering not only the wealthy and the illustrious, but a thriving middle-class, masses of immigrant communities, and an underclass of desperately poor workers.[6]

For the political theorist Fouad Ajami, this period coincides with the First Global Economy — an era marked by transnational capital, mobility of labor, a global monetary authority attained through the functioning of the gold standard, and most vivid of all, the titans of industry who loomed larger than princes and the rulers of the states. Through "imaginative cultural analogies," the drive for baseball supremacy — small towns or urban cities, East Coast or Midwest, national or transatlantic — includes the drive for wealth, fame, and the cult of celebrity. *The Clipper* called the 1884 game, "The Championship of the United States." When the Grays emerged triumphant, however, *Sporting Life* called them "World Champions." The new name stuck. The press would lay the groundwork for the 20th century's most famous sporting event, the World Series.[7]

The national press exposed how the colored championship co-existed, however unequally, with the (white) world championship. In 1871, the Chicago Uniques and Philadelphia Pythians had battled for the "Colored Championship of the United States." By the early 1880s, literary representations of "colored" ballplayers as stock "darky" characters filled daily newspapers, illustrated weeklies, and sports journals. Coinciding with them were short humorous, if not crude, stories of the newly emancipated black southern population. Grounded in the protocols of blackface minstrelsy and "negro" dialect vernacular, some baseball narratives dovetailed neatly with the middle-class fear of and desire for the colored baseballist.

The colored ballplayer reflected middle-class desires to construct, if not project, a gentlemanly image. Allegedly, the Cuban Giants did not drink liquor, smoke or chew tobacco, cuss, engage in poor sportsmanship, indulge in on-field violence or womanizing — they embodied intellect, grace, and refinement. The Trenton management (Walter I. Cook and Stanislaus Kostka Govern) carefully crafted the team's public image. Simply winning was not enough; they demanded a refined black presence as well. The *True American* reports: "The Cuban Giants appear to be gentlemanly players and they play to win all the time." They coolly abstained from complaining and publicly took controversial defeats well. Manly conduct and good playing slowly transformed Trenton's colored aggregation into one of the sporting crowd's favorites. The *True American* explains: "[T]he credit of being thoroughly disciplined must be allowed them. This is something that could not be said of clubs playing here other years. The Giants behave themselves on and off the field like gentlemen, and they deserve patronage." If respectable white spectators and sportswriters seemed unconvinced, the paper adds: "It is said that all of them are in bed at 10 o'clock every night in the week. They board at Mrs. Crusen's, on South Warren Street."[8]

While promoters, managers, and sportswriters skillfully fashioned the black image of the Cuban Giants to fill grandstands and draw standing-room-only crowds, the national press also disparaged the presence of colored clubs by circulating racist baseball images. One obvious reason reflected white anxieties about race-mixing, and the fear that the baseball sporting world might become a cultural space for social interaction. For example, the white ballplayer Tom Deasley, of the St. Louis Browns, with his drunkenness and womanizing, became a colorful character. According to *The Police Gazette*, "Tom Deasley, who got quite a reputation for mashing coons [colored women] in St. Louis, tried to mash a couple of white girls in Indianapolis but his style didn't altogether suit, and it resulted in Tom's being shoved into the cooler."[9] In this crude pun about the consumption of southern cuisine, the paper expressed views about the white woman's consumption of colored men: "Washington girls have lately acquired a taste for coon. They have taken to eloping with them, and then their dads start out with shotguns and shoot them down in the height of the honeymoon. There is no rest for our colored brethren, anyway. If the white men don't go for them the women do, and both are equally fatal." Building upon racial stereotypes that included high crimes against white women — miscegenation, lasciviousness, rape, and murder — *The Police Gazette* expanded its image-repertoire system to embrace the threatening figure of the gun-toting and razor-wielding blacks (**fig. 38**).[10]

Another example appeared in *The Globe*, a weekly colored newspaper. In the story "Base-Ball Games," John Good, a mulatto, elopes with Pauline Lewis, a young Jewess. While serving as a restaurant waiter, Good meets and begins courting Miss Lewis. Her mother condemns the relationship and forbids the daughter from seeing him. Soon afterwards, the couple disappears. After they are found living in Newark, New Jersey, Good and his wife, accompanied by the minister, set out for the Newark Police Station and present their marriage certificate. The story closes with an intriguing remark. Good pitches for the Newark Base Ball Club, which is composed of colored men. "Base-Ball Games," then, links Good to the "cullud champions of New Jersey." It also summons forth the cult of

FEB. 11. 1893.]   THE NATIONAL POLICE GAZETTE: NEW YORK.   5

Figure 38. A Colored Fiend's Work, *National Police Gazette*, **1893**

baseball celebrity to question interracial relationships and challenge the black baseball image.[11]

How colored baseballists navigate the boundary between inclusion and exclusion reveals much about 19th century sporting culture. How can they be an ambivalent object of celebrity status and derision, leisure class life and misalliance? How do sportswriters portray the Cuban Giants (or for that matter, other "colored" clubs), and why do baseball narratives — as opposed to visual images — dominate black baseball representations? By mapping social identification and differentiation, baseball representations shape national, racial, and ethnic identity.

Historian Robert E. Burk offers a succinct portrait of the period: "[T]he established lines of ethnic and racial acceptance and prohibition changed little. The owners' recalcitrance illustrated the other half of the player value equation — the need for the player force to present an appealing visual product to a 'respectable' white spectatorship." This explanation of what Burk calls "a high skilled labor-intensive entertainment industry" is a good starting point, but it is not the last word on the subject. To begin with, the terms of this explanation raise many questions that demand further explanation. Why should ballplayers be an "appealing visual product?" Why do ethnic and racial acceptance and prohibition matter? What makes a "respectable" white spectator fear colored ballplayers? Why does the sporting crowd desire them? Does this desire constitute an "appealing visual product" — or something specific to black bodies and the post-bellum Gilded Age? If we assume that social formations frame acceptance and prohibition — inclusion and exclusion — a "respectable" white spectatorship would have been severely limited in the cultural spaces or entertainment venues available them. For example, antebellum spectacles of black bodies had been objects of white fascination at least since Thomas Dartmouth Rice had "blacked up" and caricatured blacks for sport and profit, and Dr. David L. Rogers carved into the corpse of Joice Heth, an aged black woman, before 1,500 paying spectators. Previously, Heth had been exhibited by P.T. Barnum.[12]

Nor does the formula of "acceptance and prohibition" distribute itself evenly over late 19th century baseball. Some teams were white but not appealing; and some clubs were appealing but not white; some players were white but not appealing; some players were appealing but not white. But if the evidence of baseball representations is correct, black bodies intrigued not only the sporting crowd in general, but a respectable white spectatorship in particular. If the fascination with black bodies depended on "an appealing visual product," then that fascination may be about more than "the ethnocultural composition of the player force."[13]

Clearly this promising formula cannot solely explain the black body's fascination; it is only a starting point for investigation. The toughest challenge with the cultural meaning of the colored baseballist is resisting the attraction to simply settle for inclusion or exclusion, no matter how obvious it seems. Burk contends, quite rightly, that race kept many blacks from the major leagues. But he assumes, quite wrongly, that there was universal agreement as to what constituted "an appealing visual product." This is more complex.

The problem with Burk's explanation is that it limits itself, historically and culturally. For example, it does not consider how colored clubs embraced the gentlemanly image, which was crucial to the portrayal of an appealing visual product. Burk also thinks the answer resides with management's preoccupation with control over the ballplayer's image and with spectators' response to the product offered, namely a high-skill, labor-intensive entertainment industry. Club operators forced onto the game a heightened level of specialized skill and physical and mental dexterity. Skill specialization weeded out undisciplined bodies psychologically ill-suited by age, class, ethnicity, race, and gender. However, every so often an entrepreneur commodified black images into an economic windfall. The Cuban Giants, with their scientific play, aesthetic style, and perceived blackface antics, simply conjured the latest and most potent brew: combining baseball's fascination with black bodies and the strong desire to make money.

Burk readily admits the rising number of superbly talented colored ballplayers on segregated nines or sprinkled on obscure semiprofessional and professional clubs. His historical overview of colored ball does not fully explain how they fit within baseball's first revolt and subsequent retrenchment, which built upon ethnic and racial prejudices, labor rights and wages, moral corruption and redemption, contract disputes and "bounty jumpers," and "baseball slavery" or the dreaded reserve clause:

> In 1885, a group of Long Island waiters/ballplayers formed the Cuban Giants, an independent club consisting entirely of American-born born blacks but so named as not to invite dramatic attention and white retaliation. Other black clubs, including the Orions in Philadelphia and the St. Louis Black Stockings, predated the Long Island team. By 1886, black teams in New Orleans and five other cities created the Southern league of colored baseballists, only to fold soon afterward.... Cooperstown-born Bud Fowler (whose birth name was John Jackson) penetrated white professional baseball eight times with seven different franchises, and Sporting Life in 1885 admitted that only his race kept him from a major league career.

Moreover, Burk's overview does not cover how social formations and baseball representations are interwoven into the cultural fabric of the national pastime.[14]

On 2 April 1883, *The Leader* published the following: "A colored base ball club has been organized in Washington. They will play exhibition games all over the country. Most of the players are six footers, and are said to be good players." The promoter John F. Lang has been credited with organized this team, a precursor of the Cuban Giants; in fact, the team of "six footers" was called, perhaps tongue-in-cheek, the "Giants." On the other hand, the Manhattans were organized by S. K. Govern, John Lang and Charles Jones. Lang and Jones were associated with another colored club, the Orions. Lang, it appears, scheduled games and served as the team's businessman. Govern's role as manager also bears scrutiny. According to *The Bee*, colored businessman John C. Ricks implored citizens to assist Govern and the club in whatever ways they could: "Mr. Govern is a jovial as well as an energetic young man. We predict a day of pleasure and feel assured that no one will ever regret having aided in anything that will help the Manhattan Club to success."[15]

In May 1883, the Manhattans scheduled a championship series with another "colored" ball club, the Richmond Swans, managed by the colored baseballist John "Bud" Fowler. Wanting to establish a "Colored League," Fowler first contacted eastern clubs (New York City, Philadelphia, Pittsburg, Cincinnati, Baltimore, Washington, and Richmond). His plan was not new. In 1882, James H. Dudley, then captain and manager of the Richmond Swans, headed the movement. Fowler envisioned something bigger and contacted Henry Bridgewater, owner/manager of the St. Louis Black Stockings, about hosting a meeting of representatives from the leading colored organizations. Fowler's poised letter, along with optimistic correspondence from Lynchburg, Virginia, and Cincinnati, Ohio, piqued Bridgewater's interest. When the Black Stockings first toured the East, they had planned to cross bats with several colored clubs, including "the famous Manhattan club, of Washington, D.C." It never happened. Bridgewater proposed a second tour, and this time, his boys would visit Washington, Pittsburgh, and Richmond, and he could assume the mantle of organizing the "Colored League." The new league would embrace Washington, Lynchburg, Richmond, Pittsburgh, Cincinnati, St. Louis, and perhaps two other cities. It faltered again.[16]

The Manhattans consisted of colored waiters who worked at one of Saratoga's resort hotels. During the summer months, between June and August, they waited tables at the Clarendon Hotel; they also played on the hotel baseball club, and called themselves the Clarendons. On 7 July 1883, *The Globe* reported that the Clarendon, Congress, and Grand Union Hotels had organized colored base ball clubs. *The Globe* added: "A practice game was played on South Broadway, between Clarendon and Congress nines. The Clarendon Nine proved their superiority by out-batting and out-fielding their opponents at every point." Newspaper accounts provide something that *Cuban Giants, Colored Champions* cannot: a prehistory of some of the figures depicted in the photograph. The Manhattans included the following: W. H. Mahattan, J.S. Trusby, W. Jackson, Ben Boyd, Arthur Thomas, George R. Williams, J. Talbot, S. Anderson, and W. Braxton. The Manhattans would form the nucleus of the Cuban Giants Base Ball Club.[17]

How *Cuban Giants, Colored Champions* originally functioned remains something of a mystery. Given the handwritten text and clipped newspaper headers pasted onto the picture's surface, this particular image seems to have been meant for private consumption. Labeling the players and the manager, the photograph's owner commemorated two championship years. This creative act also serves to identify the Trenton organization at that specific moment. However, this photograph represents a fragmented history. Not everyone who contributed to the team's success is present. Players came and went. Nonetheless, when we consider the growing fan obsession for visual objects of their baseball heroes, the document remains important. How, then, might fans have acquired the team portrait? No ads appear in the major periodicals such as *The Sporting News*, *The Police Gazette*, and *Sporting Life*. Nor do tobacco cards (Old Judge or Allen & Ginters) depict the Cuban Giants.

Perhaps the photographic image of the *Cuban Giants, Colored Champions*, unlabelled and unidentified, served another function. Did the black image circulate as a souvenir — a commemorative picture — to reward fans toward the end of the season for their loyalty? As discussed above, *The Police Gazette* is filled with letters acknowledging the receipt of portraits and "cuts" sent to the paper. Sadly, I have uncovered only references to colored clubs or players who used the sports medium to introduce new teams, challenge clubs, and promote baseball events. *The Sporting News* did publish the promotional efforts of a well-known itinerant colored baseballist: "[John 'Bud'] Fowler goes to Cuba in October to captain the 'Cuban Giants,' a colored club now in the United States. John Jones, a colored catcher of this city, will accompany him." Considering the heroic exploits of the Cuban Giants between 1886 and 1888, one supposes that any number of promoters would have exploited the opportunity. *The Police Gazette* bears consideration in this query. Richard Fox, for instance, adored the Cuban Giants and challenged anyone willing to bet against them. But he too seemed constrained by the growing antipathy towards colored players. While the material evidence for *Cuban Giants, Colored Champions* remains buried with an undiscovered cultural artifact, the following section briefly explores other "men of mark" or "marked men," images that offer "an appealing visual product."[18]

A photo-engraved portrait of Edward G. Jackson depicts a dapper, young colored baseballist wearing a high-collared shirt and cravat. Jackson's slightly tilted head gazes to the (viewer's) right. The Missouri-born mulatto toiled as a waiter in the Garden City. Not

Figure 39. Ed Jackson, *The Tribune* (Chicago), 1888

unlike most of the player's in *Cuban Giants, Colored Champions,* Jackson seems absorbed in deep introspection (**fig. 39**).

Jackson's portrait and numerous newspaper accounts, offer an interesting case study of the sporting fraternity and race relations between 1883 and 1889. Jackson played for the Picketts, a predominantly white club and a perennial powerhouse. Jackson was the club's only colored member and played for the aggregation at least nine years. *The Sentinel,* of Milwaukee, observes: "[Jackson] is the only colored catcher with a white nine in the West, and is a fine player anywhere." Jackson's fame spread throughout the country, especially within the black sporting fraternity. Colored newspapers cover his exploits. In 1887, *The Gazette* reports:

Edward G. Jackson, the colored catcher of the Picketts in the Chicago base ball league, has the following record for the season just closed: caught 19 games, put out 106 men, assisted in putting out 38 men, made 21 errors, had 40 passed balls scored against him, had a total of 205 chances and made a general average of 702.

The Louisianan also published the story. *The Conservator* wrongly claimed Jackson to be the only colored baseballist in Chicago. *The Gazette* called him a first-class player who had no superior outside of the professionals. Jackson caught for both Chicago's Picketts and Putnams.[19]

Another interesting if not obscure figure is George Hopkins, the star pitcher for Walter l. Cohen's New Orleans Pinchbacks. Throughout the 1870s and 1880s, Cohen managed a colored aggregation variously called the Pickwick Club, W. L. Cohens, and P.B.S. Pinchbacks. The latter moniker paid tribute to Louisiana's first black governor, Pinckney Benton Stewart Pinchback, who assumed the office during the Reconstruction Period. Pinchback, a sporting man and gambler, had a special relationship with young George Hopkins, who appears to have been his protégé. Also an avid baseball fan, Pinchback, while in staying in St. Louis, helped develop Hopkins's baseball career. Hopkins lived for a time in the same residence with Pinchback, along with another future baseball star, David E. Gordon, the left-landed pitcher and power hitter for Bridgewater's Black Stockings who was nicknamed "Jumbo." Pinchback, Gordon, and Hopkins were mulattos.

George Hopkins built quite a reputation as a pitcher for the Pinchbacks in the 1880s, and in 1890, he briefly twirled for a colored club in Pensacola, Florida. In the 1890s, his celebrity status rose again when he played for the Chicago Unions. Hopkins's portrait is interesting, not only because it derives from a photograph but because Edward Elder Cooper's *Freeman*— which published the image — later used the same black image of the colored baseballist to advertise for a local department store in Indianapolis (**fig. 40**).

"Grinding Out Stylized Accounts, Studded with Hackneyed Phrases"

The evidence of sports writing remains crucial to this discussion because it provides a medium for exploring black baseball representations. During the 1880s, sportswriting grew so rapidly as a popular literary form that it forced sizable daily newspapers and weekly journals to adopt sports sections. Catering to the public demand for baseball news, newspaper barons invented a new kind of specialist: the sportswriter. Baseball historian David Quentin Voigt has contended that the sportswriters' greatest contribution was the creation of an artificial form of baseball, something vicariously enjoyed by people who could not attend a major league game. As a species of journalist, sportswriters enjoyed greater literary freedom than other staff writers. They stockpiled descriptive words and phrases, then transformed them into a language that helped ritualize the game and solidify its devotees. With this highly imaginative baseball lexicon that included terms like "wild-throwing," "muffed balls," "assists," "balks," "grounders," "passed balls," "blanked," and "whitewashed," sportswriters competed with colleagues in "grinding out stylized accounts, studded with hackneyed phrases for the consumption of fans whose intellectual demands were modest."[20]

Figure 40. George Hopkins, *The Freeman* (Indianapolis), 1890

Henry Chadwick played a seminal role not only in creating the modern game of baseball, but also in helping to facilitate the development of baseball sportswriting. Pejoratively known as the "Father of Baseball," Chadwick's style and approach became common practice. Typical accounts included descriptions of the weather, the crowd, and summaries of each inning played. However, technical advancements fostered the trend for more uniformity in reporting games; telegraphed games required efficient schemes for dispatching reports from telegraphed games. This expanded baseball accounts, as detailed summaries were followed by line score tables, summaries, and each player's record. Chadwick's sportswriting attained a high degree of development among writers who adopted an exaggerated, colorful descriptive style.[21]

Some writers developed distinctive styles using jargon, puns, and exaggeration. Typical examples culled from ball coverage of games played by the Cuban Giants include: "The Stars of New York who were Trenton's opponents had a first-class battery, but their fielders were chiefly distinguished for their ability to crowd a large number of errors into a small compass of possibilities. Fletcher, the short-stop, was a 'dandy' in the muffing line." Here's another: "It was very babyish work unbecoming a professional ball club that is supposed to be able to bear up manfully under defeat, even though the victors' skin be a shade darker than their own. On account of the Newarkers' behavior, the spectators enjoyed all the more the thorough walloping the [Cuban] Giants gave them." Finally: "To be fair it must be said [the Orientals of Highstown] can play much better ball, but the diamond fright possessed them, and Parago's delivery together paralyzed them. They could make no runs and made nothing much but errors. The Giants had a 'pudding,' and came near making a pancake of the ball." There is nothing unusual about these accounts. Such descriptions can be found throughout postbellum baseball narratives that also constructed gentlemanly images of baseball heroes, thus elevating them to the cult of celebrity.[22]

With the substantial body of baseball writing circulating in the mid–1880s, one wonders how the approach to reporting colored ball impacted the colored fan; or, at least, the colored sporting crowd. While it is easy to document mainstream black baseball literary accounts, it is much harder to track what audiences thought of them. White dailies in New York, New Orleans, Memphis, and St. Louis sporadically reported on colored clubs, sometimes announcing the contests but not the outcome. Some contests between colored and white clubs received inning-by-inning coverage, player statistics, and gossip. Meanwhile, the colored press — despite middle-class attitudes toward certain social activities outside the home and the church — saw the potential of the National Pastime for "uplifting the race." Coverage of the Cuban Giants was part of the regional correspondence to colored newspapers. In reporting such accounts, these communities expressed their civic, cultural, and social pride. *The Age* reports: "For the last two seasons the residents of the Old Dutch town owe much to the Cuban Giants for the amount of life they have given the place and the interest stimulated in the national sport." In 1887, *The Gazette* scooped *The Age* by recognizing the growing celebrity status of the Cuban Giants and their cultural value to the black national community: "The Cuban Giants, colored base ball club, claim the championship of America. Richard K. Fox, of *The Police Gazette*, offers to back them to play any club in the country from $1,000 to $10,000 for the championship of America. The Browns, of St. Louis, have refused to play." One year later, *The Gazette* promoted the "crack colored nine" as an appealing visual product: "The Cuban Giants is the name of the only colored professional base ball nine in the country. More solid enjoyment can be found in watching them play than can be found in a game between 'Baby' Anson's kickers and the New York Giants, when the Giants are winning." Colored newspapers responded to market demand; perhaps because of the growing interest in the National Pastime and the growing social exclusion expressed through baseball segregation, they felt compelled to report on the exploits of the colored baseballist.[23]

In postbellum black newspapers, baseball coverage varied from paper to paper. *The*

Freeman, The Bee, The People's Advocate, The Gazette, the *Huntsville Gazette,* and *The Free-man* (Indianapolis, IN) were a few weeklies that covered amateur, semi-professional, and professional nines; however, editorial demands coupled with column space (newspapers were rarely more than eight pages) severely limited baseball news. Some owners were fans and probably wrote significant pieces themselves. Proprietors T. Thomas Fortune (*The Free-man/ The Age*), Harry C. Smith (*The Gazette*), and Eric Elder Cooper (*The Freeman*) conceivably penned sports editorials, stories, and gossip items. Aspiring journalists (writers from literary clubs) contributing local and regional gossip to black newspaper columns (for example, "Rochester Ripples" or "Philadelphia Letter") often included local baseball gossip. While black baseball images were rare, some black newspapers published them. *The Freeman* cartoonists Moses L. Tucker and Henry Jackson Lewis drew baseball pictures. *The*

Figure 41. York Inter-State Base Ball Club, *The Cleveland Gazette,* **1890**

Gazette also published a team portrait of the York Inter-State Base Ball Club (formerly the former Cuban Giants) (**fig. 41**). For colored journalists, baseball could "uplift the race" into the heroic pantheon of men of mark, and the Cuban Giants justly merited consideration among the "Doings of the Race."

Govern's strategic collaborations with colored journalists in New York, Philadelphia, and Washington, D.C. helped define and refine the uplifting image of the Cuban Giants. In the black community, Govern was the front man. *The Bee* elaborates: "Mr. S. K. Govern made a flying trip to Philadelphia and was the guest of 'Rambler' of the Tribune, and 'Wanderer' and gave a great account of the Cuban Giants B. B. Club, which played in New York this week. Much success to him." The Cuban Giants were race men. *The Age* explains: "[T]he Cuban Giants have done the race good service. They are helping to destroy the objection to meeting colored men on an equal footing, which is the most pronounced feature of the race problem with which we have to contend." *The Bee* added that the club had done more under Govern's management to break down prejudice than any colored organization in the country.[24]

Mimesis Is Not Identity: Who Are the Cuban Giants?

Who are the Cuban Giants? That is what the mob were trying to find out last Sunday, when they chased them for their lives along the Newton Road. Had it not been for the Queens County Park people, with Manager Bright and a batch of police at their head, coming to the rescue, there would not have been a single giant left to carry the news back to Cuba. The tough mob which attend the Sunday grounds back of Williamsburg are the wrong kind of hairpins to try any fake business with, for those flannel mouthed Micks would rather fight to eat.

The above epigraph raises issues surrounding *Cuban Giants, Colored Champions*, namely, the social status and cultural meaning of black bodies. The image of the Cuban Giants, for its part, embodies both fear and desire. It demonstrates that mimesis has never been simply the production of likeness, but a mechanism for producing difference and transformation. According to the anthropologist Michael Taussig, it represents "the ability to mime, and mime well, in other words, [it] is the capacity to Other." The Cuban Giants followed an apparently established black baseball tradition that sought to entertain, but also imagined the baseball grounds as a social space to challenge black athletic inferiority. By appropriating the name "Cuban," they perhaps hoped to "uplift" the race by identifying themselves with those Cuban "freedmen" struggling against Spanish colonialism. They may have been denied admittance to the Eastern League and reviled by its clubs and fans, but the crack colored club blurred the lines between exclusion and the cult of baseball celebrity, between theatricality and scientific play, when they transformed social uplift into a battle for baseball supremacy.[25]

The Police Gazette purportedly introduces readers, for the first time, to the Cuban Giants. This assumes, of course, that fans never read other newspapers or sporting journals. The story insists on taking the mob violence of "flannel-mouthed Micks" as its principal subject matter, along with their antagonism towards the mysterious "colored" club. The paper drolly queries, "Who are the Cuban Giants?" The text does not say, nor does it specify their crime or explain the mob's angry disposition. Engaging in "any fake business," however, is the charge levied against the "Cubans." This accusation only heightens the mystery. While the fragment clearly marks black bodies as part of baseball's contested terrain, it also uncovers the racial spectacle of violence concealed beneath the humorous veneer of blackface literature.

Simply put, "Who are the Cuban Giants?" remains a rhetorical question. In 1885, the sporting crowd knew of the Cuban Giants. In October, the aggregation played the Metropolitans. Fraught with what Mitchell calls "the anxiety of misrecognition and riddled with narcissistic and aggressive fantasy," sports reporters jibed readers with clever remarks regarding their skin color. *The Times* declares: "To-morrow the Mets will probably defeat the Cuban Giants in a game of baseball, and the white-and-black game promises to be very amusing." *The Tribune* reports: "Lovers of baseball will be able to see the dark side of this popular sport at the Polo Grounds to-day. The Metropolitans will play against the Cuban Giants, the champion colored baseball club." Seeing "the dark side" of skin color in an "amusing" game unveiled an exoticism that whites had associated with the novelty of colored nines.[26]

Cuban Giants, Colored Champions belongs to a system of conspicuous consumption and sartorial display which, according to the social theorist Thorstein Veblen, was designed to signify invidious class distinctions. The postbellum Gilded Age organized "Base-Ball" around the consumption and display of commodities through which owners, players, and fans (the sporting crowd) gained prestige, identity, and standing. In this system, the more prestigious one's commodities (club ownership, sporting journals and newspapers, photography studios, saloons, gambling dens, phaeton carriages, fashionable clothing, and so on), the higher one's standing in the realm of sign value. Baseball's sartorial display parallels the early history of photography and traces the medium's technological innovations, which range from the daguerreotype to the cabinet card. The camera's power was not lost in its human subjects and, from the beginning, the leisure classes used photography to confirm or confer celebrity. Within this cultural context, baseball team photographs matter. Thus, just as words take on meaning according to their position in a differential system of language, so sign values take on meaning according to their place in a differential system of prestige and status.[27]

Team uniforms offered both players and fans tangible signs of the cult of celebrity. Uniforms were one means by which a "respectable organization established its distance from the 'appearance of poverty.'" *The Clipper* offered readers the following sneak-preview of the Metropolitans' new garb: "The uniforms for match-games will consist of dark-blue stockings, bluish-gray pants, white and polka-dot shirts and different colored caps." Emphasizing the uniform's quality, the report adds: "The material for the shirts is to be imported from England, and is identified with the colors of Keene's 'Foxhall.'" Regarding the materials from which the future uniforms of the St. Louis Browns would be tailored, *The Sporting News* states: "the material is of a genuine imported English cricket flannel and the best maufactured. They are simply immense." When the Cuban Giants made their first appearance, they wore white and red uniforms. According to the *True American*, the "pretty" uniforms "did not seem to favorably affect their work." The team played weak in the field and at bat, losing to Long Island 11 to 3. The fetishistic qualities of uniforms could have an alternative effect. *The Age* informs its predominately black reading audience: "[S]ince the [Cuban Giants] donned their new uniform they have won some twenty-nine successive games."[28]

Cuban Giants, Colored Champions restates the cult of celebrity in its pictorial code, creating with its low angle viewpoint and wide-angle an impression of monumentality and strength. The team represents an air of solemnity: collectively, the look of men touched by destiny. Baseball equipment functions as bric-a-brac or decorative ornamentation, props crucial to photographic theatricality. Consider the seemingly haphazard arrangement of the baseball equipment. Bats, a face mask, and chest protector litter the ground: their potency emphasized through aesthetic arrangement. Collectively, uniformed players and equipment transform the Cuban Giants into a tableau vivant.

If gentlemanly images of colored baseballists found particular visual expression in light-complexioned black bodies, then Stanislaus K. Govern's skillful manipulation of the baseball pose and the hierarchy of the color caste system merit consideration. Govern found race pride a stimulant sufficiently strong to brace up long enough to sit for the team photograph. Solemnly gazing towards the right side of the baseball grounds, Govern, Abraham "Abe" Harrison, and Benjamin "Ben" Boyd provide an interesting triangular arrangement of labor and management. It seems simple enough. Manager Govern sits in an armed chair, elevated slightly above Harrison and Boyd, who sit on wooden crates. Upon closer examination, their distant facial expressions contradict their body language, which ranges from informal casualness to frank uneasiness. Harrison and Boyd struggle with how best to situate their hands and legs. Harrison appears restless. Fidgeting, his right hand clasps three fingers on the left hand. Projected against the bright uniform which serves as a screen, the stark light/dark contrast between pinky finger and thumb resembles a claw. Harrison's arms rest against his inner thighs, seemingly spreading his legs apart; a bat against his right thigh. They mimic the letter "V." The backs of Harrison's angle-length shoes touch against the crate. Boyd's tightly crossed legs are pushed up against the wooden crate as well. The ballplayers are not the only things inscribed. Just below Boyd's hands, one can make out the imprinted letters on the wooden box. If labeling somehow signifies property, Govern's body seems to have escaped this designation.[29]

Govern's props — the manager's decorum and attire — seemingly distinguish him from the players and suggest refinement. His outer coat is completely buttoned, revealing only the rounded white collar and perhaps the uppermost portion of his knotted tie. He embodies the gentlemanly image. While this does not necessarily say much, considering the ballplayers' dark ties, the semi-formalized pose melds with the players around him. Skin complexion and fabric function as an abstract pattern of dark and light; the former, in effect, serving the latter. Govern's elongated head appears to float atop his white and curved collar. The collar's tonality, while accenting his dark suit, operates as a central axis for the white uniforms that seemingly radiate from it. Creating a collage-like effect, the seam of Govern's right coat sleeve, highlighted by a dark line, follows the dark line of Trusty's left thigh, giving it form. Note also how the twirler's practically silhouetted hand displays the white baseball. Similarly, his lower right arm gives definition to Harrison's upper left arm, particularly the part covered by the light shirt.

While the players wear the polo-styled baseball caps as a formal part of their uniforms, formality requires — even outdoors — that Govern remove his bowler. Or simply put, the manager mugs for the camera. He cradles the slightly tilted bowler on his left forearm, the broad upturned brim resting on exposed fingers. He is bareheaded. Neatly parted in the middle and perhaps held firmly in place by pomade, his wavy hair crowns his high-domed forehead. The mustache invokes another transatlantic (that is British) fashion statement. Thick hair covers the upper lip, terminating at the corners of the mouth. The stiff ends point slightly upward. Any unnecessary facial hair around the lower face has been shaven. Govern's right hand seems ill-at-ease. His slightly clenched fist rests awkwardly against the right thigh. His stiff verticality terminates at his torso. Not unlike the players on either side, his thighs are spread apart, implying relaxed casualness. His crossed legs suggest further comradeship. Harrison's left knee rises up to meet Govern's right knee; Boyd's right knee reaches up to touch Govern's left knee. Manager Govern is one of the boys.

There is little doubt that Govern understood the relation between image and mass circulation. The appealing visual product being sold is a mass spectacle of the New Negro itself. Govern responded to white market demand, but in part because of "negro" comedy, he was able to mask black baseball supremacy. Regarding the Cuban Giants' advent on the world stage *The Times* reports: "A nine of the ebon sons of Africa, running in all coffee shades from black Mocha to café au lait, who call themselves Cuban Giants, gave a minstrel performance on the diamond, and the Mets enjoyed it and took their cue from the colored champions." Trenton management collaborated with the sporting press, selling scientific play, aesthetic style, and blackface performance. Competing within a high-skill, labor-intensive entertainment industry, Govern's "colored" nine deployed certain protocols of blackface minstrelsy to appear in front of, and appeal to, respectable white spectators. At the same time, they communicated through baseball sports writing an in-your-face leitmotif of black cultural humor and political comment — an aesthetic style — to respectable black spectators, the black sporting crowd, and those New Negroes across the country who would never see them play. In 1888, *The Bee* observes: "[M]anager S. K. Govern stands as high with baseball managers as the best of them." The paper later observes that Govern did more to break down race prejudice than any organization among colored men in the country.[30]

The overexposed photograph contains another thematic: war. The Civil War added new terminologies to the baseball work force and tailored it in new ways. Successful baseball nines were expected to display the efficiency and espirit de corps of military units, and players were often called "troops." Uniforms became more "uniform," projecting the national unity of baseball sportsmen, while distinctive colors, insignia, and details signified a public fealty to locality and sublimation of individualism by players that did not always correspond to reality.[31] Like those of warring armies, the "weapons" of baseball performers — crossed bats which appear in baseball iconography as early as 1871— mimic the crossed sabers of the United States cavalry. Shot on location and before spectators, *Cuban Giants, Colored Champions* commemorates the spectacle of martial triumph.

Military metaphors abound. For example, the term battery, commonly associated with the pitcher and catcher, was to the ball club what the regimental battery was to the infantry. The pitcher served as the baseball squad's attillerist, laying seige to the other team's home base. *Cuban Giants, Colored Champions* situates William "Shepherd Trusty" and "Frank Miller" as an objet d'art, an artistic prop within the theatrical space of the baseball battleground. Both clutch baseballs, emblems of the profession associated with pitchers. Catchers Arthur Thomas and Clarence Williams stand between them. The catcher and pitcher, George Parago and Billy Whyte, stand and sit, respectively, nearby. Averting their gaze from the camera's eye, the batteries invoke a fiction that traces back to ancient Roman portraiture. The frozen poses conjure Roman busts, projecting a public space for viewing men in the guise of republican virtue: gravitas, dignitas, and fides. It is a formal look preserved and popularized by lithography and approrpiated by photography. *Cuban Giants, Colored Champions* recalls Matthew Brady's group portraits of military officers, representations of heroes, martyrs and landscapes that construct a common past.[32]

There is something appealing, even redeeming, about this aestheticizing reponse to a racially segregated baseball club. We look upon these ballplayers and find their social alienation beautiful, as if this iconic image is a badge of honor. Figures are caught in moments of abstraction, perhaps deep thought or reverie — in any case, most of them seem unaware of being seen. So it is with *Cuban Giants, Colored Champions*. The guise of introspection or reflection, as art historian Alan Trachtenberg relates, allows the character of the sitter's face and weight of the body to display them without distraction. "Unawareness," writes Trachtenberg, "is precisely the mode befitting the illustrious performing as American icons." As *The Age* illuminates, these colored icons of the National Pastime offer "another way of cultivating esteeem and respect for the race, and it is a good way, judging from appearances."[33]

"Judging from appearances," then, this photograph depicts melanin saturated along the riffs of the bodies of these marked men: a chemical solution fixed by varying dye stains to the paper's surface. The stiffly posed figures mimic bronze statuettes: dark skin draped in aesthetic garments obscuring the boundary between subject and object. Dark faces and hands, which appear foundational, are not only constituted through visual representation, but are really signifying elements in the discourse of racial formations. The racialist viewer, the beholder who took this as a "colored" photograph, had no difficulty grasping the polemical point of the picture, which was to counter representations of white only baseball champions. When Richard Fox and *The Police Gazette* posed the question "Who are the Cuban Giants?," they inscribed the delicate, intricate, and precarious relation of visual-verbal iconography. The team name "Cuban" and the phrase "any fake business" are as saturated with contradiction and ambivalence, which by fate or design challenges any single thread of explanation. The Cuban Giants hardly appeared from nowhere. In 1885, *The Sun* reported that the aggregation was "composed of Philadelphia, Long Branch, and Trenton colored ball tossers." *The Times* called them "a nine of colored ball tossers." Baseball's image-repertoire system penetrated and thrived in several postbellum Gilded Age print mediums: from daily to weekly newspapers, from theatrical weeklies to illustrated sporting journals, from the sporting fraternity to the ordinary baseball fans in everyday life.[34]

The apt phrase "any fake business" signifies dubious links between black bodies and the team's moniker. Whether anyone was duped by the name Cuban Giants when the team debuted in October 1885 seems debatable, presuming, of course, this was the original intention. Nor was anyone fooled the following year. *The Tribune* reports: "The Long Island nine and the Cuban Giants played on the Polo Grounds yesterday before a limited number of spectators. The latter players were remarkably dark skinned for Cubans and were rather short for giants. Late that year, *The Tribune* adds: "The 'Cuban Giants' is the name assumed by the strong colored professional club of Trenton, New Jersey." Two years later, *The Sporting News* reminded the public: "The Cuban Giants, who, by the way, are neither giants nor Cubans, but thick-set and brawny colored men, make about as stunning an exhibition of ball playing as any team in the country.... [I]t is one of the best teams in the city to see." Playing upon the racial fears of white clubs (and white spectators) who felt threatened by colored clubs, it seems, the Cubans thumbed their nose at the baseball world, while providing kranks and opponents dime museum parodies of contemporary political events.[35]

Another approach speculates about who coined the team name and, more importantly, why. In *Sol White's History of Colored Base Ball* (first published in 1906), the author recounted his baseball career, which included a stint with the Genuine Cuban Giants. White's book is a gem and one of the most significant works to come down to us from black baseball's early period. Wittingly or unwittingly, however, the book raises important issues. First, it awards Babylon, Long Island, "the distinction of being the birthplace of the first professional Colored Base Ball team in the world." Knowledgeable fans would have challenged this view — Bridgewater's famed Black Stockings offer an alternative mythological origin. Jerry Malloy's introduction to White's book frames the second example, correctly challenging the prevailing image of the team's birth and the typical explanation of its name, also derived from White. White claimed that the Cuban Giants talked gibberish to each other on the baseball field, hoping it sounded like Spanish. Moreover, jabbering in mock Spanish allowed them to avoid the disapprobation of racist white fans. However, this is an apocryphal account. White joined the team five years after its formation.[36]

Lomax links Frank P. Thompson and S. K. Govern with the image of the Cuban Giants: its birth and its unusual name. Both were social activists, contributing to the formation of the Hotel Brotherhood U.S.A. Thompson, of Philadelphia, served as headwaiter for the Howland Hotel, and Govern worked for the prestigious Clarendon House. Both managed hotel ball clubs, and they probably "crossed bats" at Long Branch, a summer playground for the wealthy. The Caribbean-born Govern served as the linchpin, and Malloy cites evidence that he managed a team called the Manhattans and had taken them to Cuba, as early as 1882. But another colored hotel nine preceded them: the Clarendon Base Ball Club. *The Advocate* reports: "The Clarendon B. B. Club is booming principally from D.C. and the management of S. K. Govern." Later, *The Globe* clarified: "The Clarendon nine is practically disbanded and is now the Manhattan Club of Washington city." The Cuban Giants ultimately derived, then, from several colored clubs: Govern's Clarendon nine and his Manhattans, Thompson's Athletics, and John F. Lang's Orions. While certainly not the prototype, the Cuban Giants aptly belong to the baseball/hotel waiter subculture.[37]

Govern seems the most likely author of the Cuban Giant's moniker. It fits into a larger context associated with the Cuban War of Independence (1868–1898). Theorist Walter Benjamin's theories of authorship and the literary techniques of work suggest behind a reader's impatience smolders that of man on the sidelines who believes he has the right to see his own interests expressed. The reader is at all times ready to become a writer, that is, a describer, but also a prescriber. Benjamin explains, "As an expert — even if not on a subject but only on the post he occupies — he gains access to authorship." As a "reader" of his times, Govern occupied a post that gained him access to authorship. Serving as baseball manager, actor, journalist, waiter, and union organizer, Govern understood the commodification of bodies as labor power, underscoring the political position of blacks in North America. Govern likely incorporated Cuba into his construction of an imagined black community. Newspapers covered the black struggle for Cuban emancipation, and they devoted copy to black intellectuals who supported the Cuban insurgency. Among them were Henry Highland Garnet and Samuel Scottron, who had founded the Cuban Anti-slavery Society.

Among the Afro-Cuban leaders of the Cuban Independence Movement was Antonio Maceo (the "Bronze Titan"), who made two important trips to New York City (1878 and 1884) and convened meetings with Garnet and other black leaders. Also interested in freeing the means of production and serving the class struggle, Govern played his part: transforming the forms and instruments of baseball production in the way desired by a progressive black intelligentsia. Govern was a race man.[38]

In 1886, the Trenton baseball community had other ideas. While the local baseball world expressed enthusiasm over the new "colored" team playing at the Chambersburg Grounds, its members cared little for the ball club's nickname. The *True American* alternately called them "Trentons" and Cuban Giants. The paper adds: "The Cuban Giants, under new management, make their first appearance this afternoon at the Chambersburg grounds." Walter I. Cook, of Trenton, New Jersey, was part of the new management. Jerry Malloy reveals that businessman Walter E. Simpson sold the team to Cook, a "scion of one of the oldest and wealthiest families on the Eastern shore." Cook's ambivalence probably had something do with the name Cuban Giants. The name was changed, at least when the team played at the home grounds: "The name of the Cuban Giants has been changed to the 'Trentons.' This is a far more appropriate name and it is hoped the club will honor the city."[39]

Why the name Trentons seemed "far more appropriate" probably had as much to do with Cook's civic pride as with the struggle he and Govern had over "access to authorship." Cook sought to create the team in his own image. He idolized the sporting life and spent his money generously on the team. The players appreciated his generosity, particularly when it came to illnesses and injuries. This represents only part of the story. Cook managed the club and scheduled games. The white press rarely mentioned Govern, who was relegated to day-to-day operations. When his name is associated with the team, it is neither as manager nor co-manager. The *Trenton American* shows that Govern umpired the team's games. While the paper initially followed Cook's lead, referring to the club as the Trenton Giants, others continued to call the team Cuban Giants. Black newspapers considered Govern the team's manager: "Mr. S. K. Govern, under whose management the Cuban Giants B. B. Club has met with such great success, receives an annual salary and they are now the leading colored of the country." And, eventually, so did the *Daily True American*. In late July, the paper was again calling them "Cuban Giants." [40]

Diamond Dust: "Quite Smart Cubans"

Cuban Giants, Colored Champions more properly belongs among tightly cropped compositions with figures wedged between the camera and the baseball grandstand wall. One crucial element found in such photographs is the presence of fans or kranks. With spectators staring down upon them, the Cuban Giants fall under the fans' watchful gaze. They wear middle-class attire — dark jackets or coats, white shirts, dark ties, and dark bowlers. Who are they? Perhaps, they represent white-collar workers: politicians, bankers, policemen, firemen, actors and theatrical employees, merchants, clerks, musicians, and skilled artisans. They may depict the sporting fraternity, gamblers, and other demimonde elements. They may be blue-collar workers, skilled or unskilled laborers, who changed clothes at their work-places, fitting themselves in their best Sunday church-going suits. Strangely, no women appear in the photograph. There was not much intermingling in the stands, but crowds typically included people from all ages, ethnicities, genders, and socioeconomic levels. While there are exaggerations as to the extent white-collar and blue-collar crowds interacted, the National Pastime attracted the broadest audience of any major spectator sport.[41]

The size of crowds in the post-bellum Gilded Age was generally quite modest. Though no reliable records exist, Steven Reiss has analyzed the three major competing leagues: the National League, the American Association, and the Player's League. However, scant attention has been given to "colored" clubs. My admittedly small sampling of games, both segregated and interracial, shows that numbers ranged between 500 and 4,000 spectators. On July 21, 1882, fully 2,000 spectators, one-third of them colored, attended the Philadelphia Orions vs. New York Metropolitans game. On May 12, 1883, the St. Louis Black Stockings crossed bats with the St. Louis Amateurs at Compton Avenue Park before about a thousand colored fans and many white spectators. On June 3, 1883, when the Black Stockings again played the Amateurs, 4,000 (mostly white) fans passed through the gates, the beautiful weather and the absence of the professionals accounting for the large gathering. On September 7, 1883, the Grand Avenues and the Black Stockings entertained about 800 people at Sportsman's Park. In another game, a racially-mixed crowd, including 1,000 colored fans, witnessed the Amateurs and the Black Stockings. In 1884 the Gordons, of Chicago, played the Milwaukee Grays, and 4,000 fans — the largest crowd ever gathered to witness a game in Milwaukee — attended. Over 3,000 people attended their second game. Nearly 2,000 attended the Gordons vs. DuBuques contest. Colored clubs playing against one another in New Orleans drew decent crowds. On August 2, 1885, the Unions defeated Cohens before 500 people. Achieving national acclaim, the Pinchbacks (formerly the Cohens) traveled north to play the Chicago Unions, and over 4,000 people attended the three-game series.[42]

According to Reiss, the size of crowds at Cuban Giants games depended on the population of the site, the quality of the competition, and the cost of attending. The game that never occurred between the Browns and Cuban Giants offers one example. When the Browns in September 1887 openly revolted against playing the colored champions, the story made national news. The team's owner, President Von Der Ahe, had arranged for his club to play an exhibition game with the Cuban Giants at West Farms, near New York. He was promised a big guarantee ($250 and half the gate receipts), expecting a crowd of 15,000. The team had other ideas. Several players presented Von Der Ahe with a letter that protested against playing colored players and refused to meet the Cuban Giants in the proposed game. In part, the letter reads: "Dear Sir: We, the undersigned members of the St. Louis Baseball Club, do not agree to play against the negroes to-morrow. We will cheerfully play against white people at any time, and think, by refusing to play, we are only doing what is right, taking everything into consideration and the shape the team is in at present." While there were claims that the Browns refused to play the Giants because many of their players were hurt and they feared losing, the Trenton management saw a large payday slip away. According to the *Post-Dispatch*, Von Der Ahe's settlement with the Giants might have reached $600. Additionally, the proprietors of the park where the game was to have been played threatened to sue Von Der Ahe for $700. Baseball drew the color line again.[43]

Late 19th century baseball resembled the postbellum business world. White owners moved their clubs frequently, while rival leagues — essentially small cartels — sprung up and competed for players and spectators. Despite the superb talent demonstrated by black segregated nines or colored players sprinkled on other professional clubs, the owners of the National League, the American Association, and the Union Association felt no need to shatter the color line by admitting black racial Others. The national press supported this white middle-class agenda and encouraged the development of separate colored leagues. *The Sporting News* reports:

> Next season an attempt should be made to form a League of colored players. Such a league, with clubs from this city, Brooklyn, Philadelphia, Pittsburg [*sic*], Washington and Baltimore, should prove successful. It costs less to run a colored club than a club of white players. They have not arrived at that point where they are paid $3000 or $4000 a season, notwithstanding the fact that there ware players among the colored men that are equal to any white players on the ball field. If you don't think so, go and see the Cuban Giants play.

If it was fashionable to attend colored championships, it was also chic to attend Cuban Giants games, despite the New Negro ballplayers' social exclusion. Baseball's popularity, along with the complex performances of black ballplayers, made the novelty of all-black professional teams one of the highlights of urban leisure-class life.[44]

The Colored Baseball Celebrity as Objet d'Art

The grandstand wall behind the team, which provides the only visible architectural structure, appears washed-out, but nonetheless situates the grayish figures firmly within the composition. Text is pasted and written across the height and width of the photograph. A clipped column heading is situated immediately above the team, centered and arranged in three rows, commemorating the team's accomplishments. The two uppermost rows consist of rectangular and unevenly cut strips. Their grayish tonality contrasts with the white grandstand walls. Derived from newspaper clippings, these strips appear to be clippings recycled from sports headlines. Literally removed from anonymous newspapers, the varying typographical styles coupled with the different fonts and sizes supports this view. Pasted directly onto the photograph, the crudely cut labels produce a collage-like effect.

The photograph partners skilled and unskilled artists and artisans: a camera operator, collage-artist, painter, and calligraphers. Perhaps it begins with the human form — the retouching or "doctoring" of the photograph. Artists' hands rearrange the space of the photograph, painting delicate, black lines around the human figures, retrieving them from overexposure. Retouching is a technical process of correcting flaws and deficiencies in a negative or positive image by adding, subtracting, or concealing tone, color and details. However, drawing on a photograph also participates in the construction of the image, not necessarily its correction. It can be decorative. In the 1870s and 1880s, for example, the fashion for decorative art swept North America. The Tile Club, a rotating group of white male artists who painted ceramic tiles, represented the organization. Recalling certain aspects of their art, the black lines drawn over the human forms in the photograph give an impression of decorative ornamentation. The pursuit of beautiful forms aptly characterizes the image's aesthetic design — yet the image is the result of the involvement of many artistic hands.

They transform the figures within the cultural space of the baseball grounds into a prized objet d'art.[45]

The players' names are conspicuously inscribed across their bodies, along the upper torso area. The lettering appears to have been done by two different hands; or at the very least, by the same hand at two different times. Beginning with the championship dates, the composition shows little regard for symmetry — the first date ("1887") and the word "And" are larger than the second date ("1888"). "Parago," "Homes," "Trusty," "Thomas," "Williams," and "Miller" mark the standing figures. "White," "Williams," "Harrison," "Boyd," "Fry," and "Allen" identify the sitting figures. The name of the non-player — "Govern. Manager" — appears in curvilinear fashion along the ground plane. Moving from left to right, the letterer's calligraphic skill appears uneven, suggesting two if not three hands.

The names "Trusty," "Thomas," and "Miller" belong to the same hand — carefully delineated and delicately rendered, they seemingly float across the body. However, the letterer appears to have skipped over the second standing figure from the right, "Williams." Perhaps not wanting to smudge the ink on the fourth standing figure, "Trusty," the letterer decided to let it dry, proceeding to the end standing figure, "Miller." "Parago" and "Homes" represent other letterers. The thickness of the letters in "Parago," and their arrangement across the figures upper chest, embodies the letterer's poise. The letters are neither too light nor too heavy. Decorative ornamentation and figure successfully meld together and are the most aesthetically pleasing. In contrast, the thickness of the letters in "Homes" suggests little control over ink and pen. The craftsmanship is amateurish: heavy and labored. Moreover, the latter name, "Homes," is misspelled; it should be "Holmes." While it was not uncommon to find names misspelled or given alternate spellings in baseball narratives and game scores, this mistake might be due to carelessness. Working beyond his or her technical skill, the letterer's craftsmanship threatens to overwhelm the figures by assuming too much writing space. At the least, the letterer's penmanship lacks subtlety; at worst, his/her mechanics struggle with eye-to-hand coordination.

On the other hand, note the consistency, size, delicacy and placement of the following names: "Williams," "Whyte," "Williams," "Harrison," "Boyd," "Fry(e)" and "Allen." It's as if the photograph's owner expressed dissatisfaction with the previous letterers, deciding instead to seek out another calligrapher. The calligraphic hand responsible for the above mentioned names attempted to reconcile the previous artistic mistakes. One senses his/her proficiency at combining calligraphic skills with aesthetic style. Note how the letters mimic the body's contour, curving ever so slightly. "White" moves along the figure's shoulders, the letters forming a delicately rendered arc. Again, note how "Williams" tilts toward the viewer, mimicking the slumping player's protruding chest. Given this uneven treatment of the lettering, different fonts, the slapdash paste-up job, and Holmes's misspelled name, this image intriguingly splits the seam between the mass culture of baseball photography and the fine art of baseball representation.

If, as Susan Sontag has suggested, "Photographs lay down routes of reference," surely the familiarity of that route builds our sense of the present and the immediate past. Photography historian Deborah Willis makes it clear that photography redefined the visual world and access to it but did not alter the visual conventions that had been used to depict racial difference. For example, Willis notes that the negative racial stereotype of the "grinning darky" is rooted in antebellum notions and idealized depictions of plantation life; yet it persists into the 21st century and renders every image of an enthusiastic black person as potentially derogatory or problematical. Photography's presumed objectivity is a key element in the historical record of black baseball images.[46]

Cuban Giants, Colored Champions is not merely a photograph made about postbellum Gilded Age baseball, nor is it simply about colored ballplayers. The image attempts to reframe our sense of the black baseball past, with the "post-humous shocks engineered by the circulation of hitherto unknown photographs." Now a constituent part of what baseball historians think about, this photograph functions as memory. Over the long run, this fiction helps, at least culturally, to lock the often-told (though incomplete) story of the colored ballplayer in our minds. Nonetheless, the picture remains a painful image when one considers its relation to racial formations and baseball representations. Sontag explains: "Ideologies create substantiating archives of images, representative images, which encapsulate common ideas of significance and trigger predictable thoughts, feelings." While *Cuban Giants, Colored Champions* carefully crafts an appealing visual product, and an important art historical object, it does not change what respectable white spectators (or any spectator for that matter) thought of colored baseballists. Hypothetically, it contains the seeds of ridicule and contempt; it embraces literary and visual forms of symbolic violence that found cultural expression in blackface minstrelsy. But the photograph could be viewed, even in the face of social exclusion, as a symbol of race pride. In other words, marked men could be imagined as men of mark.[47]

Cuban Giants, Colored Champions ultimately conjures phantom images that resurrect anxieties about the black presence during the antebellum slave period. While baseball critics cast baseball magnates as "slave" owners and white ballplayers as property to be bought and sold, appropriated representations of "negro" dialect vernacular and blackface literature restage the struggle between management and white labor. How did the postbellum figure of the colored baseballist become a symbolic substitute, a black image sacrificed on the altar of baseball capitalism? Chapter Five contemplates what "Men of Mark and Marked Men" does not; namely, how the protocols of blackface minstrelsy and blackface literature helped restage the discourse of baseball representations.

CHAPTER FIVE

"A Mirthful Spectacle": Representing Negro Comedy or Black Aesthetic Style

To sum up the [Blue Stocking vs. Pink Stocking] game in general, it need only be said that, saving the single item of color it was like other well-played games. One peculiarity, however, was noticeable, whether accidental or usual we don't know. It consisted in an irresistible propensity for tumbling head over heels when in the act of running bases or going for fly catches.[1]

The life of the stereotype resides in the death of its model, and the perceptual deadening of those who carry it in their heads as a schematic "search template" for identifying other people.[2]

Sambo has caught the baseball fever, and two clubs from Alabama and Mississippi respectively, have recently had a match in Demopolis, the Alabamians winning. "Heah now, why didn't you frow dat ball to de fust base y'rascal you?"[3]

This chapter queries: Was blackness a metaphor for the material excesses of the post-bellum Gilded Age — or for the stereotypical notion of colored base ball? One answer examines how minstrel theater penetrated the baseball sporting world, and how the business of minstrelsy paralleled the rise of professional baseball — burnt cork artists played ball, sports journalists narrated colored games as blackface farce, and colored nines engaged in "negro" comedy. It is possible to read baseball scholarship exhaustively and never arrive at a passing mention, much less an adequate treatment, of the postbellum colored ballplayer who brought to the game a "peculiar" style and becomes the object of blackness and agency in baseball representations.

Perhaps the most dramatic case of ethnic stereotypes is to be found in the melding of blackface performance and baseball representations. This image-repertoire circulated in the print medium: sports narratives, illustrations, and cartoons. W.J.T. Mitchell declares blackface minstrelsy's image-repertoire to be despicable and worthy of destruction, but he warns that racial and ethnic stereotypes seem to have a life of their own. If the life of the black baseball stereotype resides in the death of its models, as my blurring of the line between the blackface comedic mask and "colored" ballplayers wants to suggest, then who does the "image-killing" and the "image-resurrecting"? This question is best addressed by examin-

128

ing visual/verbal images, specific works that reflect on the adaptability of baseball representations.

Recently, minstrelsy has been subject to intense scholarly study. Historian Eric Lott defines blackface minstrelsy as "an established nineteenth-century theatrical practice, principally of the urban North, in which white men caricatured blacks for sport and profit." For Lott, one of its functions "was precisely to bring various class fractions into contact with one another, to mediate their relations, and finally to aid in the construction of class identities over the bodies of black people." The primary purpose of the minstrel mask may have been as much to maintain control over a potentially subversive act as to ridicule, though the blackface performers' attempts at regulation were also capable of producing an aura of blackness. Lott calls this antebellum aura "the seeming counterfeit."[4]

For literary critic Saidiya Hartman, antebellum minstrelsy represents the desire to don, occupy, or possess blackness or the black body as a sentimental resource and/or locus of excess enjoyment. According to Hartman, the fungibility of the commodity, specifically its abstractness and immateriality, enabled the black body or the blackface mask to serve as a vehicle of self-exploration, renunciation, and enjoyment. As such, black baseball representations have been replete with black bodies providing levity amid catastrophe. Baseball representations absorbed the antebellum era's stock darkey characters or low comedy types, which were readily appropriated to portray the colored ballplayer.[5]

"Most of [minstrelsy's] political content," writes historian David Roediger, "was given over to attacking emancipation, civil rights, and an alleged favoritism toward the 'nigger.'" Roediger adds, "To black up was an act of wildness in the antebellum US. Psychoanalytically, the smearing of soot or blacking over the body represents the height of polymorphous perversity, an infantile playing with excrement or dirt. It is the polar opposite of the anal retentiveness usually associated with accumulating capitalist and Protestant cultures." Minstrelsy impacted the sporting world, its forms penetrating baseball. Solomon Eytinge's *The Behemoth Club of Blackville* offers a humorous visual depiction of the colored sporting fraternity in the 1870s (**fig. 42**).[6]

The aftermath of the Civil War unleashed an outpouring of minstrelsy. In the 1870s, minstrelsy's comedic antics began to circulate in the baseball sports medium. The print media linked baseball to theater managers, promoters, burnt cork artists and the extravagant and lavish performances of blackface farce. Journalists applied the visual/verbal protocols of blackface performance to baseball sports writing. These narratives exploited the blackface mask (black skin, "negro" dialect, bulging eyes, thick lips, and toothy grins). Graphic artists working for print houses and newspapers produced baseball visual representations that appropriated burnt cork images. And finally, sportswriters misunderstood and misrepresented show how black aesthetic style represented form, fashion, expression, and action on the green diamond. These early performances were transformed into "negro" comedy.

Blackface minstrelsy not only shared the cultural stage with baseball but with the American Aesthetic Movement (1876–1887). In the search for authentic and meaningful styles, the sporting fraternity (which includes the membership of blackface minstrelsy) turned, like other Americans, towards the graphic arts, decorative objects, theatrical fashions, and literary forms that conveyed uniquely American cultural style. This style embodied what cultural historian Mary Warner Blanchard calls form, expression, and modes of

Figure 42. The Behemoth Club of Blackville, Solomon Eytinge, Jr., *Harper's Weekly*, 1870s

action and living. For U.S. citizens, in the aftermath of the Civil War, the victory of the North over the South did not eliminate the need for strong masculine figures, but it did expose the rise of the new self-stylized black male in the 1870s and 1880s. The aesthetic figure of the black male exploded onto the baseball world, its representations manifested in both the art world and in the sporting world. Figures of blackness — real and imagined — invoked social undercurrents of the era, and they helped link the aesthetic movement to the sporting world.[7] St. Louis, the Mound City, provides a unique study of race, blackface minstrelsy, and baseball that illuminates this hidden history.[8]

"Antiquated Old Fakes of the Burnt Cork Era": The "Ethiopian Dialect Business"

"The centre of the played out negro minstrel business," reports *The National Police Gazette*, "is Chicago. It is there all the antiquated old fakes of the burnt cork era find a harbor: there they form their plans, organize their new companies and thence start out on the road to tempt fate and torture the public of the newly opened up country on the borders of the wilderness." If anyone admitted blackface minstrelsy's "natural demise as a form of amusement," as the editor claimed, it was neither theater-going audiences nor the sporting fraternity. Nor was it the "wretches who maintain the torture of the minstrel business" or the "wretched performers whom they have induced to blacken their faces for profit."[9]

One way to retrieve baseball minstrelsy from this "wilderness" in both Chicago and

St. Louis is to track its visual-verbal imagery back to theatrical advertisements (**fig. 43**). There we find a billboard of signs, a heterogeneous image-text field in which "The Great Wesley Brothers" vie with theatrical others for the reading public's attention. These "negro" comedians represent the flamboyant excessiveness of the postbellum Gilded Age. Sporting top hats, plaid dusters, flared pants fastened with massive belt buckles, large-collared shirts, thickly-knotted ties, and umbrellas, the foppish blackfaced characters grinningly proclaim, "Over 200 Nights of the Greatest Success Ever Known in New York." "The Long and Short of It," as the giant and dwarf call themselves, are not alone, but are juxtaposed textually to the numerous preceding ads, particularly those devoted to agents, managers, writers, musicians, contortionists, comedians, and monster attractions.[10]

This wilderness is also related to the rise of colored baseball in St. Louis. As stated, the attention given to the Cuban Giants has cast a broad shadow over the trajectory of 19th century colored baseball. Meanwhile, the history of the Black Stockings of St. Louis (1875–1890) covers an equally complex period of at least 15 years. The Mound City provides a unique study of race, blackface minstrelsy, and baseball, in part, because of Henry Bridgewater, whose entrepreneurial relation to the Black Stockings has never been seriously considered. When the Black Stockings were referred to as Bridgewater's "blackfaced team" in 1883, the epithet revealed minstrelsy's commodification of the colored baseballist's black image. It was an image of colored baseball that Bridgewater abhorred, but colored minstrels and colored ballplayers throughout the country shared a special relation as professional entertainers. The Black Stockings and Callender Minstrels (and their progenitors, the Georgia Minstrels), for instance, had probably exchanged theatrical ideas and techniques as early as 1875. This sort of social fact is a primary piece of data that tends to be ignored. Whether "negro" comedy or black aesthetic style — the "Long and the Short of It" — black images intersected the rise of professional baseball and its collaborations with blackface minstrelsy theater.

A brief genealogy of baseball minstrelsy offers a glimpse of minstrelsy's relation to baseball based on the former's search for modern themes, and its supportive role in the sporting fraternity. As Eric Lott makes clear, the virtue of the genealogy is that it familiarizes the cultural object, revealing from a diachronic perspective, functional elements in forms that suggest a range of purposes of the black minstrels mask could

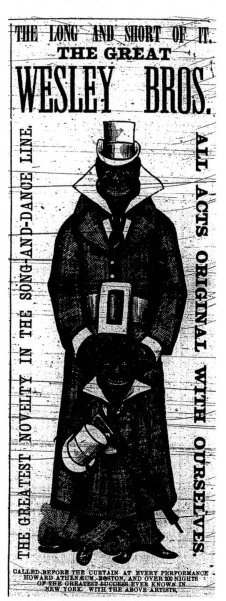

Figure 43. The Great Wesley Bros., *The Clipper*, 1882

serve, both on stage and in public. In the 1860s, professional baseball dovetailed neatly with blackface minstrelsy. Minstrel men (managers, promoters, and entrepreneurs) presented both blackface and baseball as symbols of national culture, as conspicuous displays of wealth and modernity, and as theatrical displays of their own entrepreneurial spirit. In 1869, a minstrel show promoter raised $10,000 and organized a professional baseball team: the Forest Citys, of Cleveland, Ohio. In the nation's first major league game, the Forest Citys played the Fort Wayne Kekiongas, the latter winning 2 to 0. The economic and civic aspects of minstrelsy and baseball were not lost on observers who viewed both as part of the entertainment industry. When the Cincinnati Red Stockings adopted the policy of charging fifty cents to witness every game they played in 1870, critics quipped: "The Red Stockings are professional ball players. They charge an admission fee, and the public does not lose sight of the fact that they are as much open to criticism as the performers in a circus, burnt cork artists, or the disciples of the socks and buskin."[11]

The "negro" minstrel Richard M. Hooley turned entrepreneur and baseball "krank." Hooley had begun his theatrical career with E. P. Christy's Minstrels in 1845, touring the United States and Europe. In 1860, Hooley, S. C. Campbell and G. W. H. Griffin partnered to form Hooley and Campbell's Minstrels. In 1862, they opened Hooley's New Opera House in New York City, built and equipped for the "negro-minstrel line." In the late 1860s, Hooley's Minstrels introduced baseball farce: "The Base Ball mania has broken out here in a humorous eruption, and a burlesque match will be played between the long and short nines; it will be a heavy game."

> [T]he burlesque of the champion game of base ball between the Atlantics and Unions is the most amusing. All who have never seen a genuine game should witness this, and all who are familiar with the game should also take it in. The former will be greatly amused, and the latter will learn "points" that they never dreamed of before. Every player plays "points" and sharp ones too, to the great delight of the initiated, Cool White makes an exceptionable umpire "in a horn." His decisions are without parallel, although the audience can't see it in the light.

The *Brooklyn Daily Eagle* added: "The Base Ball Match is the best thing we have seen in a long time. The fun is uproarious, and the hits very palpable. The audience insists in catching a ball occasionally, which gives them an active interest in the proceedings."[12]

Hooley had allegedly made a half million dollars before fire destroyed "the temple of the burnt cork" in 1865. By 1875, the Hooley Minstrel Company had refurbished and opened Bryan Hall as a Chicago Opera House. In 1876, Hooley started the Black Stockings of Chicago, a baseball club which his business agent organized "on the burnt cork basis." Hooley himself played first base for the minstrel nine. When they crossed bats with a picked nine of newspaper reporters in May, the "Blacks" received a severe walloping by a score of 33 to 8. Hooley would later reminisce about the good old days when he traveled through the West as a "nigger singer." It seems more than probable that the lineage of baseball minstrelsy began with Hooley's minstrels: "The burlesque Base Ball game is the best card Manager Hooley has played in some time. It is drawing immense houses."[13]

Hooley's Black Stockings and other baseball images are full of instruction for anyone who wants to think about symbols of our national culture and, more generally, of the business relationship between minstrelsy and baseball. Throughout the 1860s and 1870s, newspapers and theatrical journals covered the successes and failures of minstrel barons, not only reporting their attempts at building monopolies, but their attempts at absorbing highly skilled and talented colored troupes. They exposed how owners, managers, promoters, and performers exploited not only the artistic potential of baseball representations, but also the aesthetic possibilities of blackface imagery. As a cultural form, the aesthetic possibilities of blackface imagery went well beyond the theatrical stage or theater critic: its artistic potential had, in a very real sense, made baseball images the subject of blackface representation. The medium of the baseball landscape, in short, mediated between blackface imagery and the image of the colored baseballist.

In 1874, John Haverly's Minstrels successfully debuted at Hooley's Opera House, but their triumph was not new. "Jack" Haverly (born Christopher Heverly) had begun his career in 1864, and his success and failures reflected the period. In the postbellum Gilded Age, he formed and dissolved several minstrel partnerships. In the 1870s, Haverly recognized that he could form a monopoly by cornering the market on both white and colored minstrel performers. He recruited, hired, trained, and coached colored musical, acting, and dance talent. In 1876, Haverly bought a controlling interest in the Callender Minstrels, formerly known as the Georgia Minstrels. In Barnumesque style, the Callender Minstrels and Haverly's other troupes grew to impressive sizes, and their performances featured elaborate sets and costumes. Haverly's Mammoth Mastodon Minstrels numbered no less than 40 performers, and Callender's Minstrels traversed the country as three distinct colored troupes. Haverly outstripped competitors by more than doubling the number of performers seen in one particular act. By 1881, Haverly ran the largest colored and white minstrel troupes and owned three theaters in New York, and one each in Brooklyn, Chicago, and San Francisco. Haverly also owned two opera companies, two mining companies, an agency in London, and two sporting organizations.[14]

When Haverly's troupes toured the country, his baseball clubs also crossed bats with professional, semiprofessional, and amateur nines: "One of the adjuncts of Haverly's minstrels is its fine base ball team, which prides itself upon many victories won from strong clubs." When the minstrel aggregation performed at St. Louis in 1881, Haverly's mastodon nine played the professionals: the Louisville Eclipse and the Brown Stockings. That same year, they also played the Buffalo Bisons, who trampled them by a score of 50 to 5. Haverly's organization probably introduced the all-colored Charles Callender Minstrels to baseball comedy. During a tour to San Francisco in 1882, the Callender Minstrels played a white picked nine. In 1884, they crossed bats with Henry Bridgewater's Black Stockings of St. Louis, a prominent colored nine.[15]

Fayette Welch (Patrick Walsh) joined Hooley's Minstrels in the late 1860s and was "uproariously applauded for his imitations of darkey singing." The *Brooklyn Daily Eagle* added: "[Welch] is one of the best end men that Mr. Hooley has ever had in his company, and gives us to-day a better representation of the genuine 'nigger' than is to be found outside of Brooklyn." In 1872, the Welch, Hart & Clarke Minstrels toured Illinois and Missouri. Welch became a prominent member of the western sporting fraternity, associating with its gamblers, prizefighters, ballplayers, and sporting ladies. He joined Haverly's Minstrels when that company reorganized in 1873. As a solo entertainer, Welch performed at Deagle's Theater in St. Louis and established "a fine reputation as a burnt cork artist of the better class." During a benefit for prizefighters at Deagle's, Welch responded to six curtain calls from the raucous standing-room-only crowd. In 1875, the "renown darkey comedian" organized a burnt cork ball club. Welch's blackfaced nine crossed bats with the Red Stockings of St. Louis. They donned gorgeous uniforms of white pants, red stockings buttoned up the side, ridiculously large caps, and low shoes of extraordinary size. The Red Stockings beat them, by a score of 42 to 2: "Welch said his club (they played ten men) could have beat the Reds, but it wouldn't have looked well to beat the professionals."[16]

In 1867, Milton G. Barlow toured with the Barlow Brothers, one of the best known song and dance teams in minstrelsy. They performed on the same stage alongside Fayette Welch at the Brooklyn Opera House. In 1872, they joined (Lew) Simmons and (Edward M.) Slocum's Philadelphia Minstrels. In 1874, Barlow and George Wilson figured prominently among Haverly's Minstrels, the finest performers of the "burnt cork" profession. Barlow and Wilson performed in Haverly's organization as end-men. Following much success, the duo formed their own professional troupe in 1877; Barlow, Wilson, and Company's Minstrels toured the country for about 15 years. Among their comedic sketches was a satire on the game of baseball. In 1883, the troupe staged their baseball satire at a Cleveland-St. Louis game. It proved a great sensation, allowing blackface entertainers to further exploit the game's lucrative possibilities.[17]

Lewis Simmons, another minstrel entertainer turned baseball enthusiast, entered the act. Simmons began his career as a blackface banjo player in 1849. In 1861, he joined Hooley & Campbell's Minstrels, and in conjunction with Bob Hart organized a minstrel company in early 1863. In 1870, Lewis Simmons and Edward M. Slocum opened the Ethiopian Opera House in Philadelphia. In 1883 Simmons, William ("Billy") Sharsig, and Charlie Mason bought the Philadelphia Athletics (Mason, a former ballplayer, operated a saloon and bookie establishment; and Sharsig had organized the original Philadelphia Athletics) through a $16,000 loan that Simmons had procured from Adam Forepaugh of Forepaugh's Circus. Throughout the country, the sporting press lampooned Simmons's Athletics through baseball narratives that employed "negro" dialect and minstrelsy skits: "'That's certainly hard luck.' Says Mason. 'What do you think about it, Mr. Bones?' 'Well, I hain't got nuffin' to say.' Replies Sharsig. 'We won de championship las' year trough de 'sistance of de Metropolitans; den turned 'roun an' played a dirty mean trick on dem.'"[18]

Finally, there is Harry P. Keily, a well-known theatrical manager, actor, and tenor vocalist. The Civil War veteran had performed with prominent minstrel troupes, notably, Kelly & Leon's, Sharpley's, Campbell's Minstrels, and at the Seventh Street Opera House in Philadelphia. Keily was also connected with the Mutual Base Ball Club of New York City, serving as treasurer and manager in 1866. In 1882, he organized and managed the Leadville Blue Stockings of Leadville, Colorado. With a winning record of 34–8, his club was the baseball champion of Colorado. Keily may have also been lured westward by the Tabor Opera House, which was built in 1879. In the mid–1880s, he returned to New York City. In 1885, he umpired a benefit game between theater performers. Frank McNish and Daniel Sully agreed to meet at the Polo grounds to decide the championship of the theatrical profession.[19]

So what does this genealogy tell us about baseball minstrelsy, social segregation, the color line, coercion, and free labor? These questions clearly suggest, as Eric Lott might put it, that the ancestry of baseball minstrelsy invokes "the most virulently racist moment (the late nineteenth century) in the history of black representation." Powerful minstrel men, that is, white entrepreneurs who controlled the industry, formed a fraternal brotherhood. They thrived in the "post-emancipation economy as an instituted process" that benefited from new forms of labor that continued to be structured by race even though racial slavery ended. While this economy did not eliminate the need for cheap and coercible labor, it did problematize the overlap of race and class. With access to economic capital and the best theatrical talent (musicians, actors, comedians, dancers, and acrobats), minstrel men collaborated with other members of the sporting fraternity and fashioned the professional entertainment industry. Minstrel men financed and created new troupes, coordinated bookings and promotional aspects, traveled established circuits and created new ones, and built new theaters. Stressing socio-cultural differences with the newly emancipated blacks and their descendants, white agents of baseball minstrelsy defined freedom as a socio-economic condition which blacks did not, and could not share.[20]

The links between baseball minstrelsy and postbellum Gilded Age blacks could not have been lost on literary and visual artists. They had adopted visual codes and narrative approaches derived from the antebellum era. Framed as if on a proscenium, with the melodramatic subjects and circumstances often layered much like actors against resplendent stage settings, black images of the colored ballplayer could be mistaken for the depiction of theater and opera productions. But according to art historian Joshua Brown, artists struggled to make representation fit new situations and to provide balance for readers whose expectations and experiences were changing. Brown explains: "the new pictorial order in the making was influenced by old pictorial conventions and modes of storytelling, by the traditions of major northern publications and institutions." However, Brown has been quick to point out that literary and visual artists who had previously rendered new ways to represent black "actions and aspirations, returned to the racist conventions of the past or created new black visual types who antics mixed a dollop of affection with larger quantities of condescension and derision."[21]

"Negro" Dialect Stories and Blackface Minstrelsy: Blackface Baseball Literature

It cannot be an accident that blackface literature became wildly popular in the 1870s and 1880s, when minstrel shows were dominating the stages of America. "In the decades after the Civil War, the North's guilty nostalgia for the Old Plantation not only gave rise to the giant minstrel-show spectacles and Tom Shows," writes John Strausbaugh, "but also spurred a national craze for Negro-dialect literature, assuaged in reams of populist poetry and short stories that fed a meteoric post-war boom in the magazine industry." Strausbaugh offers a genealogy for blackface literature, a lineage of "negro dialect" authors who birthed what some scholars call a genuinely American literature. Harriet Beecher Stowe's *Uncle Tom's Cabin* (1852), Joel Chandler Harris's *Uncle Remus* stories (1870s), David Hunter Strother's *Virginia Illustrated* (1850s), Thomas Nelson Page's *In Ole Virginia* (1881), Louise Clarke-Pyrnelle's *Diddie, Dumps, and Tot* (1882), and Katherine McDowell's *Dialect Tales* (1883) attained wide popularity. Indeed, the pejorative "father of American literature," Mark Twain (Samuel Clemens) and *The Adventures of Huckleberry Finn* (1884) captured our national imagination in a vernacular voice that is, according to Shelly Fisher Fishkin, "black."[22]

Literary authors and sportswriters found inspiration in minstrelsy and "negro" dialect vernacular. Beginning in 1883, George E. Stackhouse ("Stack") worked for the *New York Daily Tribune* and became the most popular newspaper man ever connected with local baseball matters. A. B. "June" Rankin worked for the *New York Herald* between 1876 and 1889 and had entire control of the Herald's baseball coverage. Rankin's brother, William, served as sportswriter for the *New York Clipper*. Between 1882 and 1892, James C. Kennedy covered baseball for the *New York Times*. While we do not, of course, have a consistent baseball sportswriting style throughout the country prior to the 1880s, some of its work reflects the intersection of blackface literature and representations of colored ball games. Some of the earliest blackface baseball literature has yet to be unearthed, but available representations are probably based upon certain facts, and appropriate the "negro" dialect vernacular, especially with the linkages between baseball and minstrelsy.[23]

The visual/verbal protocols of minstrelsy penetrated not only baseball representations in the graphic arts, but also baseball representations in the print media. Visual and literary artists, theater promoters, and managers coalesced in the sporting world. Meeting in saloons, gambling houses, club houses, dance halls, sporting houses, newspaper offices, and ballparks, they exchanged ideas and shared strategies about how to transform baseball into a professional entertainment. Minstrelsy served a dual function. The mask of blackness represented the first uniquely American cultural aesthetic. Whether an authentic black aesthetic or the seeming counterfeit, minstrelsy infused baseball with commercial appeal: an aesthetic pedigree, so to speak, its ancestral lineage elevated the genuine colored artist to an objet d'art. Second, minstrelsy framed the history of U.S. race relations, from its mockery of abolitionists and emancipation to its lampoon of black citizenship. For white performers, blackness became a surrogate skin, something to be put on or removed, an aesthetic prosthetic fully suited for exigencies of American modernity. Blackness intersected the postbellum partnership of minstrelsy and baseball in ways that until now have not been explored.[24]

The postbellum commodification of old antebellum stereotypes — plantation "darkey" images that had dominated the blackface minstrel stage and/or out of "negro" dialect literature — began to circulate throughout the country as brands for consumer goods. While black images had appeared as commercial icons, logos, mascots, and spokespersons before the Civil War, they proliferated with the spread of plantation nostalgia in the post–Civil War era. The makers of these images intuited a basic feature of the human fascination with blackface: its vacillation between humor and derision. "Negro" stump orators were immensely popular during the 1860s and 1870s. Men like Byron Christy, Hughey Dougherty, James Unsworth, Harry Pell, Frank Morgan, Frank Bell, and Bob Hart reintroduced the orator as a political figure of Reconstruction and post–Reconstruction era black Republican leadership.[25]

Melons and Sanford's Ginger depicts a well-dressed political figure standing behind a wooden table (**fig. 44**). He sports a high collar, thickly-knotted cravat, vest, and a clawhammer coat. His sleeves are rolled from the wrists. Leaning sharply forward, to emphasize his point, his right arm extends toward the counter's roughened edge, demanding the audience's rapt attention. But there is nothing elegant about his left hand. Four thickly knuckled stubby fingers, suggestive of an unskilled laborer, press firmly against the counter. His left arm, raised at a sharp right angle, displays a pleading open hand, palm-side up. An unrolled scroll lying across the middle of the table reads, "De Melon Am King." Positioned

Melons and Sanford's Ginger.

No subject arouses the eloquence of the colored brother as does the melon, and well it may.

What more refreshing to the irritated and parched mucous membrane on a hot, sultry day than a slice of cold, ripe, luscious, black-eyed watermelon? But it has its painful side.

If the melon is sometimes full of cussedness, the antidote, SANFORD'S GINGER, is ever at hand to neutralize its venom and restore to health the disturbed functions.

This unrivaled household panacea and traveling companion is sure to check any disturbance of the bowels, instantly relieve cramps and pains, prevent indigestion, destroy disease germs in water drunk, restore the circulation when suspended by a chill—a frequent cause of cholera morbus—break up colds and fevers, and ward off malarial, contagious and epidemic influences.

Prepared with the utmost skill from Imported Ginger, Choice Aromatics and the purest and best of Medicinal French Brandy.

As a healthful Summer drink, with water, milk, iced water, lemonade, effervescent draughts and mineral water, it is the best.

It eradicates a craving for intoxicants in those addicted to their use, allays nervousness, assists digestion, promotes sleep, and builds up those reduced by disease, debility and dissipation.

Mothers worn out with the cares of maternity or the household, or when weak, nervous and hysterical, should take a dose of that delicious invigorant, SANFORD'S GINGER. No other remedy is so wholesome, palatable and safe for delicate women, young children and the aged.

Beware of worthless "gingers" offensively urged by mercenary druggists on those who call for

SANFORD'S -:- GINGER,
The Delicious Summer Medicine.

SANFORD'S -:- GINGER,
Sold by Druggists, Grocers and Dealers.

Figure 44. Melons and Sanford's Ginger, *The Globe-Democrat* (St. Louis), 1884

to the right of the scroll is an upright melon, or presumably one that has been halved, seemingly melded to the man's body and giving the illusion that his knee rests uncomfortably on the table.

While the figure of the colored orator mocks failed black political leadership, ostensibly thematized as blackface performance, it is visibly buttressed, nonetheless, by a series of metaphors that ground meaning in conspicuous consumption and sumptuary display. Is this a blackface performer or a genuine colored orator? Clothing and body parts conjure rooster's plumage. The buffoon's bullet-shaped head and receding hairline finally yield to a capacious skull. Its summit crowned with wiry curls, it looks like a rooster's crest. His vest has popped loose from the back, and the coattails rising skyward project an arched shape that also resembles a rooster's tail. Moreover, the coattails and extended arms form a sharp right with the table top, reinforcing not only the triangular composition, but the three-quarter view and the gaze of the speaker's bulging eyes. His curly locks terminate into a pointy head, yet this hairstyle recalls one of the minstrel performer's standard wig styles. His ridiculously big lips appear smeared on. A thick, white, pasty-looking ring covers the figure's lower face, roughly modeled to define and mimic lips. One is also left to ponder the mouth's relation to the gouged watermelon. "No subject arouses the eloquence of the colored brother as does the melon," the advertisement copy claims, "and well it may be." The image parallels the erosion of Reconstruction-era black empowerment (the abandonment of the 14th Amendment's egalitarian principles which were ratified on a national scale by the 1896 Plessy-Fergusson decision), which would be completed by the 1890s.[26]

A similar ambivalence surrounds the whole question of the colored baseballist as an iconic emblem of blackface baseball literature. On the one hand, "negro" dialect vernacular had penetrated baseball sports writing throughout the country by 1875. Of course, New York, Cincinnati, Chicago, Rockford, and St. Louis had professional ball clubs as early as the late 1860s and early 1870s. And sportswriters of these cities had reached a level of sophistication and cultural mastery over standard, if not mundane, inning-by-inning baseball reportage. They worked for many daily newspapers (St. Louis had at least five), and editors permitted them creative flexibility. While attending the Blue Stockings vs. Sunsets game, for instance, a sportswriter allegedly overheard this quaint exchange between colored gamblers: "Pull down yer west — dat's played out, pull down yer gweenbacks — dat's wat's de matter wid de pup." Sportswriters who incorporated real or imagined "negro" dialect vernacular into their baseball narratives would have been familiar with the national popularity and circulation of "negro" dialect stories in genteel middle-class magazines. Whether some sports journalists had literary aspirations is certainly debatable.[27]

W. J.T. Mitchell explains that "images reside within media the way organisms reside in a habitat." Where then do blackface images reside? Like organisms, they can move from one media habitat (minstrel stage) to another (sports columns). Blackface baseball literature (a combination of "negro" dialect vernacular and blackface minstrelsy) struggled to thrive and circulate in small-town newspapers where the fascination for baseball and baseball sportswriting struggled for recognition. East coast colored newspaper editors expressed ambivalence toward baseball coverage in the early 1880s; in the same period, they also resisted the denigrating images of blackface minstrelsy exploited by the national print media. When the sportswriter for the *Saginaw Morning Herald* reported the St. Louis Black Stockings vs. Saginaw Old Golds contests, this reportage represented the archaic style (inning-by-inning accounts) of the 1860s. This isn't necessarily a bad thing. Devoid of "negro" dialect vernacular and the comedic antics of blackface minstrelsy, it offered a "typical" baseball narrative: "Of the Black Stockings Rodger(s) struck to Robinson and was fielded out to first, and Davis and Sutton each went out on three strikes. Score, three to two in favor of Saginaw, and their friends felt better."[28]

But the trajectory for "negro" dialect vernacular and representative antics of minstrelsy in baseball sportswriting points to the east coast. An ideal baseball landscape to track baseball's exploitation of "negro" dialect vernacular and minstrelsy, then, is in the print media's coverage of the colored "Alpines." Between 1883 and 1887, the Alpine Base Ball Club of Brooklyn was a perennial powerhouse. Both *The Eagle* and *The Globe*, a colored weekly newspaper, reported the team's exploits. *The Globe* published highlights inserted in society columns, submitted by small-town reporters. They followed the standard format: "From the second inning the superiority of the home team was obvious. The strangers [Alpines] grew excited as the tide turned against them, so that they played worse than their natural form." Neither newspaper supported a habitat that nourished and circulated stock racist baseball images of the Brooklyn Alpines.[29]

The same observation cannot be made for New York City, where baseball accounts that appeared in *The Tribune*, *The Herald*, and *The Times* interwove "negro" dialect and blackface minstrelsy throughout baseball narratives. When the Alpines and Remsens played for the Colored Championship of Brooklyn in 1884, *The Times* engaged the players in "negro" dialect: "There has long been a bitter rivalry between the two nines, and, as one of them remarked as he entered the field 'We'll settle de question right heah.'" Another narrative linked the colored baseballist to the minstrel mask: "[T]he short stop ... stood there with his eyes as big as saucers holding on to the ball like grim death and watching the man run in from third base and scoring his run." Similarly, *The Herald* lampooned the rivalry in a literary style that would have been familiar to middle-class readers: "The Alpines were clad in gray shirts, blue trousers and polka dot stockings, while their opponents wore gray suits and blue stockings. The burly legs of Batum, the captain of the Remsens, trembled with emotion as his men strode into the field chock full of watermelon and hope." When we finally reach the heart of this narrative, we learn that the sportswriter has dramatized the entire event with crudely familiar stereotypical imagery: "Jupiter [the Remsen's catcher] put a wire mousetrap over his face and stood behind the first man at the bat, making his palms meet and part like alligator's jaws. The third ball hit the mousetrap and made his eyes wink. Then one of the Alpines was caught out and Jupiter wagged his head and see-sawed his shoulders."[30]

Baseball blackface adopted the oversized clothes minstrel performers typically wore, and their enormous shoes, which had an infantilizing effect that arrested the figure of black people in the early stages of childhood development. According to Eric Lott, "The effect perhaps explains the regularity with which observers resorted to the word 'fun' to describe their enjoyment of blacks and of blackface acts, which congruent with repeated returns to the minstrel show, may suggest ... 'the child's peculiar pleasure in constant repetition' that is the wellspring of jokes." Blackface literature, according to Lott's critique, shows that "the white male affection for blacks, [self-degradation], and infantile pleasure were conjoined by way of an imaginary racial Other." This lent itself to a widespread preoccupation in minstrel acts with oral and genital amusement. On the minstrel stage, some blackface performers shared a superstition regarding makeup of the mouth, whether painted red or left a sharp, unpainted circle of white around the lips; if this bit was badly managed, it was bad luck to take the stage: fat lips, gaping mouths, and shiny rows of teeth mattered. This "mystic or tabooed air" not only clung to blackface evocations of blackness on the minstrel stage, but it was also transferred to certain depictions of the colored baseballist on the green diamond.[31]

Such images become more pronounced when viewed as cultural allegories, conspicuous symbols of the historical forces surrounding their production and consumption. In 1883, the *Register* stages the contest of the Black Stockings vs. Rockford Reds as a cake-walk. The title transforms triumphant ballplayers into champion cake-walkers, a black cultural practice that evolved from the experiences of enslaved Africans in the United States. While the story's headline alluded to the Cake-Walk, the event linked triumphant colored ball players to victorious cake-walkers. Baseballs and cakes became interchangeable, consumable objects: "The darkies gobbled everything that took the air; no matter how wildly it flew, they 'got there Eli!' every time, and while apparently taking things easy, they were for all of that handsomely punishing the home nine." The *Globe-Democrat* illuminates: "The St. Louis Black Stockings started on an extended tour last night. They will make mince meat of the colored clubs throughout the country." Clearly, both baseball and cake-walking have something to do with leisure as consumption. They also relate to economic and social consumption: black legs gobbling up wage labor reserved, hypothetically, for white men.[32]

Donning minstrelsy's comedic mask, some sportswriters linked muffs or misplays to toothy white grins. In one narrative, the manager of the Rockford colored nine, Ben Franklin Davis, expressed rage at his team's poor performance. The sportswriter noted Davis's "double row of shining ivories" that "would make a dentist's heart ache with longing and envy." Emphasis on the black man's supposedly large lips and mouth was not new. From minstrelsy's beginnings, white performers used cosmetics to mimic huge mouths, an important part of the physical stereotype that set blacks apart from whites. Following one performance of the Georgia Minstrels in 1868, a reporter wrote: "[T]he idea of exaggeration in the delineation of African characteristics, becomes an absurdity. Mouths opening wide enough to expose the bare feet, and inimitable grins and grimaces that place their peculiar style beyond the pale of successful Caucasian competition." Billy Kersands had performed with the Callender Minstrels and successfully organized his own minstrel trope. His antics astounded the-

Figure 45. Billy Kersands, 1880s

ater spectators, in 1883, critics raved at his facial contortions and unusually large mouth (**fig. 45**). It was central to the act. Having filled his mouth with billiard balls, he performed a slick, soft shoe rendition of Stephen Foster's "Suwannee River." The correlation between large mouths, colored ballplayers, and the Cake-Walk not only related to the comedic acts of the colored ballplayer, but also fantasies about cannibalism. The fear was economic and social as well, for the colored baseballist swallowed up profits reserved for white players.[33]

Following slavery, the continuity of race as an organizing principle in the newly instituted economy of the post–Civil War era consolidated a system of social stratification. As Howard Winant notes, the economic and political "order of things" required revision and repair. Winant argues that "a lot of this work would be cultural production: the formulation of new ideas and images, new representations and interpretations, even new intellectual disciplines." In the 1870s and 1890s, the postbellum Gilded Age triumph of industrial capitalism and the economic crises — in particular, the professional sporting business — found artistic expression in the print media. *Harper's Blackville* series, Currier and Ives' *Darktown Comics*, and other illustrated periodicals effectively spread negative stereotypical ideas about the colored baseballist across the country. *Harper's Weekly*, Currier and Ives, and other print houses made it possible to preside over the death of the model — the colored baseballist — and to bring other visual-verbal images into the world. The comedic figure of the racial Other thrived in mass-produced illustrated periodicals and chromolithographic prints. "Laughing at black people amounts to a national pastime," writes Rae Beth Gordon, "and it defuses the threat represented by black virility."[34]

"Playing in the Dark": Solomon Eytinge's Baseball at Blackville

In 1883, Bridgewater's Black Stockings took the baseball sporting world by storm: "[The] colored team that has been placed in the field by Henry Bridgewater is composed of strictly first-class players." *The Chronicle*, however, called them "Bridgewater's blackfaced team," identifying them with minstrelsy's comic mask. *The Police Gazette* seized an opportunity to ridicule the "Blacks." One column notes: "The champion moke club of St. Louis, the Black Stockings, contemplate a trip to Ohio, and are anxious to know if there are any coon clubs in that state who have sufficient nerve to tackle them." Another column reports: "The Black Socks of St. Louis, the champion 'coon' club of the west, visited Cleveland ... and knocked out the Blue Stocking 'nigs' of that city." These narratives displaced the colored champions to an imagined baseball wilderness.[35]

While this wilderness conjured spaces reserved for colored communities, the colored sporting fraternity did not occupy an imaginary world. These black bodies were flesh and blood entities, struggling against marginalization. Following the Civil War and beyond, the color line exposed predominately socially segregated living conditions. In towns and cities, segregated residential patterns sprang up systematically, blocking black access to white middle-class neighborhoods. Social exclusion accelerated the emergence or growth of distinct districts and areas derided by the epithets Stagg Town, Buck Town, Darktown, Niggertown, and Blackville.[36]

According to historian Alexander Saxton, blackface minstrelsy signaled the national-

BASEBALL AT BLACKVILLE—THE "WHITE STOCKINGS" AGAINST THE "BLACK LEGS"—FIRST BLOOD FOR THE "BLACK LEGS."—[Drawn by S.A. Eytinge, Jun.]

Figure 46. Baseball at Blackville, Solomon Eytinge, Jr., *Harper's Weekly*, 1874

ization of North American theater. *Harper's* illustrator Solomon Eytinge, Jr., found inspiration in this theatrical practice. In 1874, Eytinge created the *Blackville*, which appropriated minstrelsy's visual and verbal protocols, that is, its comic mask: Negroid physical features and "negro" dialect. *Blackville* imagined a black leisure class, segregated and living along the social margins. Between 1874 and 1885, *Harper's* circulated a staggering number of Eytinge's illustrations, lampooning the Blackville family, recently emancipated following the Civil War, and its twin daughters.[37]

Solomon Eytinge's *Baseball at Blackville—The White Stockings Against the Black Legs— First Blood for the Black Legs* depicts a segregated sporting event where two colored clubs cross bats before colored spectators (**fig. 46**). Dominating the center of the composition is the White Stockings' slugger who, taking a pitch to the face, manages to hold on to his black bat. His capped head tilts backward, clearly unprepared for the smashing blow to nose and mouth. To his right squats a fat, dumpy catcher, who, with both hands cupped, braces to catch a ball that never reaches its mark. Another player stands to the left, his upper torso tilting backward, his right hand pointing upward. Perhaps he recognizes the wayward pitch, or maybe he gestures to the mishap. The pitcher's splayed arms and legs brace for what won't happen: the bat making contact with the ball. White Stockings and Black Legs players dominate the foreground, the latter lolling about in various positions, transfixed by the scene.

Baseball at Blackville is the equivalent of that other color line, late 19th century burnt cork baseball. Linked to an era of violence, disenfranchisement, and accommodation, this period of baseball history separates the burnt cork counterfeit from baseball baron Albert

Goodwill Spalding's "different color business" or "fifteenth amendment club slingers." It lays bare the synthesis of black baseball representations and modernism in the United States.[38]

Within the rectangular composition, three figures — two seated (to the left and right) and one standing in the bleacher seats — create a triangular arrangement. On the left, a player looks skyward, extending his left arm upward; to the far right, a seated player looks upward as well, raising his right arm. Other figures buttress this configuration. To the left, a player also points skyward, while another player, seated on the ground, reinforces this gesture. Occupying the middle ground, the catcher's gaze reinforces the diagonal set up by his seated teammate's tilted head. Bleacher spectators form a capstone. The standing male figure waving the handkerchief or hat serves as the apex.

The baseball grounds resemble a wide-open wilderness. No enclosed grandstand restrains the crowd, adding to the circus-like atmosphere. Men dominate the bleachers, and a mounted man on a horse watches the action. Standing or sitting spectators, fashionably attired, congregate on a grassy hill. A little boy clings to an older girl in a bonnet; a man stands behind a woman holding a parasol; a couple stands behind them; another pair rests on the knoll.

Extravagantly dressed dandies, dandizettes, and ballplayers freely intermingle. They have distinct functions: a little boy clings to an older girl in a bonnet; a man stands behind a woman holding a parasol; another couple stands behind them; the last couple, reposing on the grass, includes a woman holding a parasol. Others, more men than women, sit in the sparsely filled bleachers. It is doubtful the squat center fielder can shag fly balls or screaming line drives in either direction. Nothing restrains the spectators from interfering with the game, adding to the carnivalesque atmosphere. The mounted fan poses danger as well. Should his horse be spooked, it will trample the crowd near the bleachers. The danger for the spectators is as real for the players in this vast baseball grounds that resemble a wide-open wilderness.

Baseball at Blackville situates baseball's color line between the viewer and the image's two-dimensional surface. Functioning like minstrel show end-men, the backsides of standing and reclining players frame the truncated ground plane which doubles as a stage, and the tilted grounds, a canvas backdrop. *Baseball at Blackville* is not simply an opportunity to indulge in untroubled contemplation or ribald humor. Rather, it represents the locus of historical, political, and social practices that signify symbolic violence against the colored ballplayer.

Eytinge's *Blackville* debuted on the theatrical stage in 1883, and colored musicians were the performers. Samuel Hyers, a veteran manager, commissioned a four-act operetta called *Blackville Twins: Or Scenes on the Suwannee River*. It starred his daughters, the Hyers Sisters. Over the next fifteen years, Callender's Minstrels and other colored performers incorporated *Blackville* sketches into their acts. *The Chicago Conservator*, a colored newspaper, makes clear the connection between the theatrical sketches and Eytinge's characters: "The play is based upon the set of illustrations appearing in *Harper's Weekly* called 'The Blackville Twins.'"[39]

"Darktown Comics": *Thomas Worth's Champions of the Ball Racket*

Thomas Worth's *Champions of the Ball Racket* (1886), a lithograph for Currier and Ives's *Darktown Comics*, gives full expression to these doings on the diamond (**fig. 47**). The

THE CHAMPIONS OF THE BALL RACKET.
On the Diamond Field

Figure 47. Darktown: The Champions of the Ball Racket: On the Diamond Field, Thomas Worth, *Currier and Ives*, 1885

tilted ground plane compresses the diamond, revealing a baseball field that practically covers the horizon. It gives a full view of the participants costumed in bright and dark tones and patterns. The defensive club wears polka dots and dark stockings. The offensive team sports two-toned jockey caps and striped stockings. Both wear long-sleeved, button-down shirts and knee breeches. The pitcher, who dominates the middle ground, clutches an oversized white ball with his right hand, seemingly cradling the sphere with his left hand — the twirler's delivery hangs in the balance. Crouching, shoulders hunched and knees bent, the pitcher's gesture parodies scientific play.

Two players to the right of the pitcher cast similar poses, emphasizing the latter's overattentiveness. Bulging eyes practically pop out of their heads, and their puckering lips look like donut holes, offering perfect receptacles for the baseball. Distorted facial features, coupled with animated gestures — most with open hands and bent knees — characterize the entire squad.

These buffoonish figures display neither scientific skill nor style. For example, no defensive player challenges the base runner's move towards second base. However, the distance between first and second base hardly merits the base stealer's dismay — given the twirler's inattentiveness — yet the runner's bulging eyes and upraised hands suggest surrender. The catcher occupies an odd position behind the right-handed batter: equally careless, he stands on the wrong side of home plate. The catcher's mask offers his head little protection. This is not the only welcoming target. The defensive team's polka dot shirts conjure bull's eyes. Resembling the baseball, they too, subject the players' bodies to the batter's swing. Moreover, the polka dots on the light ground mimic bulging eyes, a metaphor that evokes both abject fear and ribald humor: the player's inability to catch the ball. Witnessing the bewildering spectacle with relative wonderment, three players in striped stockings frame the foreground. This trio, elevated above the fray, relaxes in various states of repose.

Within this rectangular composition, the third baseman, catcher, and right fielder establish a triangular grouping. On the left, a diagonal extends from the first base line to the batter. On the right, the diagonal follows the pitcher and shortstop, terminating at the third baseman. Crouching, kneeling, and reclining figures frame the bottom of this visual pyramid. *Champions of the Ball Racket* recalls *Baseball at Blackville*. An obvious figure is the bareheaded player; Worth's figure is prone, its head craning skyward. Eytinge's figure kneels; its head juts between sloping shoulders. It recalls, in a restricted sense, the iconic figure of the kneeling slave. Given the hypothetical viewer's elevated position above them, the figures giving structure to the base of the pyramid find debasement on the green diamond. *Champions of the Ball Racket* argues, quite simply, baseball does not belong to colored men.

Another image, Worth's *A Foul Tip* (1882) helped to secure, to paraphrase Lott, colored baseballists another "public hearing," with the country's rediscovery of organized colored baseball in 1882, following, no pun intended, its cultural blackout in the late 1870s (**fig. 48**). In 1882, the *New York Clipper* and *Sporting Life* followed the exploits of players

A FOUL TIP.

Figure 48. Darktown: A Foul Tip, Thomas Worth, *Currier and Ives*, 1882

like John "Bud" Fowler, and ball clubs like the Philadelphia Orions, the New Orleans Pickwicks, and the St. Louis Black Stockings; both St. Louis and New Orleans, the *New York Clipper* noted, had colored leagues. Baseball minstrelsy attained wide popularity, and minstrel show performers transformed the blackface ballplayer's "clowning" into a lucrative comedic act. Yet, the idea of early black baseball images had multiple meanings, offered economic possibilities, and measured success in terms of conspicuous consumption. But the public desire for the authentic — the real thing — also allowed black baseball entrepreneurs to pursue and own authorial voice within the highly commodified sports medium by seizing, when possible, the means of production.

A Foul Tip depicts black figures on the green diamond. It is a chaotic scene: on the right side of the baseball field, near the first base line, the central action depicts four uniformed men confronting the umpire. Heavily profiled, the figures mimic low relief sculpture. Standing atop a barrel, the umpire looks down at the disgruntled players. Looking upward, the men extend their fists toward him. To their left, four players engage in a side argument. To their right, two fights have broken out, and the players roll about on the field. A clump of spectators loll about on the grassy knoll. Separated by large empty spaces in a stage-like area, the figures are shown head-on. They emphasize the composition's geometry: the triangular arrangement is anchored at the base by the shoes of the ballplayers on the left; on the right, it is the corner of the tilted barrel. The extended players' arms (left and right), their striped knee breeches and blouses, the bent posture of the umpire, along with his striped high collar shirt and striped pants, form right angles; the apex is the tip of the umpire's head. The angularity of the players' shadows, the rhythmic arrangement of legs and arms, and the right-side of the baseball diamond help direct the viewer's eye toward the fists directed at the umpire's head.

A Foul Tip recalls Jacques-Louis David's *The Oath of the Horatii* (1784), a neoclassical painting that extolled the antique virtues of stoicism, masculinity, and patriotism. The painting depicts the Roman Horatii, male triplets destined to wage war against the Curiatti, also male triplets. Wholly supported by their father, the three Horatii brothers express their loyalty and solidarity with Rome before the battle. Although the manly associations linked to this work have nothing to do with sports, nor with ballplayers unaffected by the athletic competition, Thorstein Veblen imagined sporting events as highly-masculine affairs that transformed successful acts of aggression into make-believe wars.

Nothing is secure on the baseball grounds. What distinguishes *A Foul Tip* from other black baseball illustrations/cartoons, at least up to this period, is its hyper-instability and threat of further violence. The image captures a tension-filled moment before the free-for-all. The barrel upon which the umpire stands will turn over. One of the ballplayers will hit him; note the player to the far left who rolls his sleeve, the smallest player holding the ball in his left hand, and the two bats begging to be picked up.

The baseballists give the impression of being anatomically unfit. Not athletic men, they undermine physical dignity. Scrawny bodies, thin and wiry, are supported by bandy-legs. The figures in the background on the left possess heads that are too big for their bodies. There is no attempt at realism here. The ballplayers delight the viewer with "blackness" as spectacle, a sort of minstrelsy that turns crude counterfeits into coarse, clumsy, brute-like bodies.

Willing to display their physical prowess both against opponents and umpire out of manly duty, four players anticipate winning the colored championship. (This work's likely successor was Worth's *The Champions of the Ball Racket: At the Close of the Season.*) The bodies of angry combatants, with their resolute gaze and taut, outstretched limbs, mock both stoicism and masculinity. Thomas Worth would not have become famous without *Darktown Comics.* The symbolic violence he portrays is not the literal violence against post-bellum blacks, nor is it even the violence such an artist might subjectively feel within himself; rather, it is the violence done to the figural representations of the colored baseballists just to make a mass-produced lithograph desirable. Indeed, this desire for lithographic representations that lampooned middle-class free blacks belongs to an artistic tradition that dates back to the late 1820s and, coincidentally, parallels the birth of blackface minstrelsy. "More than two hundred Darktown lithographs were produced," writes art historian Michael D. Harris, "and most of them were issued in pairs showing black attempts at middle-class activities with absurd outcomes or failures." Perhaps the satisfaction of lampooning the colored baseballist was the satisfaction of being personally recognized and confirmed as the author of the *Darktown Comics.*[40]

"*Come in 'Yah.*

Figure 49. "Come in 'Yah," *The Republic* (St. Louis), 1888

The House of Currier and Ives was not the only establishment to depict the black image of the colored baseballist as a comedic figure with a gaping orifice, seemingly ready to gobble up and swallow anything. In the late 1880s, *The Republic* of St. Louis began to integrate visual images into baseball narratives. And when the New Orleans Pinchbacks, who claimed to be the colored champions of the country in 1888, crossed bats with the West Ends at Sportsman's Park, the newspaper had its cartoonist supply the story with cartoons. The unknown artist appropriated minstrelsy's comic mask to portray the colored baseballist as comical coacher: a wide-mouthed blackfaced figure (**fig. 49**). From the beginning of minstrelsy, blackface performers had smeared their lower faces with white or red cosmetics to give the impression they had huge mouths, an important part of the physical stereotype that set blacks apart from whites. Cartoonists did not need cosmetics to emphasis exaggeration; they went straight for pencil and pen, which permitted an exaggeration of Negroid physical features that, in a crucial way, preceded the sort of surrealistic visual imagery of animated moving pictures. The elasticity of rubbery lips recalls cartoons where lips are pulled over one's entire face. The same artist employed a similar style in producing political cartoons that mocked colored Republicans (**figs. 50, 51**).

Six Votes for Sherman, Sah!

Figure 50. "Six Votes for Sherman, Sah!" *The Republic* (St. Louis), 1888

SATURDAY MORNING, AUGUST 18, 1888.

COLORED BROTHER, Addressing Mr. Harrison—"Mr. Harrison, I'se a delegation what's come to find out how many offices you'se gwine to give the negro in case you'se elected?"
GENERAL HARRISON—"It is not the habit of Republicans to regard the nigger in the light of an office-holder, but as a voter. You do the voting and the white men will fill the offices."

Figure 51. Untitled, *The Republic* (St. Louis), 1888

"Pretty Playing" or "Looking Good": Black Aesthetic Style

Hooley's Minstrels intersected mirthful baseball narratives of early colored contests: "The dusky contestants enjoyed the game hugely, and to use a common phrase, they 'did the thing genteely.' Dinah, all eyes, was there to applaud, and the game passed off most satisfactorily. All appeared to have a very jolly time, and the little pickaninnies laughed with the rest." One approach to baseball sportswriting was to appropriate literary forms of blackface, narrating colored contests as minstrel performances, complete with comedic antics, and infused with the protocols of the blackface mask. But in such narratives — literary appropriations of blackness — colored players and symbolic figurations of blackness are markers for "the dramatic polarity created by skin color, the projection of the not me."[41]

The theatrics of the Brown Stockings baseball club are instructive. In 1886, Dave Foutz and members of Henry Bridgewater's Black Stocking set a wager. If Foutz lost the bet, the star pitcher agreed to sport a bowler and black tights on the green diamond. Foutz's antics, his surrogate blacklegs, put him on full blast. *The Sporting News* jibed: "If Dave comes out on the diamond with a plug hat on his head he had better get a mask for it, because the crowd could not resist the temptation to block for him." Foutz's blacking up could not have been lost on the sporting fraternity. Its vaudevillian performance permitted theatrical antics without the loss of major league status which proved inaccessible to Bridgewater's team. His teammate, Walter A. Latham, approved: the "nineteenth-century clown prince of baseball" would do anything for laughs. Latham was famous for his comedy in the coach's box and taunting rivals while amusing the crowd with his antics — his aesthetic style undoubtedly derived inspiration from colored players. As the recipient of the farcical put-down, Foutz's performance marked him as the seeming counterfeit and exposed affiliations with the "negro" minstrel business. But, then again, neither Foutz's nor Latham's on-field antics marked the beginning of baseball minstrelsy.[42]

One of the earliest examples of "negro" dialect vernacular in baseball sportswriting appears in 1882, when the black Philadelphia Orions crossed bats with the New York Metropolitans (white professionals). *The New York Times* derided the Orion pitcher, George Williams, as one of the game's most laughable features: he performed with "the air of a veteran." Before delivering the ball, Williams calmly surveyed the field, and in every instance, in the writer's opinion, found one of the fielders out of position. He raised his hand and in a clear voice called out to the player who was out of position: "Lay in a few more feet for dis yere man." As sure as Williams cautioned the left fielder, the batsman knocked the ball to the right field, which was the signal for an uproar by the spectators, who heartily applauded Williams for his display of good judgment. Perhaps the author's "mirthful spectacle" misrepresented the pitcher's aesthetic style, or perhaps he misinterpreted Williams's scientific understanding of the game.[43]

Some historians claim that the Cuban Giants of New York invented "negro" baseball comedy, a mix of comic pantomime and monkeyshines. According Roi Ottley and William J. Weatherby, the Trenton Cuban Giants engaged in comic pantomime and "monkeyshines" that made spectators roar with delight. The white entrepreneur and promoter John F. Lang was probably involved. One reporter called Lang the barber who had "temporarily deserted lather and razor," but he was more than a tonsorial artist. Coming from Philadelphia, where minstrelsy thrived, Lang exploited its lucrative possibilities. From 1880 to 1883, he managed the Philadelphia Orions and Manhattans of Washington, D.C., both colored nines. In 1883, he probably also introduced the Dolly Vardens of Philadelphia, the first professional women's ball club (they were also colored). Lang also financed a Chinese nine in New York. In 1886-87, he co-managed the Cuban Giants with Stanislau K. Govern, a colored baseballist and thespian. Govern served as field manager and public relations man for the colored aggregation. While Lomax links Govern to the production of the Cuban Giants' vaudevillian style, other possibilities exist. But if any team deserves credit for the innovation of "negro" baseball comedy, that dubious distinction should perhaps go to the Black Stockings. And it properly belongs, then, to baseball minstrelsy's prehistory; that is, before the Cuban Giants.[44]

But the circus atmosphere surrounding baseball may not be the deepest reason for my discomfort with "negro" comedy. Did colored players consider comical coaching a form of minstrelsy? Why did sportswriters link the boss yeller to minstrelsy's image-repertoire? Did literary and visual artists "guy" black baseball representations? While such queries demand ongoing research, my anxiety has reasons internal to image production. Sportswriters, I

A FOUL TIP.

Figure 52. A Foul Tip, Moses L. Tucker, *The Freeman* (Indianapolis), 1890

believe, donned minstrelsy's comic mask to "guy" colored ballplayers and black baseball representations. Of course, they understood the linkages between scientific play and theatricality; the sporting fraternity called it "pretty playing" or simply "looking good." But did this baseball vernacular give permission to misrepresent or misinterpret black aesthetic style? I say yes.

Moses L. Tucker's *A Foul Tip* could be viewed as a guying scene (**fig. 52**). The dude/chicken joke depicts the baseball landscape as an enclosed structure, fenced-in grounds meant to distance players from the non-paying crowd. Two colored ballplayers search for a baseball, while a rooster eyes the entire scene. The fence covers the length of the image and separates the players. The figure at the top of the planked enclosure recalls the "Kilroy Was Here" image. The stiff right arm balances his body along the top, while the left arm rests uneasily against the fence. Standing outside the grounds, the figure extends both hands outward in exasperation. His wide-legged stance mimics his splayed arms. He cannot find the baseball. The rooster's erect body, tilted head, and puffed-up neck convey a confidence lacking in the ballplayer. A thicket camouflages the baseball. Even though the triangular arrangement of figures — players and rooster — locks the ball within the viewer's sights, these players seem more interested in the fowl. They dress like ballplayers. Both sport the black and white striped, jockey-styled baseball caps. The foreground figure's long-sleeved broad-collared shirt, dark knickers, and high ankle white boots round out the dude's apparel. He appears athletic enough. His wiry upper body contrasts with his thickly muscled black legs encased in black stockings.

Hanging on the fence is "Mr. Humpa," who queries: "Whars de ball?" His teammate, "Mr. Snip," replies, "It's no use, you mouts well call de game. It's gone, don't you see dat chicken?" The rooster's swelled breast triggers to crow. Its enlarged throat, full, feathery, and round mimics the ball. In Tucker's cartoon, baseball dudes buy the absurd notion that the fowl can swallow a baseball whole.

As Mitchell has elaborated, animals are figures in scenes of visual exchange. The rooster has an almost magical relation with both the baseball dudes and the viewer. The rooster can see what we see (the dark vegetation casts an aura around the baseball); it looks us in the eye across a gulf unbridged by language, confirming what we see. The doubling pun "Foul Tip" says it all. Power has been ascribed to the rooster, but never coincides with it. Its secrets are addressed to us. The rooster defiantly faces off the baseball dude, and its sartorial dandyism is as much in evidence as that of the ballplayer. Both tilt their heads; both have angular profiles; both sport headdresses (the rooster's black cone and the ballplayer's cap); its taut wiry legs and the ballplayer's muscled calves; and its black plumage compares with the baseball uniform in making a showy display. Note the player's claw-like fingers pressed against the fence and the rooster's feet. This moment (to paraphrase Mitchell) provides a double revelation and reassurance — that human representations are true, accurate, and natural (the rooster agrees and comprehends them on its own accord), and that human power over others is secured by mastery of representations (the rooster is forced to agree, not of its own accord, but automatically).

Foul Tip belongs to the "Golden Age of American illustration," a postbellum era that witnessed the proliferation of mass-illustrated periodicals, aspiring artists searching for their place in the world of high art, new artistic techniques and styles, and modern subject matter. While Tucker's drawings translated well to the printed page, this lets neither him nor the viewer off the hook. *Foul Tip* guys both players with stereotypical Negroid features (broad noses, tumid lips, dark skin, and so on). Some colored journalists condemned Tucker's work as detrimental to the race. Harry C. Smith, editor of *The Gazette*, declared: "The illustrations would be fine for a journal printed in the South by some white man who desired to ridicule the race." *Kansas City American Citizen* editor and proprietor C.H.J. Taylor condemned Cooper: "If you have nothing else for your Mr. Tucker to do except to caricature your newspaper brethren, had you not better send him back to Georgia?" Others disagreed: "Mr. Cooper's drawings, illustrating African life and character, are refined and bespeak a high degree of genius on the part of the artist and enterprise in the person of the publisher." *Foul Tip*, it might be inferred, offered the sporting crowd an equally appealing, if not comedic, visual product.[45]

Cooper was unrepentant: "While we are averse to 'poking fun' at the Negro, still there are many traits and characteristics which will bear criticism, and which should be eliminated. This phase of the race problem will receive more attention hereafter and Mr. Tucker's gifted pen will do a share of it." Born in Atlanta, Georgia, Tucker developed his craft at the Atlanta Engraving Company, *The Georgia Cracker*, and many other periodicals. His cartoons recall crude black images that circulated widely in mainstream newspapers, magazines, journals, and advertisements. *Foul Tip's* baseball scene (the wood-planked wall secured with nail rivets, foliage and scattered rocks invoking the theatricality of a bucolic backdrop), complete with garish costumes, exaggerated Negroid features, and "negro" dialect restage the visual and verbal protocols of blackface performance.[46]

What realities exist for "negro" baseball comedy? One reality is "comical coaching," which seems to have paralleled minstrelsy's "Ethiopian dialect business." And the baseball performance of "negro" dialect recalls the verbal protocols of black minstrelsy. The coach or "boss yeller" would shout at or "guy" other players throughout the entire game. He'd give the umpire gratuitous advice as to the performance of his duties, and take special care that fans heard everything.[47]

In 1883, William Davis, the Black Stockings star pitcher, offered an intriguing performance: "the coaching of Davis was a big hit. He yelled himself hoarse, in a fog-like voice warning his men of impending danger or urging them to run the bases. 'Fo' God, you dar, you ain't runnin' a little bit! Steal dat yar base d'yer hear?'" The narration's literary style recalls Mark Twain's *The Adventures of Huckleberry Finn*. And Davis's performance was astounding: snappy antebellum "negro" dialect coupled with postbellum baseball vernacular. It had an effect because it took away any and all of the opponent's chances. But Davis was no countrified darkey: having attended Oberlin College, he belonged to the mulatto elite.[48]

Davis's performance conjured the image of a "kicker" or complainer. Others, amused by his theatrics, urged colored players to adopt the cultural practice. Such theatrics were misrepresented, if not misunderstood. Sportswriters misrepresented black aesthetic style as a novelty, but for the performers, it was not. In the 1870s and early 1880s, many critics found it impossible to believe that colored ball clubs not only played the game but played it exceptionally well. Baseball performance, then, provided public opportunities for displays of manly strength, aesthetic form, and social status. The boss yeller's ability to use words, for instance, compared favorably to displays of manly strength. Historically, black men had associated verbal contests or signifying to manliness. Being figuratively dismembered before one's friends had immense potential repercussions because of the terror of disapproval, of being proven ineffectual and therefore effeminate in the eyes of peers.[49]

The colored sporting fraternity admired the boss yeller, and his ability to use words compared favorably to displays of manly strength. For folklore anthropologist Roger D. Abrahams, such displays conferred social status. Abrahams observed:

> The verbal contests are especially important because they are indulged in by the very ones who are most conscious of their appearance of manliness. Being bested in a verbal battle in front of a group of men has immense potential repercussions because of the terror of disapproval, of being proved ineffectual and therefore effeminate in the eyes of peers.

Rather than simply view the figure of the colored ballplayer as an object that was worked over, transformed, reinvented, and re-presented, I maintain that this figure contained its own sense of the body as an objet d'art. In 1870, Lewis E. Meacham covered the Blue Stockings-Pink Stockings contest. While Meacham compared their performance to other well-played games, the sportswriter reported "one peculiarity": "It consisted in an irresistible propensity, for tumbling head over heels when in the act of running bases or going for fly catches. Sombersaults, which would have permanently doubled up and disabled a White Stocking [player], were counted as nothing by they of the colored hose, and resulted in much amusement among the spectators. Whether this practice was accidental or usual," Meacham added, "We don't know."[50]

Theatrical display or black aesthetic style found expression in St. Louis. The *Post-Dispatch* reported that the Black Stockings "played a peculiar but strong game." What did peculiar mean? During a Black Stockings contest, *The Globe-Democrat* described "numerous performances of a more or less ludicrous character." The figure of Isaac Carter, the team's star infielder, captured the reporter's attention, a mirth-provoking spectacle that convulsed the crowd with laughter.

> [Carter] was not quiet for a moment, but divided his attention between casting furtive glances at the pitcher and tapping the home plate with his bat. His motions were nervous, peculiar and indescribable. Bobbing up and down like a jerky jack-in-the box, he lost no opportunity to drum the plate. First it was one rap, then one, two, then straighten up for an instant and repeat. This performance was continuous while he occupied the bats-man's position, and was only interrupted when the pitcher delivered a ball, which was invariably struck. That it excited the risibilities of even the most cynical need scarcely be stated.

While the reporter identified two other incidents that were "superlatively" funny, it seemed clear, at least to him, that the spectators indulged in "successive ripples of merriment from the opening to the closing of the game."[51]

Carter's "nervous, peculiar and indescribable" motions conjured something entirely new: black aesthetic style. Cultural critic Rae Beth Gordon shows how colored entertainers capitalized on the fascination with new aesthetic forms. According to Gordon, in the 1870s Parisian music halls, café-concerts and the circus witnessed the coalescing of three spectacular attractions — hysteria, epilepsy, and black dance: meditative displays of the body in movement. Audiences marveled at the similarities between the hysterical body's uncontrollable epileptic contortions and the perceived excesses of agitated movement in black dance. Situating this convergence squarely in the last quarter of the 19th century, the cabaret aesthetic embodied jerky rhythms and movements that defined popular song and performance style in the period. Performers modeled their style on tics, grimaces, contortions, convulsive movements, epileptic seizures, and hysterics. Contorted corporeal poses, comical grimaces, and unabashed sexuality figured prominently in lyrics, movement, and dress. Heightening this theatrical display, some performers adopted the clown's pointy hairstyle, the same hairstyle worn by blackface performers in Paris. Others, particularly women, incorporated the distorted mouth into their performances.[52]

Carter's "bobbing up-and-down like a jerky jack-in-the box" and continuous drumming of home plate perhaps conjured the image of shaking and convulsing that 19th century science had attributed to clownism. Yet Carter was no clown; his style had method, and his ability to strategically place the baseball demonstrated technical proficiency. Some sports accounts described this display as nervousness and fear, others as a mirth-provoking spectacle. Such accounts often glossed over or downplayed technical proficiency and baseball strategy.[53]

Team uniforms fit into the equation of "pretty playing" or simply "looking good" by transforming ballplayers into aesthetic objects. Uniforms projected national unity among baseball sports. Distinctive colors, insignia, and other details signified a public fealty to locality and sublimation of individualism. They fashioned a sartorial dandyism that valorized self-containment, restraint, and description. Sartorial dandyism enhanced serious artistic and historical interests. Baseball uniforms conceivably borrowed certain theatrical effects from the historically correct costumes of Shakespearean plays, from 18th century paintings by Peter Lely or Joshua Reynolds, and from the works of Pre-Raphaelite artists and their derivative fashions. Cultural historian Talia Schaffer shows how motifs helped "fashion aestheticism by aestheticizing fashion," which in turn, transformed sporting life into a therapeutic space where colored ballplayers could heal contemporary social alienation and cultural marginalization.[54]

Baseball's quest for the aesthetic life exemplified explorations of creative subjectivity through visual formula and an accompanying self-conscious performance. In short, there was no limit to how colored ballplayers fashioned aesthetics nor how they aestheticized fashion. The Blue Stockings of Chicago, for instance, coupled their "peculiar" brand of play with their natty uniforms. They wore "a very tasty uniform, consisting of cap of broad blue and white stripes, blue shirt with a neat monogram on the breast, white flannel pants, blue stockings and regulation shoes." Their colored opponents' rig consisted of blue caps, white flannel shirt and pants, and pink stockings. Distinctive colors, insignia, and details signified a public fealty to locality and sublimation of player individualism.[55]

Baseball uniforms, not unlike military uniforms, projected the national unity of baseball sportsmen. On the green diamond, Bridgewater's Black Stockings were expected to display the efficiency and espirit de corps of military units. They allowed aggregations to distance themselves from the appearance of poverty. The "Blacks" showed themselves in good style: natty uniforms that included blue caps, white flannel jackets and trousers, red belts, and black stockings. What Blanchard calls the sense of the created self as aesthetic

Figure 53. Darktown: A Base Hit, Thomas Worth, *Currier and Ives*, 1882

object—the breaking of the boundary between person and thing—was confined to neither men nor women.[56]

When the New Orleans Pinchbacks traveled to St. Louis, to play the West Ends in 1888, they used uniforms to help project their personal identity. Designed by Frank B. Sylvester, the uniforms captured media attention: navy blue knickers, white striped caps, and white shirts with a large "P" embroidered on the right breast. *The Pelican* noted their handsome appearance in brand new uniforms, but the white sporting press derided them: "Next to a watermelon and a coon hunt, a negro likes a ball game, and they go at it with such zeal that even a policeman is compelled to stay awake." The headline read: "The Great 'Coon' Game."[57]

Like Tucker's *Foul Tip*, Thomas Worth's *A Base Hit* (1882) clearly delights in blackness as spectacle, a delight that, in the postbellum period, combines fear of and fascination with the presumably "black" male cast of clowning baseballists (**fig. 53**). In the foreground, three ballists charge an innocent bystander who has been struck in the belly by an errant a ball. Physically, the players would tower over the dwarfish spectator. Dressed in the garish baseball uniforms of the period, the tumbling and stumbling figures frame the startled well-dressed dandy in a swallow-tail coat, blouse with ruffled cuffs, and striped pants, losing his top hat. Compositionally, the vertical and horizontal rendering of the broad-striped uniforms mimics their outstretched bodies and the urgency of their physical gestures. The ballplayer in the striped bandana runs out of a shoe that has no laces, revealing a tattered stocking and exposing both heal and toes. The grinning base runner, also framed by the contorted fielders, turns second base en route to third. In the distance, on the right, another fielder dispassionately watches with folded arms. In the background, to the right, the pitcher's outstretched arms plea for the relay that never comes. Other players loll about in repose, watching the action but disinterested in the game. No figure flails his arms or jumps up and down. The umpire (a gentleman in top hat) and other players standing near home plate, calmly watch the odd turn of events.

Clearly, the composition's circus-like atmosphere inspires a certain terror as well as great affection.[58] Within this double context, the cartoon's true object and title bear consideration. According to the Cambridge Dictionary, the adjectival reference "base" means "dishonorable or immoral; of inferior quality or value; debased; or counterfeit." As previously discussed, the colored sporting man attained notoriety in the 1870s and 1880s. This figure was linked to the underworld and, in certain cases, to white women. As Eric Lott reminds us, the minstrel stage hypersexualized the black dandy, sometimes called "Long Tail Blue." A famous song, "Long Tail Blue" (1827) links sexual power to "Uncle Sam"—the coat of the black dandy—and exposes antebellum fears of racial miscegenation. Given Worth's postbellum incarnation, Lott's analysis is illuminating: "Bold swagger, irrepressible desire, sheer bodily display: in a real sense the minstrel man was the penis, that organ returning in a variety of contexts, at times ludicrous, at others rather less so." Worth takes on two phallic emblems—the umbrella and swallow tail coat—rendering their potential threat impotent, at least temporarily. The figure's comicality attempts to conceal that swagger: not only is the black dandy nattily dressed, but well-fed as well. Yet the stunted figure's potency is rendered impotent by the colliding dark ball. In short, its "base" character has taken a metaphorical hit.[59]

The story of baseball minstrelsy goes beyond masquerades of theatricality and deception. By remapping the baseball landscape and black images of self-definition and achievement within it, one learns something about performance and the black body as object d'art. Like other representations, questions of modernity and aesthetic life frame the entire period — the rise of the new self-stylized male in the 1870s and 1880s, the sporting fraternity, and its iconic images.

CHAPTER SIX

Genuine Colored Artists:
Black Legs, Black Stockings, and
Colored Baseball, 1877–1888

A game between the [St. Louis] Black Sox and the Callender's Minstrel nine will take
will take place to-morrow at Sportsman's Park.[1]

The life of the stereotype resides in the death of its model, and the perceptual deadening of those who carry it in their heads as a schematic search template for identifying other people.[2]

The "coons" of Coonville [Black Stockings, of St. Louis] have got a great nine, and
they say they have beaten everything in the country but the "Niggers" of Niggerdom,
and "Mokes" from Moketown.[3]

When the athletically inclined members of Charles Callender Minstrels challenged Henry Bridgewater's Black Stockings
Base Ball Club of St. Louis in 1884, they,
like other theatrical entertainers, wanted to
display their manly prowess (**fig. 54**). *The
Missouri Republican* reports: "They have
been eager to tackle some local club since
coming to town, and Henry Bridgewater has
arranged to accept their [call]." Having
begun an engagement at Pope's Theater
before packed galleries and a parquette filled
almost to the standing room only limit, these
"genuine colored artists" who required no
cork to give color to the bones and tam-
bourine men gave a performance which had
seldom been excelled in St. Louis. Ranging

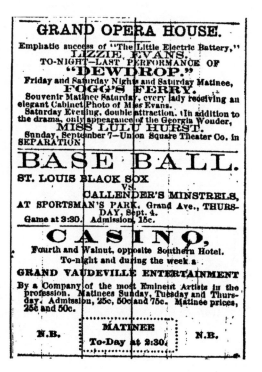

Figure 54. BASE BALL, *The Globe-Democrat*
(St. Louis), 1884

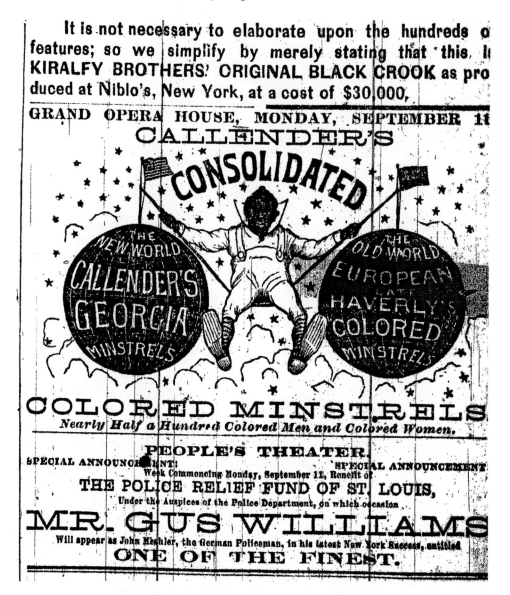

It is not necessary to elaborate upon the hundreds o
features; so we simplify by merely stating that this, l
KIRALFY BROTHERS' ORIGINAL BLACK CROOK as pro
duced at Niblo's, New York, at a cost of $30,000.

GRAND OPERA HOUSE, MONDAY, SEPTEMBER 1t
CALLENDER'S
CONSOLIDATED

THE NEW WORLD CALLENDER'S GEORGIA MINSTRELS

THE OLD WORLD, EUROPEAN LATE HAVERLY'S COLORED MINSTRELS

COLORED MINSTRELS
Nearly Half a Hundred Colored Men and Colored Women.

PEOPLE'S THEATER.
SPECIAL ANNOUNCEMENT: SPECIAL ANNOUNCEMENT
Week Commencing Monday, September 11, Benefit of
THE POLICE RELIEF FUND OF ST. LOUIS,
Under the Auspices of the Police Department, on which occasion
MR. GUS WILLIAMS
Will appear as John Mishler, the German Policeman, in his latest New York Success, entitled
ONE OF THE FINEST.

Figure 55. Callender's Consolidated Colored Minstrels, *The Globe-Democrat* (St. Louis), 1884

in hue from light cream down to dark brown, Billy Kersands, Wallace King, G. W. Hawkins, Billy Green, and others kept the audience in a constant state of good humor, the laughter at times waxing hilarious. *The Globe-Democrat* summarizes: "The Callenders are genuine darkies, and are the pick of the profession. Their singing almost invariably brings encores, and the jokes are fresh and good" **(fig. 55)**.[4]

Bridgewater's Black Stockings represented genuine colored artists as well. These high-skilled professional entertainers took the sporting world by storm in 1883 and embodied the direction that baseball barons had taken the National Pastime. Baseball accounts often misrepresented their performances on the green diamond as blackface farce, comparing them with the comedic antics of blackface minstrelsy. The *Evening Chronicle*, for instance,

called the champion colored nine "Bridgewater's Black Stockings and blackfaced team," identifying them with minstrelsy's comic mask. Yet certain sporting accounts recognized the
club's "scientific play" and its systematic strategies that took advantage of the opponent's
weaknesses. *The Globe-Democrat* observes: "[The] colored team that has been placed in the
field by Henry Bridgewater is composed of strictly first-class players." Both the Callender
Minstrels and the Black Stockings represented the colored sporting fraternity, and both
organizations embodied exemplary images of high-skilled entertainment.[5]

Was blackness a metaphor for the social excesses of the postbellum Gilded Age — or
for the cultural expressivity of the American Aesthetic Movement (1877–1887)? For U.S.
citizens in the aftermath of the Civil War, illustrated magazines, sporting journals, and
newspapers took on the spectacle of highly celebrated, if not sometimes notorious, "black"
figures. The victory of the North over the South did not eliminate the need for strong masculine figures, but it did expose the rise of the new self-stylized black male in the 1870s and
1880s. These figures exploded onto the sporting culture scene, their gendered representations being simultaneously "highbrow" and "popular"— manifested in the art world on the
one hand, and in the sporting world on the other. In general, they permitted both men and
women to sort out their personal and social identities. In particular, they incorporated the
language and visual vocabulary of black legs and black stockings into theatrical spectacles
that transformed members into celebrities. Black legs and black stockings embodied style,
what Mary Warner Blanchard calls form, expression, and modes of action and living. Clearly,
figures of blackness — real and imagined — invoked social undercurrents of the era, and they
helped link the aesthetic movement to the sporting world.[6]

Genuine Colored Artists is a story about images, the life of the colored sporting fraternity. This story, in particular, traces the lives of the Black Stockings and Callender's Minstrels through the late 19th sports medium, a complex social institution that contained not
only newspapers, sporting and theatrical journals, advertisements, cartoons and illustrations, and lithographs, but also the individuals within it, a history of practices, rituals,
habits, skills, and techniques, plus a set of material objects and spaces. As the epigraphs
suggest, racial stereotypes provide a "schematic search template" for representing colored
professional entertainers. Borrowing this apt phrase from Mitchell, I want to link blackface minstrelsy to an image-repertoire that circulated across certain media, a stockpile of
racist images of the colored sporting fraternity. While Mitchell declares blackface minstrelsy's image-repertoire to be despicable and worthy of destruction, he laments that negative racial stereotypes seem to have a life of their own. If the life of colored sporting
fraternity images resides in the death of its models, then who, in Mitchell's words, does the
image killing and image-resurrecting?[7]

"[T]he desire to don, occupy, or possess blackness or the black body as a sentimental
source and/or locus of excess enjoyment," writes literary critic Saidiya V. Hartman, "is
founded upon and enabled by the material relations of chattel slavery." For Hartman, the
fungibility of the black body, specifically its abstractness and immateriality, enabled the
blackface mask to serve as a vehicle of self exploration, renunciation, and enjoyment. Perhaps the most dramatic and colorful case of minstrelsy's comic mask is to be found in late
19th century baseball representations. The life of black sporting fraternity images has been
the subject recent scholarship — most recently important works by Michael Hatt, Michael
D. Harris, and Brian F. Le Beau — which explores visual and verbal images that absorbed

stock darkey characters or low comedy types, which were appropriated to portray genuine colored artists.[8]

What is the relation of black legs and black stockings to aesthetic style? Black legs and black stockings represent fetishistic objects, surrogate forms of blackness that helped fashion postbellum Gilded Age bodies as public spectacle. When Oscar Wilde toured North America in 1882, the Apostle of the Aesthetic Movement often encased his muscular, white legs in black silk stockings. Being the bad boy of the aesthetic movement, Wilde's theatrical effect — "black legs" — intensified certain perceptions about sensuality, humor, and corruption. Sporting journals and newspapers could not get enough of him. They mocked and obsessed over Wilde, and some readers even modeled his aesthetic image. For many critics, Oscar Wilde's aesthetic style contrasted sharply with his manly form. Yet the sporting men of St. Louis wore fashionable black silks, and those Republicans among them, linked to political corruption, would be dubbed the silk stockings. Women also wore black silks, which were expensive during the 1870s and 1880s. While one finds silk stockings associated with the aesthetics of artistic expression, they implicated women wearers with theater performers, prostitutes, and other dubious characters of the demimonde. Baseball vernacular makes clear the relation between black stockings and the body, as well. In the late 1870s, sportswriters alternately called the Black Stockings the black legs. And of course, minstrel performers, particularly burnt cork ballplayers, understood the humor embedded in blacking up not only face and hands, but other bodily appendages when necessary, to convey the aesthetics of blackness.

The monikers Black Legs and Black Stockings had multiple effects (stockings and legs were interchangeable terms). The notorious term "Blacklegs" meant professional gambler. When open gambling threatened the newly formed Southern League, for instance, *The New York Times* reminded baseballists that blacklegs had nearly killed the National League in 1877. And perhaps because Henry Bridgewater had built his wealth and political clout, in part, on gambling, the press eyed his team's nickname with suspicion. *The Globe-Democrat* laments: "The colored champions of the United States, who call themselves the Black Stockings ... deserve a better name." There was also minstrelsy's comedic mask. In 1875, Hooley's minstrels of Chicago organized a ball club called the Black Stockings. *Sporting Life* found blackface humor as well: "[T]he Black Stockings Club, a colored organization, of St. Louis, it is intimated, wear flesh colored stockings, or in other words, no hose at all." Yet the name promoted respectability and social uplift for the colored sporting fraternity, and for that reason, several colored clubs adopted the moniker.[9]

Rather than simply view the black sporting crowd as a domain where stereotypical images were worked over, transformed, reinvented, and re-presented, this domain also contains a sense of the body as an objet d'art. My search begins with Henry Bridgewater's Saloon. It was a base of operations for the Republican Party's "Colored Silk Stockings," prosperous colored men who created civic projects, hosted gala events, and plotted elections. In 1884 William Dye, Bill Curtis, Charles H. Tyler, and Bridgewater — all prominent members of the western sporting fraternity — sponsored a grand benefit for Sam Lucas, the "great Negro comedian and vocalist." Literary, dramatic, and musical talent, volunteering their services, lionized Lucas, who also had performed with Callender's Minstrels. The spectacle of this cultural icon's natty attire and collection of diamonds transformed him into an objet d'art.[10]

The St. Louis colored sporting fraternity frames Arna Bontemps's novel *God Sends Sunday* (1930). Bontemps, a black writer of the Harlem Renaissance (1917–1939), depicted a colorful male breed ornamented in embroidered shirts with knuckle-length sleeves, diamonds, and polished finger nails, box car coats, shoes with mirrors on the toes, high roller hats, and jewelry made from gold coins. James Weldon Johnson's *Black Manhattan* (1903), which also circulated during the period, identifies sports who claimed recognition through horse racing, baseball, boxing, and theater. Johnson's narrative finds sports in professional clubs, where notables of the ring, turf, diamond, and stage drew admiring crowds. They built a cult of celebrity that shared colorful images of rural and urban life, ethnocentrism, mass entertainment, and mass consumption. While agreeing with both Bontemps's and Johnson's works, I would add the relation of black style to ideas of masculinity in the 1870s and 1880s.

Historian Karen Sotiropoulos provides insight into how leisure culture may have permitted Bridgewater to build a cultural and intellectual base that nurtured young colored men and could uplift the race. In the early 20th century, social and residential segregation made it possible for New York's colored performers to establish a vibrant cultural network, providing opportunities to study the musical and theatrical talent. This world was called "Black Broadway" and "Black Bohemia," which included Ike Hines Tavern, an establishment frequented by the Cuban Giants and Callender Minstrels. Its guild-like image redefined the life of the colored community, making it possible — even stylish and respectable — to participate in America's burgeoning, if segregated, public culture.[11]

Finally, historian Wilson Jeremiah Moses referred to this provocative period of black life as "The Lost World of the New Negro." This rarely understood era, Moses asserts, emphasizes how black intellectual and literary centers developed and flourished between 1895 and 1925. Moses explains: "In the post–Reconstruction era [the term New Negro] referred to new spirit of confidence and assertiveness among recently freed masses of black southerners." This New Negro was a composite of different types that embraced more tough-minded traditions, including an awareness of black social conditions that were largely informed by the apocalyptic and moral struggles of the Civil War and Reconstruction. *Genuine Colored Artists* links the colored sporting fraternity to this rarely understood cultural milieu.[12]

Between the 1870s and 1890s, baseball representations also included the Chinese and women. These literary images are burlesque — that is, blackface images that marked the print media's fascination with female and Chinese baseballists. This segment examines how representations of "negro" dialect vernacular and minstrelsy informed other imagined baseball novelties.

The sports medium addressed baseball forms that engaged in a dialogue with baseball forms from the past. The new forms bear the multiple traces of the old forms among which they take their place. They also migrate back and forth between the singular object associated with the habitat of high art and the habitat of the mass-produced copy. There is something appealing, even redeeming, about the concept of the sports medium functioning as a place or space in which baseball forms thrive, because it addresses the black image in its native habitats. These habitats can be viewed as baseball landscapes that have the advantage of being picturesque. But why should we look upon certain black images and find their projections of social alienation beautiful? Why should we look upon the black ballplayer as if this iconic image is a badge of honor?[13]

These questions are, of course, exactly the challenges baseball representations force on us when mediating between mass-culture and high art objects; the latter engaged in the depiction of ballplayers as formal studies filled with grace, dignity, and presence — *Base Ball Player's Practicing* and *Base-Ball Vase* immediately come to mind. These works catch white ballplayers in moments of abstraction, perhaps deep thought or reverie, but certainly unaware of being seen. These works show that baseball was not confined to mass-produced images (photographs, photographically derived illustrations, woodcuts, trading cards, toys, and so on), but the sport also found visual expression in the work of painters, sculptors, and ceramicists. These works point to the significance of high art as a sports medium.[14]

Colored Baseball's Raging, Tearing, Booming Late 19th Century

As a principal exponent of the western sporting fraternity, Henry Bridgewater's image conjured prizefighting, pedestrianism (professional walking), horse racing, billiards, cycling, baseball, and gambling. His saloon entertained the era's sporting celebrities of color: pugilists Harry "Black Diamond" Woodson and Peter Jackson; the jockey Isaac Murphy; the pedestrian Frank H. Hart; the baseballist John "Bud" Fowler; and Callender musicians Billy Kersands and Sam Lucas.[15]

In the late 1800s, *The Police Gazette*, owned by Richard Fox, began publishing portrait sketches of the colored sporting fraternity, including photographs and brief biographies. Fox made the photographs available for purchase. It was sports marketing genius.[16] In the 1880s, John Woods photographed Frank Hart and Harry Woodson, both associated with Bridgewater's Black Stockings (**figs. 56, 57**). Yet portrait sketches of Bridgewater's Black Stockings remained conspicuously absent.

For Bridgewater, sporting coverage mattered because it provided a material means for circulating images of the Black Stockings' exploits. He built local relationships with the

Figure 56. Frank Hart, *National Police Gazette*, 1880s

Advance and *Tribune*, both colored newspapers, and *The Globe-Democrat*. In 1883, he served as the latter's special correspondent. Bridgewater telegraphed results throughout the country. Stylistically, his dispatches from the field belonged to the new journalism that emerged in the late nineteenth century. During this period, new ideas in representation developed, new concepts of makeup and headlines were evolving, and an infusion of new vitality was given to baseball coverage. They resonated with what Mark Twain called baseball's "outward and visible expression of the drive, and push, and rush and struggle of the raging, tearing, booming nineteenth century."[17]

The Globe's publisher, Joseph Burbridge McCullagh, has been credited with originating the word "boom," and his riverboat vernacular intensified the Black Stockings' exploits: "The Colored Champions," "The Black Stockings' Tour," "The Black Sox at Rockford," and "The Tour of the Black Socks" are exemplary. This graphic realism situated sports fans in the thick of the action: "Henry Bridgewater, manager of the St. Louis Black Stockings, telegraphed from Rockford last night that his club lost by a score of 15 to 3. [William] Davis, the pitcher, broke his finger and did not play. This leaves the nine crippled."[18]

Knowledge of history and tradition, critical insight, humor, and intimate human interest angles transformed unpretentious, if not mundane, baseball narratives into an ornate literary form: sports writing. Sports writing infused baseball narratives with jargon, puns, and exaggeration. Traditional narratives provided inning-by-inning or play-by-play accounts. The text was clean, and the adjectives few. These word pictures captured every ball struck, every ball missed, caught, and dropped. Another narrative style appropriated blackface, describing ball games as minstrel performances, complete with comedic antics, and the protocols of the blackface mask (black skin, "negro" dialect, bulging eyes, thick lips and toothy grins). Fact and fiction blurred, suggesting social collusion between sportswriters and the sporting fraternity.[19]

My examination of black sporting images begins with animals. As

Figure 57. Harry Black "Diamond" Woodson, *National Police Gazette,* **1880s**

baseball forms, animals function within a polarized logic, vacillating between virility and mischievousness. The centrality of animals to certain black sporting images is deeply linked with motives of domination, enslavement, and violence. At a minimum, such images convey the dominion of humanity over nature, figured in the animal-versus-human; at a maximum, the dominion of one human over another, expressed by the figure "man-as-animal." As Mitchell has argued, animals stand for all forms of social otherness: race, class, and gender are frequently figured in images of subhuman brutishness, bestial appetite, and mechanical servility.[20]

Roosters often traversed the boundary between baseball and blackface entertainment (**fig. 58**). By 1877, the Callender Minstrels' Bob Mack had incorporated them into his act, masquerading as a Shanghai rooster. Crowds howled at the fight parody of a monstrous cock and a real bantam rooster named "Little Dick." Bob Mack's search for authentic black comedy demonstrated how difficult it could be to represent genuine colored artists or black cultural authenticity without somehow resurrecting negative racial stereotypes. The rooster also embodied virility in baseball's high-skilled labor-intensive entertainment industry. In 1888, for example, the New York Giants installed a New Orleans game cock at the Polo Grounds as a mascot. While the Black Stockings do not appear to have been labeled roosters or cocks, some baseball narratives dubbed Bridgewater's colored nine "Blackbirds," and "mokes," and "coons."[21]

In 1883, sportswriters derided Bridgewater's club so frequently that "coon" became what Eric Lott calls a figuration of commodity, a sort of trademark assigned to the black

SOME GAME CHICKENS.

Figure 58. Some Game Chickens, Moses L. Tucker, *The* (Indianapolis) *Freeman*, 1891

images white people paid to see. While Karen Sotiropoulos makes it clear that a "coon" song craze elevated the use of the word as a mainstay of popular language, its late-nineteenth-century offstage usage to deride blacks might have begun as early as 1862. By 1880, for instance, the Callender Minstrels had performed James E. Stewart's *Mary's Gone with a Coon*, a forerunner of the coon song phenomenon that dominated the repertoire of colored and white minstrels. During the same time period, Sam Lucas wrote and composed "De Coon Dat had de Razor."[22]

Animal motifs traveled back and forth between high art and mass culture. Taboo and ritual often surrounded their appropriation and display. For example, sporting men imbued stag horns with "magical powers" and "aura." In 1877 Augustus Solari, owner of the Grand Avenue Base Ball Park in St. Louis, presented the local colored champions with a set of elk horns. Solari's gesture linked baseball to marital themes, transforming stag horns into decorative ornament. Nor was it unusual to hear colored men called bucks, an antebellum metaphor for black male slaves. Transforming black bodies into aesthetic objects took different twists. One journalist, for instance, identified a colored spectator: "A good sized buck who ornamented the pavilion." As totem animals of modernity, stags introduced colored sports to modern political life and civic responsibility. In 1882 the "Stags," a formidable colored organization, of independent tendencies, brokered political deals. Social satirist Thorstein Veblen noted, "Tangible evidences of prowess — trophies — find a place in men's habits and thoughts as an essential feature of the paraphernalia of life."[23]

The Callender Minstrels engaged in some image-killing and image-resurrecting of their own. What animal images did they resurrect? What animal images did they attempt to kill? One answer is the ape. For post–Reconstruction era critics of civil rights, the trope of the ape as the black man unmasked offered an uncanny figure of humanity motivated by lust and primal desire. It also invoked oppression, racial unrest, and sexual anxiety. When Comus-Pickwick of New Orleans commissioned Charles Briton to design Mardi Gras' *The Missing Links to Darwin's Origin of the Species* in 1872, the carnival artist caricatured Louisiana's first black governor, Pickney Benton Stewart Pinchback (the same Pinchback for whom the New Orleans ball club was named after), as the lord of all creation: a banjo-playing, Negroid-looking gorilla. Briton's work might have been inspired by Paul B. Chaillu's *Explorations and Adventures in Equatorial Africa* and *Stories in Gorilla Country* (1869). This would not be its first or last resurrection, as Edgar Rice Burroughs's *Tarzan of the Apes* (1912) and the films *King Kong* (1933) and *Planet of the Apes* (1968, 2001) have shown.

Callender's Minstrels hardly embraced the mimesis of "monkey-see monkey-do." They had evolved from the Georgia Minstrels: the word "Georgia" in the name of the minstrel troupe became a generic code of "Black" and "ex-slave." In 1828, the white minstrel performer Thomas D. Rice appropriated this image, darkening his skin with burnt cork, dancing, and singing a song called "Jim Crow." By the 1850s, the Jim Crow character had become a standard part of the minstrel show. Moreover, Callender's Georgia Minstrels differed from white minstrels in another way. They did not smear their faces with burnt cork: "It is generally known that none of this company are under the necessity of coloring their faces for a negro minstrel performance in character. They have the genuine color upon which these warm nights have no effect."[24]

By the 1860s, according to music historian Jacqui Malone, white minstrels attempted to counteract the threat of colored soldiers in the Union army by portraying them as incompetent, comically unable to perform the simplest maneuver or to obey the most elementary command. Callender's Minstrels developed and introduced a mock-military skit called the "Ginger Blues," based on a white variety house act that featured authentic black social and marching club steppers who took great pride in themselves, their uniforms, and their performances. Billy Kersands played the lead role.[25]

But cultural traces of the performative linkages between the Georgia Minstrels or Georgia Callender Minstrels, and the military-styled performers of St. Louis belong to the early 1870s. In 1868, the Missouri state legislature passed the Militia Act, which disbanded existing independent units and established an organized militia under state control. Many units of colored militia men formed in compliance with the act, including the Attuck Blues in 1871. Dress uniforms were extravagant in an attempt to outdo pre–Civil war outfits and to make a good appearance on the parade ground: "The picnic of the Attuck Blues, at Concordia Park, to-day, is an event in the minds of the colored citizens. The Blues will appear in uniform, and ample arrangements have been made for a good time." The men were required to buy their own uniforms, maintain their state-issued equipment and arms, and purchase their own camp and garrison equipment, tents, practice ammunition, flags, and instruction books. In other words, they financed their own armories. They drilled as often as three nights each week, with no pay. As previously mentioned, several colored baseballists belonged to the Attuck Blues.[26]

The Attuck Blues performed sham battles and military drills before enthusiastic crowds throughout the city. In October 1874 *The Times* wrote: "[The Attuck Blues], preceded by the Continental band, and accompanied by the Capital City guards, a colored zouave company from Springfield, Ill., paraded through the streets of the city.... The guards were handsomely dressed in their uniform of swallow tail blue coats and blue pants, were well drilled and made a creditable appearance." Their performances were highly competitive, stylish, and unique.[27]

White militias refused to compete against the Attucks Blues, but this did not stop white organizations from using blackface minstrelsy to mock them and other genuine colored artists. In 1884, the McCullough Minstrels performed at the Pickwick theatre in St. Louis. The troupe recruited a white militia and the drum corps of the National Guard to play the role of the Attuck Guards in a burlesque called "The Attic Guard Picnic." They also mocked Postlewaite's Band, a colored musical organization. Critics derided the performance as the worst the club had ever appeared in: "Whatever else the members of the McCullough club may be, God never seems to have intended them for negro minstrels."[28]

Baseball Comedy: "Antiquated Old Fakes of the Burnt Cork Era"

Callender's Minstrels pursued baseball opportunities as well. Headquartered on the east coast, they had several role models. From the mid–1870s to the mid–1880s, the troupe toured cities throughout the country that had established colored aggregations: the Alpines, West Ends, and Orions figured among eastern clubs; the Blue Stockings and Uniques played in Chicago; and the Blue Stockings, Black Stockings, Sunsets, and White Stockings represented powerhouses in St. Louis. Another St. Louis connection to the Callender's Consolidated Colored Minstrels was Johnnie Woodson, styled "the greatest living clog dancer," black or white. In 1882, the 18-year-old Woodson performed with many of the great colored entertainers of the period: Billy Kersands, Wallace King, Billy Banks, Bob Mack, Dick Little, and Virginia Armstrong. As early as 1880, Woodson performed on the stage, and the 1880 census report lists his occupation as "minstrel." According to the *Republican*: "A few ago he was a street gamin locally renowned for his ability on toe and heel—a 'talent' that then came to the notice of the manager of the colored minstrels and secured him his present engagement."[29]

In 1881, the Frohman brothers (Gustave and Charles) purchased the Callender Minstrels. Ornamenting their sets and costumes, the Frohman's transformed the group into the most lavishly produced black troupe in the world. Gustave Frohman had managed colored minstrel companies for many years. In his view, many colored entertainers possessed "eminent talent and ability." Since many colored performers had few chances to display their talent, Frohman determined to afford them as many opportunities as he possibly could. The Frohman brothers became so successful that they purchased John H. Haverly's black troupe and merged it with theirs in 1882.[30]

As with professional baseball, theatrical companies moved toward large-scale enterprise and the elimination and absorption of smaller companies. The Frohman brothers acquired the Charles Callender's Georgia Minstrels through a coup. Countering a "mutiny" with his organization, Callender entered into a five-year agreement with the Frohman's. The "mammoth minstrel project," managed by Callender, consisted of three troupes: Callender's Consolidated Colored Minstrels, Callender's Colored Minstrels, and Callender's New Colored Minstrels. Callender boasted: "the greater demand by the public for a higher class and grade of minstrel performance have prompted [him] to elevate the character of minstrelsy to a rank never before attained either by its white or its black exponents, and that the efforts in past of the genuine colored artists, who are, after all, the original exponents of native plantation minstrelsy have been accepted by the better class of the amusement public as belonging to the legitimate field of minstrelsy."[31]

There was no limit to how genuine colored artists fashioned aesthetics, and no limit to how they aestheticized fashion. Perhaps the new self-styled male embodied exchanges between colored sports, exchanges that found expression on the green diamond and on the theatrical stage. Charles Williams, Al Smith, George Freeman, Lewis Brown, C. Waters, Burel Hawkins, P. Adams, Girard and Wolf—Callender's baseball club—reinforced the sporting fraternity's manly image, proving themselves "Bohemians of the first water," whether waltzing, making a decided "mash," or making inroads on glasses of foaming lager. They also displayed military efficiency and espirit de corps—Brown, Girard and Hawkins performed with Callender's Black Zouaves. These men belonged to a cosmopolitan world where performance could invoke high art. Callender's troupe had both comedic and Shakespearean artists, and their programs often included "unusual songs" with a distinctly European character. One critic figured them as sculpted objects, "Minstrels in Bronze." If modernism demanded an elite, refined, purified objet d'art, Callender's Minstrels served as "the original in black," a vanguard that defied duplication. This curious melding of aesthetic contemplation and popular consumption embodies what Walter Benjamin termed "the destruction of the aura" endemic to modernism.[32]

Some historians (including myself) express discomfort with minstrelsy, especially its links to colored baseball. Baseball historian Phil Dixon argues that tradition marks colored baseball as vaudevillian. According to Dixon's view, colored players had opposed clowning. Yet, curiously, early twentieth century writers praised the Cuban Giants' invention of "negro" baseball comedy. Sol White and James Weldon Johnson supported this view. Having played for the Cuban Giants, White's book offers a first-hand account. Johnson's story relies on secondary sources.[33]

Although Michael Lomax correctly links actor and manager S. K. Govern to the production of the Cuban Giant's vaudevillian style, other possibilities exist. John F. Lang managed several colored nines, including the Cuban Giants. Coming from Philadelphia, where blackface minstrelsy thrived, Lang understood and exploited the burnt cork icon's lucrative possibilities. But if any team deserves credit for introducing "negro" baseball comedy, that dubious distinction goes to the Black Stockings.[34]

One form of "negro" baseball comedy was comical coaching, which recalls what theater writers dubbed as minstrelsy's "Ethiopian dialect business." Representations of comical coaching seem to counterfeit black minstrelsy. The coach or "boss yeller" (as he was called) "guys" every play — good or bad — with shouting. He gives the umpire gratuitous advice as to the performance of his duties, and takes special care that fans hear everything.

The mobility of such black images is a symptom, of course, of their indispensible role in baseball minstrelsy. In everything from "pretty playing" to simply "looking good," black images of the colored baseballist acquired forms of surplus value and excess vitality. This would be the point where, Mitchell might argue, the lives of images intersect with the love of images, which the animation of the icon is called forth by desire, attraction, need, and longing. Some sports journalists, for example, confused William Davis's style with chronic complaining or "kicking," while others urged more colored clubs to adopt this cultural practice. Sportswriters, in my view, often misrepresented black performance on the green diamond.

But the circus atmosphere surrounding colored baseball may not be the deepest reason for my discomfort with "negro" baseball comedy. My anxiety has reasons internal to image production. Did genuine colored artists consider comical coaching minstrelsy? Who melded the boss yeller to minstrelsy's image-repertoire? Did the literary and visual artists simply "guy" black baseball representations? To answer these questions, guying bears further discussion. The colored sport admired the boss yeller. His ability to use words well compared favorably to displays of manly strength. For the folklore anthropologist Roger D. Abrahams, such displays conferred social status. Abrahams observed:

> The verbal contests are especially important because they are indulged in by the very ones who are most conscious of their appearance of manliness. Being bested in a verbal battle in front of a group of men has immense potential repercussions because of the terror of disapproval, of being proved ineffectual and therefore effeminate in the eyes of peers.[35]

In 1883, *The Police Gazette* seized an opportunity to ridicule the Black Stockings. On 12 May, one column notes: "The champion moke club of St. Louis, the Black Stockings, contemplate a trip to Ohio, and are anxious to know if there are any coon clubs in that state who have sufficient nerve to tackle them." On 2 June, another column reports: "The

Black Socks of St. Louis, the champion 'coon' club of the west, visited Cleveland ... and knocked out the Blue Stocking 'nigs' of that city." These narratives displaced the colored champions to an imagined baseball wilderness.[36]

While this wilderness conjured spaces reserved for colored communities, the black sporting fraternity did not occupy an imaginary world. These black bodies were flesh and blood entities, struggling against marginalization. Following the Civil War and beyond, the color line exposed predominately socially segregated living conditions. In towns and cities, segregated residential patterns sprang up systematically, blocking black access to white middle-class neighborhoods. Social exclusion accelerated the emergence or growth of distinct districts and areas derided by the epithets Stagg Town, Buck Town, Darktown, Niggertown, and Blackville.[37]

Links between racial segregation and baseball were not lost on literary and visual artists. As promoter for the Red Stockings B.B.C. of St. Louis, the sports editor William Spink exploited the color line: wedging burnt cork nines between colored and white clubs. While the Red Stockings refused to play colored teams, Spink swayed manager Frank McNeary to rent his park grounds to them. Colored baseball struggled to escape the ideological underpinnings that sought to fix its meaning. Critics called their events novelties, in contrast to burnt cork contests, but others read them differently, stressing how first-rate colored players displayed professional style. While sportswriters thought the Black Stockings played a peculiar but very strong game, they acknowledge that opponents would have to perform their best against them to win. Others viewed them as a strong colored nine, composed of "festive Africs." If burnt corkers engaged in image-killing by casting doubt on genuine colored artists, they also engaged in image-resurrecting by reminding spectators that the baseball racket went beyond mere novelty. One question, then, asks whether the death of the model, as a means of attaining or maintaining social status, is really a language of warfare, or a means of re-appropriating conspicuous leisure.[38]

"Colored Troops": Bridgewater's Black Stockings as Stylized Celebrities

The military metaphor was evident in the rise of competitive team sports in the 1870s and 1880s. Thorstein Veblen exposed how sports embodied a means of attaining or maintaining social status. Through skilled imitation, all sports represented the cunning and chicanery of hostile combat. Sports vernacular appropriated the language of warfare, and this slang provided evidence that athletic events were substantially make-believe. Veblen wrote: "The addition to sports, therefore, in a peculiar degree marks an arrested development in man's moral nature." The true reason for the popularity of sport was its usefulness as a means of displaying conspicuous leisure.[39]

The new self-stylized male was in dialectical relation to a more persistent and visible ideal — the man as soldier. William Frederick Cody, alias Buffalo Bill, proved exemplary. Cody received this sobriquet after killing 4,280 buffalo for the Kansas Pacific Railroad in one season. He served as a scout for the United States Army. In the 1870s, Buffalo Bill created the Wild West Circus, becoming North America's biggest theater sensation in 1882. The show blurred the line between bloody carnage and comedic farce. Wearing a black velvet suit slashed with scarlet and trimmed with silver buttons and lace, Buffalo Bill's aesthetic image projected the soldier as stylized celebrity.[40]

Military vernacular also penetrated baseball representations, enhancing the ballplayer's sartorial display. Several accounts call Bridgewater's team "colored troops." Calling ballplayers "troops" was not unusual. Sportswriters borrowed the terminology from the Civil War, tailoring military terms and phrase in new ways: "To-morrow the Grand Avenues and the Black Stockings will play at Sportsman's Park. The colored troops upon this occasion are expected to turn out in force." Bridgewater's aggregation represented high-skilled professionals who, to paraphrase Veblen, contested the rival team's pluck in a substantially make-believe war.[41]

Baseball narratives situated the colored nine within an ongoing conquest drama that began on the baseball diamond. As metaphor, the diamond conjured a wealth of untapped human labor. Mining the exploits of colored clubs, including Bridgewater's Black Stockings, sports editors freely appropriated this slang: "Diamonds," "little diamond," "green diamond," "on the diamond," "diamond field," "black diamond," "diamond chips," "diamonds in the rough," "doings on the diamond,' "diamond sparks," "diamond dust," "dust from many diamonds," "diamond drift," "diamond jottings," and "a glance over the diamond fields across the continent." The metaphor's popularity coincided with the accelerated growth of South Africa's diamond mining industry in 1880. British entrepreneur Cecil John Rhodes co-founded the DeBeers Mining Company, which once controlled ninety percent of the world's diamonds. Success earned Rhodes an audience before Parliament, where he advocated using military force to secure cheap African labor. Sportswriters collapsed distinctions between blacks in the United States and South Africa. For example, *The Sporting News* writes: "The African diamonds are not the grounds of a colored baseball club."[42]

On the green diamond, Bridgewater's aggregation was expected to display the efficiency and espirit de corps of a military unit. Baseball uniforms, not unlike military uniforms, projected the national unity of baseball sportsmen. Distinctive colors, insignia, and details signified unity but also allowed organizations to distance themselves from the appearance of poverty. The Black Stockings showed themselves in good style by wearing natty uniforms that included blue caps, white flannel-jackets and trousers, red belts, and black stockings.[43]

As an objet d'art, the figure of the colored ballplayer claimed a dual function: fashioning the aesthetic of the colored dandy and aestheticizing fashion in the service of racial uplift. In 1883 the *National Tribune*, a colored weekly newspaper published by James W. Wilson, wrote the following about Bridgewater's Black Stockings: "It is a fact that there never has been, before this season, an organized, fully equipped base ball club, composed of negro men, put upon the road in regular semi-professional style."[44]

Oscar Wilde's Black Stockings and the Aesthetics of Black Legs

In 1882, *The Police Gazette* published a story called *Oscar Wilde's Legs*. It begins with a scene on a midnight train from New York to Philadelphia: a commotion awakens the journal's "religious editor." Peering through the curtain of his sleeping car, he notices move-

Figure 59. How Oscar Fooled the Boys, *National Police Gazette,* **1882**

ment in the opposite quarters. Through an opening emerges a long, black leg encircled by a jeweled garter (**fig. 59**). Out comes another leg, equally shapely, encased in a black silk stocking; it, too, is ornamented. Both limbs flutter and swing carelessly from the upper berth, thoroughly arousing him. What is attached to these legs? Some piquant beauty of the ballet, some tragic queen, Mary Anderson, Helena Modjeska or Lillian Langtry, the editor muses. The climax is enough to knock over any religious editor. The curtains open. An uncouth, long, lank, lean, and ghastly young man — yawning and stretching — stands in the aisle. The legs belong to Oscar Wilde. The editor has a sickening sensation. Recounting the awful revulsion, he seeks reassurance from other staff writers that they would have done the same thing. No takers. They conclude that the editor got sold pretty bad on Oscar's legs. And all his talk is "a dead giveaway."[45]

Oscar Wilde's Legs unveils the gendered ambivalence of black stockings. It transforms the neat leg encased in a long black silk into a multi-stable image that requires more than one name, more than one identity. Nesting within the image are both male and female. But the author remains hopeful: perhaps, it conceals woman's leg; preferably, an actress. Sadly, it belongs to "a ghastly young man." Despite perceptions of femininity and masculinity, revulsion of feeling and moral gruff, the black leg's upper body remains invisible, blurry, and unintelligible.

Eric Lott's critique of the minstrel role of blackface transvestites "acting the wench" is instructive. According to Lott, the immense popularity of cross-dressing in the blackface theater featured among other outrageous antics, "much show of leg." In the 1840s, performers such as Barney Williams and George Christy had popularized the "wench" role. At Hooley's Opera House, for instance, the "female business" of the Ebony Ballet Troupe secured a run of six weeks to good crowds. This form of male burlesque sought to maintain control over women, which witnessed a reorganization of gender roles in and out of the home. Ill-paid, irregular, or nonexistent work made husbands ineffectual breadwinners, weakening cherished patterns of patriarchal control, while wage work offered women new means of self-support. Certain masculinist traditions loosened: young women flaunted a new-found sense of power by way of stylistic excesses that paralleled the male sporting fraternity.[46]

Oscar Wilde's Legs exposes black silk stockings as fetishistic objects. One might view them as a sort of second skin, a surrogate for ones' own skin. It registers upon the surface the lascivious effects of every unbounded sexual drive to which the editor surrenders. Reaction begins with gawking and fantasizing, followed by blushing confessions. Finally, he is caught in an awkward, if not unmanly, position. *Oscar Wilde's Legs* invokes anxieties over the destruction and resurrection of images. The potency of such images resided in their agency. It exemplified the sensuous spectrum of image anxiety, conjuring figures of considerable dread.[47]

Baseball stockings typified this dread. In 1868, the Cincinnati Base Ball Club displayed eye-catching red stockings and, somewhat shockingly, much of the players' muscled legs (**fig. 60**). Critics deplored the innovation as immoral and indecent, and one writer deri-

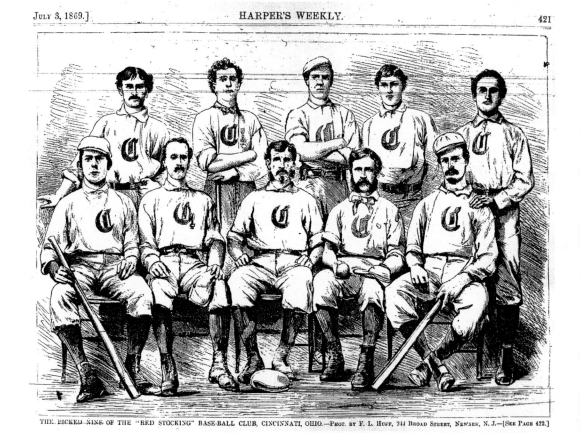

JULY 3, 1869.]   HARPER'S WEEKLY.   421

THE PICKED NINE OF THE "RED STOCKING" BASE-BALL CLUB, CINCINNATI, OHIO.—PHOT. BY F. L. HUFF, 244 BROAD STREET, NEWARK, N.J.—[SEE PAGE 422.]

Figure 60. The Picked Nine of the "Red Stocking" Base-Ball Club, *Harper's Weekly,* **1869. Front row (left to right): Charley Sweasy, Fred Waterman, Harry Wright, Asa Brainard, Charlie Gould. Back row (left to right): Dick Hurley, George Wright, Doug Allison, Cal McVey, Andy Leonard.**

sively dubbed the team "Red Stockings"—the name stuck. While some objected to the new look, other clubs adopted these theatrical, if not sartorial, vestments. In 1883, *The Globe Democrat* notes: "Red Stockings seem to be all the go. In addition to St. Louis the clubs of Louisville, Baltimore, Pittsburg, Philadelphia and Cincinnati will wear them this year."[48]

New Orleans Mardi Gras got into the act in 1882, when carnival spectators witnessed the National Pastime as a tableau vivant. One float displayed a ballpark surrounded by rails and trees, where the hats and coats of players hung. Float participants portrayed the "Silver Stockings," the "Gold Stockings," and other famous clubs.[49]

Now, this is not to imply that Wilde introduced stockings to baseball. However, his presence did make the sporting crowd, at least briefly, think differently about the game. Wilde was baseball's apostle of aestheticism. Ball clubs named themselves after him, or chose monikers like "the Aesthetics." But the sporting crowd finally concluded that his image was all flash and no substance. It appeared circumspect about the effeminacy of this tall, well-built man, with strong square shoulders, manly waist and hips.[50]

But Oscar Wilde and aesthetic style cast their broad shadow over everything, from flora to fauna. Throughout the country, baseball clubs named teams after him. *The Constitution* states: "A match game of base ball this evening between the Oscar Wildes, of Cleveland and Sun Flowers, of this city, will be hotly contested." The Oscar Wildes vanquished them. *The Republican* reports: "Last Sunday the Marions defeated the Oscar Wilde club by a score of 19 lo 18." *The Tribune* adds: "The Unknowns beat the Oscar Wilde's 8 to 4." *The Globe* reports: "The Oscar Wildes of Roxbury would like to arrange games with clubs whose average age is 15 years, the Puritans of Roxbury preferred. Address George W. Goode...." Four day later, Goode claimed that he was not the manager of the Oscar Wilde Base Ball Club. One story found him at a ball game. According to *The Clipper*, Wilde witnessed "the Clevelands and the Alleghenys on Thursday, at Pittsburg. He admired the game very much, but the uniforms were not quite to his aesthetic taste." Wilde, the "Apostle of the Aesthetic Movement," was good copy.[51]

Oscar Wilde's Legs also succeeds in promoting the aesthetic of blackness. Aesthetic tastemakers praised black silks—rather expensive in the 1880s—claiming that they were the foundation of things. Reaching a height of fashion between 1880 and 1890, both men and women wore silks. But as early as 1870, the famed Chicago White Stockings presented Ida Lewis—the famous Newport heroine—a costly pair of white stockings, fashioned curiously from rare lace, with emblems of the great American game elaborately wrought over them. The stockings (imported at a cost of $500 in gold) were accompanied by an artistically engrossed certificate of honorary membership in the baseball club. The *Cincinnati Enquirer* "jocularly acknowledged" the rage for white stockings among both women and baseballists.

> No other kind are worn up Fourth Street, and no lady of fashion would be caught in colored hose. The hard-earned victory won by the Chicago ballists in Philadelphia has confirmed fashion, and before red will 'again be the only wear,' the Cincinnatis must win their third games of the Athletics and Atlantics, and defeat the champions of the immaculate Stockings. This they mean to do.[52]

In 1877, critics also observed male apparel had begun to rival women's in gaudiness. Trendy men wore the St. James costume—black broadcloth dress coat, knee breeches, black silk stockings, and low shoes with buckles. *The Washington Bee* declared the rage for black silk stockings: "The leg never shows to better advantage than when encased in a black ribbed stocking with low and narrow clocks." The clocks on male hosiery were as "gay as peacock's tails," and elaborate enough for eight-day clocks. Rosebuds were embroidered on the dark fronts in pink and gold silk threads; the U.S. flag, coats of arms, and monograms were worked in gold threads on the instep. Miniature portraits of girlfriends, nude women, and race horses were probably embroidered onto them as well. Corrupt politicians made black silks famous, and the Republican Party dubbed the St. Louis crowd the "Silk Stockings." Ballplayers also wore them, and Bridgewater's faction was dubbed the "colored silk stockings." The New York Metropolitans manager, Jim Mutrie, introduced a new departure from baseball uniforms. His players dressed in black silk stockings, patent leather shoes, and sealskin uppers. This costume proved attractive and drew attention to players' splendid forms. Blanchard noted that the created self as aesthetic object — the breaking of the boundary between person and thing — was confined to neither men nor women.[53]

In the 1860s and 1870s, blackface minstrels wore knickers and stockings as part of their stylized costumes (the teams of James Mackin and Francis Wilson, Welby and Pearl, and the Delmanning brothers being one example). Such performers also engaged in role playing and transvestite experimentation. Crowds ogled at mesmerizing female impersonators performing as prima donnas: real artists in the production of female voices, taking on female graces, airs, and affectations, yet exhibiting nothing unnatural about their work. All the femininities could be witnessed with genuine pleasure. Wardrobes included velvet opera dresses, laced with gold and silver trimming. The white female impersonator Francis Leon establish the role so well that no successful troupe could be without one. The Callender's Georgia Minstrels also possessed first rate "leading lady" actors. Willie Lyle established himself with the troupe, replacing the 37-inch-tall Thomas Dilward ("Japanese Tommy") in the role of the colored prima donna. Lyle's visual formula and self-conscious performance compared favorably with Callender's best entertainers: Billy Kersands, Peter Devonear, and Sam Lucas.[54]

The Black Stockings' debased legs, no less than their distinct hosiery, helped make them racially offensive or outrageous. Black stockings, metaphorically speaking, conjured ostentation, immorality, and corruption. These stereotypical views proved inextricable from the aesthetic effects, and during this period we must consider shifting formations, and their shifting place within them. In public and private spaces, an emergent politics took form, and negative feelings underlying black legs and black stockings were fashioned. Rather than treat them as a stylized social backdrop that reassured the middle-class about their place in the world, stockings can be viewed as part of the performance of sartorial display.

Oscar Wilde's Legs successfully represents a vision of blackness which gives meaning to whiteness. It thematizes a socio-cultural phenomenon, metaphors that ground meaning, explanation, and blame in blackness. Wilde's counterfeit black legs could invoke the burnt cork icon, and students caricatured his aesthetic tastes by appropriating blackness. During his address at Yale College, two hundred students wearing red neckties, knee breeches, black silk stockings, and yellow sunflowers strutted into the lecture hall, following a similarly dressed black servant. Rochester students copied the prank. An elderly black man promenaded through the auditorium with a huge bouquet of flowers.[55]

Wilde was perturbed that painters and poets ignored blacks as aesthetic objects, yet the college boys aggressively racialized the "Apostle of the Aesthetic Movement," linking him to, among others, blacks in the United States. They resented the special treatment that Wilde had demanded for his black servant "Cetewayo." Cartoons ridiculed his theories as mere aping behavior and depicted blacks as his apostles. The sporting crowd considered him pretentious, labeling him the "apostle of the bogus." Perhaps critics had good reason. In 1884, *Sporting Life* avers: "Oscar Wilde's faculty of observation is poorly developed. He says the national game of America is euchre. He overlooked baseball and poker entirely."[56]

Oscar Wilde's Legs is not simply an indictment of the sporting fraternity; the story also provides insight into image-resurrecting, those relations that produced the cultural commodity of blackness. The story, in other words, unveils blackness as a vast profusion of ambiguous signs that, like the comedic minstrel mask itself, shaped the socio-cultural experience of blackness even as participants absented it. This was especially true for genuine colored artists, who struggled to transform the black body's image into heroic display that illuminated the purpose of the diminished copy.[57]

There were other genuine colored artists. The enterprising businessman John F. Lang introduced two new colored nines to the green diamond: one aggregation of women, and a team of Chinese men. Lang was an entrepreneur. For years, he had organized, financed, and promoted colored baseball clubs. What we know about the Orions, Manhattans, and Cuban Giants suggests that both organizations proved to be lucrative investments. Lang also organized a colored nine comprised only of six-footers. Lang may have had connections to the minstrel stage, which prospered in Philadelphia. The Eleventh Street Opera House, the oldest and one of the most famous homes of minstrelsy, opened in 1854; the Ethiopian Opera House opened in 1870. Lang may have learned much from the performers, and perhaps encouraged his teams to engage in similar displays of extravagant showmanship. When his Philadelphia Orions crossed bats with the Washington Long Branch Club, also colored, sportswriters stressed that it was an "amusing game." The *New York Daily Tribune* published the following: "The contestants conducted themselves more like negro minstrels on picnic than baseball players." In 1885, Lang introduced "Lang's Colored Giants," precursor to the Cuban Giants; nearly every man was 6 feet tall, and Lang planned for them to only play white men. As a businessman and promoter, Lang was no stranger to the print media. His advertisements and promotions circulated in the newspapers of sporting towns throughout the United States and Upper Canada.[58]

Other Baseball Landscapes: "Miss Harris's Base-Ball Nine"

"Miss Harris's Base-Ball Nine" is a story about the Dolly Vardens, black Philadelphians who formed the first professional women's baseball club.[59] It follows Captain Ella Harris and "Dolly Varden No. 1," who are to give an exhibition game against "Dolly Varden No. 2." Traveling to Chester, Pennsylvania, a reporter finds the team along with a number of persons, white and black, lounging in the Lamokin Woods. Captain Ella Harris suddenly emerges on the scene, epitomizing the Dolly Varden's. Miss Harris, "a dusky damsel," wears a red and white jockey cap, a short, tight-fitting pink and white sheeny calico dress, and cricket shoes. She carries a base-ball bat over her right shoulder and makes her way across the green with "manly strides." The scarlet ribbon suspended on the bosom of the uniform denotes her status as captain. In "a loud, theatrical aside"—spoken in "negro dialect"— Harris expresses frustration with Dolly Varden No. 2: "Well, I nevah! I declare them Philadelphians ain't come yet, and we won't be able to have dat match nohow." Gaudily dressed — one in a calico scarlet dress trimmed with white, another pink trimmed with yellow, another blue trimmed with white, and all wearing red and white peaked caps — the "colored" girls startle the woods with "the yells of half a hundred ragged little darkies." Some carry bats, some croquet hoops and mallets, and one or two ropes, which impaired the stateliness of their triumphal march. Dolly Varden No. 1 marches down to a hollow in the glade to hold an indignation meeting.[60]

The reporter transforms this scene into blackface performance, complete with blacked-up characters, "negro dialect," comedic antics, social violence, and gender cross-dressing — Dolly Varden No. 2 comprises "wimmen," and Captain Harris's team are "men." Harris gathers the players for an intra-squad game. "Cord Patten," Harris directs one player, "you stand dar kase we wants you to be our umpire. I'll stand hyar kase I'm goin' to be short stop. Mollie Johnson, you'll be furst base...." And so it goes until every player has been positioned. When the ground has been measured off, Harris discovers a knot in the rope and "promptly" pulls a razor from her pink stocking and cuts the obstacle. To give the Philadelphia Vardens time "to come up," their opponents organize a game of skipping-rope. One jealous onlooker calls them "high-toned." Another spectator points to the catcher Ella Johnson: "Jes you look at her trying to show her shape. Ain't she jes lovely." Responding to her companion, another women declares, "If I was a man and had my girl gwine foolin' and monkeyin' like dem I would hab nuffin to do wid her." When finished skipping, the team amuses itself by pitching the ball at each other. One woman gets hit in the upper lip, but it does not seem to swell any bigger than it was before. The Dolly Varden's No. 2 did not appear until a late hour, apparently missing the train to Chester, Pennsylvania.

There is nothing particularly unusual about the outcome of this story. Baseball narratives are filled with stories about railroad schedules, late arrivals, and missed trains causing cancelled and rescheduled games. For example, *The Register* reports: "The St. Louis Colored ball players failed to put in an appearance on the afternoon train and consequently there was no game this afternoon." However, the early addition missed out: "The St. Louis Black Stockings reached this city yesterday afternoon in spite of the report in the papers to the contrary. They missed the early train, but made the city on the Kenosha division, arriving a few moments before 5 o'clock." Obviously, late train arrivals for "colored" female baseballists were no exception.[61]

Then again, the real interest of this story is not missed trains, but the fact that Miss Ella Harris's gender identity is so unstable. Like other baseball narratives of colored clubs, this story is an assemblage of historical fact and fancy invoking the blackface tradition of American literature. The countrified Miss Harris, the central figure, represents a rustic baseball hero: a comedic darkey testing the limits of freedom and individuality. Romantically and sentimentally respectful of the game that she plays for a living, Miss Harris's homespun wisdom invokes common-sense, competence, toughness, and impatience. What she seems does not warrant inquiry, but what the reporter needs from her should solicit the reader's attention. Harris is the furthest thing from femininity, so far away as to be not womanly but manly. Moving with manly strides over the greensward and carrying a baseball bat over her right shoulder, Harris stomps across the baseball landscape. A veritable mountain woman, Captain Harris commands the Dollie Varden's No. 1 with tribal efficiency. She positions them strategically on the baseball diamond. An ambivalent figure, Harris is threatening if not dangerous: she conceals a deadly razor in her pink baseball stockings. Blackface performer, like the tight-fitting pink and white "sheeny" calico dress, maps her body. Harris's "negro dialect" is construed as alien, made deliberately unintelligible by spellings contrived to deize it. It fits perfectly within the blackface literary tradition, romantic stories about black characters of the Old South. While the baseball uniform and scarlet ribbon suspended on her bosom seemingly give feminine form to Harris's body, she remains an "apparition" in a flaming baseball cap. Casting ambivalence on her femininity, the figure's face, skin complexion, and hair texture remain masked. One might expect that the female baseballist would be out of place in the blackface literary tradition, but the surprise is the ease with which it works. No matter how insistently the story reassures us that black female baseballists are pure fiction, though, the historicity of the Dolly Vardens makes the rightness and plausibility of that black presence overwhelming.[62]

Celestial Baseballists and Chinese Burlesque

According to historian Robert C. Toll, blackface entertainment's most exotic foreigners were Asians. "Although they were rarely seen in most of the country in the mid-nineteenth century," writes Toll, "the California gold rush brought white Americans, including minstrels, in contact with the Chinese. Different from Americans in race, language, and culture, the Chinese became a part of the minstrelsy's minor curiosities. Although they referred to the Chinese only occasionally, minstrels consistently presented them as totally alien." Contributing to the blackface image-repertoire, and to the vogue for Chinese burlesque, Bret Harte and Mark Twain wrote a dramatic play based on Harte's poem "Ah Sin, the Heathen Chinee" (1877). The narrative is told through the gambler Bill Nye, who attempts to cheat the antagonist Ah Sin at euchre, a popular card game. Proving more than Nye's match, Ah Sin masks his card-playing expertise and cheating skills — he smiles "inscrutably," and the white Americans he plays with can't read his facial expressions. Ah Sin does not speak in the poem; rather, the poem is written/spoken about him, in "plain language" by "Truthful James."[63]

"Ah Sin, the Heathen Chinee" offers a classic example of American Orientalism, a discursive creation of an imagined Orient. The Western identity gets to speak and produce images and ideas about the Oriental identity, which does not get to talk back. Lang's successes led him to organize an "Asiatic nine," seeking to capitalize on any eye-catching group and offering them up as baseball curiosities.[64]

Many Chinese looking for fame and broken fingers apply for positions on the team. The response is overwhelming, so Lang must refuse a large number of applicants. The selected "heathens" are to be captained by Loo Hing, "a rugged-looking little laundryman, who has worked in nearly every laundry in the city, and has sufficient command of English profanity to manage even an American baseball team." Having seen baseball played in San Francisco and Chicago, Captain Loo longs to engage in the sport. After practicing two days, the agile "Celestials" acquire the art of stopping "hot grounders," making "double plays," and finding fault with the umpire's decisions. When asked how soon the team would be ready to play, Loo softly replies: "Chinaman him glab on plenty quick." He adds: "Chinamen him got plenty blains." However, the team wouldn't play before June.[65]

Known for its candid comments, *The Police Gazette* observes:

> The scheme will, no doubt, prove quite a success, as there are thousands who would go to see the 'heathens' play just out of idle curiosity. A similar scheme was started several years ago by a Philadelphian. On that occasion two teams of young ladies were selected, and for awhile, until the novelty wore off, considerable money was made. The Chinamen will never develop into scientific ball players, but if they only get sufficient knowledge of the game to understand general principles, it will be all that is necessary, as no one expects to see more than a miserable attempt at ball playing.

Newspaper stories about Lang's baseball racket border on the absurd, with negative stereotypical associations linking Chinese comedic antics (as opposed to "negro" comedic antics) and the players' initiation into the mysteries of the game.[66]

Lang uniforms his Chinese nine in exotic costumes: white knee-breeches, various colored silk jackets, black felt hats bound with ribbon the color of the jacket, and regular Chinese shoes with cork soles. During the first practice session, Lang positions his players: Wah Lung, pitcher; Wah Lee, catcher; Ki Yung, short stop; Ki Chung, first base; Sing Gee, second base; Sing Ling, third base; Hong Kong, center field; Hop Lee, right field; and Ah Sin, left field. Thus positioned, Lang gives the bat to Lee Yaw, and instructs him to hit the ball gracefully. Eyeing the bat with suspicion, Yaw handles it as if it were a "flat-iron." The pitched ball hits him in the stomach, and he "opens his Celestial mouth," yelling loudly as he drops the bat. After Lang urges Yaw to again pick up the willow, the second pitch, to Yaw's amazement, connects with the bat's bigger end. The ball bounds thirty feet. Lang shouts for him to run to first base. Ki Chung, the first baseman, sees his countryman running toward him. Thinking that Yaw is angry, Ki runs toward the nearest fence and disappears. The remaining players rush for the ball, as if it was "a dead rat and they were starved."

The farce continues the next day. Lang gives them explicit commands about what to do and how to do it. Wah Lung pitches to Sam Weng, the team's captain, but the ball strikes Weng in the stomach. Lang decides to show them how to strike the ball and hits one to the outfield, where seven players converge, knocking over the center fielder. When they resume their positions, Lang's foul tip strikes catcher Wah Lee in the mouth, "shutting that useful member and one eye up in a flash." However, Lee refuses to wear a catcher's mask: "Makee me lookee too damn much like a doggy." The carnage continues, and the Chinese club becomes the walking wounded. Hong Kong breaks a finger while catching a "fly" ball; Hop Lee stumbles over a stone, tearing his breeches; and Ah Sin, who climbs over a fence into an adjoining watermelon patch to recover a "far" ("foul") ball, is bitten by a Jersey bull dog. At day's end, the players storm Lang's house and demand higher wages, which they receive. Swearing by Confucius and a dozen lesser Celestial gods that they are at last fully satisfied, the players vow to forfeit their precious pigtails if they should ever strike again.

Two day later, Lang's team appears in specially designed baseball uniforms. The results are worse. Wah Lung pitches to Ki Chung. When the former reaches out to strike at Wah's curve ball, Ki whacks catcher Wah Lee alongside the head, inflicting an ugly welt. Lang roars with laughter, to the consternation of Wah, who swears at him in broken Chinese. They only practice twice more. Lang strikes the ball toward pitcher Wah Lung, who thinks the ball soft and attempts to grab it. When the ball slips through his long, slim fingers and strikes him in the stomach, Wah doubles up like a jack knife. Ah Sin attempts to catch a "high" fly and breaks his nose. The banged-up players, broken noses and fingers, and mangled members demand $20 per week and expenses (including laundry bills). Lang refuses, choosing instead to leave them to their own devices.[67]

Lang's baseball novelty was hardly innovative nor the final word. In 1878, Hartford, Connecticut had a Chinese baseball nine, and by 1888, the sporting craze for Chinese baseball clubs had emerged throughout the country. The *Boston Globe* reports: "The game in the Union Grounds next Monday between two Chinese nines will be one of the funniest base ball events of the season." In Chicago, fourteen Chinese laundrymen crossed bats at Thirty-Third Street, near Stewart Avenue. According to *The Chicago Tribune*, the prize was "a barrel of rum and five pounds of opium." Again in Chicago, the Pi Pittahs of Chicago and the Vanquishers of the Dragon from San Francisco clashed at League Park. *The Chicago Tribune* reports:

> The Vanquishers of the Dragon, attired in dark blue shirts, went to bat first. The Pi Pittahs, dressed in white shirts, nerved themselves for action like novices in war facing their first fire of musketry.... Whenever they saw the ball coming they faced it heroically. They let it strike them wherever it pleased — in the face, or body, or legs. As a rule they fell when it hit them, and the ball, ricocheting on another player, bowled him over too. Thus there was the spectacle of all the players lying prone upon the field, like nine pins.[68]

The motivation for these racial stereotypes of Chinese baseballists seems clear enough: the threat of Chinese labor. The *Los Angeles Times* observes: "The Chinamen residing in Philadelphia are organizing base ball clubs. Thus does Chinese cheap labor seek to play out American civilization on the diamond field." Lang would have disagreed. Being ridiculed or demeaned in the national press would not come cheap. The Chinese baseballists demanded higher wages and expenses. Amusing images of emasculated and effeminate Chinamen — long slim fingers — mask the threat of deceitful "bias-eyed strikers," who prove more than Lang's match. According to *The Police Gazette*, Lang found the strikes for higher wages more than even his patience could stand. The Celestial baseballists represented a tough job lot. The story described the strikes as unethical, pre-planned events; the secret sessions were held in Wash-Tub Tommy's laundry, where chuckles of devilish delight were heard from the sidewalk. The story recommends that the next contractor must do more than simply put the players through their poses; he must also teach them the American maxim that "Honesty is the best policy." Something more is going on here than baseball burlesque: these stories also reveal the surplus value of stereotypical images, the notion that even performers found ways to outwit white employers. Thus, it seems, Lang's team emerged as champions of the baseball racket.[69]

Promoters like John F. Lang and his ilk (the McCullough's and Jack Haverly included), exploited the relationship between genuine colored artists (or entertainers) and blackface minstrelsy. Regarding the Black Stocking vs. Callender game, the *Post-Dispatch* announced: "To-morrow (Thursday) afternoon, at Sportsman's Park, there will be one of the most amusing affairs of the week, this being the game of base-ball between Harry Bridgewater's St. Louis Black Sox, the champion colored club of the United States, and the Callender Minstrel team, which is composed of a number of excellent and clever base-ball tossers." On the previous day, the Callender Minstrels attended the St. Louis vs. Indianapolis contest. Neither newspapers nor theatrical and sporting journals published detailed baseball accounts of the Black Stockings vs. Callender Minstrels contest. Before the contest, Postlewaite's Band entertained spectators with a promenade concert. *The Sunday Sayings* is the only newspaper to report that the Black Stockings won: "The Black Socks did up the Callender Minstrels last Wednesday at Sportsman's Park to the tune of 'There's a new coon in town."[70]

The native habitats of the black image reveal something about the process by which genuine colored artists is pictured. While cultural performances were not necessarily meant as direct political statements, the social context in which they were often represented rendered them so. Sartorial expression and language represented a subversive refusal to be subservient. Black aesthetic style functioned within the same cultural and political places as complex signs of authenticity, technological, and economic power, enforcing a sense of collective identity that was itself passionately contested. Standard readings of the black images discussed here typically reduce them to a particularly modernist commercial gaze that transforms the figures into a commodity and the viewer/reader into a leisure-class consumer. But these representations say more than that. And once we contextualize cultural expressivity, considering the sports medium, the totality of signifiers from black legs to black stockings, we cannot help but view the black image as part of a larger process by which black entertainers appropriated, transformed, and reinscribed coded oppositional meanings onto styles derived from leisure-class life.

Coda: A Glance Over the Diamond Fields of the Continent

This afternoon the Black Stockings, colored, who have become famous by reason of their many victories will meet the Grand Avenues at the Sportsman's Park.[1]

The typical ekphrastic text might be said to speak to or for a semiotic "other"—an image, visual object, or spectacle—usually *in the presence* of that object. The point of view of the text is the position of a seeing and speaking subject in relation to a seen and usually mute object. But suppose the "visual other" was not merely represented by or "made to speak" by a speaking subject? Suppose that the "other" spoke for [him]self, told [his] own story, attempting "an ekphrasis of the self"?[2]

On 13 May 1883, Henry Bridgewater's Black Stockings debuted at Sportsman's Park against the Grand Avenues, an all-white club. The contest was highly anticipated: "The Black Stockings and the Grand Avenues meet at the Sportsman's Park on Sunday next. The colored champions will return from their triumphant tour during the latter part of the week." This game was culturally significant. Located on the west side of Grand Avenue at Dodier Street, Sportsman's Park was home to the Brown Stockings. Even though the white-washed structure was built entirely of wood (like other late 19th century ballparks), the park was more luxurious than most others. In 1882, the permanent seating capacity was 6,000, although crowds were sometimes more than double that amount. The grandstand stretched approximately from first to third base. In 1883, Chris Von Der Ahe, the team's owner, introduced a new invention patented by Alexander Graham Bell—the telephone—to establish a connection between the ball park and the club's downtown headquarters. This technological innovation enabled the team to report events on the ball field as fast as they occurred and also allowed them to post the scores of other games in progress, which were relayed to St. Louis by telegraph.[3]

For Black Stockings fans around the country, the wired results were disappointing. *The Police Gazette* quipped: "The St. Louis Blackbirds, after an extended tour, in which they played ten games, returned to their homes, and encountered the Grand Avenue club of St. Louis, who polished them up to the queen's taste, putting them away to a tune of 6 to 0." Notwithstanding nursery rhyme imagery that transformed the game's outcome into a crude racial joke, newspapers admitted that Bridgewater's boys played a fair game and batted well, but threw away opportunities with injudicious base-running. Injuries cost them as well. Catcher Joseph Harris hurt his thumb badly attempting to stop a wild pitch. Following the accident, pitcher William Davis had to moderate his pace. The players also looked rather worse for the wear. Having been on the go for nearly a month and playing games daily, the team had been unable to launder their soiled uniforms. However, their play was first-class — the Black Stockings out-batted the Grand Avenues, but lost the game in the field.[4]

Despite the colored nine's performance, Bridgewater's team achieved national fame. This was partly due to the larger forces of modernization reshaping American life. Telegraph and telephone technologies enabled sports columns, if they so desired, to map the baseball landscape's uncharted territory. Midwifed by technology Bridgewater's baseball narratives entered daily sporting life. This historical moment found expression through the innovation of the baseball bulletin-board. *The Chronicle* observes: "When the championship season opens the immense blackboard at the extreme corner of the grounds will be used as a bulletin board on which will be posted the score of all games being played by the clubs of the American Association." Clearly, this figuration of blackness reconstructed time and space: "The huge telegraph bulletin worked admirably at the Sportsman's Park yesterday, the games at other points being chronicled by innings." *The Chronicle* summarizes: "The immense bulletin-board in the far corner of the Grand Avenue Park was generally admired, yesterday. It is the neatest thing of the kind in the country." Bulletin-board technology was only one of the novel constraints and opportunities introduced during the postbellum era.[5]

The bulletin-board's importance begins with its insistence on taking baseball images — specifically, the progress of multiple games on a national scale — as its principal subject matter. While this might seem obvious from the standpoint of common sense, 21st century scoreboards are comparatively mundane objects. Today's baseball fans expect jumbo-tron scoreboards to track the progress of games, provide player portraits and statistical records, insert freeze-frame/moving pictures, and offer instant-replays. For postbellum baseball fans, gamblers, and journalists, the bulletin-board-telegraph-telephone medium emerged as a new innovation. While the Brown Stockings played on the road, and another club played at Sportsman's Park, fans could follow their heroic exploits; or they could simultaneously monitor several contests. However, it could prove a conundrum. *The Republican* humorously reports:

> A new line of comedy was introduced at Sportsman's Park yesterday. The small boy who marks up the "telegraph," in response to the Republican's suggestions, indulged in goose-eggs of the antediluvian size. When the fifth inning was reached the blackboard gave out, and he had to finish the innings on the other side.

This fan-friendly medium was no idle phenomenon; the highly interactive technology was baseball business. For gamblers, the new bulletin-board raised the stakes, expanding the baseball landscape's space, time, and site of enunciation. No longer would betting apply only to local baseball grounds where spectators witnessed the game. The medium facilitated pool betting from long and short distances, high-rollers gambling on innings, players, and performances they would never behold. It was boom or bust.[6]

Bridgewater's special dispatches appeared throughout the 1883 baseball season, in both local and national newspapers. They belong to the new journalism that emerged during the last three decades of the 19th century, a period when new ideas in news coverage and presentation were developing, new concepts of makeup and headlines were evolving, and an infusion of new vitality was given to baseball coverage. Also during this period, advertising expanded and newspaper promotion began to appear. According to historian Charles C. Clayton, Joseph B. McCullagh's *Globe-Democrat* exemplified the changes taking place in American newspapers. "Little Mack" was the architect of the new journalism and set the example for comprehensive coverage, both local and national. His sensationalism preceded both Joseph Pulitzer and William Randolph Hearst. His formula comprised six parts: an aggressive news policy both for local and national news; crusades and stunts; a vigorous, outspoken editorial page; an impressive physical size of the paper with more pages; liberal use of illustrations; and a promotion policy for the paper. Credited with originating the word "boom" in the connotation with which it has become familiar, McCullagh's steamboat river culture vernacular also became a favorite for describing St. Louis baseball. The *Globe-Democrat* and other newspapers embraced Bridgewater's role as special correspondent.[7]

Symbolic figurations of blackness are — as shown — markers for fascination and horror; spirituality and sensuousness; corruption and aesthetics. None is more telling than the bulletin-board, an immense rectangular slab that rose like a black monolith on the baseball landscape — a rather foreboding, yet solemn object that made the unknown familiar and the familiar unknown. Not unlike the bulletin-board, Bridgewater's dispatches — a black voice in the wilderness — invoked the colored baseballist. Images, not language, are the main currency of baseball representations, and Bridgewater's narratives fashioned a black image of the colored baseballist that until now remained relatively unknown. Bridgewater deployed the tools of journalism and the aesthetics of style to produce graphic narratives that were as performative as any black Republican speech. As "special correspondent," he dispatched at least twenty-six telegrams — 70 games have been documented with 15 played at home (St. Louis) and 39 on the road, with a record of 47 wins and 23 defeats. Carefully crafting an image of the Black Stockings as "famous," Bridgewater engaged in Barnumesque tactics by promoting a product already successfully tested on the baseball market. By mediating black images that countered negative stereotypes in the sports medium, he established the fact of black humanity through promoting baseball representations worthy of elevation in the baseball pantheon.[8]

While Bridgewater's narratives insisted that racial exclusion had restricted the upward mobility of colored baseballists, his club transformed the figure into an object of racial uplift. They mapped baseball's uncharted wilderness and blazed new trails for the colored sporting fraternity. His commentary is filled with complex reflections typically absent from sports accounts. But they emerged from a cultural position of baseball consciousness very similar to standard accounts that white journalists had claimed as essential to traversing the baseball landscape. Thus, these descriptive textual strategies associated with vision and space played a double role as symptoms of both lack and plentitude, unveiling of time, memory, history, and direct access to sensory actuality.[9]

Bridgewater's narratives between the object being addressed (the 1883 championship season of the Black Stockings) and a listening/reading subject (the sports fan) who (if ekphrastic hope is fulfilled) will be made to see the Black Stockings through the sports medium of the writer's voice. According to Mitchell, ekphrasis is stationed between two "othernesses," and two forms of (apparently) impossible translation and exchange: (1) the conversion of the visual representation into a verbal representation, either by description or ventriloquism; and, (2) the reconversion of the verbal representation back into the visual object in the reception of the listener/reader. As Mitchell has explained, "the working through" of ekphrasis and the other is more like a triangular relationship than a binary one — it must be pictured as a ménage a trios in which the relations of self and other, text and image, are triply inscribed. "If ekphrasis typically expresses a desire for a visual object (whether to possess or praise)," writes Mitchell "it is also typically an offering if this expression as a gift to the reader."[10]

For Bridgewater, black images engaged in mediation, as a material means for communicating the sporting fraternity's political, economic, and spiritual concerns. He worked the bulletin-board-telegraph-telephone medium to full effect. Newspaper contacts mattered. Bridgewater established relationships with P.H. Murray and J.W. Wilson, colored proprietors of the *St. Louis Advance* and *The National Tribune* newspapers. He was savvy enough to work the sporting press (not unlike William P. Johnson, of the Blue Stockings) in general, including the *Globe-Democrat*, owned by Joseph Burbridge McCullagh. Bridgewater's narratives typified the graphic image used to frame baseball representations as an assemblage of staged scenes linked in an episodic structure that confined temporality of the Black Stockings.[11]

The natural place to start this investigation of the black image of the colored baseballist begins with sports gossip. Thousands of sports gossip columns survive from the period. Columns headers like *Base Ball Notes, Diamond Dust, Diamond Chips, Sporting Notes, Tips, Minor Games*, and so on mediated between readers and black image. In this cultural context, brief narratives devoted to the Black Stockings provide unprecedented access to uncharted territory, a baseball wilderness paralleled, perhaps, only by the Cuban Giants and Walter L. Cohen's Pinchbacks of New Orleans.[12]

Bridgewater's Black Stockings: Colored Champions of the United States

Henry Bridgewater was born at Jefferson Barracks, below St. Louis, on the Mississippi River, 17 December 1844. Named in honor of former President Thomas Jefferson, the military post was established in 1826 as the country's first "Infantry School of Practice." Bridgewater's mother worked as a seamstress for Major Wheaton, a surgeon in the regular army, stationed at that post. Slaves were often rented out to the military installation. Bridgewater and his mother, Cecelia, both mulattos, were probably slaves. Bridgewater's original name was Henry Meyers Biggs; he acquired "Bridgewater" from his mother's second husband whom she married when Henry was 5 years old (A census report of 1850 identifies him as "Henry Myers," not yet taking his father's surname). In 1854, Henry's mother moved from St. Louis to Weston, Missouri. From Weston, the family moved back to St. Louis, but moved again, going to Fulton, Illinois, where they lived for 3 years. In 1859 they went to Chicago,

Figure 61. Henry Bridgewater, *The Republican* (St. Louis), 1890

and an 1860 federal census report shows the family living in the Third Ward. Bridgewater's stepfather, Elijah, a 34-year-old barber, was listed as head of the family. The 16-year-old worked as a waiter. In 1861, Henry Bridgewater, as attendant to a regimental surgeon, went to the front with the Federal Army and remained in his service until the end of the Civil War.

Bridgewater returned to Missouri and began running the river as a cabin boy, waiter, and barber until he left that business to open a saloon. Failing in this line, he returned to the steamboat river culture (the city directory lists his occupation as "river man"), remaining at that until 1874, his last trip being made as a porter on the steamer Red Wing, running between St. Louis and St. Paul. Bridgewater returned to the saloon business in 1874, eventually owning several establishments and accumulating a large fortune. Bridgewater was described as a tall, slender man, with an unusually keen and shrewd face of most changeable expression, and of a quick and decisive manner of speech (**fig. 61**).[13]

In an interview with a Dayton, Ohio, sportswriter, Bridgewater claimed to have been a professional baseballist since 1871. While the press was relatively silent on colored baseball in the early 1870s, the staggering number of organized colored nines in St. Louis suggests that Bridgewater spent much of his leisure time playing, managing or betting on baseball. His claims to professional baseballist dovetailed neatly with the formation of the professional league. But what aggregation(s) did Bridgewater play for? What board of directors did he serve? Why did he choose the Black Stockings? And what cultural practices permitted celebrity status within the baseball fraternity in general and the colored sporting fraternity in particular?

The press, as mentioned, often sensationalized links between steamboat river culture and black life. Crime, vice, and corruption figured prominently. Journalists created headlines lurid enough to attract attention, reporting the folkloric exploits of gunslingers, outlaws, and roustabouts. Colored youths, perhaps not unlike their white counterparts, expressed fascination with them. While playing with a pistol, for instance, Conroy Kenard claimed the title "black Jesse James," before accidentally killing himself. Heroic tales could be found in baseball narratives. Sportswriters reported, for instance, that the colored Anchor Line club came up the Mississippi from New Orleans to cross bats with the Athletics, a colored team in St. Louis. Before about 400 spectators, the Athletics defeated the Anchor Line Club by a score of 17–16. According to Cecil Brown, colored roustabouts were particularly fond of the Anchor Line steamers because they were noted for their speed, sumptuous cuisine — and prostitution. The colored sporting fraternity found a perfect theme in the "boom" of riverboat culture.[14]

From the early to mid–1870s, Henry Bridgewater, Charles H. Tyler, Louis Helms, and James W. Wilson labored as riverboat men. Wilson changed careers in the mid–1870s and became the proprietor of the *National Tribune*. He extolled Bridgewater's attempts to elevate the Black Stockings in the baseball sporting world. Whenever wage labor revolts occurred among colored roustabouts, the brotherhood probably counted these men among them. But river men not only fought the barons of the steamer companies, they also fought violently among themselves over politics, gambling, and women. During an altercation on the steamer New Orleans, Louis Helms nearly died from a dagger wound. Helms, along with Tyler and Bridgewater, formed the management triumvirate of the Black Stockings. Perhaps the closest to Tyler, Bridgewater regarded him as a mentor. While both men opened saloons in the early 1870s, Tyler's entrepreneurial efforts proved successful; Bridgewater's triumph came in the mid–1870s, and by 1878 they had formed a business partnership. This relationship likely included the sponsorship of baseball clubs — after all, Bridgewater's economic success, civic efforts, and political muscle dovetailed neatly with flourishing colored ball clubs. Significantly, these men — exceedingly close friends — were mulattos.[15]

Sports journalists often mediated a baseball landscape that overflowed with gamblers, politicians, saloonkeepers, businessmen, and ballpark managers. It was often incestuous. Al and William Spink worked for the *Globe Democrat* and *The Republican* respectively, but they also served as official scorers and promoters for the St. Louis Reds and the Brown Stockings. Al Spink credited himself with naming the Browns. It became their mission to "boom the game" by emphasizing promptness and fair play. The Black Stockings' archive challenges this view, by exposing how sportswriters covered the colored champions. While newspapers situated them firmly within the Missouri baseball landscape, the circulation reach of the *Globe-Democrat* covered a frontier territory bordering on the West and Southwest. Publisher "Little Mack" McCullagh regarded this wilderness as part of his territory, extending north into Southern Iowa, Illinois, and Indiana to the point where the paper competed with Chicago newspapers. Eastward, it stretched to the Wabash River, which was the dividing line for the Cincinnati papers. To the West, it reached the Rocky Mountains; to the Southwest, into most of Texas; and then South as far as New Orleans.[16]

Little is known of the Black Stockings of the 1870s, and that which is known has been extracted from many newspapers. Even though the first mention of the aggregation appeared in 1875, the colored club may have been around much earlier. Between 1875 and 1877, they played both white and colored nines. The aggregation split with the Olives (white), winning 15–14 and losing 20–12; they played the Eccentrics of St. Louis and the Brown Stockings of Belleville, Illinois (both white), winning 6–1 and losing 20–4 respectively. In 1876, newspapers reported several contests: the "Blacks" defeated the famed Uniques of Chicago, by a score of 15 to 6; twice, they defeated the Brown Stockings, of St. Louis (colored), 24–2 and 15–3; twice, they beat the Independence Club of Topeka, Kansas (colored), 18–14 and 22–19; the club beat the Red Stocking Juniors, of St. Louis (white) by a score of 15–3; they split with the Blue Stockings of St. Louis (colored), losing 30–19, and winning 15–9; they whitewashed the Atlantics, of St. Louis (colored) by a score of 8–0. In 1877, sports editors published the results of only three games: the Black Stockings defeated the Nonpareil of St. Louis (white) by a score of 17–10; they defeated Our Boys of St. Louis (white), 6–4; and finally, they scheduled to play the Hartfords (colored), of St. Louis for the local colored championship. Game results failed to appear in any newspaper.[17]

Why were colored clubs ignored or poorly covered by the local press? One answer argues that they claimed neither professional nor semi-professional status. This honorific title belonged to baseball's "high skilled labor-intensive entertainment industry," which Baseball's High Culture jealously guarded. Colored baseballists crossed bats on weekends. Young, colored working-class men labored during the week. Playing ball also required flexible working schedules. While serving as barbers, house servants, coachmen, and waiters guaranteed regular wages, such professions also provided them with opportunities to practice. In short, only white clubs mattered. Another answer, then, specifically considers the St. Louis Brown Stockings. According to J. Thomas Hetrick, sportswriters and promoters devoted attention to transforming the club into a profitable business venture and civic project. However, neither economics nor civic virtue nor social exclusion hampered black aesthetic style: "pretty playing" or simply "looking good." Emphasizing new uniforms was not fortuitous. *The Chronicle* reported that for the Black Stockings vs. Blue Stockings contest of 1881, both clubs would be wearing brand new uniforms. As black baseball images of the newspaper sports medium, colored baseballists nonetheless understood the pecuniary relation of conspicuous consumption and sumptuary display.[18]

Mapping the uncharted territory of colored baseballists challenges our understanding of the politics of social exclusion. Typically, baseball reportage of colored clubs was no more than a few lines of copy. It appeared on Fridays, Saturdays, Sundays, or Mondays. No manager or player names or game statistics appear. Only rarely did game results turn up. On 17 June 1882, for example, *The Chronicle* announces: "Two colored clubs are going to play ball at the Reds' Park Sunday next. They call themselves the Black and Yellow Stockings." Sifting through sports columns of five daily newspapers revealed neither inning-by-inning coverage nor box scores. Only one paper mentions the scheduled game. When the Black Stockings and Yellow Stockings cross bats again, the same paper announces the game and again fails to report the outcome. It would seem that sports fans find little interest in reading about colored clubs, which implies that journalists and sports columns have little need to take them too seriously. One might safely conclude that when colored clubs played, the avid sports reader expected little or no information. But there is more than one fundamental lesson to be learned from this example, and that is the severe limitations of newspapers, sportswriters, sports columns, and avid sports readers in the midst of the baseball landscape medium.[19]

Following a four-year dry spell, between 1881 and 1882, local newspapers renewed their coverage on the city's colored clubs: the Lindells, the Hartfords, the Blue Stockings, the Yellow Stockings, and the Black Stockings. In 1881, *The Clipper* suggested a Colored Championship of St. Louis be contested by the Red Stockings, the Brown Stockings, and the Black Stockings. The McNeary family profited from the colored concession. According to Al Spink, the McNeary's were the city's architects of organized baseball. In the 1860s, Thomas McNeary leased a piece of ground at Compton Avenue and the Missouri Pacific Railway tracks. He "fitted it up for baseball purposes, covering the field with a coat of blue grass and making the surface as level as a billiard table." Originally called Red's Park for the Red Stockings Club, and owned by the McNeary's, William Spink renamed the ball grounds "Compton Avenue Park" in 1881.[20]

Money mattered. For the business world in general and park owners in particular, it proved advantageous, if not lucrative, to exploit the labors of colored clubs as extra income. For instance, when it became clear that Black Stockings vs. Blue Stockings represented the colored championship, the McNeary's seized the opportunity to boost profits and sold the idea to sportswriters who promoted two highly interesting contests for one admission fee. The *Globe-Democrat* reports: "Manager McNeary ... has arranged to give his patrons the worth of their money to-day." Fans unfamiliar with colored clubs were assured: "The colored lads play surprisingly well, and those who witness the contest will see proof of their efficiency." Over 1,500 spectators witnessed the double-header: the Black Stockings vs. the Blue Stockings in the opener, the Red Stockings vs. the Nationals of East St. Louis, Champions of Southern Illinois, in the night-cap. In "a close and exciting game," the "Blacks" defeated the "Blues" by the score 14–10. Adding that they were two first-class clubs, the

Globe-Democrat found it expedient, perhaps for the gambling establishment, to provide box scores. This was rare. Given the perceived excessiveness of baseball reportage to the exclusion of "more interesting matter," colored baseball reportage was likely to be the first casualty.[21]

In 1882, the white baseballist Tom Dolan reorganized the Black Stockings. He had played for the Chicago White Stockings, Buffalo Bisons, Baltimore Orioles, St. Louis Brown Stockings, and the city's Red Stockings or Maroons. According to *The Post-Dispatch*, "The Black Stocking Club (colored), recently organized by Dolan, are anxious to meet the Browns. They are said to be fine players."[22] Another account noted that the young ballplayer had partnered with his father, John Dolan, a saloonkeeper who catered to a black clientele. On 12 October, the *Globe-Democrat* announced, "To-day's game at the Red Stocking Park will be a purely political one, the Black Stocking colored nine meeting a white nine of Democrats known as the Union Blues." Reporting the game's outcome the next day, a rare occurrence, the newspaper described it as "the most interesting of the season. Every seat in the park was occupied. The Black Stocking colored team beat the Democratic Union Blues by a score of 7 to 4."[23] According to the report, "Mr. Dolan says the Blacks can beat the Browns, or come very near beating them, and he is just dying to get a game with the latter. He says his men will play them at anytime or place." Dolan's fantasy was not without foundation: in 1882, the "Browns" finished fifth in a six-team league. His perception of colored baseball supremacy projected an offensive image that could cast doubt over the marketability of the white professionals, and their worthiness as a civic project deserving financial support. Dolan's fantasy of besting the lackluster "Browns" seemed incomprehensible to the sporting fraternity.[24]

Nothing prepared the sporting world for Henry Bridgewater's baseball media debut. He was a "principal exponent of the western sporting fraternity," and *The Republican* acknowledged him as "the well-known boniface Henry Bridgewater." When he assumed control of the Black Stockings, the situation was precipitous because the Dolan clan bankrolled the team. In 1882, Bridgewater pilfered their best players, recruited others both locally and nationally, and appropriated the team's moniker. *The Republican* reports: "[Bridgewater] has secured a team of the very best players to be found amongst the local colored clubs, and will have a notability in the person of [John "Bud"] Fowler, the famous colored pitcher from New Orleans, who has been playing there in the Colored League games, and is a most effective man in the position, he having also pitched for several white nines in Canada."[25]

Bridgewater's desire to secure a team of the best talent was not only foundational to postbellum Gilded Age capitalism but also to the black image of the colored baseballist. In 1882, Bridgewater envisioned controlling the modes of production. As stated, the colored baseballist had hoped to establish a Colored League. One report identified Washington, Lynchburg, Richmond, Pittsburgh, Cincinnati, St. Louis, and perhaps two other cities. But Bridgewater's scheme was bigger: it embraced East and West. It was colored baseball's Holy Grail. While he had been quiet about plans, evidence suggests communication with western clubs. The *Elgin Morning Frank* reported that the colored baseball convention scheduled for May 1883 included representatives from Denver, Leadville, Colorado Springs, Longmout, Fort Collins, Greeley, Idaho Springs, and Lawson. While Bridgewater's Colored League never materialized, it briefly appeared in 1886. On 18 December 1886, *The Sport-*

ing News invoked Bridgewater's baseball celebrity, claiming (perhaps wrongly) that his vision had mapped out this successful journey: "[T]he Colored Base Ball League is now organized. Henry Bridgewater, who piloted the famous St. Louis Black Stockings through the country in 188[3], should again come to the front. He had the most successful club ever."[26]

"A Formidable Colored Organization, of Independent Tendencies"

Solomon Eytinge's humorous portrayal of colored institutions can be seen in *The Behemoth Club of Blackville* (**fig. 42**). Fashionable colored men cram into an all-male club house. It is a tightly compacted space. The room is sparsely furnished, containing one table and five chairs. In the background, a long fancy mirror partitioned into three panels rests above a mantelpiece. A window illuminates the room. On the same wall hangs a framed sign: "Rules: No Gentleman Blackballed Can Be Whitewashed." Twelve bodies of various ages, shapes, and sizes fill the space. While precisely delineated, they piece together an entangled web of human forms melded together through white, gray, and black tonalities. To the far left two men sitting at a table hold decorated stoneware mugs and pay rapt attention to the monocled figure standing before them. One man glares admiringly at his image in the mirror, forming the apex of this pyramid. This narcissist is not alone — his head along with those of two other figures are framed by the other two mirror panels. Behind this grouping, another seated figure in black top hat holds a walking stick in his mouth. Two background figures stand near the mirror, one wears a derby and the other is bareheaded. A young boy drives a wedge between them. He carries a serving tray of refreshments, filled with decorated stoneware mugs and a large bottle. Three other men, to the near right, one sitting and two standing, look out the window, gawking at a smiling female passerby, who returns their gaze. The foreground is dominated by a seated figure, slouching in his chair. Like a stage director, Eytinge has strategically staged his colored cast before the viewer.

Making the connection between *The Behemoth Club of Blackville* and newspaper stories about the colored sporting fraternity of St. Louis is not too difficult. Henry Bridgewater, prosperous and politically powerful, could count himself among the city's important New Negroes in his connection to the Republican Party. Mediating between racial uplift and the colored sporting fraternity, he relied heavily on his clout as a political boss. The most powerful saloonkeepers in the "Bloody Third," also called "Deep Morgan," were William T. Curtis, Henry Bridgewater, and James Ray. In 1882, Bill Curtis, "Bad Jim" Ray, Charles H. Tyler, A. Irwin, and other colored sporting men belonged to the Stags, "a formidable colored organization, of independent tendencies." As Cecil Brown has shown, the Stag Club had political associations. Colored saloons and barbershops functioned as sports mediums where white political bosses came to give speeches. Bridgewater collaborated with the Stags on various civic and cultural projects. Acquiescing to the politics of racial accommodationalism, 20 years before Booker T. Washington's 1895 Atlanta Compromise Address, Bridgewater embraced and promoted colored institutions.[27]

While white politicians visited Bridgewater's Saloon, the Democrats controlled the city's baseball parks. Bridgewater needed them. Chris Von Der Ahe, the McNeary Brothers, and Al Spink were Democrats. In 1873, the McNeary's organized and financed the Red

Stockings. Von Der Ahe served as chairman of the Eighth Congressional District Committee. In 1880 Von Der Ahe, Spink, Democratic Congressman John J. O'Neil, and other prominent sporting men formed the Sportsman's Park Club and Association. The Spinks under the auspices of the St. Louis Baseball Association promoted many other ball clubs and helped reorganize the Brown Stockings. Von Der Ahe purchased the team, and this effectively ended the Association, which was absorbed by the Sportsman's Park Club and Association.[28]

How did the institution of the colored social club fashion the Black Stockings? Did politics impact them? Could the black image of the colored baseballist invoke the threat of a behemoth? What is a behemoth? According to the Oxford English Dictionary, the Latin word derives from the Hebrew form "b'hemoth" *or* "b'hemah," which means beast. It appears in the Old Testament Book of Job, 40:15–24: "Behold now, the behemoth, which I made as well as thee; He eateth grass as an ox." But the Hebrew word is most likely a folk etymology of the ancient Egyptian "pehemau," which literally means "water-ox," the name for the hippopotamus. *The Behemoth Club of Blackville* deploys the term to full peekaboo effect, a verbal imagery that gives a visual playing field to the fort-da game of now you see it, now you don't. The human figures within the composition have been transformed into monstrous hybrids. Take the two figures seated to the far left. The man wearing the hat is a brutish characterization in profile: the sullen facial expression intensified by the sloping forehead, the droopy eye, flared nostril, and thick-down-turned lips. His head overlaps the figure sitting immediately before him. The silhouette practically obscures the facial features. His elongated cranium melds with the other head, becoming a monstrous form incapable of being concealed. Note how the curve of the hat continues with the shape of the man's bald pate, how one figure leans forward and the other leans back, and how the angled shoulders mimic one other. To the far right, the erect figure with cigarette in hand exemplifies the imagery of man-as-animal imagery. Cast in profile, the derby-wearing dude's dark clothing and position against the wall practically silhouettes him. The umbrella near his lower torso dangles from the left hand, extending to the floor not unlike a bushy tail.[29]

Not unlike *Base Ball in Blackville*, *The Behemoth Club of Blackville* is not simply a funny picture, but a two-dimensional image of blackface performance. It embodies a postbellum plantation myth, humorous "countersigns," nostalgic black images of a simpler time, before the trauma of Civil War and the turmoil of Reconstruction. They are meant to help mediate a world imagined as turned-up-side-down. According to Joshua Brown, the postbellum era made a concerted effort to construct a postwar visual culture based on racial inequality. Brown writes that the Blackville Comics offered readers across the country a continuous supply of buffoonish images of freed people: "The appearance of black politicians in positions of power a few years after the end of slavery represented a truly radical formation on the American social landscape," writes historian Eric Foner, "especially the South. Not only was the old ruling class stripped of political power, but most Reconstruction office-holders, whether white or black, now depended for their positions on the votes of former slaves. Many contemporary observers truly believed that they were living through a revolution." As Reconstruction crumbled and racial violence escalated, however, demeaning black images of the behemoth proliferated as well.[30]

Henry Bridgewater remained, throughout his life, a staunch Republican. But as Cecil Brown makes clear, many young colored males in 1883 — including Bridgewater's baseball protégés — might have had little reason to vote Republican. The Republican Party continued to enslave blacks because they had neither fair representation in party decisions and patronage equal their voting strength, nor a fair share of political offices. Colored journalists and politicians dissented. The distinguished politician James Milton Turner, when asked about black loyalty, replied: "The negroes have never belonged to the Republican Party.... That party has used and controlled their votes, but have given very little in return and now the negroes propose to announce their claim." Nonetheless, sportswriters continued to link colored clubs to the Republican Party.[31]

While colored social clubs sponsored athletic competitions and colored nines, they also employed young boys to perform menial duties in their club houses and saloons. However, these social spaces were subject to police raids, shootings, stabbings, and other forms of violence. Bridgewater's Saloon offers an example. On 13 August 1881, William Scott, a colored boy fifteen years old, who had been working at Bridgewater's Saloon, broke into the establishment, stole $10 and a revolver, and was later arrested. Following his confession, Scott led police officers to $6.50 of the money and the revolver. Bridgewater's Saloon, according to newspapers, functioned as a breeding ground for criminal activity. On the other hand, it was the world where members of the colored sporting fraternity rubbed elbows and shared libations with celebrities of the era. For young boys like William Scott, Bridgewater helped sustain an alluring public space for colored males to gather.[32]

The Behemoth Club of Blackville demands additional scrutiny. Occupying the center of the composition, around which action evolves, is a young servant boy. The dreamy-eyed figure stares directly at the viewer. Light from the window illuminates the left side of his puckish face. His carefully modeled head projects against the backdrop of two large human figures that dissolve into an amorphous white space that doubles as an aura, giving closer scrutiny to the boy's head. His heavy eye lids convey an epicanthic fold, contrasting sharply with his broad, fleshy nose and tumid lips. The boy deports himself with dignity, the sack cloth suit and bow tie ornamenting his body. Delicate black marks give form to the bow tie and open up onto the surrounding white space, melding the head and flanking bodies. Given the strong contrast between the black neck and the white tie, the head appears severed. In fact, all the figures — the contrast between white high collared shirts and the strongly modeled heads — conjure decapitation. Why is the boy the central figure? Maybe the focus is not him. Maybe it is the floating heads. The aura of whiteness surrounding the two mugs on the tray is further intensified when projected against the subtle cross-hatching of the boy's coat. The heads resting on stark-white-collared shirts, like the beverages on the tray, are served on platters.

Journalists were not alone in staging minstrel scenes where black figures performed for the delectation of white readers. Graphic artists engaged in similar cultural practices. Solomon Eytinge inserted a black figure as surrogate within the composition. Because whites don't appear in the Blackville Comics, this figure dons the comedic mask of blackface minstrelsy. Eytinge was notorious for adding compositional black figures that seem estranged from the action. Note the seated man in the top hat holding a walking stick pressed against his mouth. His stove pipe hat barely fits his head. His unkempt hair, to the left and right sides of the head, emerges from beneath the hat and conjures a broom. The eyes bulge from his head. Without the eyes, highlighted cheeks, nose, and lips, the entire face would be a blackened mass. Thick, rubbery lips wrap themselves around the handle of the walking stick.

Finally, the club sign reads "Rules: No Gentleman Blackballed Can Be Whitewashed." The sign not only references the practice of "blackballing" unwanted applicants but also invokes the racial pun: Washing an Ethiopian White. Black bodies dramatically losing their skin pigmentations as a result of a cleaning process, or in this case, being liberally brushed with white paint, are frequently found in 19th-century advertisements and published as magazine illustrations for middle-class consumption. Eytinge used white collars and platters as both a way of adding pictorial and dramatic interest and as a means of distancing middle-class consumption from black bodies. Being "whitewashed," then, functions as a derogatory term referring to blacks who had embraced what is imagined as "white" culture over their own. Perhaps, the behemoth conjures a black image of the colored sporting fraternity's inability to attain whiteness.[33]

An Immense Black Bulletin-Board Within the Imagination

Bridgewater had limited opportunities to dictate what went across telegraph or telephone wires. Nor could he control how sports journalists felt or interpreted dispatches devoted to his club's exploits. While translation was crucial to game results, the ability to transcribe them effectively was quite a different matter from the representation of baseball reality. When the club traveled to Dayton, Ohio, for instance, Bridgewater dispatched the outcome and other crucial matters: "The Black Stockings played a second game at Dayton, yesterday, defeating the Dayton Club on a score of 8 to 5 in ten innings. In the game on Thursday [Lewis] Canter [of the Black Stockings], one of their best batsmen, was struck by a ball on the hip and so badly hurt that he had to be carried from the field." This gritty image could be juxtaposed to other baseball images, revealing forms of expression rarely seen in visual representations. The ardent respect given to Bridgewater's account suggests an astonishing authority and shows that the author followed specific guidelines — as a special correspondent would.[34]

McCullagh built on his own news service and trained hundreds of correspondents. He sternly enforced 48 specific rules, one demanding that any news worth printing was worth paying telegraphic tolls on. He provided detailed instructions for preparing copy and filing stories: "Let your matter be free from comment. Don't use the first person. Don't lug in 'your correspondent' when it is possible to avoid doing so." Other rules dealt with instructions for specific kinds of news. While specific instructions for baseball coverage do not appear among them, one senses a growing fascination for colored baseballists. Under McCullagh's direction, sports editor Al Spink provided colorful headlines: "The Colored Champions," "The Black Stockings' Tour," "The Black Sox at Rockford," "Black Stockings at St. Louis Amateurs," "The Tour of the Black Socks," "An Amusing Game Between Colored Clubs at Sportsmen's Park," and "The Black Stockings Decisively Defeat the Grand Avenue Nine." Similarly, Bridgewater's dispatches situated the reader in the thick of the colored championship and were noted for their graphic realism: "Henry Bridgewater, manager of the St. Louis Black Stockings, telegraphed from Rockford last night that his club lost by a score of 15 to 3. [William] Davis, the pitcher, broke his finger and did not play. This leaves the nine crippled." One can only imagine Spink's gains and losses from gambling on the Black Stockings.[35]

This is not to suggest that the relations of word and image are incapable of complex meanings. On the contrary, the ekphrastic hope embedded in the bulletin-board not only requires an understanding of baseball imagery but the dispatcher's translation of its verbal message into an understandable baseball language. Within this context, the word dispatch functions both as noun and verb. As a verb, it means to send, transmit, express, forward, consign, and remit; as in the case of official messages, or of the immediate sending of troops to their destination, or the like. The word is thus used as a substantive of written official reports of events, battles, and the like, sent by ambassadors and generals. Euphemistically, it means to kill, murder, execute, slaughter, and destroy. As a noun, it functions as an official (especially military or diplomatic) report. It also represents a journalist's report sent to newspaper; it is the act of dispatching or the fact of being dispatched. As discussed, baseball has been mediated by military metaphors, visual/verbal imagery dispatched to and from the baseball battlefield.

The effect of these metaphors is, of course, more complex than simply the "veiling" of the National Pastime's civic spirit. Reducing the archive of the Black Stockings to simply a series of military maneuvers is at once outlandish in its failure to view the narratives as part of the "high skilled labor-intensive entertainment industry" and is absolutely on point in its revelation of military imagery often used to describe them. The archive insists that the players were "colored" troops and "dusky" warriors; they were wounded, crippled, and carried off the battlefield; the team's battery engaged in military maneuvers, "a rifle-shooting exercise"; whether winning or losing games on the baseball battlefield, they fought nobly; martial triumphs championed the "colored" nine as being militarily prepared or "out in force." The hyperbole of this baseball imagery enforces a mode of critical realism, while defending the listener/reader against (or preventing) an unbearable (or voyeuristic) access to genuine landscapes of war and conquest. In short, the composite nature of the dispatch (both text and image) that helps give Bridgewater's Black Stockings their sense of gritty realism was produced through a complex set of references to other media in baseball's culture of vision and representation.[36]

Playing an innovative role in the representation of baseball performance and the communication of ball games, this "immense blackboard" demonstrates that there are no "pure" media. The *Globe-Democrat* reports: "This year the Western Union Telegraph Company will have offices in the director's box and in the reporter's stand at the base ball park." The bodies of fans, gamblers, and sportswriters sitting in pool parlors, occupying newsrooms, or waiting in business establishments designed to carry professional games would invariably react, at some point, to what came across the wires. The Black Stockings vs. Grand Avenues caught the national sports media's attention. If one can imagine what it would be to smile knowingly at an exciting report delivered over the wires, one can understand how fans reacted when the Grand Avenues (the St. Louis Browns' reserve team) finally broke the game open by scoring runs in the final three innings. One can also begin to see something of the fascination in the problem of ekphrasis, the verbal representation of visual representation.[37]

I offer, as example, the Southern League game between Atlanta and Augusta. On Wednesday afternoon, 15 April 1885, the produce and cotton exchange is "packed to suffocation with citizens of all classes," watching the reports from the baseball games. Atlanta's Oglethorpe Park, originally built for the International Cotton Exposition (1881), is transformed into the Atlanta Baseball Exchange, which contains four boards, one for each day, with special wires running into the grandstand of each park. The bulletin boards report the contests inning-by-inning. One board reports the Augusta-Atlanta game in detail and, according to newspaper accounts, "photographs" the images perfectly. "Every ball struck, and every ball missed is cheered by Atlanta's fans, before the cheers of Augusta's fans have died away. Mr. Williams, operator for the Western Union, reports the game faultlessly, and Manager Stephen's arrangements are all that can be asked. Tomorrow's game will be similarly reported."[38]

Obviously, the Atlanta-Macon game could never be made visible over the baseball bulletin-board. A verbal representation cannot represent — that is, make present — its object the same way a visual representation can. The bulletin-board (the telegraph or telephone, or the sports column for that matter) may refer to the game, describe it, invoke it, but it can never bring its visual presence before the fans in the way that spectators witness the game on the field. Words can "cite" baseball events, but never "sight" them. What are fans left with? How does a bulletin-board "photograph" the actions of the game? One answer suggests that the bulletin-board is an intrusive "thing," embodying the "shock of the new." It is not like being at the game, nor like gathering at the offices of the St. Louis *Globe-Democrat*, and waiting for each inning to be recorded over the telegraph. It is not like the daily sports column that fans eagerly anticipated in cities like St. Louis, where papers published morning, afternoon, and evening editions. It is not like columns found in weekly sports journals that circulated old material, even though some might consider it new. Its closest equivalent is the pool parlor, the betting establishment where the sporting fraternity receives minute-by-minute accounts of several ball games from across the country. However, respectable fans presumably avoid such places. The bulletin-board could be viewed, then, as an offending image, like persons found guilty by association with the wrong kinds of people, values, or materials.[39]

Such deceptive practices were hardly innovative. On 4 July 1877, the Atlanta Champions and the Chattanooga Olympics, both colored nines, cross bats in Memphis. The Champions defeat the Olympics, 25 to 19. The Olympics take their defeat badly and, growing angry and malicious, try to embroil the Atlanta crowd in a row. This attempt fails. The losing team's mischievousness takes a different tactic. P. S. Cannon, of the Olympic club, telegraphs *The Constitution*: "Olympics beat the Atlantics; score 25 to 19." It was not until the Atlanta club had returned home that they "learned of the cowardly revenge which had been taken by the defeated base ballers." *The Constitution* adds: "So far as the deportment of the Atlanta colored club is concerned, we have nothing to indicate that is was not correct and gentlemanly. We hope that Chattanooga will give a better reception to others who may visit her in the future."[40]

Mediating between the viewer/listener and the "thing" itself, telegraphic operators transmitted baseball accounts in the familiar vernacular. *The Picayune*, as example, presented the local sporting crowd with an illuminating account of how baseball language, peg-board games, the photograph, and the bulletin-board nested within the baseball landscape medium:

> [T]he games the Atlantas play away from home are reported in detail on a large black-board, and with pegs numbered to represent the men, the game be reached as closely as if the spectator were actually on the ground. For instance, peg. No. 1 represents Cahill. It is stuck in the home plate when he goes to bat; if he hits a safe ball his peg is moved up to first base, or as

many bases as he makes. Then peg No. 2, representing Goldsby, is stuck at home plate and manipulated same way. When a runner or batter is put out his peg is retired, and so on to the end.

The bulletin-board mediated between enthusiastic fans and telegraphic dispatches. It functioned as a baseball diamond where numbered and moveable pegs doubled as players, creating the perception that fans were witnessing the game. Transforming the baseball mind into an immense black-board, memory's sensory channels photographed the game's action instantaneously by mapping the telegraph operator's oral performance onto a visual structure.[41]

Serving as a special correspondent to the *Globe-Democrat* and other newspapers, Bridgewater's dispatches from the field were the best rhetorical weapons for black images of authenticity, virtue, and judiciousness. Yet telegraphing sports news had its challenges. Game results, for example, could suffer misrepresentation. On 19 June 1883, the *Register* reported that the Redford Reds had defeated the Black Stockings, 15 to 3. The *Globe-Democrat* followed suit, claiming that Bridgewater had "telegraphed from Rockford last night that his club lost by a score of 15 to 3." The sports column was incorrect. Cross-checking box scores generally comprised of two rows, one for each club, but several newspapers differed on which team represented the home club. Sometimes, box scores placed the home nine in the bottom row. Other times, the home club was determined by coin toss. Bridgewater dispatched another telegraph: "The Black Sox won in Rockford by a score of 15 to 3 on Monday; the report was received differently." Simply put, the score results had been inverted. Moreover, the narrative provides no clues as to the game's progress. It concludes, rather ambiguously, that the game ended with the score standing in favor of the home nine. Whether this dispatch had been intentionally or accidentally changed, the game's misrepresentation served as a mean-spirited joke on the colored boys.[42]

What could the Rockford sports column have meant beyond the pleasures of ridiculing Bridgewater's Black Stockings, an absurd gesture that had temporarily obscured the reality from the baseball world? Both St. Louis and Chicago papers had portrayed the Black Stockings as the "home nine." No retraction appeared. However, the column header for the second game, "The Coons Carry Off the Cake," is instructive. While the *Register* conceivably viewed this episode as an innocuous transgression, the reputations of Bridgewater's Black Stockings and perhaps the gambling establishment were on the line. Bridgewater's second dispatch carefully side-stepped both issues. He understood that embarrassing the Rockford Reds, an all-white club, might get picked up by the sporting press and alienate potential competitors. Several games had been prescheduled with professional and semi-professional white clubs. Having them cancelled to prove a point was not good business. Gate receipts mattered. Race also mattered. Spectator violence towards visiting clubs came with the territory. To provoke needless hostility against his team was suicidal. Bridgewater shrewdly added both human faces and dramatic storylines to his barebones dispatches; what historian William L. Van DeBurg has called, "setting the literary record straight by distancing victim from villain." Colored journalism was determined to have its opinions matter, and Bridgewater's accounts proved compelling, his descriptions political and symbolic, sometimes beyond anything the baseball sporting would have imagined.[43]

Bridgewater's dispatches from the field, especially Upper Canada, are significant because they document his club's second professional tour, a symbolic journey to be sure, one of socio-political significance, if not a capitalist enterprise. From 25 June to 3 July, the Black Stockings spent two remarkable weeks battling Canadian clubs. A telegram from Guelph, Ontario, evoked an ominous beginning: the Black Stockings lost to the Maple Leafs by the score of 11–1, owing to their want of a substitute for their disabled pitcher (fans knew from earlier reports that William "Bud" Davis, the team's "phenomenal pitcher," had broken his finger. Davis reinjured his hand). The Canadian excursion produced 16 games against all-white clubs: the "colored boys" winning 11 of the contests. Prior to Independence Day, the Black Stockings defeated the Maples Leafs by a score of 5–4. Bridgewater's patriotic dispatch was picked up nationally, appearing in over 14 newspapers. The *Arkansas Mansion*, a colored newspaper, expressed its pride in the Black Stockings, especially the management triumvirate of Holmes, Tyler, and Bridgewater, celebrating the organization as the only professional colored ball club in the United States.[44]

What made the extended stay in Upper Canada depended on the accommodations that Guelph's relatively large and thriving colored population could offer. Historically, Guelph had been the site of early 19th-century black enslavement and, after 1812, a site for the Underground Railroad. During his early career, Moses Fleetwood Walker had played for the celebrated Tecumseh Club, of Upper Canada. But opportunities for pool or other gambling probably proved lucrative as well. Bridgewater considered gambling on prizefights, dogfights, billiards, bicycle races, and baseball part of the sporting life. His players gambled. On the first leg of the professional tour at Rockford, Illinois, one of the St. Louis nine boasted that he would have bet $100 that the Rockford would not have touched third base if not for an error.[45]

Exploring the archive of Bridgewater's Black Stockings remains an ambitious cultural project because the level of public attention given to this colored club had no precedent across the country. Additionally, the number of sports accounts dedicated to his professional nine is staggering. Much of it, black images aside, may be summarized under the thematic of pretty playing. For example, performative descriptions link both dandies and dudes to enumeration, simply telling baseball stories and providing copious detail. "Very tall, powerful and free-moving," "good batting," "running bases with good facility," "making dives and slides in professional style," "playing beautifully," "prettily uniformed, wearing suits of all white and black stockings," "gentlemanly and quiet," "chronic kickers," "injudicious base running," "horrible," "fumbling a hot grounder," and "muffing and slipping and sprawling": all these vernacular forms have close parallels to standard baseball images found in sports columns across the baseball landscape. The majority of sports accounts covering the Black Stockings derive from contests against white clubs. Towards the beginning of the 1883 season, the epic journey of the Black Stockings had already become enmeshed within the sporting network of the Mound City and beyond, and the various images circulating in the print media were mediated through material objects already understood by the sporting fraternity. Bridgewater's Black Stockings are, then, true exemplars of black images as matter. There are no baseball images without baseball objects — black bodies embodied in material form, in things, primarily newspapers and sporting journals — seemingly creating themselves, and creating the social formations that they signified on the baseball landscape.[46]

"Baseball managers," according to the *Pelican*, "are like editors in one respect at least. They come in contact with more people who 'know it all' in running either a nine or a newspaper, than it is possible to keep track of." Whether Bridgewater thought this or compared himself to journalists is another story. In 1883, he was interviewed by *The Dayton Democrat* (an especially rare find), acknowledging the reality of social exclusion, and aspiring to build colored institutions:

> Our team was organized with a view to entering a colored league, which was talked of some last winter. Originally we did not intend to play any but colored nines which were to have composed this league. When the league failed to organize we were compelled to make engagements with teams composed of white players. We only have one engagement for the season with a colored nine, and that is at Cleveland.

Bridgewater called Dayton's white team "too old." Speaking as an experienced baseball man, he candidly observed that certain players "could not hold a place in any other nine in the country." He buttressed his criticism: "I know what I am talking about. I have been playing professional base ball for about twelve years, but there are players on your nine that played ball before I was born. You need young men to play base ball."[47]

Bridgewater's spectacle of old teams and young men trumpets the golden age of colored baseball in an era of declining civil rights. When the club owner asserted his knowledge of the game and directed the sportswriter's attention to the talent-laden club under his management — the colored aggregation would defeat the famed Dayton club four games out of five — he understood its future significance. We assume that Bridgewater was simply thinking of baseball, but he put forth broader considerations, and he could as easily have been talking about the peculiarity of capitalist commodity production and the tragedy of the modern hero. The figure of the young colored ballplayer isn't merely "read" or interpreted as a sign, symptom, or allegory, and it isn't merely acted upon as if it were dude or dandy. Bridgewater's assessment treats it both as commodity and the tragedy that it signifies, both as a sign of the postbellum Gilded Age and the postbellum Gilded Age itself. That is why the early image of black baseball is best described as a new patterning of race relations, not just in the sense of the politics of self-making but at the level of creating some space within the institutions and social relationships that threatened to dominate its life.

Chapter Notes

Preface

1. Mitchell, W.J.T. *What Do Pictures Want?* (Chicago: The University of Chicago Press, 2005); Scott, James C. *Domination and the Arts of Resistance: Hidden Transcripts* (New Haven: Yale University Press, 1990).

2. Morrison, Toni. *Playing in the Dark* (Cambridge: Harvard University Press, 1992), 38.

3. Benjamin, Walter. *The Work of Art in the Age of Its Technological Reproducibility and Other Writings on Media* (Cambridge: The Belknap Press of Harvard University, 2008), 195–225; Snead, James. A. *Figures of Division: William Faulkner's Major Novels* (New York: Methuen, 1986), x–xi.

Introduction

1. Neil Harris, "The Gilded Age Reconsidered Once Again," *Archives of American Art Journal* 23, no. 4 (1983): 8–18.

2. Henri Focillon, *The Life of Forms in Art* (New York: Zone Books, 1992); W.J.T. Mitchell, *The Last Dinosaur Book* (Chicago: University of Chicago Press, 1998).

3. Mitchell, *The Last Dinosaur Book*, 53–54.

4. Focillon, *The Life of Forms in Art*, 32.

5. Richard Brilliant, *Portraiture* (London: Reaktion Books, 1997), 46.

6. W.J.T. Mitchell, *What Do Pictures Want?* (Chicago: University of Chicago Press, 2005), 272.

7. Bruce Chadwick, *When the Game Was Black and White: The Illustrated History of the Negro Leagues* (New York: Abbeville Press, 1992).

8. Mitchell, *What Do Pictures Want?*, 91; Steven Riess, *City Games: The Evolution of American Urban Society and the Rise of Sports* (Urbana: University of Illinois Press, 1991), 15–16, 117–123.

Chapter One

1. Christopher Robert Reed, *Black Chicago's First Century*, Vol. I, 1833–1900 (Columbia: University of Missouri Press, 2005), 177; E. Ann Kaplan, *Trauma Culture* (New Brunswick: Rutgers University Press,

2005), 67; "Base Ball," *The Inter-Ocean* (Chicago), July 17, 1874.

2. W.J.T. Mitchell, *What Do Pictures Want?* (Chicago: University of Chicago Press, 2005), 91.

3. Mitchell, *What Do Pictures Want?*, 94.

4. In 1965, I first heard Malcolm X use the word "black." He had helped define black in social, political, and cultural terms. In the 1970s, my awareness of racial terminology was further complicated. I recall a magazine cartoon that depicted an integrated cocktail party. A white man asks a black man the following: "What are you people calling yourselves lately?" Working in a university setting over the past thirty years, I remain fascinated, if not absorbed, by the range of designations that students, faculty, and staff continue using to label people of color, publicly and privately. It has not been uncommon to hear "Negro," "colored," "black," "Afro-American," and "African-American." These designations, except the last one, were used in the late nineteenth-century, suggesting their seeming timelessness. In this book, their usage might appear confusing or inconsistent. This is not my intent. When I apply the label "colored," it refers to the polite middle-class term shared between whites and people of color. Both "colored" and "Negro" suggest physiognomic characteristics; the latter implying more Negroid features: dark brown skin, tightly-curled hair, broad nose, and thick lips; the former, a lighter complexion, curly to straight hair, and relatively thin nose and lips. Negro could be pejorative, that is, a derogatory comment used to insult an insubordinate colored person. However, these designations could apply to any person of color. The designation "black" has been contextualized within a late twentieth-century framework, burdened by personal social, political, and cultural meanings.

5. "A Colored Game," *The Times* (Chicago), October 12, 1875.

6. Ray Schmidt, "The Golden Age of Chicago Baseball," *Chicago History* 28, no. 2 (Winter 2000): 40; Leslie A. Heaphy, "Early Black Teams in Chicago," *Black Baseball And Chicago,* ed. Leslie A. Heaphy, 7–17 (Jefferson, NC: McFarland, 2006), 8–9.

7. Neil Harris, "The Gilded Age Reconsidered Once Again," *Archives of American Art Journal* 23, no. 4 (1983): 8–18.

8. W.J.T. Mitchell, *Picture Theory* (Chicago: Uni-

versity of Chicago Press), 83. "Metapictures make visible the impossibility of a strict metalanguage, a second-order of representation that stands free of its first-order target. They also reveal the inextricable weaving together of representation and discourse, the imbrications of visual and verbal experience. It the relation of the visible and the readable is (as Foucault thought) an infinite one, that is, if 'word and image' is simply the unsatisfactory name for an unstable dialectic that constantly shifts its location in representational practices, breaking both pictorial and discursive frames and undermining the assumptions that underwrite the separation of the verbal and visual disciplines, then theoretical pictures may be mainly useful as de-disciplinary exercises." "The Sporting World," *The Tribune* (Chicago), August 24, 1870; "The Green Diamond," *Globe-Democrat* (St. Louis), July 10, 1876; "Base Ball from a Colored Point of View," *The Tribune* (Chicago), August 24, 1870.

9. "Base Ball from a Colored Point of View," *The Tribune* (Chicago) August 24, 1870.

10. "Police," *The Tribune* (Chicago), July 10 and 13, 1858.

11. Herbert Asbury, *The Gangs of Chicago* (originally published as *Gem of the Prairie: An Informal History of the Chicago Underworld*, New York: Knopf, 1940, reprint DeKalb: Northern Illinois University Press, 1986), 100–101; Ancestry.com; Cynthia Marie Blair, "Vicious Commerce: African American Women's Sex Work and the Transformation of Urban Space in Chicago, 1850–1915" (Ph.D. diss., Harvard University, 1999), 259–260; John J. Flinn, *History of the Chicago Police* (Chicago: Police Book Fund, 1887; repr., New York: AMS Press, 1973), 108.

12. Robin D. G. Kelly, *Race Rebels: Culture, Politics, and the Black Working Class* (New York: The Free Press, 1996), 47–49.

13. Mitchell, *What Do Pictures Want?*, 91; Steven Riess, *City Games: The Evolution of American Urban Society and the Rise of Sports* (Urbana: University of Illinois Press, 1991), 15–16, 117–123; "The Umpire Does His Best," *New York Times*, August 11, 1886; "Umpire McQuaid's Mysterious Disappearance Accounted For," *Sporting News*, August 30, 1886; "Alas Poor Umpires!," *Sporting News*, October 4, 1886; "Notes About Clubs and Players," *The Tribune* (New York), April 25, 1887; "Caught on the Fly," *Sporting News*, September 20 and 27 1886, September 10, 1887.

14. "Dusky Dolly Vardens of Chester Give An Exhibition," *New York Times*, May 18, 1883; "Chicago Doings," *The Globe* (New York), September 20, 1884; "Life in New York City," *Daily Eagle* (Brooklyn), February 10, 1884; Angela Davis, *Blues Legacies and Black Feminism* (New York: Vintage Books, 1998), 44.

15. "Notes and Comments," *Sporting Life* November 14, 1883; "A Base-Ball Burlesque," *New York Times*, September 23, 1883.

16. "Libel Suit Against the Times," *The Democrat* (St. Louis), October 23, 1874.

17. Asbury, *The Gangs of Chicago*, 106.

18. Ancestry.com; Asbury, *The Gangs of Chicago*, 140–141; Clifton R. Wooldridge, *Hands Up! In the World of Crime* (Chicago: Police Publishing, 1901).

19. "Kent Held Them Down," *The American Nashville*, June 5, 1886, 4.

20. https://www.gfg.com/baseball/n172.shtml; http://murraycards.com/cards/reprint_newissues.html.

21. "Female Baseballists," *The Constitution* (Atlanta), July 16, 1886.

22. "Indecent Advertising," *The Times* (New York), June 20, 1886; "Female Baseballists," *The Constitution*, July 16, 1886. In 1873 the United States Congress passed the first national obscenity legislation — the Comstock Law — which marked a historically new federal involvement in fighting vice. It accelerated censorship by enlarging the category of "obscene literature" to include all printed matter, and, for the first time, made it a crime to circulate information about contraception or abortion.

23. Neil Harris, *Building Lives: Constructing Rites and Passages* (New Haven: Yale University Press, 1999), 62.

24. The turf war over Comiskey Park is traceable to the city's changing demographics during the 19th century, which culminated in the Chicago race riots of 1919. "White gangs from the neighborhood of 59th and Wentworth Avenue — including some of the tough Irish who belonged to Ragens Colts, a notorious 'athletic club' sponsored by a politician named Frank Ragen who found its members' proficiency in intimidation useful — objected to black youths using the park's baseball diamonds. Ball games in the park often led to gang fights, which were usually broken up by park policemen." Robert K. Landers, *An Honest Writer: The Life and Times of James T. Farrell* (San Francisco: Encounter Books, 1999), 34–44.; Harris, *Building Lives*, 120.

25. Reed, *Black Chicago's First Century*, 178–179. Among the occupations listed for people of color: coachman, domestic servant, hotel waiter, barber, blacksmith, saloonkeeper, barkeeper, city laborer, hotel waiter or cook, railroad employee, saloon porter, "seaman," janitor, seamstress, restaurant waiter, "mining," tailor, laundress, physician, drayman (cart driver), butcher, house painter and whitewasher, tobacco manufacturing, teamster, house carpenter, Methodist minister, shoe maker, dress maker, school teacher, plasterer, farmer, and real estate agent.

26. "The Colored Electors," *The Tribune* (Chicago), June 30, 1870.

27. *Ibid.*, 187; Thekla Ellen Joiner, *Sin in the City: Chicago and Revivalism, 1880–1920* (Columbia: University of Missouri Press, 2007).

28. Joiner, *Sin in the City*, 129–131.

29. "The Base Ball Championship," *The Tribune* (Chicago), July 5, 1868.

30. Mitchell, *What Do Pictures Want?*, 214–215; "A Satisfied Look," *Daily Eagle* (Brooklyn), May 30, 1881.

31. Kelly, *Race Rebels*, 49–50; "Base Ball," *The Tribune* (Chicago), August 23, 1867; Eugene H. Cropsey, *Crosby's Opera House* (Madison, N.J.: Farleigh Dickinson University Press, 1999), 332; Frederick Francis Cook, *Bygone Days in Chicago* (Chicago: Cook Press, 2007), 210.

32. "Police," *The Tribune* (Chicago), July 10, 1858.

33. Edwin Atlee Barber, *The Pottery Porcelain of the United States* (New York: Putnam, 1893), 220–224;

Ellen Paul Denker, "Parian Porcelain Statuary: American Sculptors and the Introduction of Art in American Ceramics," *Ceramics in America 2002*, ed. Robert Hunter (Milwaukee, WI: Chipstone, 2002), 62–79.

34. Alice Cooney Frelinghuysen, *American Porcelain: 1770–1920* (New York: The Metropolitan Museum of Art, 1989); James M. DiCelrico and Barry J. Pavelee, *The Jersey Game* (New Brunswick, NJ: Rutgers University Press, 1991); Susan James-Gadzinski and Mary Mullen Cunningham, *American Sculpture in the Museum of American Art of the Pennsylvania Academy of the Fine Arts* (Philadelphia: Museum of American Art of the Pennsylvania Academy of the Fine Arts, 1997); *The Royal City of Susa*, ed. Prudence O. Harper, Joan Aruz, and Francoise Tallon (New York: Harry N. Abrams, 1992).

35. "Close of the Detroit Tournament," *The Times* (Chicago), August 21, 1867.

36. Peter L. Bernstein, *The Power of Gold: The History of an Obsession* (New York: John Wiley, 2000).

37. Michael D. Lomax, *Black Baseball Entrepreneurs, 1860–1901* (Syracuse: Syracuse University Press, 2003), 17; Lawrence D. Hogan, *Shades of Glory: The Negro Leagues and the Story of African-American Baseball* (Washington: National Geographic, 2006); "Pythian and Olympic," *Daily Eagle*, September 6, 1867; "Sporting News," *Daily Eagle*, September 4, 1869.

38. Bridget T. Heneghan, *Whitewashing America: Material Culture and Race in the Antebellum Imagination* (Jackson: University of Mississippi Press, 2003), 132–136; Eric Lott, *Love and Theft: Blackface Minstrelsy and the American Working Class* (Oxford: Oxford University Press, 1993).

39. "St. Louis In Splinters," *Daily Globe-Democrat* (St. Louis), April 18, 1874; "Colored Jealousy," *The Republican* (St. Louis), August 20, 1877; "Notes About Town," *The Republican* (St. Louis), July 29, 1881; "A Fight in Clabber Alley Over a Yellow Girl," *The Republican* (St. Louis), June 8, 1882; "The St. Louis Black Socks Gallantly Down the Cleveland Blues," *The Leader* (Cleveland), May 10, 1883; "Diamond Chips," *The Republican* (St. Louis), April 25, 1884; "Shot and Killed," *Globe-Democrat*, April 26, 1884.

40. *The Lakeside Directory of Chicago, 1874–75* (Chicago: Williams, Donnelly, 1875); "Chicago Voter Registration, 1892" (ancestry.com); 1870 Federal Census Report (ancestry.com).

41. "Concerning Saloons," *The Tribune* (Chicago), July 7, 1870; Ted Vincent, *Mudville's Revenge: The Rise and Fall of American Sport* (Lincoln: University of Nebraska Press, 1994), 101.

42. "Base Ball from a Colored Point of View," *The Tribune* (Chicago), August 24, 1870; "Base Ball," *The Times* (St. Louis), September 5, 1875.

43. Mitchell, *What do Pictures Want?*, 216–217; "The National Game," *The Tribune* (Chicago), July 9 and 10, 1870, August 5, 1870; "The Sporting World," *The Tribune* (Chicago), September 6, 1870, October 2, 9, 16, 23, and 30, 1870; "Games and Pastimes," *The Tribune* (Chicago), June 13, 23, and 25, 1871.

44. Mitchell, *What do Pictures Want?*, 216–217; Mitchell, *Picture Theory*, 194–197.

45. Schmidt, "The Golden Age of Chicago Base-ball," *Chicago History*, 40; "First Day of the Dexter Park July Racing Meeting," *The Tribune* (Chicago), July 2, 1869; "Presentation of the Prizes in the Amateur Billiard Tournament," *The Tribune* (Chicago), July 8, 1869; "Tenth Contest for the Billiard Championship of Illinois," *The Tribune* (Chicago), March 24, 1870; "Base Ball," *The Tribune* (Chicago), March 24, 1870; "Rat Killing," *The Tribune* (Chicago), April 3, 1870.

46. Vincent, *Mudville's Revenge*, 127.

47. "Sporting Notes," *The Republican* (Chicago), July 1, 1871.

48. "On Tour," *The Register*, August 27, 1870.

49. "Blue vs. Pink," *The Republican* (Chicago), August 23, 1870; "Colored Base Ballists," *The Evening Journal* (Chicago), August 24, 1870.

50. "Base-Ball," *The Times* (Chicago), August 13, 1874.

51. "The National Game," *The Register* (Rockford, IL), July 23, 1870; "The Colored Clubs," *The Register*, August 6, 1870; "Colored Clubs," *The Register*, August 20, 1870.

52. "Announcements," *The Tribune* (Chicago), August 14 and 24, 1870; "Games to Come," *The Times* (Chicago), August 20, 1870; "The Proposed Tournament," *The Times* (Chicago), August 25, 1870; "Sporting Matters," *The Tribune* (Chicago), May 14, 1870; "The Blue Stockings," *The Tribune* (Chicago), September 21, 1870.

53. "The Blue Stockings," *The Times* (Chicago), September 23, 1870.

54. "Base Ball Matters," *The Evening Journal* (Chicago), September 16, 1870.

55. "The Amateur Tournament," *The Evening Journal*, September 17, 1870.

56. "Sporting," *The Times* (Chicago), September 17, 1870.

57. *Ibid.*

58. "White vs. Blacks," *The Republican* (Chicago), September 28, 1870; Alfred H. Spink, *The National Game* (St. Louis: national Game Publishing, 1910; repr. Carbondale: Southern Illinois University Press, 2000), 337.

59. "The Amateur Championship," *The Tribune*, October 2, 1870.

60. "Base Ball," *The Times* (Chicago), October 6, 1870; "Sporting," *The Tribune* (Chicago), September 21 and 28, 1870; "The Blue Stockings," *The Times* (Chicago), September 21 and October 8, 1870; "The Sporting World," *The Tribune* (Chicago), October 6 and 7, 1870; "Base-Ball Items," *The Times* (Chicago), October 7, 1870; "The Colored Electors," *The Tribune* (Chicago), June 30, 1870.

61. "The Uniques," *The Tribune* (Chicago), September 19, 1871.

62. "The Colored Championship," *The Times* (Chicago), May 31, 1871.

63. James Brunson, "Henry Bridgewater's Black Stockings, 1881–1889," *Base Ball: A Journal of the Early Game* 1, no. 2 (2007), 12–26.

64. "Colored Men's Match Games," *The Tribune* (Chicago), September 17, 1871; "Sporting Gossip," *The Evening Journal*, September 18, 1871; "Base Ball," *The Inquirer* (Philadelphia), September 18, 1871; "The

Uniques," *The Tribune* (Chicago), September 19, 1871; "Condensed Locals," *The Evening Star* (Washington, DC), September 11, 1871; "Condensed Locals," *The Evening Star*, September 12, 1871.

65. "The Uniques," *The Tribune* (Chicago), September 19, 1871.

66. "Games to Come Off," *The Inter-Ocean*, July 17, 1874; "The Week's Sport," *The Times* (Chicago), August 16, 1871; "The Base Ball Tournament" *The Inter-Ocean*, August 15, 1874.

67. "Uniques vs. Napoleons," *The Times* (Chicago), September 12, 1874.

68. "Colored Champions," *The Times* (St. Louis), May 13, 1876.

69. Eric Foner, *Forever Free: The Story of Emancipation and Reconstruction* (New York: Knopf, 2005), 181–184.

Chapter Two

1. Chicago's DuSable Museum of African American History has a collection of Lewis's original drawings, including both pencil and pen and ink works. One finely rendered drawing titled *Blocking Progress* shows two young colored ballplayers, in traditional baseball uniforms, conversing with an old colored farmer who is holding a shotgun. His concern is that several ballplayers have transformed his field into a baseball grounds. In the background are six other players. Was Lewis making a social statement about baseball's modern impact on the younger and older generations?

2. "The Green Diamond," *Globe-Democrat* (St. Louis), July 10, 1876. The exact dates demarcating Reconstruction are not universally agreed upon. American historian Eric Foner frames the period between 1863 and 1877, beginning with the Emancipation Proclamation and ending with southern "Redemption and "home rule," the equivalent to white rule. Other historians point to 1883 as the end of Reconstruction, the year that the United States Supreme Court declared the Civil Rights Act of 1875 unconstitutional.

3. "The Sporting World," *The Tribune* (Chicago), August 24, 1870.

4. David R. Roediger, *The Wages of Whiteness* (London: Verso, 1995).l

5. W.J.T. Mitchell, *Picture Theory* (Chicago: University of Chicago Press, 1994), 45.

6. Lott, *Love and Theft*, 137–139.

7. Lomax, *Black Baseball Entrepreneurs*, xxiv–xxvi.

8. "How They Play Base Ball," *The Gazette* (Cleveland), June 21, 1888; "Sports," *The Globe* (St. Louis), April 30, 1875; "Ball and Bat," *The Globe* (St. Louis), May 4, 1875; Phil Dixon and Patrick J. Hannigan, *The Negro Baseball Leagues, a Photographic History, 1863–1955* (Mattituck, NY: Amereon House, 1992), 18; David R. Roediger, *The Wages of Whiteness* (London: Verso, 1993), 124; Lott, *Love and Theft*, 3; William J. Mahar, *Behind the Burnt Cork Mask* (Urbana: University of Illinois Press, 1999).

9. Cecil Brown, *Stagolee Shot Billy* (Cambridge: Harvard University Press, 2003), 13, 70.

10. Victor Turner, *Dramas, Fields, and Metaphors: Symbolic Action in Human Society* (Ithaca: Cornell University Press, 1974).

11. Mitchell, *What Do Pictures Want?*, 204.

12. *Ibid.*, 207–213. The late nineteenth-century sports medium was a complex social institution that contained not only sport and theater journals, newspapers, advertisements, cartoons, illustrations, and lithographs, but also the individuals within it, a history of practices, rituals, and habits, skills and techniques, and a set of material objects and spaces. "All About Town," *The Times* (St. Louis), December 18, 1873; "St. Louis in Splinters," *The Globe* (St. Louis), May 5, 1874; "Colored Mass Meeting," *The Democrat* (St. Louis), December 3, 1873; "St. Louis in Splinters," *Globe-Democrat*, May 5, 1878.

13. "Negro Emancipation," *The Globe* (St. Louis), September 6, 1874; Timothy J. Gilfoyle, *City of Eros: New York City, Prostitution, and the Commercialization of Sex* (New York: Norton), 15.

14. "St. Louis In Splinters," *The Globe* (St. Louis), May 5, 1874; "Amusements," *The Times* (St. Louis), January 3, 1875.

15. Charles C. Clayton, *"Little Mack": Joseph B. McCullough of the St. Louis Globe-Democrat* (Carbondale: Southern Illinois University Press, 1969), 85; Brown, *Stagolee Shot Billy*, 215, 245.

16. Wilson Jeremiah Moses, "The Lost World of the Negro, 1895–1919: Black Literary and Intellectual Life Before the 'Renaissance,'" *Black American Literature Forum* 21, no. 1–2 (Spring-Summer 1987): 61–84; "Local Short Stops," *The Democrat*, September 17, 1873; "Ira Aldridge Club," *The Democrat*, December 14, 1873; "Local Brevities," *The Republican* (St. Louis), May 30, 1874; "Negro Emancipation," *Daily Globe*, August 4, 1874; "Our Colored Schools," *Globe Democrat*, August 13, 1878.

17. Brown, *Stagolee Shot Billy*, 122.

18. *Ibid.*, 79–80; "The Fifteenth Amendment," *Post Dispatch*, April 2, 1875.

19. "Local Gambling," *The Chronicle* (St. Louis), September 9, 1881; "Short Stops," *Globe-Democrat*, August 9 and 30, 1875, June 6 and August 30, 1876; "Gossip," *Globe-Democrat*, June 10, 1875; "Local Gossip," *Globe-Democrat*, May 8, 1876; "Tips," *The Republican* (St. Louis), July 24, 1876; "Base Ball," *The Republican* (St. Louis), August 7, 1876; "Kind to Coons," *The Republican* (St. Louis), May 17, 1881; "Mild Censorship," *The Republican* (St. Louis), May 15, 1876; "All About Town," *The Times* (St. Louis), March 28, 1875; "Up and Down Town," *Post Dispatch*, April 6, 1874.

20. J. A. Dacus and James W. Buel, *A Tour of St. Louis; or, The Inside Life of a Great City* (St. Louis: Western Publishing, 1878), 412–418; "City Politics," *Globe-Democrat*, April 6, 1875; Harris, "The Gilded Age Reconsidered Once Again," *Archives of American Art Journal*, 8–18.

21. "Other Games," *The Republican* (St. Louis), June 28, 1875.

22. "City Politics," *Globe-Democrat* (St. Louis), April 6, 1875; Wilson Jeremiah Moses, *The Wings of Ethiopia* (Ames: Iowa State University, 1990), 201–218.

23. Brown, *Stagolee Shot Billy*, 93–98.

24. "Local Short Stops," *Globe-Democrat*, July 13,

1873; "Cut with a Knife," *Globe-Democrat*, March 15, 1876; "A Dangerous Colored Woman," *Globe-Democrat*, March 22, 1876; "St. Louis," *The Gazette*, February 16, 1884; D.R. Sneddeker, "Regulating Vice: Prostitution and the St. Louis Social Evil Ordinance, 1870–1874," *Gateway Heritage* 11, no. 2 (1990): 20–47.

25. Brown, *Stagolee Shot Billy*, 105–115; "A Raid on the concert Saloons," *The Democrat* (St. Louis), August 15, 1873; "Local Brevities," *The Republican* (St. Louis), October 11, 1874; "The Demi-Monde," *The Democrat*, March 16, 1873; "The City News," *The Chronicle*, August 15, 1881.

26. "Local Short Stops," *The Democrat*, August 28, 1873; "Total Depravity," *The Times* (St. Louis), July 28, 1879; "Amusements," *The Democrat*, July 2, 1872.

27. Mitchell, *What Do Pictures Want?*, 34.

28. Brown, *Stagolee Shot Billy*, 71–72; "St. Louis In Splinters," *Globe-Democrat*, April 18, 1874; "Colored Jealousy," *The Republican* (St. Louis), August 20, 1877; "Notes About Town," *The Republican* (St. Louis), July 29, 1881; "A Fight in Clabber Alley Over a Yellow Girl," *The Republican* (St. Louis), June 8, 1882; Mitchell, *What Do Pictures Want?*, 295.

29. *Ibid.*, 88; L. O. McMurray, *To Keep The Waters Troubled* (Oxford: Oxford University Press, 1998), 53.

30. "The Colored Champions," *The Times* (St. Louis), June 13, 1876; "Local Short Stops," *Globe-Democrat*, May 14, 1873; "Colored Mass Meetings," *Globe-Democrat*, December 6, 1873; "Colored Citizens," *Globe-Democrat*, June 12, 1875.

31. "Base Ball," *Republican*, September 9, 1875; Mitchell, *What Do Pictures Want?*, 90–94.

32. "Base Ball — Miscellaneous," *The Times* (St. Louis), August 31 and September 6, 1875; "Base Ball Brevities," *Globe-Democrat*, July 29, 1876; "Short Stops," *Globe-Democrat*, May 16 and August 16, 1876; "The Colored Clubs," *Globe-Democrat*, June 14, 1876; "The Green Diamond," *Globe-Democrat*, July 10, 1876; "Base Ball," *The Republican* (St. Louis), July 10, 1876; "Tips," *Globe-Democrat*, July 24, 1876; "Diamond Dust," *Globe-Democrat*, August 1, 1877.

33. "Sports," *Globe-Democrat*, April 25, 1875; "Waving the Willow," *Globe-Democrat*, April 29, 1875; "The Sporting World," *Globe-Democrat*, April 17, 1876; "Ball and Bat," *Post Dispatch*, April 27, 1874; "Local Gossip," *Globe-Democrat*, April 9, 1876. The Red Stockings organization, as example, initially limited rentals to college and store nines, and then only by the day.

34. "Sporting News," *The Inter-Ocean*, May 10, 1875; "Base Ball," *The Republican* (St. Louis), September 7 and 9, 1875; "The Colored Teams," *Globe-Democrat*, September 13, 1875; "Willow and Leather," *Globe-Democrat*, June 16, 1876; "The Colored Clubs," *Globe-Democrat*, September 7, 1875.

35. "Enquirer Shrieks," *Globe-Democrat*, July 8, 1876; "Gossip," *The Globe*, May 9, 1875; "Local Ball Items," *The Republican* (St. Louis), May 20, 1876; "Enquirer Shrieks," *Globe-Democrat*, July 8, 1876; "Base Ball Brevities," *The Times* (St. Louis), August 15, 1880; "Base Ball," *The Clipper*, September 2, 1882; "The Colored Teams," *Globe-Democrat*, September 13, 1875; "The Rival Colored Clubs on the Green Diamond," *The Times* (St. Louis), September 13, 1875; "A

Game Between Crack Colored Nines," *The Times* (St. Louis), August 31, 1875.

36. "The Colored Teams," *Globe-Democrat*, September 13, 1875; "The Rival Colored Clubs on the Green Diamond," *The Times* (St. Louis), September 13, 1875.

37. "Base Ball Brevities," *The Times* (St. Louis), August 15, 1880; "Base Ball," *The Clipper*, September 2, 1882

38. "The Amateurs' Day," *The Times* (St. Louis), May 15, 1876; "Short Stops," *Globe-Democrat*, May 16, 1876; "Base Ball Notes," *The Times* (St. Louis), June 15, 1876; "Dusky Tossers," *The Times* (St. Louis), May 16, 1876.

39. "The Green Diamond," *Globe-Democrat*, July 10, 1876; "Base Ball Brevities," *Globe-Democrat*, July 29, 1876; "Base Ball," *Elgin Morning Frank* (Elgin, IL), July 17, 1883; "Base Ball Notes," *The Times* (St. Louis), June 14, 1876.

40. "A Game Between Crack Colored Nines," *The Times* (St. Louis), August 31, 1875.

41. "Base Ball," *The Times* (St. Louis), December 9, 1874; "A Chat with Chapman," *The Tribune*, May 2, 1875.

42. Larry Bowman, *Before the World Series* (DeKalb: Northern Illinois University Press, 2002), 25–26.

43. "Gossip," *The Globe*, May 9, 1875; "Local Ball Items," *The Republican*, May 20, 1876; "Enquirer Shrieks," *Globe-Democrat*, July 8, 1876.

44. "The Contest for the Belt," *The Times* (St. Louis), September 25, 1879; "The Great Walk," *The Police Gazette*, October 4, 1879; "A 'Smoked Irishman' Wins the Belt," *The Globe* (Boston), December 28, 1879; "The Wheel," *The Republican* (St. Louis), August 27, 1882; "General Sporting Notes," *The Republican* (St. Louis), September 4, 1882.

45. Lomax, *Black Baseball Entrepreneurs*, 38–49; "Base Ball," *The Republican* (St. Louis), October 5, 1874; "The National Game," *Globe-Democrat*, March 1, 1876; "Base Ball To-Day," *Globe-Democrat*, April 16, 1876; "Base Ball," *Globe-Democrat*, April 20, 1876; "Base Ball To-Day," *Globe-Democrat*, April 30, 1876; "Base Ball To-Day," *Globe-Democrat*, June 15, 1876.

46. *Gould's St. Louis Directory for 1872–73* (St. Louis, 1872); *Gould's St. Louis Directory for 1875* (St. Louis, 1875); *Gould's St. Louis Directory for 1876* (St. Louis, 1880); "Shots and Stars," *The Times-Journal* (St. Louis), May 19, 1879; Cyprian Clamorgan, *The Colored Aristocracy of St. Louis* (Columbia: University of Missouri Press, 1999), 13–15.

47. Lomax, *Black Baseball Entrepreneurs*, 34; "Local Short Stops," *The Democrat*, March 1, 1873; "That $10,000 Dinner," *The Democrat*, August 23, 1873.

48. *Ibid.*

49. "Base Ball Brevities," *The Globe* (St. Louis), September 6, 1874; "Miscellaneous," *The Tribune* (Chicago), September 6, 1874; "Base Ball: Uniques vs. Napoleons," *The Tribune* (Chicago), September 12, 1874.

50. *Gould's St. Louis Directory for 1870–71* (St. Louis, 1871); *Gould's St. Louis Directory for 1872–3* (St. Louis, 1872).; *Gould's St. Louis Directory for 1875* (St. Louis, 1875).

51. "Sessinghaus-Frost," *The Republican* (St. Louis), February 5, 1881.

52. "Base Ball Notes," *The Daily Times*, July 29, 1876; "Base Ball Brevities," *St. Louis Daily Globe-Democrat*, July 29, 1876; "Craps," *The Republican* (St. Louis), September 3, 1882.

53. "Diamond Chips," *The Republican* (St. Louis), September 20, 1884.

54. "Enterprise and Success," *The Globe* (St. Louis), May 17, 1874; "Local Gossip," *Globe-Democrat* (St. Louis), August 11, 1875.

55. "Ball of the Empire Boys," *Globe-Democrat*, January 26, 1876; S. A. Floyd, Jr., "A Black Composer in Nineteenth-Century St. Louis," *19th-Century Music* 4, no. 2 (1980): 121–133.

56. Frank Snowden, *The Image of the Black in Western Art*, Part I (Cambridge: Harvard University Press, 1976), 161–164; Peter P. Hinks, *To Awaken My Afflicted Brethren: David Walker and the Problem of Slave Resistance* (University Park: Pennsylvania State University Press, 1997); Mitch Kachum, "Before the Eyes of all Nations: African-American Identity and Historical Memory at the Centennial Exposition of 1876," *Pennsylvania History* 65, no. 3 (1998): 300–323.

57. "Rev. J.C. Learned's Lecture on Blue Stockings," *Post Dispatch*, January 6, 1875: "Blue Stockings," *The Globe*, January 6, 1875.

58. *Gould's St. Louis Directory for 1876* (St. Louis, 1876); "Local Short Stops," *Daily Democrat*, March 27, 1873; "The Ninth Ward Republican," *Globe-Democrat*, August 5, 1876; "The Colored Troops," *The Daily Times*, October 21, 1874; "St. Louis in Splinters," *Globe-Democrat*, November 3, 1876.

59. John Viessman, "They Also Served: Missouri's Black Militias," *Bear Facts* 31, no. 2. (February 2007); "The Colored Press Association," *The Western Recorder* (Lawrence, KS), July 20, 1883.

60. "Military," *Globe-Democrat*, September 19, 1878; David T. Burbank, *Reign of the Rabble: The St. Louis General Strike of 1877* (New York: Augustus M. Kelley, 1966), 129–133.

61. "How We Gamble," *The Republican* (St. Louis), June 13, 1887.

62. "A Gambling Carnival," *The Chronicle* (St. Louis), October 29, 1881; "Another Gambling Raid," *The Democrat*, September 23, 1873.

63. "Police Court," *Democrat*, July 30, 1873; *Gould's St. Louis Directory for 1870–71*; *Gould's St. Louis Directory for 1876*; *Gould's St. Louis Directory for 1883–84*; "Colored Children Turned Out of the Gamble School," *Democrat*, September 2, 1873; "Colored Mass Meeting," *Democrat*, December 2, 1873; "Hayes and Wheeler Flag Raising," *Globe-Democrat*, August 9, 1876.

64. "Base Ball Notes," *The Daily Times*, June 14, 1876; Asbury, *The Gangs of Chicago*, 140–171; 1870 Federal Census Report (ancestry.com).

65. "A Colored Game," *The Times* (Chicago), October 12, 1875;

66. "Colored Clubs — St. Louis Wins," *Globe-Democrat*, July 12, 1876; "The Colored Champions," *Globe-Democrat*, July 13, 1876; "Diamond Dust," *Globe-Democrat*, August 1, 1877; "Base Ball Notes," *The Republican* (St. Louis), September 10, 1877.

67. "Local Lines," *Globe-Democrat*, August 6, 1877; "Diamond Dust," *Globe-Democrat*, May 5, 1878; Lomax, *Black Baseball Entrepreneurs*, 30.

Chapter Three

1. The cartoon appeared in *The Freeman* (Indianapolis), August 7, 1890.

2. Mitchell, *What Do Pictures Want?*, 105.

3. Wilson Jeremiah Moses, "The Lost World of the New Negro, 1895–1919: Black Literary and Intellectual Life Before the 'Renaissance,'" *Black American Literature Forum* 21, no. 1–2 (Spring-Summer 1987): 63.

4. "Base Hits," *The Republican* (St. Louis), August 7, 1881; "Around Various Bases," *The Picayune*, January 15, 1887.

5. Barbara L. Webb, "The Black Dandyism of George Walker: A Case Study in Genealogical Method," *The Drama Review* 45, no. 4 (Winter 2001): 15.

6. Esther Leslie, "Flaneurs in Paris and Berlin," *Histories of Leisure*, ed. Rudy Koshar (Oxford: Berg, 2002), 61–77.

7. Brown, *Stagolee Shot Billy*, 219–225; Kelly, *Race Rebels*, 7–11.

8. Moses, "The Lost World of the New Negro," 63.

9. *Ibid.*, 61–84

10. *Online Etymology Dictionary*, http://www.etymoline.com/index; "Severe On The Dudes," *The Times* (St. Louis), August 22, 1883; "A Real Live Dude Interviewed — Definition of a New Species," *Post Dispatch*, April 16, 1883; "The Agony of the Dude," *The Times* (New York), May 6, 1883; "Saratoga Hotels Ready," *The Times* (New York), June 27, 1883; "Habits of Dude Society," *The Tribune* (Du Quoin, IL), June 21, 1883.

11. "City News," *The Freeman* (Indianapolis), September 15, 1888; "Panorama," *The Freeman* (Indianapolis), May 25, 1889.

12. Mary Warner Blanchard, *Oscar Wilde's America: Counterculture in the Gilded Age* (New Haven: Yale University Press, 1998), 31.

13. *Ibid.*, 61; *The Gazette*, July 18, 1885; "Our Man About Town," *The Gazette*, July 25, 1885; "City Department," *The Gazette*, October 23, 1886; Gerber, *Black Ohio and the Color Line, 1860–1915*, 135–136.

14. "Local Gossip," *The Gazette*, September 1, 1883; *The Gazette*, May 10, 1884; "Our Man About Town," *The Gazette*, July 24, 1884; *The Gazette*, April 1, 1885.

15. "Owlets," *The Gazette*, July 5, 1884; "City News," *The Gazette*, July 5, 1884; "Our Man About Town," *The Gazette*, March 28 and May 2, 1885.

16. "The St. Louis Black Socks Gallantly Down the Cleveland Blues," *The Leader*, May 10, 1883.

17. "A Victory For The Black Stockings," *The Republican* (St. Louis), April 25, 1883.

18. "Our Man About Town," *The Gazette*, May 16, 1885, January 30, 1886, February 19 and October 29, 1887.

19. "Our Man About Town," *The Gazette*, March 28, May 9 and December 26, 1885.

20. "Base Ball Notes," *The Gazette*, April 25, 1885; "Our Man About Town," *The Gazette*, March 21 and August 16, 1885.

21. Walter Benjamin, *The Arcades Project*, trans. Howard Eiland and Kevin McLaughlin (Cambridge: Belknap Press, 1999), 447–448; David A. Gerber, *Black Ohio and the Color Line, 1860–1915* (Urbana: University of Illinois Press, 1976), 182.

22. *The Gazette*, March 21, 1885; "Our Man About Town," *The Gazette*, April 11 and November 28, 1885.

23. "Sporting Gossip: The Home Colored Team and the Black Stockings," *The Leader*, April 25, 1883.

24. *The Gazette*, May 3, 1884; *The Gazette*, July 26, 1884; "Geneva, O.," *The Gazette*, September 29, 1883; Gerber, *Black Ohio and the Color Line, 1860–1915*, 82–83, 182–184.

25. "Sporting Gossip: Disputed Claim," *The Leader*, April 9, 1883; "Sporting Gossip: The Colored Boys," *The Leader*, May 7, 1883.

26. "The St. Louis Black Socks Gallantly Down the Cleveland Blues," *The Leader*, April 10, 1883; "Local Gossip," *The Gazette*, September 1, 1883; "Geneva, O.," *The Gazette*, September 29, 1883.

27. "Owl Club," *The Gazette*, September 8, 1883; Gerber, *Black Ohio and the Color Line, 1860–1915*, 85.

28. "Local Gossip," *The Gazette*, November 17, 1883, and May 10, 1884; "Billiards at the Owl Club," *The Gazette*, September 8, 1883; "Our Man About Town," *The Gazette*, May 10, 1884.

29. Thorsten Veblen, *The Theory of the Leisure Class* (New York: Macmillan, 1899; repr. New York: Penguin, 1994), 32.

30. *Ibid.*, 10–11.

31. Mitchell, *Picture Theory*, 333–335.

32. Whitney Davis, *Replications: Archaeology, Art History, Psychoanalysis* (University Park: Pennsylvania State University Press, 1996), 206–207.

33. "Base Ball," *The Gazette*, August 25, 1883; *The Gazette*, September 22, 1883; "Geneva, O.," *The Gazette*, September 29, 1883; "Base Ball," *The Gazette*, October 6, 1883; *The Gazette*, October 13, 1883; "Local Gossip," *The Gazette*, October 27, 1883.

34. "Local Luncheon," *The Gazette*, April 12, 1884; *The Gazette*, April 26, 1884; "Local Gossip," *The Gazette*, May 3, 1884; "Base Ball," *The Gazette*, July 19, 1884.

35. "City Department," *The Gazette*, August 16, 1886, and April 23, 1887; "No Title," *The Gazette*, May 28, 1887; *The Gazette*, May 25, 1889.

36. *The Gazette*, August 30, 1885; "Lakewood, N.Y.," *The Gazette*, August 1, 1885; "Base Ball," *The Picayune*, June 17, 1886; "The Unions Defeat the Pickwicks," *The Pelican*, April 25, 1887; *The Gazette*, April 23, 1887; *The Gazette*, August 27, 1887; "Rakings," *The Pelican*, June 4, 1887.

37. "Local," *The Gazette*, July 12, 1884; *The Gazette*, July 26, 1884; "Local Notes," *The Gazette*, August 30, 1884; *The Gazette*, May 2, 1885; *The Gazette*, April 23, 1887; *The Gazette*, May 28, 1887.

38. "Local Gossip," *The Gazette*, September 8, 1883; "Our Man About Town," *The Gazette*, October 12, 1889; *The Gazette*, August 29, 1885.

39. "Read This and Remember," *The Gazette*, August 30, 1884; "Local Gossip," *The Gazette*, December 1, 1883; Gerber, *Black Ohio and the Color Line, 1860–1915*, 84.

40. *Ibid.*

41. "Eureka Ball Chips," *The Gazette*, November 24, 1883; Gerber, *Black Ohio and the Color Line, 1860–1915*, 183–184.

42. *The Gazette*, May 3, 1884; "The Excelsior's Concert," *The Gazette*, March 14, 1885; "Lakeview, N.Y.," *The Gazette*, August 1 and 29, 1885.

43. "Local Gossip," *The Gazette*, September 9, 1883; "Local Luncheon," *The Gazette*, April 19, 1884; "Our Man About Town," *The Gazette*, April 11, 1885, and October 12, 1889; "Pinched to Death," *The Gazette*, October 3, 1885.

44. Gerber, *Black Ohio and the Color Line, 1860–1915*, 130–133.

45. "Read and Remember This," *The Gazette*, August 30, 1884; "Our Man About Town," *The Gazette*, March 21, 1885; "'Z' Club," *The Gazette*, June 18, 1886; *The Gazette*, May 12, 1888.

46. *The Gazette*, June 15, 1889; "Brooklyn Items," *The Age* (New York), June 29, 1889; "The Ball Game," *The Gazette*, September 14, 1889.

47. "We Have the Dude," *Post-Dispatch*, May 5, 1883.

48. "Base Ball Notes," *Daily Eagle* (Brooklyn), June 15, 1887.

49. "Ball-Players Fined for Intemperance," *Tribune* (New York), June 15, 1887; "Doings of the Race," *The Gazette*, April 30, 1887; "The National Game," *Daily Eagle*, June 26, 1887; "Baseball," *The Appeal* (Memphis), April 17, 1888; "The Diamond," *The Freeman* (Indianapolis), January 5, 1889; "The Smoky City Boys," *Sporting News*, April 23, 1887; "Buffalo's Colored Player," *Sporting News*, April 20, 1889.

50. Kelly, *Race Rebels*, 214–216.

51. Brown, *Stagolee Shot Billy*, 87–91.

52. "The flaneur is allied to the dandy, but where the usually aristocratic dandy is known for his immaculate attention to dress and a desire for self-display (and self-publicity, hence renowned such as Count Alfred D'Orsay, Prince de Sagan, and Beau Brummel), the flaneur is anonymous, passing by unnoticed, a product of hearsay. Or, he never appears simply as a flaneur, but other guises: as poet, journalist, critic, detective, spy, shopper, gambler or crook." Esther Leslie, "Flaneurs in Paris and Berlin," *Histories of Leisure*, 61–77; Brown, *Stagolee Shot Billy*, 23, 91–92.

53. "Pistol Practice by a Colored Man," *The Republican*, February 19, 1887; Arna Wendell Bontemps, *God Sends Sunday* (Washington, DC: Washington Square Press, 2005), 54; John Russell David, "Tragedy in Ragtime: Black Folktales from St. Louis" (Ph.D. diss., St. Louis University, 1976), 213; Brown, *Stagolee Shot Billy*, 86–92.

54. "John Anderson's Death," *The Democrat*, March 14, 1873; "A Low Murder," *The Democrat*, April 30, 1873; Brown, *Stagolee Shot Billy*, 55; Mitchell, *What Do Pictures Want?*, 138–140.

55. "The Dude of Saratoga," *The Post* (Washington, DC), August 3, 1883; "Saratoga Locals," *The Globe* (New York), July 19, 1884.

56. "New Jersey Summer Resorts," *The Globe* (New York), August 18, 1883; "Social Gossip," *The Globe* (New York), August 18, 1883; "Personals," *The Bee*, April 28, 1883; "Chicago Correspondence," *The Globe* (New York), April 12, 1884.

57. "Ashbury Park and Ocean Grove," *The Globe* (New York), September 8, 1883; "A Presentation at Saratoga," *The Globe* (New York), September 8, 1883; "Chicago Letter," *The Globe* (New York), January 6, 1883; "Saratoga Locals," *The* Globe (New York), September 6, 1884; Errol G. Hill and James V. Hatch, *A History of African American Theatre* (Cambridge: Cambridge University Press, 2003), 112–113; "Negro Minstrelsy," *The Clipper*, January 7, 1882.

58. "The Colored Press," *Globe-Democrat*, July 12, 1883.

59. "Lathered," *Daily Eagle*, July 10, 1883; "Saratoga Letter," *The Globe* (Boston), July 28, 1883; "Ashbury Park and Ocean Grove," *The Globe* (New York), July 26, 1884; "Men Who Paint and Powder," *The Globe* (New York), August 3, 1884; "Chicago," *The Gazette*, February 16, 1884; "Topeka's New Club," *Sporting News*, March 29, 1886; "Caught on the Fly," *Sporting News*, May 21, 1887.

60. "Various Town Topics," *The Times* (St. Louis), September 3, 1880; "Notes About Town," *The Republican* (St. Louis), August 21, 1882.

61. "The Rahzer," *The Post*, January 21, 1883.

62. "The National Game," *The Police Gazette*, May 26, 1883; "The Hartfords Beat the West Ends by a Close Shave," *The Courant* (Hartford, CN), September 15, 1883; "Sporting Gossip," *The Leader*, April 30, 1883; "The National Game," *The Police Gazette*, June 9, 1883; "Miss Harris's Base-Ball Nine," *The Times* (New York), May 18, 1883; "On the Fly," *Sporting Life*, May 20, 1883.

63. A Base Hit: Frank Larkin Held for the Grand Jury," *Daily Eagle*, June 1, 1883; "Razors in the South," *The Times* (New York), November 19, 1883; "An Assault With A Razor," *The Times* (New York), April 17, 1877; "The Suicidal Mania," *The Times* (New York), May 20, 1887; "Suicide of a Bank Cashier," *The Times* (New York), August 16, 1877; "Badly Slashed," *The Tribune* (Chicago), August 25, 1877; "Suicide of a Southern Gentleman," *The Times* (New York), February 17, 1880; "A Jealous Husband's Fury," *The Times* (New York), February 28, 1880; "A Wife's Terrible Crime," *The* Times (New York), January 12, 1880; "The Suicidal Mania," *The Times* (New York), January 7, 1883; "Horrible Double Murder," *The Post*, February 9, 1883; "The Judson Tragedy," *The Courant*, March 26, 1883; "A Razor This Time," *The Globe* (Boston), May 7, 1883; "A Colorado Tragedy," *The Post*, August 13, 1883.

64. Richard Ohmann, *Selling Culture* (New York: Verso, 1996), 220, 259–264; "Our Famous Tonsorialist," *The Police Gazette*, October 1, 1892.

65. In 1888, Frederick Ives invented the halftone, a photomechanical printing process. Ives devised a method that allowed him to break up the continuous tones of the photographic image into a pattern of dots that could be printed in relief. Intermediate tones in the original photographic image were imitated in the halftone image by the variations in the sizes of the dots that made up the resulting reproduction. Light grays were reproduced as small dots, dark grays reproduced as large dots. When viewed from a distance, the eye would blend the different-sized dots and produce in the mind the illusion that one could see shades of gray in an image that in reality only contained black or white.

66. "Oscar Wilde," *The Picayune*, June 17, 1882. Oscar Wilde expressed surprise that American painters and poets paid so little attention to "the negro as an object of art." However, the New Negro aesthete hardly needed an endorsement from "The Apostle of Modern Art." As early as 1885, *The Freeman* and *The Gazette* ran illustrated advertisements for hair care products that depicted a black man, guaranteeing to transform his curly locks into straight hair. "Anti-Curl," *The Freeman* (New York), September 26, 1885; "Anti-Curl," *The Gazette*, December 5, 1885.

67. "Our Famous Tonsorialist," *The Police Gazette*, October 1, 1892; "Sidney A. Clark, Sport," *The Police Gazette*, September 26, 1891.

68. Veblen, *The Theory of the Leisure Class*, 166.

Chapter Four

1. From 1880 to 1885, the national press reported the emergence of several colored teams, including the Manhattan B.B.C., the Philadelphia Orions, the Louisville Mutuals, the St. Louis Black Stockings, the Chicago Gordon B.B.C., the Memphis Eclipse, the Unions, and the W.L. Cohens of New Orleans, LA. From this point on, I will abbreviate the title and refer to the photograph as "Cuban Giants, Colored Champions."

2. "New York Notes," *The Bee* (Washington, DC), August 25, 1888; "The Base Ball Field," *The Age*, September 1, 1888; "The Base Ball Champions," *The Age*, September 15, 1888.

3. "A Color Line in Baseball," *The Times* (New York), September 12, 1887; "Some Good Ball Playing," *True American* (Trenton, NJ), May 29, 1886; "Caught on the Fly," *Sporting News*, June 28, 1886; "Our Philadelphia Letter," *The Bee*, June 12, 1886.

4. "The National Game," *The Police Gazette*, September 27, 1887. In 1876, the English firm of Lock and Whitfield issued a series of portrait albums of famous contemporaries "photographed from life" under the title "Men of Mark." Ten years later, black author William J. Simmons published a similarly styled volume devoted to black Americans called *Men of Mark: Eminent, Progressive, And Rising* (1886). The title serves as inspiration for this book.

5. "The Base Ball Champions," *The Age*, September 15, 1888; David Nemec, *The Beer and Whiskey League: The Illustrated History of the American Association — Baseball's Renegade Major League* (Guilford, CT: Lyons Press, 2004). See the photographic images on pages 27, 37, 58, and 70 as examples. Team photographs depicting the players in external settings, particularly at the base ball grounds are traceable to the first professional team, the Cincinnati Red Stockings,

in 1870. See Michael Gershwin's *Diamonds: The Evolution of the Ballpark* (Boston: Houghton and Mifflin, 1999), 5.

6. Bowman, *Before the World Series*, 50.

7. Bowman, *Before the World Series*, 198; Fouad Ajami, "Their Gilded Age—And Ours," *The National Interest* 63 (Spring 2001): 37–47.

8. "Base Ball Briefs," *True American*, May 21, 1886; "The Giants Win," *True American*, May 13, 1886.

9. "Our National Game," *The Police Gazette*, June 7, 1884.

10. "Our National Game," *The Police Gazette*, August 9, 1884.

11. Lomax, *Black Baseball Entrepreneurs*, 75; "Love in Black and White," *The Police Gazette*, May 12, 1883; "Notes and Comments," *The Globe* (New York), May 24, 1884; "Base-Ball Games," *The Times* (New York), May 30, 1884.

12. Burk, *Never Just A Game*, 88; Benjamin Reiss, "P.T. Barnum, Joice Heth and the Antebellum Spectacle of Race," *American Quarterly* 51, no. 1 (March 1999): 78–107; "Dissection of Joice Heth-Precious Humbug Exposed," *The Sun* (New York), February 26, 1836.

13. Burk, *Never Just A Game*, 89.

14. *Ibid.*, 88–89.

15. "Sporting Gossip," *The Leader*, April 2, 1883; "Locals," *The Bee*, May 5, 1883.

16. "Base Ball Notes," *The Post* (Washington, D.C.), April 12 and 28, May 6, 1883; "Nine to Nothing," *The Post*, April 26, 1883; "Nationals-Molineaux," *The Post*, May 30, 1883; *The Conservator* (Chicago), December 23, 1882; "The Black Sox," *The Republican* (St. Louis), April 15, 1883; "The Colored League," *The Republican* (St. Louis), May 16, 1883.

17. "Saratoga Gossip," *The Globe* (New York), July 7, 1883.

18. "Henry Moor Reinstated," *Sporting News*, August 9, 1886.

19. "A Close Call," *The Sentinel* (Milwaukee), July 16, 1883; *The Gazette*, December 10, 1887; *The Gazette*, May 19, 1888.

20. David Quentin Voigt, *American Baseball*, Volume 1 (University Park: Pennsylvania State University Press, 1983).

21. Voigt, *American Baseball*, 197.

22. "Seventeen to Three," *True American*, August 21, 1886; "Trenton Beats Newark," *True American*, May 13, 1887; "Fairly Jumped On," *True American*, September 6, 1887.

23. "Base Ball Around New York," *The Age*, July 28, 1888; "Cuban Giants to the Front," *The Gazette*, January 21, 1887; "How They Play Base Ball," *The Gazette*, July 21, 1888.

24. "Going To Summer Resorts: News," *The Bee*, July 3, 1886; "Base Ball," *The Age*, April 14, 1888; "New York Notes," *The Bee*, August 4, 1888.

25. Michael Taussig, *Mimesis and Alterity* (New York: Routledge, 1993), 19; "Our National Game," *The Police Gazette*, June 12, 1886; "Base Ball Tips," *True American*, July 21, 1886; "Base Ball Briefs," *True American*, July 30, 1886.

26. Mitchell, *What Do Pictures Want?*, 296; "Notes of the Game," *The Times* (New York), October 1 and 4, 1885; "Notes of the Game," *The Tribune* (New York), October 5, 1885.

27. Heinz K. Henisch and Bridget A. Henisch, *The Photographic Experience, 1839–1914* (University Park: Pennsylvania State University Press, 1994), 244; Jean Baudrillard, *America*, trans. Chris Turner (New York: Verso, 1998).

28. *The Clipper*, January 14, 1882; "Caught on the Fly," *Sporting News*, May 10, 1886; "The Base Ball Champions," *The Age*, September 15, 1888.

29. Lomax, *Black Baseball Entrepreneurs*, 5–6.

30. "The Cuban Giants Beaten," *The Times* (New York), October 6, 1885; "New York Notes," *The Bee*, July 28, 1888; "New York Doings," *The Bee*, August 4, 1888.

31. Burk, *Never Just A Game*, 24.

32. Alan Trachtenberg, *Reading American Photographs* (New York: Hill and Wang, 1989), 46; Mary Panzer, *Matthew Brady and the Image of History* (Washington: Smithsonian, 1997).

33. "Baseball Around New York," *The Age*, July 28, 1886.

34. "The National Game," *The Sun*, October 6, 1885; "Notes of the Game," *The Times* (New York), October 1, 1885.

35. "Games in and Around the City," *The Tribune* (New York), July 3, 1886; "Caught on the Fly," *Sporting News*, August 2, 1886; *Sporting News*, September 5, 1888.

36. Baseball historian Jerry Malloy declares: "Despite the occasional minor errors in White's text ... , his account of the first twenty years of black professional baseball has withstood the scrutiny of subsequent historical research." *Sol White's History of Colored Base Ball, With Other Documents On The Early Black Game, 1886–1936*, ed. Jerry Malloy (Lincoln: University of Nebraska Press, 1995), lviii.

37. Lomax, *Black Baseball Entrepreneurs*, 50; *Sol White's History of Colored Base Ball*, lviii-lxi; "From the Springs," *The Globe*, August 11, 1883; "Saratoga," *The People's Advocate* (Washington, D.C.), July 28, 1883; *The New York Times* referred to Lang, who was white, as a Philadelphia barber. Lang's deep pockets and Barnumesque tendencies—the infusion of blackface performance into baseball—marked his circus-style showmanship.

38. "Samuel R. Scottron," *The Gazette*, June 4, 1887; *The Booker T. Washington Papers*, Volume 8, 1904–06, ed. Louis R. Harlan and Raymond W. Smock (Urbana: University of Illinois Press, 1979), 31. Samuel R. Scottron was born in Philadelphia in 1843 and resided in Brooklyn until the Civil War, when his father sent him into the South as a sutler for a black regiment. After an unsuccessful attempt running a grocery business, Scottron opened a barbershop. He invented and patented Scottron's Adjustable Mirror and formed a partnership in New York to sell it. He eventually sold more household items, including an extension cornice. During the 1870s, Scottron was active in the anti-slavery movement and was a founder of the Cuban Anti-Slavery Society. Philip S. Foner, *Antonio Maceo: The "Bronze Titan" of Cuba's Struggle for Independence* (New York: Monthly Review Press,

1977); Walter Benjamin, *Reflections*, ed. Peter Demetz (New York: Schocken Books, 1978), 225–228.

39. Jerry Malloy, "The Birth of the Cuban Giants," *Out of the Shadows: African American baseball from the Cuban Giants to Jackie Robinson*, ed. Bill Kirwin (Lincoln: University of Nebraska Press, 2005), 1–80; "Base Ball Briefs," *True American*, May 28, 1886.

40. Malloy, "The Birth of the Cuban Giants," *Out of the Shadows*, 1; "The Giants Win," *True American*, May 13, 1886; "Four to One," *True American*, July 17, 1886; "Another Victory Scored," *True American*, July 19, 1886; "Our Philadelphia Letter," *The Bee*, June 12, 1886.

41. Steven Riess, *City Games: The Evolution of American Urban Society and the Rise of Sports* (Urbana: University of Illinois Press, 1991), 223.

42. Riess, *City Games*, 223; "The Colored Orions Badly Defeated by the Metropolitan Team," *The Times* (New York), July 21, 1882; "Baseball," *The Clipper*, July 29, 1882; "The Compton Avenue Contest," *Globe-Democrat*, May 21, 1883; "Base-Ball Information," *Post-Dispatch*, September 8, 1883; "Won by One Run," *Globe-Democrat*, June 4, 1883; "Gordon B.B.C. Beat," *The Gazette*, May 17, 1884; "Diamond Chips," *Post-Dispatch*, May 20, 1884; "The Chicago Colored Champions Defeated by the Milwaukees," *The Journal* (Milwaukee), July 7, 1884; "DuBuques, 6; Gordons, 3," *Globe-Democrat*, September 15, 1884; "The Unions Defeat the Cohens," *The Picayune*, August 3, 1885; "Unions, 4; Pinchbacks, 1," *The Picayune*, August 22, 1888; "Minor Games. Pinchbacks 6; Unions, 5," *The Inter-Ocean*, August 23, 1888.

43. Riess, *City Games*, 40; "That Revolt: A Dramatic Account of the Mutiny Among the World's Champions," *Post-Dispatch*, September 13, 1887; "A Color Line in Baseball: The St. Louis Browns Refuse To Play With The Cuban Giants," *The Times* (St. Louis), September 12, 1887; "Clips and Chips," *Post-Dispatch*, September 12, 1887; "That Revolt: A Dramatic Account of the Mutiny Among the World's Champions," *Post-Dispatch*, September 13, 1887; "Color-Line Drawn Again," *The Freeman* (New York), September 17, 1887.

44. "The Gorhams and the Cuban Giants Battling For It," *Sporting News*, September 1, 1888.

45. *Encyclopedia of Photography* (New York: Crown, 1984); Helmut Gernsheim, *Creative Photography: Aesthetic Trends, 1839–1960* (Boston: Book Mart & Art Shop, 1962); Ronald Pisano, *The Tile Club* (New York: Harry N. Abrams, 1999); Lionel Lambourne, *The Aesthetic Movement* (London: Phaidon Press, 1996).

46. Susan Sontag, *Regarding the Pain of Others* (New York: Farrar and Strauss, 2003), 85; Deborah Willis and Carla Williams, *The Black Female Body, A Photographic History* (Philadelphia: Temple University Press, 2002).

47. Sontag, *Regarding the Pain of Others*, 86.

Chapter Five

1. "Base Ball from a Colored Point of View," *The Tribune* (Chicago), August 24, 1870.

2. Mitchell, *What Do Pictures Want?*, 298.

3. "Fact and Comment," *The Constitution* (Atlanta), August 5, 1877.

4. Lott, *Love and Theft*, 3.

5. Saidiya V. Hartman, *Scenes of Subjection: Terror, Slavery, and Self-Making In Nineteenth-Century America* (Oxford: Oxford University Press, 1997), 21–27.

6. David R. Roediger, *The Wages of Whiteness: Race and the Making of the American Working Class* (London: Verso, 2007).

7. Blanchard, *Oscar Wilde's America*, 3.

8. "Sports," *The Globe* (St. Louis), April 30, 1875.

9. "Stage Whispers," *The Police Gazette*, December 20, 1882.

10. "The Great Wesley Bros.," *The Clipper*, January 7, 1882.

11. Lott, *Love and Theft*, 22; "Base Ball," *Daily Eagle*, July 29, 1870.

12. "Amusements," *Daily Eagle*, August 30, 1867; "Amusements," *Daily Eagle*, November 6, 1868.

13. "Great Success of Hooley's Minstrels," *Daily Eagle*, September 30, 1862; "Theatricals in Brooklyn," *Daily Eagle*, September 7, 1863; "Amusements," *Daily Eagle*, August 26, 1867; "Amusements," *Daily Eagle*, August 28, 1867; "Amusements," *Daily Eagle*, August 29, 1867; "Sports," *The Globe* (St. Louis), April 30, 1875; "Hooley's Opera House," *Daily Eagle*, May 3, 1867; "The Stage," *Daily Eagle*, May 23, 1874; "Hooley's Chicago Opera House," *Daily Eagle*, December 19, 1870; "Fun on the Field," *The Times* (Chicago), May 15, 1876; "Sporting," *The Inter-Ocean*, May 27, 1876.

14. "Hooley's Opera House," *Daily Eagle*, November 25, 1874; "'Jack' Haverly is Dead," *The Times* (New York), September 29, 1901.

15. "Base Ball Notes," *The Republican* (St. Louis), October 24, 1881; "Fly Tips," *The Republican* (St. Louis), October 25, 1881; "Baseball," *The Clipper*, May 6, 1881, and December 30, 1882; "Black Sox vs. Callender's Minstrels," *Globe-Democrat* (St. Louis), September 4, 1884.

16. "Sports," *The Globe* (St. Louis), April 30, 1875.

17. "Brooklyn Opera House," *Daily Eagle*, May 20, 1871; "Amusements," *The Republican* (St. Louis), August 25, 1874; "Haverly's Minstrels," *Globe-Democrat*, September 3, 1875; "Amusements," *The Republican* (St. Louis), March 21, 1876.

18. "Our National Game," *Police Gazette*, April 26, 1884; "In New Hands," *The Times* (New York), October 30, 1887.

19. "Theatrical Ball Players," *The Times* (St. Louis), June 23, 1885; "Baseball Champions of Colorado: The Leadville Blues of 1882," *Journal of Sport History* 4, no. 10 (1977): 51–77.

20. Lott, *Love and Theft*, 36; Howard Winant, *The World is a Ghetto: Race and Democracy Since World War II* (New York: Basic Books, 2001), 93–95.

21. Joshua Brown, *Beyond the Lines; Pictorial Reporting, Everyday Life, and the Crisis of Gilded Age America* (Berkeley: University of California Press, 2002), 70–74; Foner, *Forever Free*, 152–155.

22. John Strausbaugh, *Black Like You* (New York; Penguin Books, 2006), 165; Shelly Fisher Fishkin, *Was Huck Black?* (New York: Oxford University Press, 1993), 4.

23. Spink, *The National Game*, 324–351.

24. Robert C. Toll, *Blacking Up: The Minstrel Show in Nineteenth Century America* (New York: Oxford University Press, 1974), 169–170.

25. Strausbaugh, *Black Like You*, 276; "The Fifteenth Amendment," *Daily Eagle*, April 4, 1870; "A Colored Orator," *Daily Eagle*, March 16, 1875; "Civil Rights," *Daily Eagle*, March 31, 1875.

26. Winant, *The World is a Ghetto*, 102.

27. Mitchell, *What Do Pictures Want?*, 216; "Dusky Tossers," *The Times* (St. Louis), June 16, 1876.

28. "Base Ball," *The Herald* (Saginaw, MI), May 1, 1883.

29. Mitchell, *What Do Pictures Want?*, 216; "Newark Notes," *The Globe* (New York), May 24, 1884.

30. "The Colored Clubs Amuse a Small Crowd at the Polo Grounds," *The Herald* (New York), May 30, 1884; "The Colored Championship of Brooklyn Settled," *The Times* (New York), Oct. 1, 1884; "When Greek Meets Greek," *The Herald* (New York), October 4, 1884.

31. Lott, *Love and Theft*, 143–144.

32. In 1876, one of the earliest exhibitions of the Cake Walk was given as part of the American Centennial Exhibition in Philadelphia. The dance was also known as the "chalk-line walk" or "walk-around," and the prize was an enormous cake for the winning couple. Questions remain as to the true origin and purpose of the Cake Walk. "The Coons Carry off the Cake," *The Register* (Rockford, IL), June 20, 1883; "Sporting," *Globe-Democrat*, April 27, 1883.

33. "Fought Nobly, on the Diamond — Rockford Takes the Banner — A Picnic for Spectators," *The Register*, July 11, 1884; "Annual Excursion of the Brooklyn City Guard," *Daily Eagle*, August 24, 1868; "Amusements," *Globe-Democrat*, March 27, 1883.

34. Winant, *The World is a Ghetto*, 86–109; Rae Beth Gordon, "Natural Rhythm: La Parisienne Dances with Darwin: 1875–1910," *Modernism/modernity* 10, no. 4 (November 2003): 634.

35. "Diamond Dust," *Globe-Democrat*, April 19, 1883; "Base Ball," *The Chronicle*, April 8, 1883; "The National Game," *The Police Gazette*, May 12 and June 2, 1883.

36. Charles Mills, *The Racial Contract* (Ithaca: Cornell University Press, 1997); Leon Litwack, *Trouble in Mind: Black Southerners in the Age of Jim Crow* (New York: Knopf, 1998), 235–236; Brown, *Stagolee Shot Billy*, 102.

37. Alexander Saxton, *The Rise and Fall of the White Republic* (London: Verso, 1996), 166; Henry Clay Lukens, "American Literary Comedians," *Harper's New Monthly Magazine*, April 1890, 783–797; Albert Bigelow Paine, *Thomas Nast: His period and His Pictures* (New York: Macmillan, 1904); William Winter, *Old Friends; Being Literary Recollections of Other Days* (New York: Moffat, Yard, 1909); Albert Parry, *Garrets and Pretenders: A History of Bohemianism in America* (New York: Covici, Friede, 1933).

38. "The Colored Club," *The Republican* (St. Louis), September 9, 1875; "Dusky Ball Tossers," *The Times* (St. Louis), May 15, 1876.

39. "The Blackville Twins," *The Conservator* (Chicago), September 8, 1883; "Local Gossip," *The Gazette*, October 20, 1883; "Chicago," *The Gazette*, December 8, 1883.

40. John Berger, *Selected Essays*, 104–105; Harris, *Colored Pictures*, 62–62.

41. "Base Ball," *Daily Eagle*, October 17, 1862; Toni Morrison, *Playing in the Dark: Whiteness and the Literary Imagination* (Cambridge: Harvard University Press, 1992), 38.

42. "Caught on the Fly," *The Sporting News*, September 13, 1886; Russell Wolinsky, "Arlie Latham: 19th Century Clown Prince of Baseball," National Baseball Hall of Fame. http://209.23.71.87/library/columns/rw_040618.htm.

43. "The Colored Orions Badly Defeated by the Metropolitan Team," *The Times* (New York), July 21, 1882.

44. *The Negro in New York*, ed. Roi Ottley and William J. Weatherby (New York: The New York Public Library, 1967), 147–148; "Our Philadelphia Letter," *The Bee*, June 12, 1886; "Saratoga Letter," *The Globe* (Boston), August 18, 1883; "Mask in an Ancient City," *The Age*, March 2, 1889.

45. "The Point Well Taken," *The Freeman* (Indianapolis), February 14, 1891; "An Indecent Egotist," *The Gazette*, December 12, 1891; *The Freeman* (Indianapolis), April 5, 1890.

46. *The Freeman* (Indianapolis), June 8, 1889.

47. "Amusements," *The Democrat* (St. Louis), October 28, 1873.

48. "Pinchbacks Won Again," *The Republican* (St. Louis), August 27, 1888.

49. "Base Ball," *The Herald* (Saginaw, MI), May 1, 1883; "Fun at the Park," *The Free Press* (Detroit), June 23, 1883.

50. Roger D. Abrahams, *Deep Down in the Jungle* (Chicago: Aldine Publishing, 1970), 56; "Topics," *The Times* (St. Louis), August 15, 1880; "Craps," *The Post-Dispatch*, February 21, 1881; "The Colored Race," *The Gazette*, October 23, 1886; "More Race Doings," *The Gazette*, June 4, 1887; "Base Ball from a Colored Point of View," *The Tribune* (Chicago), August 24, 1870.

51. "An Amusing Game Between Colored Clubs at Sportsman's Park," *Globe-Democrat*, August 13, 1883.

52. Gordon, "Natural Rhythm: La Parisienne Dances with Darwin: 1875–1910," *Modernism/modernity*, 617–656.

53. The French neurologist and psychiatrist Jean-Martin Charot (1825–1893) took an interest in the women's malady then called hysteria, which he believed was a mental disorder with physical manifestations, resulting from a weak neurological system. Once set off by a traumatic event like an accident, hysteria was then progressive and irreversible. It proceeded through several phases, one being "clownism." Gordon, "Natural Rhythm: La Parisienne Dances with Darwin: 1875–1910," *Modernism/modernity*, 626.

54. Burk, *Never Just A Game*, 24; Talia Schaffer, "Fashioning Aestheticism by Aestheticizing Fashion: Wilde, Beerbohm, and the Male Aesthetes' Sartorial Codes," *Victorian Literature and Culture* 28, no. 1 (2000): 39–54.

55. Blanchard, *Oscar Wilde's America*, 3; Burk, *Never Just A Game*, 24.

56. "Rah for Our Black Socks," *The Republican*, August 12, 1883; "The National Game," *The Police Gazette*, May 6, 1883.

57. "Rakings," *Weekly Pelican* (New Orleans), March 26, 1887; "They Fought Nobly," *The Republican* (St. Louis), August 26, 1888; "Rakings," *Weekly Pelican*, April 16, 1887; "Rakings," *Weekly Pelican*, April 23, 1887; Lott, *Love and Theft*, 101.

58. Lott, *Love and Theft*, 24–25.

59. *Ibid.*, 25–26; *Ibid.*, 120–121.

Chapter Six

1. "Sporting," *Globe-Democrat*, September 3, 1884.

2. Mitchell, *What Do Pictures Want?*, 212–213.

3. "Our National Game," *The Police Gazette*, June 14, 1883.

4. "Base Ball Notes," *The Republican* (St. Louis), October 24, 1881; "Fly Tips," *The Republican* (St. Louis), October 25, 1881; "Amusements," *Globe-Democrat*, March 28, 1883.

5. "Base Ball," *The Evening Chronicle* (St. Louis), April 8, 1883; "Base Ball," *The Evening Chronicle* (St. Louis), April 8, 1883; Richard J. Puerzer, "From Scientific Baseball to Sabermetrics," *NINE: A Journal of Baseball History and Culture* 11, no. 1 (2002): 34–48; "Diamond Dust," *Globe-Democrat*, April 19, 1883.

6. Blanchard, *Oscar Wilde's America*, 3.

7. Reiss, *City Games*, 15–16; Mitchell, *What Do Pictures Want?*, 212–213, 295. "[A medium] is not just a set of materials, an apparatus, or a code that 'mediates' between individuals. It is a complex social institution that contains individuals within it, and is constituted by a history of practices, rituals, habits, skills and techniques, as well as by a set of material objects and spaces (stages, studios, easel painting, television sets, laptop computers). A medium is as much a guild, a profession, a craft, a conglomerate, a corporate entity as it is a material means for communicating." Late nineteenth century baseball, as a sports medium, is exemplary.

8. Hartman, *Scenes of Subjection*, 21.

9. "The Black Stockings Decisively Defeat the Grand Avenues Nine," *Globe-Democrat*, August 29, 1883; "On the Fly," *Sporting Life*, May 20, 1883; "Sporting," *Inter-Ocean*, May 27, 1876.

10. "Topics," *The Times* (St. Louis), August 15, 1880; "Craps," *The Post-Dispatch*, February 21, 1881; "The Colored Race," *The Gazette*, October 23, 1886; "More Race Doings," *The Gazette*, June 4, 1887; "St. Louis Items," *The Gazette*, April 26, 1884; "St. Louis, MO.," *The Gazette*, May 10, 1884; Eileen Southern, "The Origin and Development of the Black Musical Theater: A Preliminary Report," *Black Music Research Journal*. 2 (1981–1982): 1–14; James Weldon Johnson. *Black Manhattan* (New York: Knopf, 1930; repr., New York: Da Capo Press, 1991), 91–92.

11. Sotiropoulos, Karen. *Staging Race: Black Performers in Turn of the Century America* (Cambridge, Massachusetts, and London, England: Harvard University Press, 2006).

12. Moses, *The Wings of Ethiopia*, 201–218.

13. Henri Focillon, *The Life of Forms in Art* (New York: Zone Books, 1992), 26–27.

14. Shelly Mehlman Dinhofer, *The Art of Baseball* (New York: Harmony Books, 1990).

15. "The Future Great," *The Freeman* (Indianapolis), May 3, 1890.

16. In 1889, *The Police Gazette* carried the column "Our Famous Tonsorialists," which portrayed colored sporting men. These portrait sketches represented the colored sporting fraternity with the insignia of affluence and authority. The sports journal rivaled *Harper's Weekly* for the best artists. Among the artists working for Fox were George E. McEvoy, Matt Morgan, Charles Kendrick, Paul Cusachs, George White, and John Woods.

17. Charles C. Clayton, *"Little Mack" Joseph B. McCullagh of the St. Louis Globe-Democrat* (Carbondale: Southern Illinois University Press, 1969); Joel Zoss and John Bowman, *Diamonds in The Rough: The Untold History of Baseball* (Chicago: Contemporary Books, 1996), 67.

18. "The Black Sox At Rockford," *Globe-Democrat*, June 19, 1883; Clayton, *"Little Mack,"* 85.

19. "Base Ball," *The Morning Herald* (Saginaw, MI), April 30, 1883; "Base Ball," *The Morning Herald*, May 1, 1883; "The Dust of Four Diamonds," *The Constitution*, April 16, 1885; "Sports and Pastimes," *Daily Eagle* (Brooklyn), July 3, 1879; "A New Sensation in Base Ball Circles — Sambo as a Ball Player and Dinah as an Emulator — Unknown of Weeksville vs. Monitor of Brooklyn," *Daily Eagle*, July 29, 1870.

20. W.J.T. Mitchell, *Picture Theory* (Chicago: University of Chicago Press, 1994), 333–335.

21. Burk, *Never Just A Game*, 88; Sotiropoulos, *Staging Race*, 113; "Minstrels in Bronze," *The Evening Chronicle*, March 27, 1883; "The National Game," *The Police Gazette*, May 12, June 2 and 9, 1883; "Base Hits," *The Times* (St. Louis), May 8, 1875. "Moke" refers to a broken down horse or donkey.

22. Hill, *A History of African American Theatre*, 141; Sotiropoulos, *Staging Race*, 91; Roediger, *The Wages of Whiteness*, 97–100; Lott, *Love and Theft*, 48–49;

23. "Base Ball," *The Republican* (St. Louis), July 30, 1876; "Diamond Chips," *The Republican* (St. Louis), April 25, 1883; Veblen, *The Theory of the Leisure Class*, 7–15.

24. Hill, *A History of African American Theatre*, 110; "Amusements," *The Republican* (St. Louis), May 26, 1874.

25. Jacqui Malone, *Steppin' on The Blues* (Urbana: University of Illinois Press, 1996), 135.

26. "Local Short Stops," *Globe-Democrat*, July 17, 1873; "Local Brevities," *The Republican* (St. Louis), October 7, 1874.

27. John Viessman, "They Also Served: Missouri's Black Militias," *Bear Facts* 31, no. 2 (February 2007); "The Colored Press Association," *The Western Recorder* (Lawrence, KS), July 20, 1883; "The Colored Troops," *The Times* (St. Louis), October 21, 1874.

28. "The McCullough Minstrels," *The Republican* (St. Louis), March 29, 1884.

29. "Notes," *The Republican* (St. Louis), September 10, 1882.

30. "Music-Drama-Minstrelsy," *The Gazette*,

December 2, 1883; "Negro Minstrelsy," *The Clipper*, February 11, 1881.

31. "Negro Minstrelsy," *The Clipper*, September 23 and 30, 1881; "The One Great Minstrel Event of the Age," *The Clipper*, September 30, 1881.

32. *Walter Benjamin, Selected Writings*, Volume 3, ed. Michael W. Jennings (Cambridge, MA: Belknap Press, 2002); Sampson, *The Ghost Walks*, 50; "Colored Nabobs," *The Post Dispatch*, May 16, 1883; Johnson, *Black Manhattan*, 76–77; "Amusements," *The Republican* (St. Louis), May 26, 1884; Minstrels in Bronze," *The Evening Chronicle*, May 27, 1883; "One of the Finest," *The Globe* (New York), May 19, 1883; "Baseball," *The Clipper*, December 30, 1882.

33. "Base Ball and Athletics," *Globe-Democrat*, July 3, 1887; "How They Play Baseball," *The Gazette*, June 21, 1888; Dixon and Hannigan, *The Negro Baseball Leagues*, 18.

34. "Saratoga Letter," *The Globe* (Boston), August 18, 1883; "Mask in an Ancient City," *The Age* (New York), March 2, 1889; "Our Philadelphia Letter," *The Bee* (Washington, D.C.), June 12, 1886.

35. Abrahams, *Deep Down in the Jungle*, 56.

36. "The National Game," *The Police Gazette*, May 12 and June 2, 1883.

37. "The National Game," *The Police Gazette*, May 12, 1883; Leon Litwack, *Trouble in Mind: Black Southerners in the Age of Jim Crow* (New York: Knopf, 1998), 235–236; Brown, *Stagolee Shot Billy*, 102.

38. "Sports," *St. Louis Globe*, April 30, 1875; "Ball and Bat," *Daily Globe*, May 4, 1875; "Other Games," *Globe-Democrat*, September 5, 1875; "The Rival Colored Clubs on the Green Diamond," *The Daily Times*, September 13, 1875; "Diamond Chips," *Post Dispatch*, April 30, 1885; "Diamond Chips," *The Republican* (St. Louis), April 25, 1885; "The Colored Clubs," *The Globe-Democrat*, June 14, 1876.

39. Veblen, *The Theory of the Leisure Class*, 156–7; Larry Smith, "Thorstein Veblen on Sports in America," *Social Text* 16 (Winter 1986–1987): 176–183.

40. Blanchard, *Oscar Wilde's America*, 3–7; Louis S. Warren, "Cody's Last Stand: Masculine Anxiety, the Custer Myth, and the Frontier of Domesticity in Buffalo Bill's Wild West," *Western Historical Quarterly* 34, no. 1 (Spring 2003): 49–70; Paul Reddin, *Wild West Shows* (Urbana: University of Illinois Press, 1999).

41. "Diamond Dust," *The Globe-Democrat*, August 21, 1883; "To-day's Games," *The Globe-Democrat*, April 25, 1883.

42. "Funny Cracks," *The Sporting News*, July 12, 1886; "The Transvaal," *The Republican* (St. Louis), August 19, 1877; Brian Roberts, *Cecil Rhodes: Flawed Genius* (London: Hamish Hamilton, 1987).

43. Burk, *Never Just A Game*, 24; "Rah for Our Black Socks," *The Republican*, August 12, 1883.

44. "Diamond Chips," *The Republican* (St. Louis), May 4, 1883.

45. "Oscar Wilde's Legs," *The Police Gazette*, December 30, 1882.

46. Lott, *Love and Theft*, 159–168; "Farewell Night of Hooley's Minstrels," *Daily Eagle*, June 13, 1868; "Concerning Burlesque, Opera, Female Men, Salaries, Men, Managers, and Mokes," *Daily Eagle*, June 6, 1871.

47. "Mr. Wilde's Thrilling Legs," *Daily Eagle*, January 22, 1882.

48. "Diamond Dust," *The Globe Democrat*, March 27, 1883; Christopher Devine, *Harry Wright, the Father of Professional Base Ball* (Jefferson, NC: McFarland, 2003); Stephen D. Guschov, *The Red Stockings of Cincinnati* (Jefferson, NC: McFarland, 1998); National Baseball Hall of Fame, "Parts of the Uniform: Stockings." *Dressed to the Nines: A History of the Baseball Uniform*, http://baseballhalloffame.org/exhibits/online_exhbits/online_exhbibits/dressed_tothe nines/stockings.htm.

49. "The Carnival," *The Picayune*, February 22, 1882.

50. Blanchard, *Oscar Wilde's America*, 27; *The Police Gazette*, April 8, 1882; "Diamond Dust," *The Globe-Democrat*, September 26, 1883; "Oscar Wilde, the Esthete," *Daily Eagle*, January 4, 1882; "Dalton Doings," *The Constitution*, June 11 and 14, 1882; "Notes," *The Republican* (St. Louis), April 17, 1882; "Gossip of the Game," *The Tribune* (Chicago), June 4, 1882; "Never Give Up," *The Globe* (Boston), July 23, 1888; "Senators Win," *The Globe* (Boston), July 27, 1888; "On the Fly," *Sporting Life*, May 13, 1883.

51. "Dalton Doings," *The Constitution*, June 11 and 14, 1882; "Gossip of the Game," *The Tribune* (Chicago), June 4, 1882; "Never Give Up," *The Globe* (Boston), July 23, 1888; "Senators Win," *The Globe* (Boston), July 27, 1888; "Notes," *The Republican* (St. Louis), April 17, 1882; *The Clipper*, April 29, 1882.

52. "Fashions for Gentlemen," *The Times* (Chicago), July 20, 1876; "The White Stockings Poeticized," *The Tribune* (Chicago), July 3, 1870; "All the Rage," *The Tribune* (Chicago), September 29, 1870.

53. "Notes About Town," *The Republican* (St. Louis), August 8, 1877; "The Knee Breeches Question," *The Post*, October 28, 1883; "The Freaks of Fashion," *The Times* (St. Louis), June 23, 1879; "Expensive Stockings," *The Bee*, January 6, 1883; "The Silk Stockings," *The Evening Chronicle*, October 10, 1882; "Political Gossip," *The Evening Chronicle*, November 3, 1882; "Republican Harmony in Missouri," *The Times* (St. Louis), January 26, 1884; "The Colored Voters," *The Republican* (St. Louis), March 24, 1884; "Silk Stockings and Hoodlums," *The Globe-Democrat*, September 26, 1883; "The National Game," *The Police Gazette*, May 6, 1883.

54. Blanchard, *Oscar Wilde's America*, 20; Henry T. Sampson, *The Ghost Walks: A Chronological History of Blacks in Show Business, 1865–1910* (Methuen, NJ: Scarecrow Press, 1988), 24; "Amusements," *The Republican* (St. Louis), September 2, 1877; "The Minstrel World," *Daily Eagle*, November 11, 1883; "Dramatic," *Daily Eagle*, December 23, 1872; "At Hooley's: The Georgias," *Daily Eagle*, August 8, 1874.

55. Curtis Marez, "The Other Addict: Reflections on Colonialism and Oscar Wilde's Opium Smoke Screen," *ELH* 64, no. 1 (1997): 257–287.

56. "Notes and Comments," *Sporting Life*, February 13, 1884; "Oscar Wilde and His Negro Valet," *The Times* (New York), July 9, 1882; Rose Snider, "Oscar Wilde's Progress Down East," *The New England Quarterly* 13, no. 1 (March 1940): 7–23; Ellen Crowell, "The

Picture of Charles Bon: Oscar Wilde's Trip Through Faulkner's Yoknapatawpha," *Modern Fiction Studies* 50, no. 3 (Fall 2004): 614; Curtis Marez, "The Other Addict: Reflections on Colonialism and Oscar Wilde's Opium Smoke Screen," *ELH* 64, no. 1 (1997): 7; Schaffer, "Fashioning Aestheticism By Aestheticizing Fashion: Wilde, Beerbohm, And the Male Aesthetes' Sartorial Codes," *Victorian Literature and Culture*, 39–54; "The National Game," *The Police Gazette*, January 28, 1882. This comical epithet refers to Cetshwayo kaMpande (1826–1884), the King of the Zulu nation from 1872 to 1879. His name also has been transliterated as Cetawayo, Cetewayo, Cetywajo, and Ketchwayo. In 1879, the British defeated Cetschwayo and captured and torched his capital. In 1882, he was deposed and exiled in London. The association between Wilde's servant and Cetshwayo derives from this period.

57. Lott, *Love and Theft*, 100–115.

58. "Base Ball," *The Sentinel* (Trenton, NJ), June 24, 1882; "Baseball Games," *Daily Tribune* (New York), September 13, 1882; "Diamond Dust," *Globe-Democrat*, April 7, 1883; "Colored Champions," *The Times* (New York), June 23, 1883; "Sporting," *The Times* (Los Angeles), April 7, 1883; "Sporting Gossip," *The Leader*, April 6, 1883; "Sporting," *Globe-Democrat*, April 9, 1883; "Dots from Different Diamonds," *The Picayune*, September 2, 1885.

59. "Sporting Notes," *Daily Mercury* (Guelph, Ontario), May 22, 1883. "Philadelphia has two colored female base ball clubs, and may be said to be considerably ahead."

60. "Miss Harris's Base Ball Nine," *The Times* (New York), May 18, 1883; Gail Ingham Berlage, *Women in Baseball: The Forgotten History* (London: Praeger, 1994), 24–32.

61. "No Ball To Day," *The Register* (Rockford, IL), June 18, 1883; "Black Socks Badly Beaten," *The Register*, June 19, 1883.

62. "The Dolly Varden Nine," *Morning Herald* (Baltimore), May 19, 1883.

63. Toll, *Blacking Up*, 169–170; Harte's popular narrative poem "Plain Language from Truthful James" had been originally published in the *Overland Monthly*. It was pirated and popularized under the name "The Heathen Chinee." Twain and Harte collaborated on a dramatic version that managed only 35 performances as the writers could not agree on needed revisions.

64. Ibid, 170–171.

65. "The Diamond Field," *The Times* (St. Louis), April 9, 1883; "A Chinese Base-Ball Club," *The Times* (St. Louis), April 10, 1883; "Sporting," *Globe-Democrat*, April 8, 1883.

66. "The National Game," *The Police Gazette*, April 28, 1883

67. "A Chinese Ball Club," *The Leader*, April 6, 1883; "Base Ball," *The Leader*, April 7, 1883; "Chinese not a Success in Philadelphia," *The Leader*, April 16, 1883; "Base Ball," *The Evening Chronicle* (St. Louis), April 18, 1883; "Base Ball Notes," *Enquirer* (Cincinnati), May 20, 1883.

68. "In General," *The Constitution*, April 26, 1878; "Home Runs," *The Globe* (Boston), September 14, 1888; "John Chinaman Plays Base-Ball," *Daily Tribune* (Chicago), August 5, 1888; "Oriental Ball Tossers," *Daily Tribune*, September 2, 1888.

69. *The Times* (Los Angeles), April 7, 1883; "The National Game," *The Police Gazette*, May 10, 1883; Richard Slotkin, *The Fatal Environment* (Norman: University of Oklahoma Press, 1994). During the California Gold Rush, between 1851 and 1860, over 40,000 Chinese miners came to the United States. In the 1860s, the Central Pacific Railroad recruited large labor gangs, many on five-year contracts, to help build the Transcontinental Railroad. On May 6, 1882, Congress passed the Chinese Exclusion Act, which followed 1880 revisions to the Burlingame Treaty of 1868. Both allowed the U.S. to suspend Chinese immigration, and Congress quickly implemented the law. For ten years, the act excluded all Chinese laborers from immigrating to the United States. In 1884, further amendments tightened the provisions that allowed previous immigrants to leave and return. In 1892, The Geary Act clarified this for another 10 years; and again in 1902, with no fixed date.

70. "The Black Sox-Callender Game," *Post-Dispatch*, September 3, 1884; "Cracks for the Cranks," *The Sunday Sayings* (St. Louis), September 7, 1884.

Coda

1. "To-Day's Games," *Daily Globe Democrat*, August 22, 1883

2. Mitchell, *Picture Theory*, 184.

3. "Diamond Dust," *Globe Democrat*, May 9, 1883; John Snyder, *Cardinals Journal* (Cincinnati: Emmis Books, 2006). The baseball diamond had been laid out at Grand and Dodier as early as 1866.

4. "The National Game," *The Police Gazette*, June 9, 1883; "The Colored Champions," *The Republican* (St. Louis), May 14, 1883. The nursery rhyme's origin is disputed. Some critics argue that the English poem "Sing a Song of Six Pence" appeared in *Tom Thumb's Pretty Song Book*, Volume II (1744). Others believe it was written earlier by poet George Stevens, to satirize the English Poet Laureate Henry James Pye. However, the nursery rhyme itself may date to the English Medieval Period.

5. "Base Ball," *The Chronicle*, May 5, 1883; "Diamond Chips," *The Republican* (St. Louis), May 16, 1883; "Base Ball," *The Chronicle*, May 16, 1883.

6. Regarding Recreation Park, home of the Detroit Wolverines, *The Free Press* reports, "The bulletin-board is in position, and all the scores of the league games will be displayed thereon." "Fair Balls," *The Free Press*, May 1, 1883. "The Emerald Diamond," *The Republican* (St. Louis), April 9, 1883; "Working the Pool Rooms; Tapping the Wires — Thousands of Dollars Paid Out in Wrong Dispatches," *The Sporting Life*, October 15, 1883; "A Base Ball Exchange," *Globe-Democrat*, March 26, 1882.

7. Clayton, *"Little Mack,"* 85. According to McCullagh, the word came to him from a Mississippi riverboat pilot, whom he once heard exclaim as he looked upon the river overflowing its banks and sweeping everything before it, "By Jove, she's a-booming."

8. "Diamond Dust," *Globe Democrat*, July 14, 1883.

9. Mitchell, *Picture Theory*, 186.

10. *Ibid.*, 163–164.

11. Mitchell, *What Do Pictures Want?*, 212–215.

12. "*Narration as enumeration*. We need to be mindful of the whole panoply of figures that link narration to counting, recounting, 'giving an account,' (in French, *conte*), 'telling' and 'tallying' a numerical total, and the relation between 'stories' and 'storage.' Description particular is often treated as the textual site of greatest wealth, an unbounded cornucopia of rich detail, rendered in the rhetoric of the copiousness." Mitchell, *Picture Theory*, 195.

13. "The Money Paid," *The Republican* (St. Louis), July 20, 1890.

14. Brown, *Stagolee Shot Billy*, 45; "Diamond Chips," *The Republican* (St. Louis), June 9, 1884; "Shot in the Heel," *The Republican* (St. Louis), June 8, 1882; "Smith and 'Daisy George,'" *Globe-Democrat*, October 13, 1881; "All for Love," *The Republican* (St. Louis), April 7, 1882; "Two Dusky Maidens," *The Republican* (St. Louis), August 7, 1882; "Splinters," *Globe-Democrat*, September 11, 22, and 26, 1881.

15. "Incipient Riot," *The Democrat*, September 30, 1873; "Where is Brown?," *The Republican* (St. Louis), March 31, 1882.

16. Spink, *The National Game*, 41–48; J. Thomas Hetrick, *Chris Von Der Ahe and the St. Louis Browns* (Landham, MD: Scarecrow, 1999), 6–7.

17. "Gossip," *Globe-Democrat*, May 15, 1876; "Tips," *Globe-Democrat*, June 19, July 3, and August 7, 1876; "Base Ball," *Globe-Democrat*, July 24, 1876; "Base Ball Brevities," *Globe-Democrat*, July 29, 1876; "Local Lines," *Globe-Democrat*, August 1, 1876, and August 6, 1877; "Base Ball," *The Republican* (St. Louis), August 7, 1876; "Minor Games," *Globe-Democrat*, September 25, 1876; "Tips," *The Republican* (St. Louis), June 18, 1877; "Base Ball Notes," *The Republican* (St. Louis), September 10, 1877.

18. "Base Hits," *The Republican* (St. Louis), August 7, 1881; "Sporting Notes," *The Chronicle*, August 12, 1881; Hetrick, *Chris Von Der Ahe and the St. Louis Browns*, 7. "Base Ball Brevities," *The Times* (St. Louis), August 15, 1880. In 1883, *The New York Globe* reported that Adam Lewis, formerly of the Lindell Hotel of St. Louis, had become chief hall man of the Congress Hotel. "Saratoga Gossip," *The Globe* (New York), July 7, 1883; "Hotel Waiter's Strike," *The Chronicle*," September 23, 1882; "Notes About Town," *The Republican* (St. Louis), September 24, 1882.

19. Inspired by the success of the Cincinnati Red Stockings, many "Stockings" clubs, black and white, continued the tradition. "Base-Ball," *The Chronicle*, June 17, 1881.

20. *Ibid.*, 346, 400.

21. "Base Ball," *Globe-Democrat*, August 14, 1881; "Base Ball," *Globe-Democrat*, August 14, 1881; *The Globe-Democrat* called the Red Stockings "semi-professionals" and the Nationals "amateurs."

22. "Sporting," *The St. Louis Post-Dispatch*, September 4, 1882.

23. *Ibid.*, 346, 400; Brown, *Stagolee Shot Billy*, 65; "Diamond Dust," *Globe-Democrat*, October 15,

1882; "Diamond Dust," *Globe-Democrat*, October 16, 1882.

24. "Diamond Dust," *Globe-Democrat*, March 27 and September 4, 1882; Hetrick, *Chris Von Der Ahe and the St. Louis Brown*, 13; "Sporting," *The Post-Dispatch*, September 4, 1882; "Craps: A Raid By the Police on a Negro Gambling House," *The Republican* (St. Louis), September 3, 1882.

25. "Base Ball," *The Republican* (St. Louis), November 12, 1882; "Meyer's Beaten at a Mile," *Globe-Democrat*, November 12, 1882; "Base Ball Notes," *Post-Dispatch*, November 11, 1882.

26. "Diamonds," *Elgin Morning Frank* (Elgin, IL), May 10, 1883; "Diamonds," *Elgin Frank*, May 10, 1883; "The Colored League," *The Republican* (St. Louis), May 16, 1883; "On The Fly," *The Sporting News*, December 18, 1886; "Colored Baseball League Formed," *The Gazette*, January 15, 1887.

27. Bridgewater's desire to develop black institutions belonged to a larger push towards self-empowerment and racial-uplift. Since 1881, black residents of St. Louis had been trying to build an industrial arts school for "colored" boys. Along with Bill Curtis and James Milton Turner, Bridgewater attempted to purchase land in Kirkwood, an affluent white suburb. Whites protested when they discovered the owner, Mrs. Annie S. Cairns, had threatened to sell the property and a fashionable seminary for white women to a "syndicate of wealthy Negroes." The new school would have been named in Bridgewater's honor. Bad publicity about his being a "notorious saloonkeeper" forced him to withdraw support. Brown, *Stagolee Shot Billy*, 79–80; "Notes," *Globe-Democrat*, October 28, 1882; "Colored Journalism," *The Chronicle*, August 17, 1881; "A School Teacher's Revenge: The Aristocrats of a St. Louis Suburb Greatly Shocked," *The Times* (St. Louis), July 9, 1890; "Given Up By The Negroes," *The Times* (New York), November 3, 1891.

28. Hetrick, *Chris Von der Ahe and the St. Louis Browns*, 6–7.

29. *Oxford English Dictionary*, OED Online ed, s.v. "behemoth."

30. Foner, *Forever Free*, 157–184; Michael Rogin, *Blackface, White Noise* (Berkeley: University of California Press, 1996), 114.

31. Brown, *Stagolee Shot Billy*, 81; "The Negro Politician," *Sedalia Democrat*, August 8, 1883.

32. "Notes About Town," *The Republican* (St. Louis), August 13, 1881.

33. Jean Michel Massing, "From Greek Proverb to Soap Advert: Washing the Ethiopian," *Journal of the Warburg and Courtauld Institutes* 58 (1995): 180–201.

34. "Diamond Dust," *Globe-Democrat*, July 7, 1883.

35. "The Black Sox at Rockford," *Globe-Democrat*, June 19, 1883.

36. Mitchell, *Picture Theory*, 92–93; "dispatch," http://encyclopedia.jrank.org. Dispatch derives from either the Italian "dispacciare" or the Spanish "despachar." The French word (*despeechier* which means "to set free") came into English as despeech, which was in use from the fifteenth century until dispatch was introduced. Mary Blanchard Warner observes:

"Only a cataclysm as profound as war between brother and brother could temporarily have suppressed the visibility and continuity of the soldier/hero in a culture formed from a revolutionary war ethos. Never entirely disappearing as a cultural value, soldierly manhood, nonetheless, was a contested model during the years after the Civil War." Warner, *Oscar Wilde's America*, 4.

37. "[T]he search for the essence of a medium, what Clement Greenberg saw as the task of the modernist avant-garde, is a utopian gesture that seems inseparable from the artistic deployment of any medium. The issue of media purity arises when a medium becomes self-referential and renounces its function as a means of communication or representation." Mitchell, *What Do Pictures Want?*, 215; "Diamond Dust," *Globe-Democrat*, March 27, 1883; Mitchell, *Picture Theory*, 152.

38. "The Dust of Four Diamonds," *The Constitution* (Atlanta), April 16, 1885.

39. Mitchell, *Picture Theory*, 152; "On the Fly," *The Sporting Life*, June 24, 1883; Mitchell, *What Do Pictures Want?*, 131; *The Clipper*, July 21, 1883. Telegraphing sports news had its challenges. Hustlers and gamblers discovered that they could tap telegraph wires, enabling them to forward bogus information so their partners in crime could steal from bookmakers. The film *The Sting*, starring Robert Redford and Paul Newman, offers the perfect example.

40. "A Mean Trick Played Upon Strangers in Chattanooga," *The Constitution*, July 7, 1877.

41. "Notes," *The Courier-Journal* (Louisville, KY), August 7, 1884; "Base Ball," *The Picayune*, July 6, 1885;

Mitchell, *Picture Theory*, 152; Mark Cooper, *Baseball Games: Home Versions of the National Pastime, 1860s-1960s* (Atglen, PA.: Schiffer Publishing, 1995), 31–33.

42. "Diamond Dust," *Globe Democrat*, June 19, 1883; "Diamond Chips," *The Republican*, June 20, 1883.

43. Bridgewater appears to have dispatched the results to Chicago newspapers. *The Daily Inter-Ocean* carried the story. "The Coons Carry Off the Cake," *The Register*, June 20, 1883; William L. Van DeBurg, *Hoodlums: Black Villains and Social Bandits in American Life* (Chicago: University of Chicago Press, 2004), 87; "Red and Black," *The Inter-Ocean*, June 19, 1883; "The Tour of the Black Socks," *Globe-Democrat*, June 20, 1883; "A Game At Rockford," *The Inter-Ocean*, June 20, 1883.

44. "Black Sox Left," *The Republican* (St. Louis), June 26, 1883; "Notes," *Guelph Mercury* (Guelph, Ontario), June 27, 1883; "Sporting Notes," *Guelph Mercury*, June 28, 1883; "Base Ball," *Guelph Mercury*, July 3, 1883; "Diamond Dust," *The Globe* (St. Louis), July 2, 1883; "B.B.C. of St. Louis," *Arkansas Mansion* (Little Rock), July 28, 1883.

45. "The Coons Carry of the Cake," *The Register*, June 20, 1883.

46. Mitchell, *What Do Pictures Want?*, 104–105.

47. "Base Ball: The Black Stocking-Dayton Game Today," *The Dayton Democrat*, May 7, 1883; "Meyer's Beaten At A Mile," *Globe-Democrat*, November 12, 1882; "Base Ball," *The Republican* (St. Louis), November 12, 1882; "Base Ball Notes," *Post-Dispatch*, November 11, 1882.

Bibliography

Primary Sources

The Age (New York)
The American Nashville (Nashville)
The Appeal (Memphis)
The Bee (Washington)
The Chronicle (St. Louis)
The Clipper (New York)
The Conservator (Chicago)
The Constitution (Atlanta)
The Courant (Hartford)
Daily Eagle (Brooklyn)
Daily Globe-Democrat (St. Louis)
Daily Mercury (Guelph, Ontario)
The Democrat (St. Louis)
Enquirer (Cincinnati)
The Evening Chronicle (St. Louis)
The Evening Journal (Chicago)
The Evening Star (Washington)
The Free Press (Detroit)
The Freeman (Indianapolis)
The Freeman (New York)
The Gazette (Cleveland)
The Globe (Boston)
The Globe (New York)
Gould's St. Louis Directory
The Herald (New York)
The Herald (Saginaw, MI)
The Inquirer (Philadelphia)
The Inter-Ocean (Chicago)
The Journal (Milwaukee)
The Lakeside Directory of Chicago
The Leader (Cleveland)
Morning Frank (Elgin, IL)
Morning Herald (Baltimore)
The National Police Gazette (New York)
The Pelican (New Orleans)
The People's Advocate (Washington)
The Picayune (New Orleans)
The Post (Washington)
The Post Dispatch (St. Louis)
The Register (Rockford, IL)
The Republican (Chicago)
The Republican (St. Louis)

The Sentinel (Milwaukee)
The Sentinel (Trenton)
Sporting Life (Philadelphia)
The Sporting News (St. Louis)
The Sun (New York)
The Sunday Sayings (St. Louis)
The Times (Chicago)
The Times (Los Angeles)
The Times (St. Louis)
The Times (New York)
The Tribune (Chicago)
The Tribune (Du Quoin, IL)
The Tribune (New York)
The Western Recorder (Lawrence, KS)
True American (Trenton)
Weekly Pelican (New Orleans)

Secondary Sources

Abrahams, Roger D. *Deep Down in the Jungle*. Chicago: Aldine Publishing, 1970.

Asbury, Herbert. *The Gangs of Chicago*. Originally published as *Gem of the Prairie: An Informal History of the Chicago Underworld*. New York: Knopf, 1940. Reprint, DeKalb: Northern Illinois University Press, 1986.

Barber, Edwin Atlee. *The Pottery Porcelain of the United States*. New York: Putnam, 1893.

Baudrillard, Jean. *America*. Translated by Chris Turner. New York: Verso, 1998.

Benjamin, Walter. *Reflections*. Edited by Peter Demetz. New York: Schocken Books, 1978.

_____. *The Arcades Project*. Translated by Howard Eiland and Kevin McLaughlin. Cambridge, MA: Belknap Press, 1999.

Berlage, Gail Ingham. *Women in Baseball: The Forgotten History*. London: Praeger, 1994.

Bernstein, Peter L. *The Power of Gold: The History of an Obsession*. New York: John Wiley, 2000.

Blair, Cynthia Marie. "Vicious Commerce: African American Women's Sex Work and the Transformation of urban Space in Chicago, 1850–1915." PhD diss., Harvard University, 1999.

Blanchard, Mary Warner. *Oscar Wilde's America, Counterculture in the Gilded Age.* New Haven: Yale University Press, 1998.

Bontemps, Arna Wendell. *God Sends Sunday.* Washington, DC: Washington Square Press, 2005.

The Booker T. Washington Papers, Volume 8, 1904–1906, edited by Louis R. Harlan and Raymond W. Smock. Urbana: University of Illinois Press, 1979.

Bowman, Larry. *Before the World Series.* DeKalb: Northern Illinois University Press, 2002.

Brilliant, Richard. *Portraiture.* London: Reaktion Books, 1997.

Brown, Cecil. *Stagolee Shot Billy.* Cambridge: Harvard University Press, 2003.

Brown, Joshua. *Beyond the Lines: Pictorial Reporting, Everyday Life, and the Crisis of Gilded Age America.* Berkeley: University of California Press, 2002.

Brunson, James. "Henry Bridgewater's Black Stockings, 1881–1889." *Base Ball: A Journal of the Early Game* 1, no. 2 (2007): 12–26.

Burbank, David T. *Reign of the Rabble: The St. Louis General Strike of 1877.* New York: Augustus M. Kelley, 1966.

Chadwick, Bruce. *When the Game Was Black and White: The Illustrated History of the Negro Leagues.* New York: Abbeville Press, 1992.

Clamorgan, Cyprian. *The Colored Aristocracy of St. Louis.* Columbia: University of Missouri Press, 1999.

Clayton, Charles C. *"Little Mack": Joseph B. McCullagh of the St. Louis Globe-Democrat.* Carbondale: Southern Illinois University Press, 1969.

Cook, Frederick Francis. *Bygone Days in Chicago.* Chicago: Cook Press, 2007.

Cropsey, Eugene H. *Crosby's Opera House.* Madison, NJ: Farleigh Dickinson University Press, 1999.

Crowell, Ellen. "The Picture of Charles Bon: Oscar Wilde's Trip Through Faulkner's Yoknapatawpha." *Modern Fiction Studies* 50, no. 3 (Fall 2004): 595–631.

Dacus, J.A., and James W. Buel. *A Tour of St. Louis; or, The Inside Life of a Great City.* St. Louis: Western Publishing, 1878.

David, John Russell. "Tragedy in Ragtime: Black Folktales from St. Louis." PhD diss., St. Louis University, 1976.

Davis, Angela. *Blues Legacies and Black Feminism.* New York: Vintage Books, 1998.

Davis, Whitney. *Replications: Archaeology, Art History, Psychoanalysis.* University Park: Pennsylvania State University Press, 1996.

Denker, Ellen Paul. "Parian Porcelain Statuary: American Sculptors and the Introduction of Art in American Ceramics." In *Ceramics in America 2002,* edited by Robert Hunter, 62–79. Milwaukee, WI: Chipstone, 2002.

Devine, Christopher. *Harry Wright, the Father of Professional Base Ball.* Jefferson, NC: McFarland, 2003.

DiCelrico, James M., and Barry J. Pavelee. *The Jersey Game.* New Brunswick, NJ: Rutgers University Press, 1991.

Dinhofer, Shelly Mehlman. *The Art of Baseball.* New York: Harmony Books, 1990.

Dixon, Phil, and Patrick J. Hannigan. *The Negro Baseball Leagues: A Photographic History.* Mattituck, NY: Amereon House, 1992.

Fishkin, Shelly Fisher. *Was Huck Black?: Mark Twain and African-American Voices.* New York: Oxford University Press, 1993.

Flinn, John J. *History of the Chicago Police.* New York: AMS Press, 1973.

Floyd, S. A., Jr. "A Black Composer in Nineteenth-Century St. Louis." *19th-Century Music* 4, no. 2 (1980): 121–133.

Focillon, Henri. *The Life of Forms in Art.* New York: Zone Books, 1992.

Foner, Eric. *Forever Free; The Story of Emancipation and Reconstruction.* New York: Knopf, 2005.

Foner, Philip S. *Antonio Maceo: The "Bronze Titan" of Cuba's Struggle for Independence.* New York: Monthly Review Press, 1977.

Frelinghuysen, Alice Cooney. *American Porcelain: 1770–1920.* New York: The Metropolitan Museum of Art, 1989.

Gerber, David A. *Black Ohio and the Color Line, 1860–1915.* Urbana: University of Illinois Press, 1976.

Gernsheim, Helmut. *Creative Photography: Aesthetic Trends, 1839–1960.* Boston: Book Mart & Art Shop, 1962.

Gershwin, Michael. *Diamonds: The Evolution of the Ballpark.* Boston: Houghton and Mifflin, 1999.

Gilfoyle, Timothy J. *City of Eros: New York City, Prostitution, and the Commercialization of Sex.* New York: Norton, 1992.

Gordon, Rae Beth. "Natural Rhythm: La Parisienne Dances with Darwin: 1875–1910." *Modernism/modernity* 10, no. 4 (November 2003): 617–656.

Guschov, Stephen D. *The Red Stockings of Cincinnati.* Jefferson, NC: McFarland, 1998.

Harris, Michael D. *Colored Pictures, Race and Visual Representation.* Chapel Hill: University of North Carolina Press, 2003.

Harris, Neil. "The Gilded Age Reconsidered Once Again." *Archives of American Art Journal* 23, no. 4 (1983): 8–18.

_____. *Building Lives: Constructing Rites and Passages.* New Haven: Yale University Press, 1999.

Hartman, Saidiya V. *Scenes of Subjection: Terror, Slavery, and Self-Making In Nineteenth-Century America.* Oxford: Oxford University Press, 1997.

Hatt, Michael. "'Making a Man of Him': Masculinity and the Black Body in Mid-Nineteenth-

Century American Sculpture." *Oxford Art Journal* 15, no. 1 (1992): 21–35.

Heaphy, Leslie A. "Early Black Teams in Chicago." In *Black Baseball And Chicago*, edited by Leslie A. Heaphy, 7–17. Jefferson, NC: McFarland, 2006.

Heneghan, Bridget T. *Whitewashing America: Material Culture and Race in the Antebellum Imagination*. Jackson: University of Mississippi Press, 2003.

Henisch, Heinz K., and Bridget A. Henisch. *The Photographic Experience, 1839–1914*. University Park: Pennsylvania State University Press, 1994.

Hill, Errol G., and James V. Hatch. *A History of African American Theatre*. Cambridge: Cambridge University Press, 2003.

Hinks, Peter P. *To Awaken My Afflicted Brethren: David Walker and the Problem of Slave Resistance*. University Park: Pennsylvania University Press, 1997.

Hogan, Lawrence D. *Shades of Glory: The Negro Leagues and the Story of African-American Baseball*. Washington, DC: National Geographic, 2006.

International Center of Photography Encyclopedia of Photography. New York: Crown Publishers, 1984.

James-Gadzinski, Susan, and Mary Mullen Cunningham. *American Sculpture in the Museum of American Art of the Pennsylvania Academy of the Fine Arts*. Philadelphia: Philadelphia Museum of American Art, 1997.

Johnson, James Weldon. *Black Manhattan*. New York: Knopf, 1930. Reprinted, New York: Da Capo Press, 1991.

Joiner, Thekla Ellen. *Sin in the City: Chicago and Revivalism, 1880–1920*. Columbia: University of Missouri Press, 2007.

Kachum, Mitch. "Before the Eyes of all Nations: African-American Identity and Historical Memory at the Centennial Exposition of 1876." *Pennsylvania History* 65, no. 3 (1998): 300–323.

Kaplan, E. Ann. *Trauma Culture*. New Brunswick, NJ: Rutgers University Press, 2005.

Kelly, Robin D. G. *Race Rebels: Culture, Politics, and the Black Working Class*. New York: The Free Press, 1996.

Lambourne, Lionel. *The Aesthetic Movement*. London: Phaidon, 1996.

Landers, Robert K. *An Honest Writer: The Life and Times of James T. Farrell*. San Francisco: Encounter Books, 1999.

Leslie, Esther. "Flaneurs in Paris and Berlin." *Histories of Leisure*, edited by Rudy Koshar, 61–77. New York: Berg, 2002.

Litwack, Leon. *Trouble in Mind: Black Southerners in the Age of Jim Crow*. New York: Knopf, 1998.

Lomax, Michael D. *Black Baseball Entrepreneurs, 1860–1901*. Syracuse: Syracuse University Press, 2003.

Lott, Eric. *Love and Theft: Blackface Minstrelsy and the American Working Class*. Oxford: Oxford University Press, 1993.

Lukens, Henry Clay. "American Literary Comedians." *Harper's New Monthly Magazine*, April 1890, 783–797.

Mahar, William J. *Behind the Burnt Cork Mask*. Urbana: University of Illinois Press, 1999.

Malloy, Jerry. "The Birth of the Cuban Giants." *Out of the Shadows*. Lincoln: University of Nebraska Press, 2005.

Malone, Jacqui. *Steppin' on The Blues*. Urbana: University of Illinois Press, 1996.

Marez, Curtis. "The Other Addict: Reflections on Colonialism and Oscar Wilde's Opium Smoke Screen." *ELH* 64, no. 1 (1997): 257–287.

McMurray, L.O. *To Keep The Waters Troubled*. Oxford: Oxford University Press, 1998.

Mills, Charles. *The Racial Contract*. Ithaca: Cornell University Press, 1997.

Mitchell, W.J.T. *The Last Dinosaur Book*. Chicago: The University of Chicago Press, 1998.

_____. *Picture Theory: Essays on Verbal and Visual Representation*. Chicago: University of Chicago Press, 1994.

_____. *What Do Pictures Want?* Chicago: University of Chicago Press, 2005.

Morrison, Toni. *Playing in the Dark: Whiteness and the Literary Imagination*. Cambridge: Harvard University Press, 1992.

Moses, Wilson Jeremiah. "The Lost World of the Negro, 1895–1919: Black Literary and Intellectual Life Before the 'Renaissance.'" *Black American Literature Forum* 21, no. 1–2 (Spring-Summer 1987): 61–84.

_____. *The Wings of Ethiopia*. Ames: Iowa State University Press, 1990.

National Baseball Hall of Fame. "Parts of the Uniform: Stockings." *Dressed to the Nines: A History of the Baseball Uniform*. http://baseballhalloffame.org/exhibits/online_exhbits/online_exhbits/dressed_to the nines/stockings.htm.

The Negro in New York, edited by Roi Ottley and William J. Weatherby. New York: New York Public Library, 1967.

Nemec, David. *The Beer and Whiskey League; The Illustrated History of the American Association — Baseball's Renegade Major League*. Guilford, CT: Lyons Press, 2004.

Ohmann, Richard. *Selling Culture*. New York: Verso, 1996.

Paine, Albert Bigelow. *Thomas Nast: His Period and His Pictures*. New York: Macmillan, 1904.

Panzer, Mary. *Matthew Brady and the Image of History*. Washington, DC: Smithsonian, 1997.

Parry, Albert. *Garrets and Pretenders: A History of Bohemianism in America*. New York: Covici, Friede, 1933.

Pisano, Ronald. *The Tile Club*. New York: Harry N. Abrams, 1999.

Puerzer, Richard J. "From Scientific Baseball to Sabermetrics," *NINE: A Journal of Baseball History and Culture* 11, no. 1 (2002): 34–48.

Reddin, Paul. *Wild West Shows.* Urbana: University of Illinois Press, 1999.

Reed, Christopher Robert. *Black Chicago's First Century,* Vol. I, 1833–1900. Columbia: University of Missouri Press, 2005.

Reiss, Benjamin. "P.T. Barnum, Joice Heth and the Antebellum Spectacle of Race." *American Quarterly* 51, no. 1 (March 1999): 78–107.

Ribowsky, Mark. *A Complete History of the Negro Leagues, 1884–1955.* New York: Birch Lane Press, 1995.

Riess, Steven. *City Games: The Evolution of American Urban Society and the Rise of Sports.* Urbana: University of Illinois Press, 1991.

Roberts, Brian. *Cecil Rhodes: Flawed Genius.* London: Hamish Hamilton, 1987.

Roediger, David R. *The Wages of Whiteness.* London: Verso, 1993.

The Royal City of Susa. Edited by Prudence O. Harper, Joan Aruz, and Francoise Tallon. New York: Harry N. Abrams, 1992.

Saxton, Cecil Alexander. *The Rise and Fall of the White Republic.* London: Verso, 1996.

Schaffer, Talia. "Fashioning Aestheticism By Aestheticizing Fashion: Wilde, Beerbohm, and the Male Aesthetes' Sartorial Codes." *Victorian Literature and Culture* 28, no. 1 (2000): 39–54.

Schmidt, Ray. "The Golden Age of Chicago Baseball." *Chicago History* 28, no. 2 (Winter 2000): 38–59.

Slotkin, Richard. *The Fatal Environment.* Norman: University of Oklahoma Press, 1994.

Smith, Larry. "Thorstein Veblen on Sports in America." *Social Text* 16 (Winter 1986–1987): 176–183.

Sneddeker, D. R. "Regulating Vice: Prostitution and the St. Louis Social Evil Ordinance, 1870–1874." *Gateway Heritage* 11, no. 2 (1990): 20–47.

Snider, Rose. "Oscar Wilde's Progress Down East." *New England Quarterly* 13, no. 1 (March 1940): 7–23.

Snowden, Frank. *The Image of the Black in Western Art,* Part I. Cambridge: Harvard University Press, 1976.

Sontag, Susan. *Regarding the Pain of Others.* New York: Farrar and Strauss, 2003.

Sotiropoulos, Karen. *Staging Race: Black Performers in Turn of the Century America.* Cambridge: Harvard University Press, 2006.

Southern, Eileen. "The Origin and Development of the Black Musical Theater: A Preliminary Report." *Black Music Research Journal* 2 (1981–1982): 1–14.

Spink, Alfred H. *The National Game,* St. Louis: National Game Publishing, 1910. Reprinted, Carbondale: Southern Illinois University Press, 2000.

Strausbaugh, John. *Black Like You.* New York: Penguin, 2006.

Taussig, Michael. *Mimesis and Alterity.* New York: Routledge, 1993.

Toll, Robert C. *Blacking Up: The Minstrel Show in Nineteenth Century America.* New York: Oxford University Press, 1974.

Tractenberg, Alan. *Reading American Photographs.* New York: Hill and Wang, 1989.

Turner, Victor. *Dramas, Fields, and Metaphors: Symbolic Action in Human Society.* Ithaca: Cornell University Press, 1974.

Veblen, Thorsten. *The Theory of the Leisure Class.* New York: Macmillan, 1899. Reprinted, New York: Penguin, 1994.

Viessman, John. "They Also Served: Missouri's Black Militias." *Bear Facts* 31, no. 2 (February 2007).

Vincent, Ted. *Mudville's Revenge: The Rise and Fall of American Sport.* Lincoln: University of Nebraska Press, 1994.

Voigt, David Quentin. *American Baseball: From the Gentleman's Sport to the Commissioner System.* University Park: Pennsylvania State University Press, 1983.

Walter Benjamin, Selected Writings, Volume 3, Edited by Michael W. Jennings. Cambridge, MA: Belknap Press, 2002.

Warren, Louis S. "Cody's Last Stand: Masculine Anxiety, the Custer Myth, and the Frontier of Domesticity in Buffalo Bill's Wild West," *Western Historical Quarterly* 34, no. 1 (Spring 2003): 49–69.

Webb, Barbara L. "The Black Dandyism of George Walker; A Case Study in Genealogical Method," *The Drama Review* 45, no. 4 (Winter 2001): 7–24.

Willis, Deborah and Carla Williams, *The Black Female Body, A Photographic History.* Philadelphia: Temple University Press, 2002.

Winant, Howard. *The World is a Ghetto: Race and Democracy Since World War II.* New York: Basic Books, 2001.

Winter, William. *Old Friends; Being Literary Recollections of Other Days.* New York: Moffat, Yard, 1909.

Wolinsky, Russell. "Arlie Latham: 19th Century Clown Prince of Baseball." National Baseball Hall of Fame. http://209.23.71.87/library/columns/rw_040618.htm.

Wooldridge, Clifton R. *Hands Up! In the World of Crime* (Chicago: Police Publishing, 1901.

Zang, David. *Fleet Walker's Divided Heart.* Lincoln: University of Nebraska Press, 1995.

Zoss, Joel and John Bowman, *Diamonds in The Rough: The Untold History of Baseball.* Chicago: Contemporary Books, 1996.

Index

Numbers in *bold italics* indicate pages with photographs.